Nutshell Series

of

WEST PUBLISHING COMPANY

P.O. Box 64526

St. Paul, Minnesota 55164–0526

Accounting—Law and, 1984, 377 pages, by E. McGruder Faris, Late Professor of Law, Stetson University.

Administrative Law and Process, 2nd Ed., 1981, 445 pages, by Ernest Gellhorn, Dean and Professor of Law, Case Western Reserve University and Barry B. Boyer, Professor of Law, SUNY, Buffalo.

Admiralty, 1983, 390 pages, by Frank L. Maraist, Professor of Law, Louisiana State University.

Agency-Partnership, 1977, 364 pages, by Roscoe T. Steffen, Late Professor of Law, University of Chicago.

American Indian Law, 1981, 288 pages, by William C. Canby, Jr., Adjunct Professor of Law, Arizona State University.

Antitrust Law and Economics, 2nd Ed., 1981, 425 pages, by Ernest Gellhorn, Dean and Professor of Law, Case Western Reserve University.

Appellate Advocacy, 1984, 325 pages, by Alan D. Hornstein, Professor of Law, University of Maryland.

Art Law, 1984, 335 pages, by Leonard D. DuBoff, Professor of Law, Lewis and Clark College, Northwestern School of Law.

Banking and Financial Institutions, 1984, 409 pages, by William A. Lovett, Professor of Law, Tulane University.

Church-State Relations—Law of, 1981, 305 pages, by Leonard F. Manning, Late Professor of Law, Fordham University.

List current as of January, 1985

Civil Procedure, 1979, 271 pages, by Mary Kay Kane, Professor of Law, University of California, Hastings College of the Law.

Civil Rights, 1978, 279 pages, by Norman Vieira, Professor of Law, Southern Illinois University.

Commercial Paper, 3rd Ed., 1982, 404 pages, by Charles M. Weber, Professor of Business Law, University of Arizona and Richard E. Speidel, Professor of Law, Northwestern University.

Community Property, 1982, 423 pages, by Robert L. Mennell, Former Professor of Law, Hamline University.

Comparative Legal Traditions, 1982, 402 pages, by Mary Ann Glendon, Professor of Law, Boston College, Michael Wallace Gordon, Professor of Law, University of Florida and Christopher Osakwe, Professor of Law, Tulane University.

Conflicts, 1982, 469 pages, by David D. Siegel, Professor of Law, Albany Law School, Union University.

Constitutional Analysis, 1979, 388 pages, by Jerre S. Williams, Professor of Law Emeritus, University of Texas.

Constitutional Power—Federal and State, 1974, 411 pages, by David E. Engdahl, Professor of Law, University of Puget Sound.

Consumer Law, 2nd Ed., 1981, 418 pages, by David G. Epstein, Professor of Law, University of Texas and Steve H. Nickles, Professor of Law, University of Minnesota.

Contract Remedies, 1981, 323 pages, by Jane M. Friedman, Professor of Law, Wayne State University.

Contracts, 2nd Ed., 1983, 425 pages, by Gordon D. Schaber, Dean and Professor of Law, McGeorge School of Law and Claude D. Rohwer, Professor of Law, McGeorge School of Law.

Corporations—Law of, 1980, 379 pages, by Robert W. Hamilton, Professor of Law, University of Texas.

Corrections and Prisoners' Rights—Law of, 2nd Ed., 1983, 384 pages, by Sheldon Krantz, Dean and Professor of Law, University of San Diego.

Criminal Law, 1975, 302 pages, by Arnold H. Loewy, Professor of Law, University of North Carolina.

Criminal Procedure—Constitutional Limitations, 3rd Ed., 1980, 438 pages, by Jerold H. Israel, Professor of Law, University of Michigan and Wayne R. LaFave, Professor of Law, University of Illinois.

Debtor-Creditor Law, 2nd Ed., 1980, 324 pages, by David G. Epstein, Professor of Law, University of Texas.

Employment Discrimination—Federal Law of, 2nd Ed., 1981, 402 pages, by Mack A. Player, Professor of Law, University of Georgia.

Energy Law, 1981, 338 pages, by Joseph P. Tomain, Professor of Law, University of Cincinnatti.

Environmental Law, 1983, 343 pages by Roger W. Findley, Professor of Law, University of Illinois and Daniel A. Farber, Professor of Law, University of Minnesota.

Estate Planning—Introduction to, 3rd Ed., 1983, 370 pages, by Robert J. Lynn, Professor of Law, Ohio State University.

Evidence, Federal Rules of, 1981, 428 pages, by Michael H. Graham, Professor of Law, University of Miami.

Evidence, State and Federal Rules, 2nd Ed., 1981, 514 pages, by Paul F. Rothstein, Professor of Law, Georgetown University.

Family Law, 1977, 400 pages, by Harry D. Krause, Professor of Law, University of Illinois.

Federal Estate and Gift Taxation, 3rd Ed., 1983, 509 pages, by John K. McNulty, Professor of Law, University of California, Berkeley.

Federal Income Taxation of Individuals, 3rd Ed., 1983, 487 pages, by John K. McNulty, Professor of Law, University of California, Berkeley.

Federal Income Taxation of Corporations and Stockholders, 2nd Ed., 1981, 362 pages, by Jonathan Sobeloff, Late Professor of Law, Georgetown University and Peter P. Weidenbruch, Jr., Professor of Law, Georgetown University.

Federal Jurisdiction, 2nd Ed., 1981, 258 pages, by David P. Currie, Professor of Law, University of Chicago.

Future Interests, 1981, 361 pages, by Lawrence W. Waggoner, Professor of Law, University of Michigan.

Government Contracts, 1979, 423 pages, by W. Noel Keyes, Professor of Law, Pepperdine University.

Historical Introduction to Anglo-American Law, 2nd Ed., 1973, 280 pages, by Frederick G. Kempin, Jr., Professor of Business Law, Wharton School of Finance and Commerce, University of Pennsylvania.

Immigration Law and Procedure, 1984, 345 pages, by David Weissbrodt, Professor of Law, University of Minnesota.

Injunctions, 1974, 264 pages, by John F. Dobbyn, Professor of Law, Villanova University.

Insurance Law, 1981, 281 pages, by John F. Dobbyn, Professor of Law, Villanova University.

Intellectual Property—Patents, Trademarks and Copyright, 1983, 428 pages, by Arthur R. Miller, Professor of Law, Harvard University, and Michael H. Davis, Professor of Law, Cleveland State University, Cleveland-Marshall College of Law.

International Business Transactions, 2nd Ed., 1984, 476 pages, by Donald T. Wilson, Professor of Law, Loyola University, Los Angeles.

Introduction to the Study and Practice of Law, 1983, 418 pages, by Kenney F. Hegland, Professor of Law, University of Arizona.

Judicial Process, 1980, 292 pages, by William L. Reynolds, Professor of Law, University of Maryland.

Jurisdiction, 4th Ed., 1980, 232 pages, by Albert A. Ehrenzweig, Late Professor of Law, University of California, Berkeley, David W. Louisell, Late Professor of Law, University of California, Berkeley and Geoffrey C. Hazard, Jr., Professor of Law, Yale Law School.

Juvenile Courts, 3rd Ed., 1984, 291 pages, by Sanford J. Fox, Professor of Law, Boston College.

Labor Arbitration Law and Practice, 1979, 358 pages, by Dennis R. Nolan, Professor of Law, University of South Carolina.

Labor Law, 1979, 403 pages, by Douglas L. Leslie, Professor of Law, University of Virginia.

Land Use, 1978, 316 pages, by Robert R. Wright, Professor of Law, University of Arkansas, Little Rock and Susan Webber, Professor of Law, University of Arkansas, Little Rock.

Landlord and Tenant Law, 1979, 319 pages, by David S. Hill, Professor of Law, University of Colorado.

Law Study and Law Examinations—Introduction to, 1971, 389 pages, by Stanley V. Kinyon, Late Professor of Law, University of Minnesota.

Legal Interviewing and Counseling, 1976, 353 pages, by Thomas L. Shaffer, Professor of Law, Washington and Lee University.

Legal Research, 4th Ed., 1985, approximately 425 pages, by Morris L. Cohen, Professor of Law and Law Librarian, Yale University.

Legal Writing, 1982, 294 pages, by Dr. Lynn B. Squires and Marjorie Dick Rombauer, Professor of Law, University of Washington.

Legislative Law and Process, 1975, 279 pages, by Jack Davies, Professor of Law, William Mitchell College of Law.

Local Government Law, 2nd Ed., 1983, 404 pages, by David J. McCarthy, Jr., Professor of Law, Georgetown University.

Mass Communications Law, 2nd Ed., 1983, 473 pages, by Harvey L. Zuckman, Professor of Law, Catholic University and Martin J. Gaynes, Lecturer in Law, Temple University.

Medical Malpractice—The Law of, 1977, 340 pages, by Joseph H. King, Professor of Law, University of Tennessee.

Military Law, 1980, 378 pages, by Charles A. Shanor, Professor of Law, Emory University and Timothy P. Terrell, Professor of Law, Emory University.

Oil and Gas, 1983, 443 pages, by John S. Lowe, Professor of Law, University of Tulsa.

Personal Property, 1983, 322 pages, by Barlow Burke, Jr., Professor of Law, American University.

Post-Conviction Remedies, 1978, 360 pages, by Robert Popper, Professor of Law, University of Missouri, Kansas City.

Presidential Power, 1977, 328 pages, by Arthur Selwyn Miller, Professor of Law Emeritus, George Washington University.

Procedure Before Trial, 1972, 258 pages, by Delmar Karlen, Professor of Law Emeritus, New York University.

Products Liability, 2nd Ed., 1981, 341 pages, by Dix W. Noel, Late Professor of Law, University of Tennessee and Jerry J. Phillips, Professor of Law, University of Tennessee.

Professional Responsibility, 1980, 399 pages, by Robert H. Aronson, Professor of Law, University of Washington, and Donald T. Weckstein, Professor of Law, University of San Diego.

Real Estate Finance, 2nd Ed., 1985, approximately 300 pages, by Jon W. Bruce, Professor of Law, Vanderbilt University.

Real Property, 2nd Ed., 1981, 448 pages, by Roger H. Bernhardt, Professor of Law, Golden Gate University.

Regulated Industries, 1982, 394 pages, by Ernest Gellhorn, Dean and Professor of Law, Case Western Reserve University, and Richard J. Pierce, Dean and Professor of Law, University of Pittsburgh.

Remedies, 2nd Ed., 1985, 325 pages, by John F. O'Connell, Professor of Law, Western State University College of Law, Fullerton.

Res Judicata, 1976, 310 pages, by Robert C. Casad, Professor of Law, University of Kansas.

Sales, 2nd Ed., 1981, 370 pages, by John M. Stockton, Professor of Business Law, Wharton School of Finance and Commerce, University of Pennsylvania.

Schools, Students and Teachers—Law of, 1984, 409 pages, by Kern Alexander, Professor of Education, University of Florida and M. David Alexander, Professor, Virginia Tech University.

Sea—Law of, 1984, 264 pages, by Louis B. Sohn, Professor of Law, University of Georgia, and Kristen Gustafson.

Secured Transactions, 2nd Ed., 1981, 391 pages, by Henry J. Bailey, Professor of Law Emeritus, Willamette University.

Securities Regulation, 2nd Ed., 1982, 322 pages, by David L. Ratner, Dean and Professor of Law, University of San Francisco.

Sex Discrimination, 1982, 399 pages, by Claire Sherman Thomas, Lecturer, University of Washington, Women's Studies Department.

Torts—Injuries to Persons and Property, 1977, 434 pages, by Edward J. Kionka, Professor of Law, Southern Illinois University.

Torts—Injuries to Family, Social and Trade Relations, 1979, 358 pages, by Wex S. Malone, Professor of Law Emeritus, Louisiana State University.

Trial Advocacy, 1979, 402 pages, by Paul B. Bergman, Adjunct Professor of Law, University of California, Los Angeles.

Trial and Practice Skills, 1978, 346 pages, by Kenney F. Hegland, Professor of Law, University of Arizona.

Trial, The First—Where Do I Sit? What Do I Say?, 1982, 396 pages, by Steven H. Goldberg, Professor of Law, University of Minnesota.

Unfair Trade Practices, 1982, 444 pages, by Charles R. McManis, Professor of Law, Washington University, St. Louis.

Uniform Commercial Code, 2nd Ed., 1984, 516 pages, by Bradford Stone, Professor of Law, Detroit College of Law.

Uniform Probate Code, 1978, 425 pages, by Lawrence H. Averill, Jr., Dean and Professor of Law, University of Arkansas, Little Rock.

Water Law, 1984, 439 pages, by David H. Getches, Professor of Law, University of Colorado.

Welfare Law—Structure and Entitlement, 1979, 455 pages, by Arthur B. LaFrance, Dean and Professor of Law, Lewis and Clark College, Northwestern School of Law.

Wills and Trusts, 1979, 392 pages, by Robert L. Mennell, Former Professor of Law, Hamline University.

Workers' Compensation and Employee Protection Laws, 1984, 248 pages, by Jack B. Hood, Former Professor of Law, Cumberland School of Law, Samford University and Benjamin A. Hardy, Former Professor of Law, Cumberland School of Law, Samford University.

Hornbook Series

and

Basic Legal Texts

of

WEST PUBLISHING COMPANY

P.O. Box 64526

St. Paul, Minnesota 55164–0526

Administrative Law, Davis' Text on, 3rd Ed., 1972, 617 pages, by Kenneth Culp Davis, Professor of Law, University of San Diego.

Agency and Partnership, Reuschlein & Gregory's Hornbook on the Law of, 1979 with 1981 Pocket Part, 625 pages, by Harold Gill Reuschlein, Professor of Law Emeritus, Villanova University and William A. Gregory, Professor of Law, Georgia State University.

Antitrust, Sullivan's Hornbook on the Law of, 1977, 886 pages, by Lawrence A. Sullivan, Professor of Law, University of California, Berkeley.

Civil Procedure, Friedenthal, Kane and Miller's Hornbook on, Student Ed., 1985, approximately 750 pages, by Jack H. Friedental, Professor of Law, Stanford University, Mary K. Kane, Professor of Law, University of California, Hastings College of the Law and Arthur R. Miller, Professor of Law, Harvard University.

Common Law Pleading, Koffler and Reppy's Hornbook on, 1969, 663 pages, by Joseph H. Koffler, Professor of Law, New York Law School and Alison Reppy, Late Dean and Professor of Law, New York Law School.

Conflict of Laws, Scoles and Hay's Hornbook on, Student Ed., 1982, 1085 pages, by Eugene F. Scoles, Professor of Law,

List current as of January, 1985

University of Illinois and Peter Hay, Dean and Professor of Law, University of Illinois.

Constitutional Law, Nowak, Rotunda and Young's Hornbook on, 2nd Ed., Student Ed., 1983, 1172 pages, by John E. Nowak, Professor of Law, University of Illinois, Ronald D. Rotunda, Professor of Law, University of Illinois, and J. Nelson Young, Professor of Law, University of North Carolina.

Contracts, Calamari and Perillo's Hornbook on, 2nd Ed., 1977, 878 pages, by John D. Calamari, Professor of Law, Fordham University and Joseph M. Perillo, Professor of Law, Fordham University.

Contracts, Corbin's One Volume Student Ed., 1952, 1224 pages, by Arthur L. Corbin, Late Professor of Law, Yale University.

Corporate Taxation, Kahn's Handbook on, 3rd Ed., Student Ed., Soft cover, 1981 with 1983 Supplement, 614 pages, by Douglas A. Kahn, Professor of Law, University of Michigan.

Corporations, Henn and Alexander's Hornbook on, 3rd Ed., Student Ed., 1983, 1371 pages, by Harry G. Henn, Professor of Law, Cornell University and John R. Alexander, Member, New York and Hawaii Bars.

Criminal Law, LaFave and Scott's Hornbook on, 1972, 763 pages, by Wayne R. LaFave, Professor of Law, University of Illinois, and Austin Scott, Jr., Late Professor of Law, University of Colorado.

Criminal Procedure, LaFave and Israel's Hornbook on, Student Ed., 1985, approximately 1300 pages, by Wayne R. LaFave, Professor of Law, University of Illinois and Jerold H. Israel, Professor of Law University of Michigan.

Damages, McCormick's Hornbook on, 1935, 811 pages, by Charles T. McCormick, Late Dean and Professor of Law, University of Texas.

Domestic Relations, Clark's Hornbook on, 1968, 754 pages, by Homer H. Clark, Jr., Professor of Law, University of Colorado.

Economics and Federal Antitrust Law, Hovenkamp's Hornbook on, Student Ed., 1985, approximately 375 pages, by Herbert

Hovenkamp, Professor of Law, University of California, Hastings College of the Law.

Environmental Law, Rodgers' Hornbook on, 1977 with 1984 Pocket Part, 956 pages, by William H. Rodgers, Jr., Professor of Law, University of Washington.

Evidence, Lilly's Introduction to, 1978, 486 pages, by Graham C. Lilly, Professor of Law, University of Virginia.

Evidence, McCormick's Hornbook on, 3rd Ed., Student Ed., 1984, 1155 pages, General Editor, Edward W. Cleary, Professor of Law Emeritus, Arizona State University.

Federal Courts, Wright's Hornbook on, 4th Ed., Student Ed., 1983, 870 pages, by Charles Alan Wright, Professor of Law, University of Texas.

Federal Income Taxation of Individuals, Posin's Hornbook on, Student Ed., 1983 with 1985 Pocket Part, 491 pages, by Daniel Q. Posin, Jr., Professor of Law, Southern Methodist University.

Future Interest, Simes' Hornbook on, 2nd Ed., 1966, 355 pages, by Lewis M. Simes, Late Professor of Law, University of Michigan.

Insurance, Keeton's Basic Text on, 1971, 712 pages, by Robert E. Keeton, Professor of Law Emeritus, Harvard University.

Labor Law, Gorman's Basic Text on, 1976, 914 pages, by Robert A. Gorman, Professor of Law, University of Pennsylvania.

Law Problems, Ballentine's, 5th Ed., 1975, 767 pages, General Editor, William E. Burby, Late Professor of Law, University of Southern California.

Legal Writing Style, Weihofen's, 2nd Ed., 1980, 332 pages, by Henry Weihofen, Professor of Law Emeritus, University of New Mexico.

Local Government Law, Reynolds' Hornbook on, 1982, 860 pages, by Osborne M. Reynolds, Professor of Law, University of Oklahoma.

New York Practice, Siegel's Hornbook on, 1978, with 1981–82 Pocket Part, 1011 pages, by David D. Siegel, Professor of Law, Albany Law School of Union University.

Oil and Gas, Hemingway's Hornbook on, 2nd Ed., Student Ed., 1983, 543 pages, by Richard W. Hemingway, Professor of Law, University of Oklahoma.

Poor, Law of the, LaFrance, Schroeder, Bennett and Boyd's Hornbook on, 1973, 558 pages, by Arthur B. LaFrance, Dean and Professor of Law, Lewis and Clark College, Northwestern School of Law, Milton R. Schroeder, Professor of Law, Arizona State University, Robert W. Bennett, Professor of Law, Northwestern University and William E. Boyd, Professor of Law, University of Arizona.

Property, Boyer's Survey of, 3rd Ed., 1981, 766 pages, by Ralph E. Boyer, Professor of Law, University of Miami.

Property, Law of, Cunningham, Whitman and Stoebuck's Hornbook on, Student Ed., 1984, 916 pages, by Roger A. Cunningham, Professor of Law, University of Michigan, Dale A. Whitman, Dean and Professor of Law, University of Missouri–Columbia and William B. Stoebuck, Professor of Law, University of Washington.

Real Estate Finance Law, Osborne, Nelson and Whitman's Hornbook on, (successor to Hornbook on Mortgages), 1979, 885 pages, by George E. Osborne, Late Professor of Law, Stanford University, Grant S. Nelson, Professor of Law, University of Missouri, Columbia and Dale A. Whitman, Dean and Professor of Law, University of Missouri, Columbia.

Real Property, Burby's Hornbook on, 3rd Ed., 1965, 490 pages, by William E. Burby, Late Professor of Law, University of Southern California.

Real Property, Moynihan's Introduction to, 1962, 254 pages, by Cornelius J. Moynihan, Professor of Law, Suffolk University.

Remedies, Dobb's Hornbook on, 1973, 1067 pages, by Dan B. Dobbs, Professor of Law, University of Arizona.

Secured Transactions under the U.C.C., Henson's Hornbook on, 2nd Ed., 1979, with 1979 Pocket Part, 504 pages, by Ray D.

Henson, Professor of Law, University of California, Hastings College of the Law.

Securities Regulation, Hazen's Hornbook on the Law of, Student Ed., 1985, approximately 665 pages, by Thomas Lee Hazen, Professor of Law, University of North Carolina.

Torts, Prosser and Keeton's Hornbook on, 5th Ed., Student Ed., 1984, 1286 pages, by William L. Prosser, Late Dean and Professor of Law, University of California, Berkeley, Page Keeton, Professor of Law Emeritus, University of Texas, Dan B. Dobbs, Professor of Law, University of Arizona, Robert E. Keeton, Professor of Law Emeritus, Harvard University and David G. Owen, Professor of Law, University of South Carolina.

Trial Advocacy, Jeans' Handbook on, Student Ed., Soft cover, 1975, by James W. Jeans, Professor of Law, University of Missouri, Kansas City.

Trusts, Bogert's Hornbook on, 5th Ed., 1973, 726 pages, by George G. Bogert, Late Professor of Law, University of Chicago and George T. Bogert, Attorney, Chicago, Illinois.

Urban Planning and Land Development Control, Hagman's Hornbook on, 1971, 706 pages, by Donald G. Hagman, Late Professor of Law, University of California, Los Angeles.

Uniform Commercial Code, White and Summers' Hornbook on, 2nd Ed., 1980, 1250 pages, by James J. White, Professor of Law, University of Michigan and Robert S. Summers, Professor of Law, Cornell University.

Wills, Atkinson's Hornbook on, 2nd Ed., 1953, 975 pages, by Thomas E. Atkinson, Late Professor of Law, New York University.

Advisory Board

LEGAL RESEARCH

IN A NUTSHELL

By

MORRIS L. COHEN
Librarian and Professor of Law,
Yale Law School

FOURTH EDITION

ST. PAUL, MINN.
WEST PUBLISHING CO.
1985

50 West Kellogg Boulevard
P.O. Box 64526
St. Paul, Minnesota 55164–0526

Printed in the United States of America

Library of Congress Cataloging in Publication Data

Cohen, Morris L., 1927–
Legal research in a nutshell.

(Nutshell series)
Includes bibliographical references and index.
1. Legal research—United States. I. Title.
II. Series.
KF240.C54 1984 340'.072073 84–21929

ISBN 0–314–83243–2

Cohen Legal Research 4th Ed. NS

To Gloria Cohen

*

PREFACE

The growing interest in American legal research, both in the professional and lay communities, has led to a proliferation of new guides to legal bibliography and research techniques. Over the last fifteen years, *Legal Research in a Nutshell,* in three successive editions, has provided a basic introduction to this increasingly complex mass of materials. This fourth edition continues that function for a new generation of students and scholars, and for all who seek to know the law.

The literature of American law is rich and varied and has a long and distinguished history. Its primary sources contain the rules of human behavior by which our society is governed; its ingenious finding tools provide access to the mass of chronologically published decisions and statutes; and its wide ranging secondary sources illuminate the law by study of its past, its present, and its future.

Legal literature, reflecting and shaping the continuing struggle for justice and order, is part of our total cultural heritage. But knowledge of its forms and skill in its use are even more certainly an essential part of the lawyer's basic training and equipment. This epitome of American legal bibliography is designed primarily to assist the student in achieving such knowledge and skill. Since this *Nutshell* is not intended to be a reference tool in the usual sense, footnotes and most bibliographic detail have been omitted or placed in the Appendices. For more detailed references, the reader can use Cohen and Berring, *How to Find the Law,* 8th ed. (1983) or its abridged edition, *Finding the Law* (1984).

For best effect, readings in the *Nutshell* should be followed by exposure to the actual sources described herein, in a library setting. The problem book for *How to Find the Law,* by Elizabeth Slusser Kelly and Lynn Foster (1983), or its projected successor by Lynn Foster and Nancy P. Johnson (1985), is recommended for this purpose. Those exercises can be supplemented by more analytical legal method problems, or through legal writing assignments.

Since the publication of the first edition of this manual, the nature of legal research and the forms of legal material have undergone many changes and will undoubtedly continue to incorporate new developments in information technology. Computerized legal research and the use of microforms are becoming accepted in law libraries and are described herein where relevant. While the essential publications and processes remain familiar, bibliographic advances are significantly improving the nature and effectiveness of legal research. The maximum potential inherent in both traditional and modern research techniques can only be realized by an adequate understanding of the form and content of legal literature. This guide is designed to facilitate such an understanding.

For their permission to reproduce exhibits from their respective publications, the author acknowledges the kindness of the American Association of Law Libraries, the Bureau of National Affairs, Capitol Services, Inc., Commerce Clearing House, Inc., the Congressional Information Service, Congressional Quarterly, Information Access Company, Lawyers Co-operative Publishing Company, Oceana Publications, Inc., Fred B. Rothman & Co., Shepard's Citations/ McGraw-Hill, Inc., Sweet & Maxwell, Ltd., the Edward Thompson Company, the West Publishing Company, and the H.W. Wilson Company.

The author wishes to express his gratitude to colleagues at the Yale Law School Library for their support in preparation of this new edition, and to Cynthia Arkin, Karen Bragg, Elyse Fox, Stephen R. Hildrich, Kent McKeever, Diana Moses, Kent Olson, Laura Praglin, Sara Robbins, and Kay Webb, who helped directly in its revision. Special thanks are given to Kent Olson, who helped edit the book in all its stages, and to Sara Robbins who prepared the index. And to those who are introduced to legal research through these pages, I offer my hope that their use of the book will justify the investment.

MORRIS L. COHEN

New Haven, February, 1985

*

OUTLINE

APPENDICES

*

LEGAL RESEARCH

IN A NUTSHELL

*

CHAPTER I

INTRODUCTION

The forms and usages of law books are varied and, taken in their entirety, may appear at first view somewhat confusing. However, for a simpler perspective, legal literature can be divided into three broad categories: (a) primary sources; (b) search books or finding tools; and (c) secondary materials.

Primary Sources. We can define the primary sources as those recorded rules of human behavior which will be enforced by the state. They include statutes passed by legislatures, decisions of courts, decrees and orders of executives, and regulations and rulings of administrative agencies.

American law today, as so construed, has a number of characteristics which should be noted for their pervasive bibliographic significance.

It is subject to constant change through tens of thousands of new decisions and new statutes issued each year, requiring regular and prompt supplementation and updating.

Its development is marked, however, by a quest for certainty and stability, as reflected in the doctrine of *stare decisis,* which gives most law books a continuing relevance long beyond their initial publication.

It derives from many governmental agencies (judicial, legislative and executive) and from a variety of jurisdictions (the federal government, fifty states, a host of local counties, cities and towns, and even some international agencies, whose rules may be accepted by tribunals here). This variety of law-making bodies vastly multiplies the bibliographic sources of law in this country.

Its judicial system embodies hierarchies of courts (typically including, in each jurisdiction, a number of trial courts, one or more intermediate appeal courts, and a high court, usually the *Supreme Court* of the jurisdiction). This system includes a process of appellate review whereby appeal courts may be called upon to review the decisions of lower courts and even the acts of the legislative and executive branches.

The contents of its legal publications differ in their relative authority—some are binding, others only persuasive in various degrees, and some lacking any formal legal force—leading to the need for careful evaluation by the user.

Its forms are issued *chronologically* in either official or unofficial publications, requiring some means of access by subject to enable the researcher to find the law applicable to a particular factual situation.

Federal and state statutes and appellate court decisions are the most important primary authorities. Traditionally they were the only primary sources of law, administrative materials being considered secondary forms since their authority *derived* from the legislature. Only in recent generations, by virtue of their great impact on the legal system, have administrative regulations, orders, and decisions been treated as primary sources.

The primary sources relevant to any problem may range in time from the first enactments of law-making bodies to the most recent decisions, statutes and rulings. A current decision may be based on a precedent many generations old; an executive order may stem from a statute of another century. Since primary sources retain legal effect until expressly overruled or repealed, it is necessary that even the earliest sources remain accessible. The accessibility of the *latest* legal sources is also, as we have seen, an inherent requirement of effective legal research.

Finding Tools. Because of the great number of decisions and statutes issued since the beginning of our legal history and because of their chronological method of publication, the researcher needs some means of subject access into this large body of law. The effective operation of the doctrine of precedent requires that prior decisions be easily available. In legal research, as in other aspects of the lawyer's work, one must employ what should be a highly developed sense of relevance—a keen appreciation of what is legally and factually relevant to a particular problem. Without a topical approach to legal sources, one could not find existing statutes or decided cases in point. A varied group of finding tools, typically issued by specialized private publishers, provides such access. This includes digests of decisions, citators, encyclopedias, phrasebooks, annotated statutory compilations, looseleaf services, indexes, and computerized research systems such as LEXIS and WESTLAW.

Such research tools may themselves lack legal authority, but they provide the means of locating the primary sources of authority.

Secondary Materials. Secondary sources are the last major component of legal bibliography. These include textbooks, treatises, practice manuals, commentaries, restatements, and periodicals which explain and describe the law for the practitioner, the scholar and the student. They vary widely in quality, form and authority, ranging from monumental treatises by great academic scholars to superficial tracts by hack writers. Encyclopedias are usually considered to be secondary sources, although some scholars prefer to treat them primarily as case finders and cast them with the finding tools and search books.

Although these works lack legal authority in a formal sense, some have a persuasive influence on the law-making process by virtue of the prestige of their authors or the recognized quality of their scholarship. Access to these materials is usually provided by their internal subject indexes, although a variety of separate indexes have been developed for periodicals, and some guides and bibliographies are available for texts and treatises.

LAW LIBRARIES

There are varied types of law libraries, serving many kinds of readers who are engaged in legal research for different reasons and with different approaches. These collections range in size and purpose from the million-volume libraries at the Harvard Law School and the Law Library of Congress to the law office library of a thousand volumes serving a few practicing lawyers. Law libraries are also found in court houses, government agencies, corporations, bar associations, and even within some public libraries.

Regardless of differences in size, purpose and clientele, most law libraries have a great deal in common. The following are the usual components of the larger law libraries, arranged somewhat arbitrarily into the three main categories of legal material:

Primary Sources

Administrative decisions and rulings

Administrative rules and regulations

Constitutions

Executive documents

Judicial reports

Statutes—session laws and codes

Treaties

Finding Tools

Bibliographies and research guides

Citators

Computerized research services

Digests of case law

Indexes to statutes and legislative history

Looseleaf services

Periodical indexes

Word and phrase books

Secondary Materials

Administrative reports and studies

Appellate records and briefs

Attorneys General opinions

Bar association reports and proceedings

Biographies of lawyers and judges

Commentaries, histories and surveys of law

Constitutional conventions and documents

Dictionaries

Directories of lawyers and law firms

Encyclopedias

Fiction and anecdotes relating to law

Foreign and comparative legal sources

Form books

International legal sources

Legislative history

Periodicals

Practice and procedure manuals

Reference books—legal and general

Restatements of the Law

Sourcebooks of historical documents

Texts, treatises and monographs

Trials

Access to the contents of law libraries may be facilitated in several ways: law librarians, who are often trained bibliographic specialists, offer expert direction; the specialized indexes and finding tools described herein provide access to the primary sources of law; bibliographies of many kinds list specific types of legal sources; and the card catalog, that most neglected and ingenious tool of information retrieval, aids in identifying and locating most of the library's collection. The advent of the computer has added another means of access to the contents of law libraries.

AIDS TO RESEARCH

Because legal research differs from research in general, several special aids are recommended. For an understanding and mastery of the language of the law, a good law dictionary is a necessity for the beginning student. See Chapter IX, Secondary Materials, at pages 316–317 below, for specific suggestions.

To cope with the complex shorthand of legal citations, guides to proper citation form and usage are available. *A Uniform System of Citation,* published by the Harvard Law Review Association (13th ed., 1981) and commonly referred to as the *Bluebook,* is the generally accepted standard.

Abbreviations of many kinds are widely used in legal writing, and aids to their meanings are frequently needed. The *Bluebook* contains many explanatory lists of abbreviations. *Black's Law Dictionary* includes the most extensive coverage of abbreviations, but lacks many references to current reporters, session laws and statutory compilations which are covered well in the *Bluebook.*

The following specialized aids to abbreviations are also recommended:

D.M. Bieber, *Dictionary of Legal Abbreviations Used in American Law Books* (William S. Hein, 1979).

D.M. Bieber, *Current American Legal Citations with 2100 Examples* (William S. Hein, 1983).

M.D. Powers, *The Legal Citation Directory* (Franas Press, 1971).

D. Raistrick, *Index to Legal Citations and Abbreviations* (Abingdon, England, Professional Books, 1981).

Legal sources have been more fully described and listed than those of perhaps any other literature. The bibliographic approaches of legal research are more sophisticated than those of perhaps any other discipline. New developments of information science have further improved access to the law, particularly by microfacsimiles and computerized search services. However, the practitioners of legal research have never fully exploited the tools at hand. The widespread failure to use the many aids and shortcuts now available leads to that sad by-product of bibliographic ignorance—needless waste of valuable time and effort.

CHAPTER II

JUDICIAL REPORTS

Law reports, containing the decisions of courts, form one of the two great sources of legal authority. The reports consist primarily of *appellate* decisions, but some also include decisions rendered by *trial* courts on issues of law. Although statutes appear direct and imperative, they are often ineffective until construed or interpreted by judges and actually applied to particular situations.

The development of the recording of judicial decisions has been related to the quest for certainty in the law. Those seeking to achieve regularity in the impact of legal rules soon came to realize the value of recording the decisions of particular legal controversies. Such records provide guidance to later tribunals when faced with similar cases, and also aid in preventing further disputes.

Karl Llewellyn formulated the following reasons for the doctrine of precedent:

> " . . . laziness as to the reworking of a problem once solved; the time and energy saved by routine, especially under any pressure of business; the values of routine as a curb on arbitrariness and as a prop of weakness, inexperience and instability; the social values of predictability; the power of whatever exists to produce expectations and the power of expectations to become normative . . . that curious, almost universal sense of justice which

urges that all men are properly to be treated alike in like circumstances." Llewellyn, "Case Law", 3 *Encyclopaedia of the Social Sciences* 249 (1930).

From its beginnings, law reporting facilitated the achievement of those purposes, particularly the search for predictability in law. Written records made it possible to evaluate the future impact of the law and the conduct of individuals influenced thereby. Whether or not that was the original rationale of law reporting, it certainly has been its most important by-product.

The earliest evidence of law reporting in England closely follows the Norman conquest of 1066; scattered records of judicial decisions exist from that period. The *Plea Rolls,* beginning with Richard I in 1189, contain fragmentary reports, which have been republished and cited in later works. Many of the oldest cases, however, remain only in the synthesis of early legal texts, such as those by Glanville (c. 1190) and Bracton (c. 1250).

The next collection of English judicial reports is found in the *Yearbooks,* which cover the long period from 1285 to 1537. These reports were actually written in court, by either law students or lawyers. Some represent verbatim transcripts of the proceedings; others are brief summaries of the decisions. In their entirety they constitute a great body of legal literature, which has been edited and republished in scholarly series by the Selden Society and similar groups.

Following the *Yearbooks* came the *nominative* reporters, that is, court reports named for the particular individual who recorded or edited them. The earliest known reporter was probably James Dyer, whose reports were published around 1550 and covered cases from 1537. Plowden's *Reports*, which were first published in 1571, are considered among the finest and most accurate, while the reports of Sir Edward Coke are perhaps the most influential of that period. The nominatives continued until modern English law reporting began in 1865 with the establishment of the *Law Reports*, a quasi-official series of annual reporters for each of the four major English courts. These and other current English reporters are discussed more fully in Chapter X below.

By virtue of our common legal history, the English legal system still has a special relevance in this country. The American colonies inherited the English common law and a legal tradition of statutes, cases, customs, and attitudes. This inheritance was made express in many of the newly independent states by the enactment of laws adopting the English common law and statutes as part of the law of the state. These *reception statutes* excluded, however, those portions of English law which were considered repugnant to the American experience. Although we have increasingly gone our separate ways, English laws and legal scholarship have continued to exert a persuasive influence here. The development of English law reporting has similarly shaped our own experience in that regard.

The reporting of court decisions is affected by the hierarchical structure of the judicial system at both the federal and state levels in this country. Typically, litigation begins in one of a variety of trial courts.

The jurisdiction of these courts may be based on a geographical unit (e.g. the U. S. District Courts in the federal court system, or county courts in many states), on the type of case they hear (e.g. the U. S. Claims Court, or, in the states, family courts, probate courts, criminal courts, etc.), or often on a combination of the two factors. The trend in modern court reform is toward more unified systems in which trial courts have broad subject coverage, rather than systems utilizing many separate specialized courts.

Appeals from the decisions of trial courts are generally taken to an intermediate appellate court (e.g., the U. S. Court of Appeals on the federal level and similar tribunals on the state level). The highest court in each jurisdiction (the Supreme Court of the United States and the supreme courts of the various states) will hear appeals from the intermediate appellate courts, but under certain circumstances may take cases directly from the trial court. In a few special situations the high court may function as a court of original jurisdiction, i.e., hear a case in the first instance. The rules of jurisdiction vary from state to state, but the federal courts and their rules are increasingly used as models in state court reorganizations.

AMERICAN FEDERAL LAW REPORTING

Reports of the U.S. Supreme Court

The early development of American reports followed the pattern of the British reports of the same period. While nominative reporting was still the common practice in England, the first American reports were also issued under the name of individual reporters, beginning with Kirby's *Reports* in Connecticut in 1789.

Official court reporting, that is, the publication of reports pursuant to statutory direction, did not begin until 1804 when Massachusetts, New York and Kentucky authorized official reports for their respective courts. The *United States Reports* started in 1790 as a private venture, but became official in 1817 and continues today as the official edition of United States Supreme Court decisions. Alexander J. Dallas was the Court's first official reporter and issued the first four volumes of the *U.S. Reports*, covering the period from 1790 to 1800. The first volume of his reports, however, does not contain federal Supreme Court decisions, but rather decisions from several Pennsylvania courts.

Citations to cases in the early volumes of the *U.S. Reports* must include the name of the particular reporter, such as *Marbury v. Madison*, 5 U.S. (1 Cranch) 137 (1803). A list of the early official reporters for the Supreme Court follows.

Nominative Reports			**U.S. Reports**
Dallas	1–4	(1790–1800)	1–4
Cranch	1–9	(1801–1815)	5–13
Wheaton	1–12	(1816–1827)	14–25
Peters	1–16	(1828–1842)	26–41
Howard	1–24	(1843–1860)	42–65
Black	1–2	(1861–1862)	66–67
Wallace	1–23	(1863–1874)	68–90

After volume 90 (1874), cases are normally cited only by volume number of the *U.S. Reports*. Thus the official citation of *Roe v. Wade,* a 1973 decision on abortion, is 410 U.S. 113 (1973), meaning the case beginning on page 113 of volume 410 of the *U.S. Reports.* The opening page of the official report of *Roe v. Wade* appears below in Exhibit 1.

ROE *v.* WADE 113

Syllabus

ROE ET AL. *v.* WADE, DISTRICT ATTORNEY OF DALLAS COUNTY

APPEAL FROM THE UNITED STATES DISTRICT COURT FOR THE NORTHERN DISTRICT OF TEXAS

No. 70–18. Argued December 13, 1971—Reargued October 11, 1972—Decided January 22, 1973

A pregnant single woman (Roe) brought a class action challenging the constitutionality of the Texas criminal abortion laws, which proscribe procuring or attempting an abortion except on medical advice for the purpose of saving the mother's life. A licensed physician (Hallford), who had two state abortion prosecutions

and presented justiciable controversies. Ruling that declaratory, though not injunctive, relief was warranted, the court declared the abortion statutes void as vague and overbroadly infringing those plaintiffs' Ninth and Fourteenth Amendment rights. The court ruled the Does' complaint not justiciable. Appellants directly appealed to this Court on the injunctive rulings, and appellee cross-appealed from the District Court's grant of declaratory relief to Roe and Hallford. *Held:*

1. While 28 U. S. C. § 1253 authorizes no direct appeal to this Court from the grant or denial of declaratory relief alone, review is not foreclosed when the case is properly before the Court on appeal from specific denial of injunctive relief and the arguments as to both injunctive and declaratory relief are necessarily identical. P. 123.

2. Roe has standing to sue; the Does and Hallford do not. Pp. 123–129.

(a) Contrary to appellee's contention, the natural termination of Roe's pregnancy did not moot her suit. Litigation involving pregnancy, which is "capable of repetition, yet evading review," is an exception to the usual federal rule that an actual controversy

Exhibit 1: The official *U.S. Reports*, showing the beginning of the official syllabus.

A similar form of citation, including case name and date, is used for all court reports, whether state or federal, official or unofficial. In practice, most attorneys include in their citations parallel references to the unofficial reports for the convenience of their readers, although that is not strictly necessary.

In addition to the official *U.S. Reports,* there are also two privately published editions of the Supreme Court's decisions which provide special research aids and supplementary material not in the official edition. These unofficial editions, described below, reproduce the same text of decisions as the official reports. They include more decisions than the official by occasionally publishing decisions rendered by Supreme Court justices sitting on circuits of the U.S. Court of Appeals, which may not have been reported officially. Since the unofficial reports usually include references to the citation of the official report, the researcher can cite directly to the official text. This is sometimes facilitated by a method called "star paging" which superimposes the official pagination on the text of the unofficial report by marginal references. See Exhibit 2.

718 93 SUPREME COURT REPORTER 410 U.S. 134

nant view, following the great common-law scholars, has been that it was, at most, a lesser offense. In a frequently ⊥135 cited ⊥ passage, Coke took the position that abortion of a woman "quick with childe" is "a great misprision, and no murder." [24] Blackstone followed, saying that while abortion after quickening had once been considered manslaughter (though not murder), "modern law" took a less severe view.[25] A recent review of the common-law precedents argues, however, that those precedents contradict Coke and that even post-quickening abortion was never established as a common-law crime.[26] This is of some importance because while most American courts ruled, in holding or dictum, that abortion of an unquickened fetus was not criminal under their received common law,[27] others followed ⊥136 Coke in stating that abor⊥tion of a quick fetus was a "misprision," a term they translated to mean "misdemeanor." [28] That their reliance on Coke on this aspect of the law was uncritical and, apparently in all the reported cases, dictum (due probably to the paucity of common-law prosecutions for post-quickening abortion), makes it now appear doubtful that abortion was ever firmly established as a common-law crime even with respect to the destruction of a quick fetus.

4. *The English statutory law.* England's first criminal abortion statute, Lord Ellenborough's Act, 43 Geo. 3, c. 58, came in 1803. It made abortion of a quick fetus, § 1, a capital crime, but in § 2 it provided lesser penalties for the felony of abortion before quickening, and thus preserved the "quickening" distinction. This contrast was continued in the general revision of 1828, 9 Geo. 4, c. 31, § 13. It disappeared, however, together with the death penalty, in 1837, 7 Will. 4 & 1 Vict., c. 85, § 6, and did not reappear in the Offenses Against the Person Act of 1861, 24 & 25 Vict., c. 100, § 59, that formed the core of English anti-abortion law until the liberalizing reforms of 1967. In 1929, the Infant Life (Preservation) Act, 19 & 20 Geo. 5, c. 34, came into being. Its emphasis was upon the destruction of "the life of

24. E. Coke, Institutes III *50.

25. 1 W. Blackstone, Commentaries *129–130.

26. Means, The Phoenix of Abortional Freedom: Is a Penumbral or Ninth-Amendment Right About to Arise from the Nineteenth-Century Legislative Ashes of a Fourteenth-Century Common-Law Liberty?, 17 N.Y.L.F. 335 (1971) (hereinafter Means II). The author examines the two principal precedents cited marginally by Coke, both contrary to his dictum, and traces the treatment of these and other cases by earlier commentators. He concludes that Coke, who himself participated as an advocate in an abortion case in 1601, may have intentionally misstated the law. The author even suggests a reason: Coke's strong feelings against abortion, coupled with his determination to assert common-law (secular) jurisdiction to assess penalties for an offense that traditionally had been an exclusively ecclesiastical or canon-law crime. See also Lader 78–79, who notes that some scholars doubt that the common law ever was applied to abortion; that the English ecclesiastical courts seem to have lost interest in the problem after 1527; and that the preamble to the English legislation of 1803, 43 Geo. 3, c. 58, § 1, referred to in the text, *infra*, at 718, states that "no adequate means have been hitherto provided for the prevention and punishment of such offenses."

27. Commonwealth v. Bangs, 9 Mass. 387, 388 (1812); Commonwealth v. Parker, 50 Mass. (9 Metc.) 263, 265–266 (1845); State v. Cooper, 22 N.J.L. 52, 58 (1849); Abrams v. Foshee, 3 Iowa 274, 278–280 (1856); Smith v. Gaffard, 31 Ala. 45, 51 (1857); Mitchell v. Commonwealth, 78 Ky. 204, 210 (1879); Eggart v. State, 40 Fla. 527, 532, 25 So. 144, 145 (1898); State v. Alcorn, 7 Idaho 599, 606, 64 P. 1014, 1016 (1901); Edwards v. State, 79 Neb. 251, 252, 112 N.W. 611, 612 (1907); Gray v. State, 77 Tex.Cr.R. 221, 224, 178 S.W. 337, 338 (1915); Miller v. Bennett, 190 Va. 162, 169, 56 S.E.2d 217, 221 (1949). Contra, Mills v. Commonwealth, 13 Pa. 631, 633 (1850); State v. Slagle, 83 N.C. 630, 632 (1880).

28. See Smith v. State, 33 Me. 48, 55 (1851); Evans v. People, 49 N.Y. 86, 88 (1872); Lamb v. State, 67 Md. 524, 533, 10 A. 208 (1887).

Exhibit 2: Star paging, as illustrated in an unofficial report of *Roe v. Wade.*

The *Supreme Court Reporter*, one the two major unofficial reports, begins with volume 106 of the *U.S. Reports* and incorporates the West Publishing Company's key number digest system, which indexes the significant points of law in all reported decisions in a unique classification scheme of broad legal topics and detailed subtopics. (The key number system will be more fully discussed in Chapter III below.) Decisions appearing in the *Supreme Court Reporter* and in all of West's other reporters are preceded by headnotes containing short abstracts of the legal issues in the case. Each headnote is classified by the name of the digest topic and sub-topic numbers (called *key* numbers) which are assigned to that point of law in the case. The opening page of *Roe v. Wade* as it appears in the *Supreme Court Reporter* at 93 S.Ct. 705 is shown in Exhibit 3 below and illustrates these headnotes.

410 U.S. 113 **ROE v. WADE** **705**

Cite as 93 S.Ct. 705 (1973)

410 U.S. 113, 35 L.Ed.2d 147

Jane ROE, et al., Appellants,

v.

Henry WADE.

No. 70–18.

Argued Dec. 13, 1971.

Reargued Oct. 11, 1972.

Decided Jan. 22, 1973.

Rehearing Denied Feb. 26, 1973.

See 410 U.S. 959, 93 S.Ct. 1409.

Action was brought for a declaratory and injunctive relief respecting Texas criminal abortion laws which were claimed to be unconstitutional. A

declaratory aspects of case attacking constitutionality of Texas criminal abortion statutes where case was properly before Supreme Court on direct appeal from decision of three-judge district court specifically denying injunctive relief and the arguments as to both aspects were necessarily identical. 28 U.S.C.A. § 1253.

2. Constitutional Law ⚿**42.1(3), 46(1)**

With respect to single, pregnant female who alleged that she was unable to obtain a legal abortion in Texas, when viewed as of the time of filing of case and for several months thereafter, she had standing to challenge constitution-

---

unconstitutional; that prior to approximately the end of the first trimester the abortion decision and its effectuation must be left to the medical judgment of the pregnant woman's attending physician, subsequent to approximately the end of the first trimester the state may regulate abortion procedure in ways reasonably related to maternal health, and at the stage subsequent to viability the state may regulate and even proscribe abortion except where necessary in appropriate medical judgment for preservation of life or health of mother.

Affirmed in part and reversed in part.

Mr. Chief Justice Burger, Mr. Justice Douglas and Mr. Justice Stewart filed concurring opinions.

Mr. Justice White filed a dissenting opinion in which Mr. Justice Rehnquist joined.

Mr. Justice Rehnquist filed a dissenting opinion.

1. Courts ⚿**385(7)**

Supreme Court was not foreclosed from review of both the injunctive and

93 S.Ct.—45

3. Courts ⚿**383(1), 385(1)**

Usual rule in federal cases is that an actual controversy must exist at stages of appellate or certiorari review and not simply at date action is initiated.

4. Action ⚿**6**

Where pregnancy of plaintiff was a significant fact in litigation and the normal human gestation period was so short that pregnancy would come to term before usual appellate process was complete, and pregnancy often came more than once to the same woman, fact of that pregnancy provided a classic justification for conclusion of nonmootness because of termination.

5. Federal Civil Procedure ⚿**331**

Texas physician, against whom there were pending indictments charging him with violations of Texas abortion laws who made no allegation of any substantial and immediate threat to any federally protected right that could not be asserted in his defense against state prosecutions and who had not alleged

Exhibit 3: The unofficial *Supreme Court Reporter*, showing the West Publishing Company's key number system of headnotes.

The other unofficial reporter is the *United States Supreme Court Reports, Lawyers' Edition*, published by the Lawyers Co-operative Publishing Company. *Lawyers' Edition*, as it is called, contains headnotes similar to West's, with its own numbering system, and includes legal analyses in the form of annotations to a few of the more important decisions. Indexes preceding the text of the annotation provide detailed access to the annotation by subject, court and jurisdiction. The annotations in volumes 1–31 of *Lawyers' Edition 2d* are supplemented with later citations and comments in a separate volume entitled *Lawyers' Edition (2d series) Later Case Service.* Beginning with volume 32, each volume of reports contains a supplementary pocket part in the back of the volume for this purpose. Preceding each annotation is an insert entitled *Total Client-Service Library References* which refers users to coverage on the same topic in other Lawyers' Co-op tools, such as the *U.S. Supreme Court Digest, Lawyers' Edition,* and *American Jurisprudence 2d,* etc.

The texts of the Supreme Court's decisions are, of course, identical with those in the other two editions, but unlike the *Supreme Court Reporter, Lawyers' Edition* contains all Supreme Court decisions since 1791. Also, only this reporter carries summaries of the arguments of counsel, which may offer a better understanding of the court's decision.

Exhibits 4, 5, 6 and 7 show the opening page of *Roe v. Wade* in *Lawyers' Edition,* the beginning of the annotation, and the summary of the arguments of counsel.

147

[410 US 113]
JANE ROE et al., Appellants,

v

HENRY WADE

410 US 113, 35 L Ed 2d 147, 93 S Ct 705, reh den 410 US 959, 35 L Ed 2d 694, 93 S Ct 1409

[No. 70–18]

Argued December 13, 1971. Reargued October 11, 1972. Decided January 22, 1973.

SUMMARY

An unmarried pregnant woman who wished to terminate her pregnancy by abortion instituted an action in the United States District Court for the Northern District of Texas, seeking a declaratory judgment that the Texas criminal abortion statutes, which prohibited abortions except with

ment, (5) the Texas criminal abortion statutes were void on their face, because they were unconstitutionally vague and overbroad, and (6) the application for injunctive relief should be denied under the abstention doctrine (314 F Supp 1217). All parties took protective appeals to the United States Court of Appeals for the Fifth Circuit, which court ordered the appeals held in abeyance pending decision on the appeal taken by all parties to the United States Supreme Court, pursuant to 28 USCS § 1253, from the District Court's denial of injunctive relief.

SUBJECT OF ANNOTATION

Beginning on page 735, infra

Validity, under Federal Constitution, of abortion laws

Briefs of Counsel, p 730, infra.

Exhibit 4: The *Lawyers' Edition* report, showing the first page of its summary of *Roe v. Wade*.

ANNOTATION

VALIDITY, UNDER FEDERAL CONSTITUTION, OF ABORTION LAWS

by

Sheldon R. Shapiro, J.D.

TOTAL CLIENT-SERVICE LIBRARY® REFERENCES

1 AM JUR 2d, Abortion § 1.5
1 AM JUR OF PROOF OF FACTS 15, Abortion and Miscarriage
US L ED DIGEST, Abortion § 1; Constitutional Law § 526; Statutes § 18
ALR DIGESTS, Abortion §§ 1–3; Constitutional Law §§ 445, 452, 525; Statutes § 29
L ED INDEX TO ANNO, Abortion
ALR QUICK INDEX, Abortion
FEDERAL QUICK INDEX, Abortion

Consult POCKET PART in this volume for later case service

Exhibit 5: The opening page of the annotation in *Lawyers' Edition* on the validity of abortion laws, showing references to the subject in other Lawyers Co-op research tools.

INDEX

TABLE OF COURTS AND CIRCUITS

Consult POCKET PART in this volume for later case service

Exhibit 6: Subject index and table of courts and jurisdictions for the *Lawyers' Edition* annotation on abortion.

I. Preliminary matters

§ 1. Introduction

[a] Scope

This annotation[1] collects and analyzes the federal and state cases determining[2] whether, as a matter of federal constitutional law,[3] abortion[4] laws[5] are valid.

[b] Related matters

Indefiniteness of language as affecting validity of criminal legislation or judicial definition of common-law crime—Supreme Court cases. 96 L Ed 374, 16 L Ed 2d 1231.

Homicide based on killing of unborn child. 40 ALR3d 444.

Right of action for injury to or death of woman who consented to illegal abortion. 36 ALR3d 630.

Woman upon whom abortion is committed or attempted as accomplice for purposes of rule requiring corroboration of accomplice testimony. 34 ALR 3d 858.

Action for death of unborn child. 15 ALR3d 992.

Entrapment to commit or attempt abortion. 53 ALR2d 1156.

Pregnancy as element of abortion or homicide based thereon. 46 ALR 2d 1393.

Necessity, to warrant conviction of abortion, that fetus be living at time of commission of acts. 16 ALR2d 949.

Admissibility, in prosecution based on abortion, of evidence of commission of similar crimes by accused. 15 ALR2d 1080.

1. The annotation at 28 L Ed 2d 1053 is hereby superseded.

2. Dealing solely with cases which purport to determine federal constitutional issues as to the validity of abortion laws, the annotation does not discuss cases which merely present such issues without determining them.

3. For purposes of this annotation, if a particular issue involving the constitutionality of an abortion law is the type of issue which could arise either under the Federal Constitution or under a state constitution, and if the court, in discussing its decision of such issue, does not specify whether the decision is based upon the Federal Constitution or upon a state constitution, it is assumed, in the absence of any indication by the court to the contrary, that the decision is based upon the Federal Constitution.

4. This annotation is concerned solely with laws expressly referring to "abortion" or "miscarriage," the two terms having been treated by the courts as synonymous. This annotation is not, however, concerned with laws dealing generally with contraception or birth control, without dealing specifically with abortion; moreover, even if a contraception or birth control law consists in part of a reference to abortion, but if a court determines the constitutionality of the law only insofar as it relates to contraception or birth control, without discussing that part of the law referring to abortion, such a case is not included herein.

5. For present purposes, the term "laws" includes municipal ordinances as well as state and federal statutes, but does not include mere administrative action.

Exhibit 6: Cont'd.

730 ROE v WADE
35 L Ed 2d 147

JANE ROE et al., Appellants,

v

HENRY WADE

Reported in this volume: p 147, supra.

Holding: Texas criminal abortion statutes held unconstitutional.

Annotation: p 735, infra.

BRIEFS AND APPEARANCES OF COUNSEL

Sarah Weddington, of Austin, Texas, reargued the cause and, with **James R. Weddington,** also of Austin, Texas, **Roy Lucas, Norman Dorsen,** both of New York City, **Linda N. Coffee, Fred Bruner,** and **Roy L. Merrill, Jr.,** all of Dallas, Texas, filed briefs for appellants:

Plaintiffs Doe have standing to challenge the Texas abortion law and they do present a case or controversy. The Does are complaining not of a future, anticipated injury resulting from the unavailability of legal abortions, but of the effect that unavailability is currently having upon their marital relationship. Flast v Cohen, 392 US 83, 20 L Ed 2d 947, 88 S Ct 1942; Investment Co. Institute v Camp, 401 US 617, 28 L Ed 2d 367, 91 S Ct 1091; Epperson v Arkansas, 393 US 97, 21 L Ed 2d 228, 89 S Ct 266.

The fact that plaintiff Roe was forced to continue her pregnancy pending determination of her suit and could not then obtain a safe abortion does not moot the appeal, particularly in light of the class allegations. Southern Pacific Terminal Co. v ICC, 219 US 498, 515, 55 L Ed 310, 31 S Ct 279; Moore v Ogilvie, 394 US 814, 816, 23 L Ed 2d 1, 89 S Ct 1493; Gaddis v Wyman, 304 F Supp 713, 717, affd mem sub nom Wyman v Bowens, 397 US 49, 25 L Ed 2d 38, 90 S Ct 813; Kelly v Wyman, 294 F Supp 887, 890, 893, affd sub nom Goldberg v Kelly, 397 US 254, 257, 25 L Ed 2d 287, 90 S Ct 1011; United States v W. T. Grant Co. 345 US 629, 633, 97 L Ed 1303, 73 S Ct 894.

The abortion statute directly curtailed the physicians' interests in providing adequate medical advice and treatment for patients. These interests are aspects of liberty, property, and association directly protected by the Fourteenth and First Amendments. The opportunity to pursue one's profession is encompassed within the concepts of liberty and property. Willner v Committee on Character and Fitness, 373 US 96, 102, 103, 10 L Ed 2d 224, 83 S Ct 1175, 2 ALR3d 1254; Slochower v Board of Higher Educ. 350 US 551, 100 L Ed 692, 76 S Ct 637; Greene v McElroy, 360 US 474, 492, 3 L Ed 2d 1377, 79 S Ct 1400; Birnbaum v Trussell, 371 F2d 672.

The physician class has standing to assert the rights of patients to seek the medical care of induced abortion. Griswold v Connecticut, 381 US 479, 14 L Ed 2d 510, 85 S Ct 1678; United States ex rel. Williams v Zelker, 445 F2d 451; Crossen v Breckenridge, 446 F2d 833; Truax v Raich, 239 US 33, 60 L Ed 131, 36 S Ct 7; Pierce v Society of Sisters, 268 US 510, 69 L Ed 1070, 45 S Ct 571, 39 ALR 468; Eisenstadt v Baird, 405 US 438, 31 L Ed 2d 349, 92 S Ct 1029; YWCA v Kugler, 342 F Supp 1048; Abele v Markle, 452 F2d 1121; Poe v Menghini, 339 F Supp 986.

Injunctions against future enforcement of state criminal statutes are proper even absent a showing of bad-faith enforcement for the purpose of discouraging protected rights. Ex parte Young, 209 US 123, 52 L Ed 714, 28 S Ct 441; Truax v Raich, 239 US 33, 60 L Ed 131, 36 S Ct 7; Terrace v Thompson, 263 US 197, 68 L Ed 255, 44 S Ct 15; Hygrade Provision Co. v Sherman, 266 US 497, 69 L Ed 402, 45 S Ct 141.

Plaintiffs Roe and Doe were not in any sense involved in the pending pros-

Exhibit 7: The page showing a portion of the briefs of counsel in *Lawyers' Edition.*

The complete citation of the abortion decision, reflecting all three texts, is *Roe v. Wade,* 410 U.S. 113, 93 S.Ct. 705, 35 L.Ed.2d 147 (1973). This form is widely used, although technically the official citation is sufficient. The "2d" in the citation of *Lawyers' Edition* indicates that those reports are now in a second series, an arbitrary numbering technique employed by most publishers of court reports. When the volumes of a reporter reach a certain number (usually volume 300, but in the case of *Lawyers' Edition,* volume 100), the publisher starts a second series and begins numbering from volume 1 again (usually for commercial reasons). If a reporter is in its second series, that must be indicated in its citation in order to distinguish it from the same volume number in the first series.

The bound volumes of these three reporters are usually the last form of publication of Supreme Court decisions. The following services provide the text of such decisions much sooner:

Looseleaf Services. Two unofficial commercial publications, issued in looseleaf form, publish the Supreme Court's decisions on the day after they are announced, so that many of their subscribers have them within forty-eight hours. These looseleaf services are *U.S. Law Week,* published by the Bureau of National Affairs, and *Supreme Court Bulletin,* published by Commerce Clearing House. Both of these publishers issue looseleaf services on other legal topics as well, and these will be discussed in detail in Chapter VII below. In addition to the prompt publication and delivery of the text of the decisions themselves, *U.S. Law Week* and *Supreme Court Bulletin* provide information about court calendars, dockets, motions, arguments, and general court news. They are extremely valuable to practitioners before the Supreme Court and of interest to legal researchers generally as a source of current information on the business of the Court. *U.S. Law Week* also includes another volume called *General Law*, which summarizes important weekly legal developments of all kinds—state and federal; judicial, legislative and administrative. Most of the decisions appearing in the *General Law* volume are in abstract form, but their full text can be requested from the publisher of the service by subscribers.

Slip Decision. Several weeks after the unofficial looseleaf services appear, the official slip decision of the Supreme Court is issued by the Court itself and reaches subscribers any time from two to four weeks after decision date. This is the first official and authoritative text of the decisions, but its pages are not numbered in final form. Each slip decision is a separate pamphlet, paginated individually. Slip decisions are available by subscription from the U.S. Government Printing Office. They are accumulated until there are enough for publication together as the advance sheet (or preliminary print, as it is officially called) of the official *U.S. Reports.*

Advance Sheets. Each of the reporters of the Supreme Court's decisions (and many other court reports) issues a preliminary booklet, which contains the Court's latest decisions in a temporary form. These pamphlets are called "advance sheets" and are issued periodically to provide the text of decisions before publication of a complete bound volume. The pagination of the advance sheets is the same as that in the bound volume, so that cases can be cited from the advance sheet exactly as they will appear when finally published.

The advance sheets of *Supreme Court Reporter* and *Lawyers' Edition* are issued faster than the official preliminary print, and all three include the unique features of the series to which they belong. The preliminary print is the authoritative text of the Court's decisions until the bound volume of the *U.S. Reports* appears. *Supreme Court Reporter* incorporates West's unique key number digest and other West finding aids; the *Lawyers' Edition* advance sheet provides several Lawyers Co-op research aids and cross-references to other publications in its "Total Client-Service Library", although it does not contain the annotations or the summaries of briefs and arguments found in the bound volume.

Computer Services

LEXIS and WESTLAW, the two computer research services, provide the full text of all Supreme Court decisions, as well as decisions from other courts, faster than their publication in most traditional printed sources.

Lower Federal Court Reporting

During most of the nineteenth century, decisions of the U.S. District Courts and the U.S. Circuit Courts of Appeals were issued in over 200 separate series of nominative reports. Virtually every federal court published its own series, and bibliographic chaos resulted from the impossibility of locating the reports of many courts anywhere but in their own locales or in the largest law libraries. Finally, between 1894 and 1897 the West Publishing Company published a thirty volume series which included over 20,000 of these decisions under the title *Federal Cases.* This closed set incorporated virtually all important lower federal court decisions from 1789 to 1880, arranged in alphabetical sequence by case name.

In 1880, West initiated its *Federal Reporter* to publish decisions of both the district and circuit courts. In 1932, with the increasing volume of litigation in the federal courts, West began another series of federal reports called *Federal Supplement.* Since that time, *Federal Supplement* has published selected U.S. District Court decisions, leaving the *Federal Reporter* to cover the decisions of the various U.S. Circuit Courts of Appeals, now called U.S. Courts of Appeals. (A map indicating the states that make up each circuit is set out as Exhibit 8 on page 31.)

Federal Reporter and *Federal Supplement* now include decisions from a number of specialized federal courts as well. The coverage of special courts by these reporters has changed several times, but presently the *Federal Reporter* includes decisions of the U.S. Temporary Emergency Court of Appeals. The *Federal Supplement* includes decisions of the U.S. Court of International Trade (formerly the U.S. Customs Court), the Special Court under the Regional Rail Reorganization Act, and the rulings of the Judicial Panel on Multidistrict Litigation.

Since the decisions of the lower federal courts do *not* appear in official editions, other than as individual slip decisions issued by the courts themselves (with very limited distribution), *Federal Reporter*, *Federal Supplement*, and the other unofficial reporters described below are essential for research in federal law.

In 1940, West began another series, *Federal Rules Decisions*, which publishes selectively a limited number of lower federal court decisions (not published in *Federal Reporter* or *Federal Supplement*) which deal with procedural matters. Typically, these decisions are from cases decided under the Federal Rules of Civil or Criminal Procedure. *Federal Rules Decisions* also contains proceedings of judicial conferences, and occasional speeches or articles dealing with procedural law in the federal courts. Its bound volumes are preceded by the usual West advance sheets, and both its bound volumes and advance sheets contain all of the West reporter research aids (classified headnotes, key number digest, etc.).

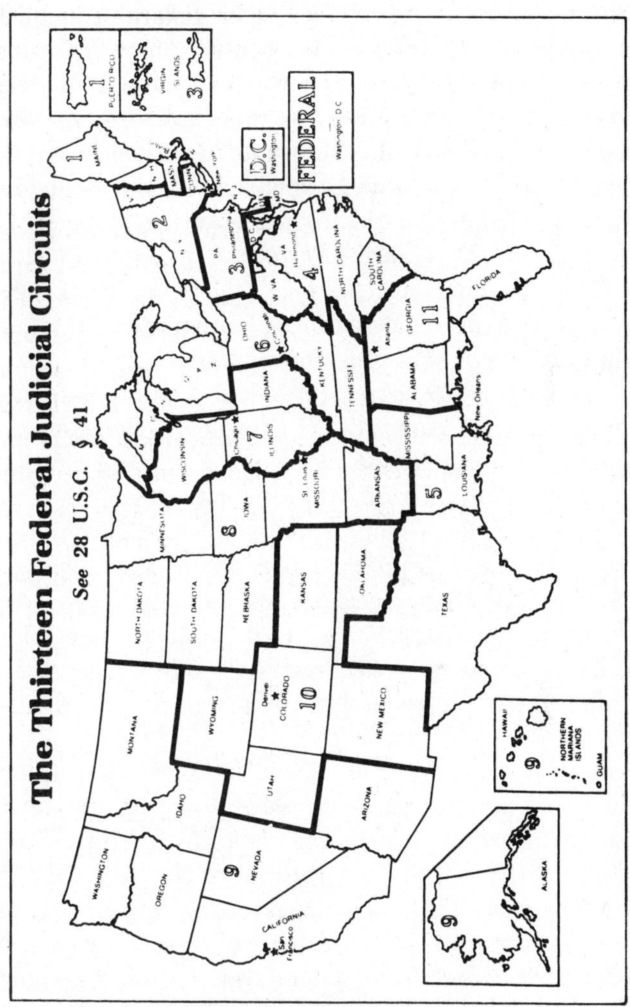

Exhibit 8: The Thirteen Federal Judicial Circuits (as defined in 28 *U.S. Code* § 41).

In more recent years, the West Publishing Company has been adding a number of other reporters in specialized subject fields of federal law. These new selective reporters include the following: *Military Justice Reporter* (1977–date), containing decisions from the U.S. Court of Military Appeals, and the Courts of Military Review for the Army, Navy & Marines, Air Force and Coast Guard; *Bankruptcy Reporter* (1979-date), containing decisions of the U.S. Bankruptcy Courts, and decisions from all other federal courts relating to bankruptcy law; and *United States Claims Court Reporter* (1982–date), containing decisions of the Claims Court (formerly the Court of Claims), and reprinting decisions from the Supreme Court and the Court of Appeals for the Federal Circuit in review of the Claims Court. West also publishes *Education Law Reporter* (1982–date), including federal *and* state court decisions on education law along with occasional articles on that subject; and *Social Security Reporting Service* (1983–date), also including both federal and state decisions in *that* field.

Federal Case News is issued by West as a weekly advance pamphlet service *summarizing* important federal decisions before they appear in the advance sheets of the various federal reporters. Although the actual text of the decisions is not given, and bound volumes are not issued, it is a useful service for following current developments in the federal courts.

Another potential source of lower federal court decisions in full text, with descriptive articles on each case published, is *A.L.R. Federal* (Lawyers Co-operative

Publishing Company, 1969-date). This is a companion set to the older *American Law Reports* series (popularly known as *A.L.R.*), which prior to 1969 included a selection of both state and federal cases. *A.L.R.*, *A.L.R. Federal*, and their predecessors are more fully described on pages 49–51 below.

The two computer services now widely used in legal research, LEXIS and WESTLAW, provide additional sources of decisions from the federal courts. LEXIS includes some decisions which may never be published in the reporters; WESTLAW includes many before they are issued in advance sheets. These services will be described further in Chapter III, Case-Finding.

Finally, it should be noted that unofficial topical reporters and looseleaf services also publish federal court decisions, either in full text or in abstracted form, for the many subject fields covered by such services. The topical reporters are described at pages 51–52 below, and looseleaf services are treated more fully in Chapter VII.

STATE REPORTS

American state reports are published in two forms: as *official* reports, which are issued by the courts themselves as the authoritative text of their decisions, and as *unofficial* reports. There are two *general* unofficial reporting systems—West Publishing Company's comprehensive National Reporter System, and Lawyers Co-operative Publishing Company's selective *American Law Reports.* As noted above for federal reporters, there are also a number of other specialized reporters of more limited subject coverage, some of which include state court decisions as well, and the two computerized legal research services, LEXIS and WESTLAW, both of which provide extensive coverage of state decisions.

Official Reports. The official reports are important to the researcher because they are authoritative and must be cited in legal briefs and memoranda. Citation to the unofficial report is optional (although desirable) and should follow the official reference. The unofficial reports, however, are very widely used and cited, because of their superior research aids, fuller coverage and faster publication, and because many states have now discontinued their official reports.

National Reporter System. West's National Reporter System consists of a series of regional reporters which collectively publish most of the decisions issued by the appellate courts of the fifty states. It is the most comprehensive approach to law reporting and for some states includes more decisions than the official reports. Although the system suffers to some extent from its huge scope and bulk, West's key number case-finding device has kept it fairly manageable. To simplify storage and preservation of the set in libraries, West has also produced an ultra-microfiche edition of the first series of the National Reporter System, and has begun gradual inclusion of the second series in this format.

The National Reporter System divides the country into seven regions: Atlantic, North Eastern, North Western, Pacific, South Eastern, Southern and South Western. The decisions of the appellate courts of the states in each of these regions are published together in one series of volumes. These series have been supplemented by West with separate reporters for the two most litigious states, *California Reporter,* and *New York Supplement,* which also include selected lower court decisions. These nine reporters, together with West reporters for other states, and the various West federal court reporters described above, comprise a uniform system tied together by the key number indexing and digesting scheme. Exhibit 9 shows which states are included in each region of the reporter system. Appendix A gives a complete list of the contents of each reporter and its date of inception.

The original rationale of the National Reporter System was that contiguous states shared similar legal development and therefore lawyers in one state would be interested in the law of adjacent states. Despite changes in the country which have tended to undermine this theory, the venture has flourished, largely because of the speed of publishing; the greater number of decisions as compared with the official reports; and the case-finding advantages of the key number system. In addition, advance sheets for each of these reporters bring the decisions to lawyers much faster than do the official reporters, which rarely offer such service. After four or five advance sheets appear, they are reissued on better paper in a bound volume with the same pagination. The superseded advance sheet can then be discarded.

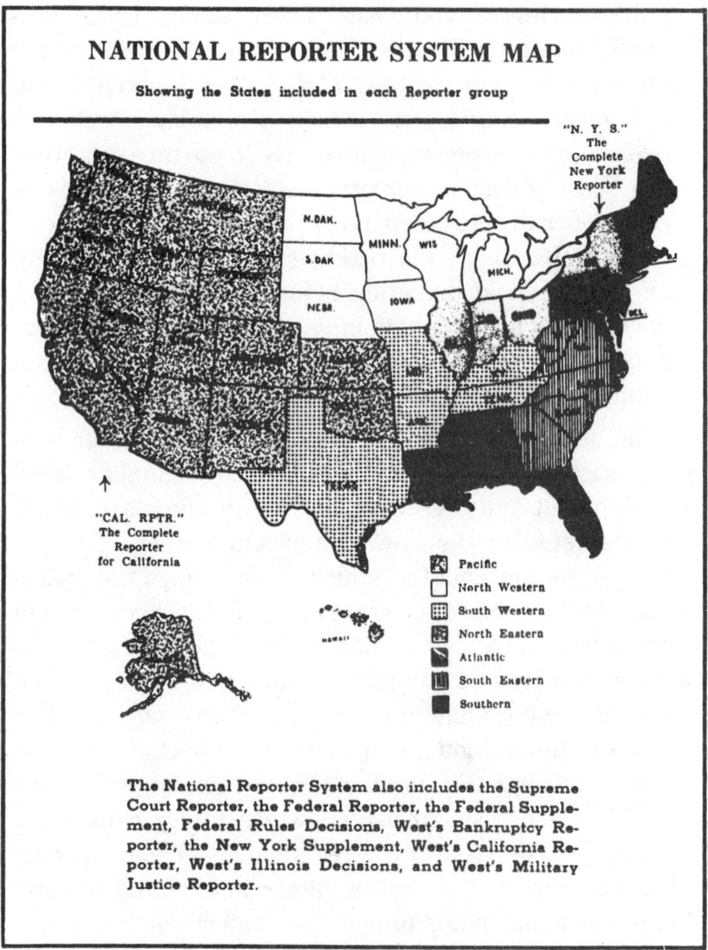

<u>Exhibit 9</u>: National Reporter System map, showing states included in each reporter.

By analyzing a single decision in a National Reporter volume or an advance sheet, one can get a general idea of the make-up of an appellate decision, as well as of the special reporting aids which West provides for its subscribers. Such analysis would reveal the following items illustrated in Exhibit 10:

Title or case name.

Official citation if available.

Other identifying data: docket number, date of decision, name of court and jurisdiction.

Synopsis or brief descriptive paragraph of the case: its holding, how it arose, facts, etc.

Brief statement of decision and notation of dissent or concurrence, if any.

Headnotes summarizing the points of law discussed in the case, with the identifying key numbers of the digest system.

Syllabus by the Court, if provided.

Names of counsel and judges.

Full text of opinion, decision, and dissents or concurrences, if any.

Reference, by number of headnote, to the section of the opinion which discusses the point of each headnote.

STATE, EX REL. LEIS v. OUTCALT

Cite as, Ohio, 438 N.E.2d 443

It is undisputed that the state has a legitimate interest in regulating obscenity. The extent to which they choose to regulate it, however, is a matter for the General Assembly. Moreover, inasmuch as there is no common law obscenity—and, indeed, no common law crime [12]—it is for the legislature to declare what actions in this area constitute criminal conduct. Our role is to determine whether this is a legitimate exercise of discretionary power. Today's decision, however, not only establishes a common law crime, but disregards the presumption of constitutionality afforded legislative enactments, and, in effect, shifts the burden of proof to the General Assembly to justify its actions.[13]

Underlying today's holding is the mistaken belief that a vote of unconstitutionality in this case is a vote against obscenity. While eliminating obscenity is certainly a laudable goal, it is not within the power of this court to rewrite legislative enactments. A judiciary should not sit as a super legislature to judge the wisdom or desirability of legislative policy determinations.[14] Nevertheless, the majority has done precisely this in substituting its judgment for the General Assembly's.

The General Assembly, and not this court, is empowered with the responsibility for determining how to combat obscenity. It is our duty to decide whether the disputed classification has any rational basis—not whether it comports with this court's perception of how the fight against obscenity is to be waged. I am satisfied that the instant classification is reasonable enough to meet the low level of judicial review traditionally afforded non-suspect classifications. See *Vostack v. Axt* (S.D. Ohio E.D. 1981), 510 F.Supp. 217 [22 O.O.3d 360]; *Holloway v. Brown* (1980), 62 Ohio St.2d 65, 403 N.E.2d 191 [16 O.O.3d 47]; *Massachusetts Bd. of Retirement v. Murgia* (1976), 427 U.S. 307, 96 S.Ct. 2562, 49 L.Ed.2d 520; *Dandridge v. Williams* (1970), 397 U.S. 471, 90 S.Ct. 1153, 25 L.Ed.2d 491; *Breard v. Alexandria* (1951), 341 U.S. 622, 71 S.Ct. 920, 95 L.Ed. 1233 [46 O.O. 74]. In short, I cannot acquiesce in an attempt to elevate moralistic pronouncements to the status of enduring constitutional principles. I therefore respectfully dissent.

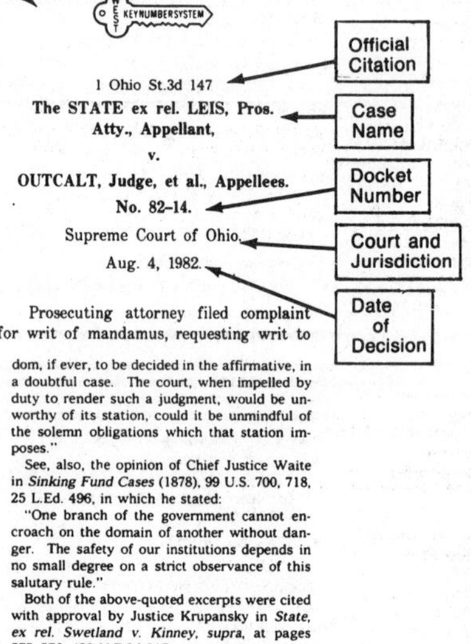

1 Ohio St.3d 147

The STATE ex rel. LEIS, Pros. Atty., Appellant,

v.

OUTCALT, Judge, et al., Appellees.

No. 82–14.

Supreme Court of Ohio.

Aug. 4, 1982.

Prosecuting attorney filed complaint for writ of mandamus, requesting writ to

12. See R.C. 2901.03(A) which states as follows: "No conduct constitutes a criminal offense against the state unless it is defined as an offense in the Revised Code."

13. The following excerpt exhibits the attempt by this court to switch the burden of proof: "The fact that this section of law may adversely affect a person's employment, by itself, constitutes *neither a valid defense to the crime nor a valid reason for exemption from prosecution.*" (Emphasis added.) See, also, fn. 6, *supra*, and the quote contained therein.

14. As Chief Justice John Marshall observed in *Fletcher v. Peck* (1810), 6 Cranch (10 U.S.) 87, 128, 3 L.Ed. 162:

"The question, whether a law be void for its repugnancy to the constitution, is, at all times, a question of much delicacy, which ought seldom, if ever, to be decided in the affirmative, in a doubtful case. The court, when impelled by duty to render such a judgment, would be unworthy of its station, could it be unmindful of the solemn obligations which that station imposes."

See, also, the opinion of Chief Justice Waite in *Sinking Fund Cases* (1878), 99 U.S. 700, 718, 25 L.Ed. 496, in which he stated:

"One branch of the government cannot encroach on the domain of another without danger. The safety of our institutions depends in no small degree on a strict observance of this salutary rule."

Both of the above-quoted excerpts were cited with approval by Justice Krupansky in *State, ex rel. Swetland v. Kinney, supra,* at pages 575–576, 433 N.E.2d 217.

Exhibit 10: A decision of the Supreme Court of Ohio as reported in the *North Eastern Reporter.*

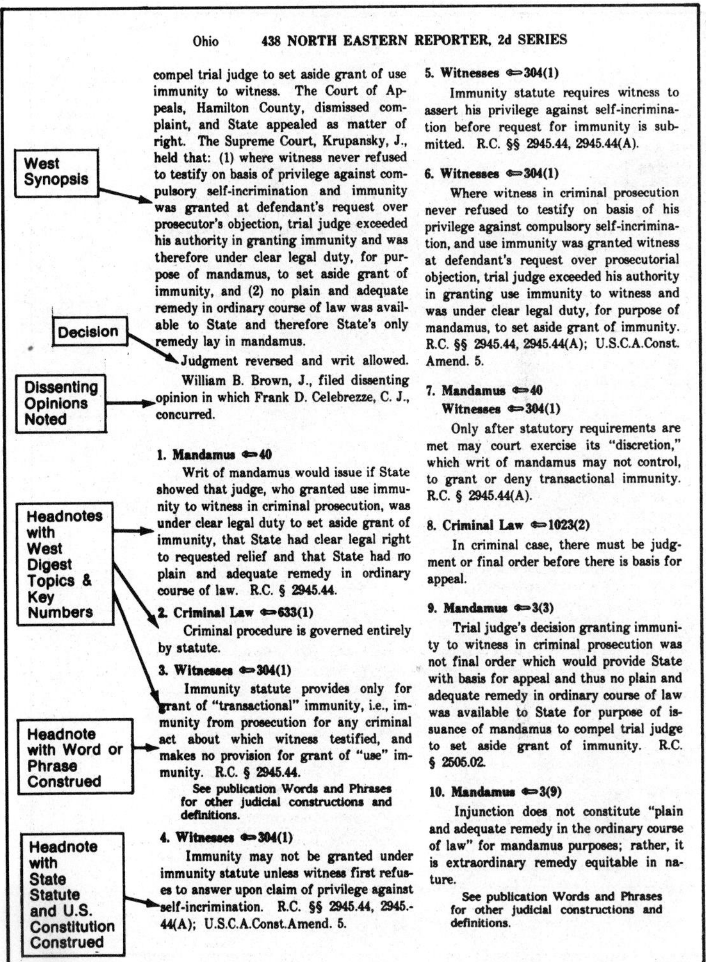
Ohio 438 NORTH EASTERN REPORTER, 2d SERIES

compel trial judge to set aside grant of use immunity to witness. The Court of Appeals, Hamilton County, dismissed complaint, and State appealed as matter of right. The Supreme Court, Krupansky, J., held that: (1) where witness never refused to testify on basis of privilege against compulsory self-incrimination and immunity was granted at defendant's request over prosecutor's objection, trial judge exceeded his authority in granting immunity and was therefore under clear legal duty, for purpose of mandamus, to set aside grant of immunity, and (2) no plain and adequate remedy in ordinary course of law was available to State and therefore State's only remedy lay in mandamus.

Judgment reversed and writ allowed.

William B. Brown, J., filed dissenting opinion in which Frank D. Celebrezze, C. J., concurred.

1. Mandamus ⟹40

Writ of mandamus would issue if State showed that judge, who granted use immunity to witness in criminal prosecution, was under clear legal duty to set aside grant of immunity, that State had clear legal right to requested relief and that State had no plain and adequate remedy in ordinary course of law. R.C. § 2945.44.

2. Criminal Law ⟹633(1)

Criminal procedure is governed entirely by statute.

3. Witnesses ⟹304(1)

Immunity statute provides only for grant of "transactional" immunity, i.e., immunity from prosecution for any criminal act about which witness testified, and makes no provision for grant of "use" immunity. R.C. § 2945.44.

See publication Words and Phrases for other judicial constructions and definitions.

4. Witnesses ⟹304(1)

Immunity may not be granted under immunity statute unless witness first refuses to answer upon claim of privilege against self-incrimination. R.C. §§ 2945.44, 2945.44(A); U.S.C.A.Const.Amend. 5.

5. Witnesses ⟹304(1)

Immunity statute requires witness to assert his privilege against self-incrimination before request for immunity is submitted. R.C. §§ 2945.44, 2945.44(A).

6. Witnesses ⟹304(1)

Where witness in criminal prosecution never refused to testify on basis of his privilege against compulsory self-incrimination, and use immunity was granted witness at defendant's request over prosecutorial objection, trial judge exceeded his authority in granting use immunity to witness and was under clear legal duty, for purpose of mandamus, to set aside grant of immunity. R.C. §§ 2945.44, 2945.44(A); U.S.C.A.Const. Amend. 5.

7. Mandamus ⟹40
Witnesses ⟹304(1)

Only after statutory requirements are met may court exercise its "discretion," which writ of mandamus may not control, to grant or deny transactional immunity. R.C. § 2945.44(A).

8. Criminal Law ⟹1023(2)

In criminal case, there must be judgment or final order before there is basis for appeal.

9. Mandamus ⟹3(3)

Trial judge's decision granting immunity to witness in criminal prosecution was not final order which would provide State with basis for appeal and thus no plain and adequate remedy in ordinary course of law was available to State for purpose of issuance of mandamus to compel trial judge to set aside grant of immunity. R.C. § 2505.02.

10. Mandamus ⟹3(9)

Injunction does not constitute "plain and adequate remedy in the ordinary course of law" for mandamus purposes; rather, it is extraordinary remedy equitable in nature.

See publication Words and Phrases for other judicial constructions and definitions.

Exhibit 10: *North Eastern Reporter* decision (Continued).

STATE, EX REL. LEIS v. OUTCALT

Cite as, Ohio, 438 N.E.2d 443

11. Criminal Law ⟹1024(1)

State does not have basis for appeal in criminal case from decision affecting nonparty when defendant has already been acquitted.

Syllabus by the Court

Immunity is erroneously granted to a witness when the witness has not refused to answer on the basis of his privilege against self-incrimination, and the prosecuting attorney has not requested the court to order the witness to answer.

This action arises out of events which occurred during the trial of James Schultz in the Hamilton County Common Pleas Court. During the trial, Donald E. Hope was called as a witness for the defense. Before any questions were asked Hope, counsel for the defendant moved the court for a grant of immunity for Hope. Hope never asserted his Fifth Amendment privilege against self-incrimination. Over the assistant prosecutor's objection, appellee, Judge Peter Outcalt, granted Hope "use" immunity. Hope then testified that he committed the crime for which the defendant was on trial, and the defendant was acquitted. Hope has been indicted for the crime about which he testified, and that case is pending before the Hamilton County Common Pleas Court.

Appellant, Simon Leis, Jr., prosecuting attorney, filed a motion for leave to appeal appellee's decision granting Hope immunity, and the motion was denied. Appellant also filed a complaint for a writ of mandamus in the Court of Appeals, requesting a writ to compel appellee to set aside his grant of immunity. Appellee's motion to dismiss the complaint was granted by the Court of Appeals.

This cause is now before this court upon appeal as a matter of right.

Simon L. Leis, Jr., Pros. Atty., and Leonard Kirschner, Asst. Pros. Atty., for appellant.

G. Ernie Ramos, Jr., Cincinnati, for appellee Judge Outcalt.

KRUPANSKY, Justice.

[1] A writ of mandamus will issue if appellant shows appellee is under a clear legal duty to perform the requested act, that appellant has a clear legal right to the requested relief and that appellant has no plain and adequate remedy in the ordinary course of the law. See, *e.g., State, ex rel. Heller v. Miller* (1980), 61 Ohio St.2d 6, 399 N.E.2d 66 [15 O.O.3d 3], paragraph one of the syllabus.

I.

Inasmuch as appellee was without authority to grant the witness use immunity, appellee is under a clear legal duty to set aside his decision granting immunity.

[2] In this state, criminal procedure is governed entirely by statute. *Municipal Court of Toledo v. State, ex rel. Platter* (1933), 126 Ohio St. 103, 184 N.E. 1, paragraph one of the syllabus. A court's sole authority for granting immunity is regulated by R.C. 2945.44, which provides in relevant part:

"(A) In any criminal proceeding in this state, if a witness refuses to answer or produce information on the basis of his privilege against self-incrimination, the court of common pleas of the county in which the proceeding is being held, unless it finds that to do so would not further the administration of justice, shall compel the witness to answer or produce the information, if both of the following apply:

"(1) The prosecuting attorney of the county in which the proceedings are being held makes a written request to the court of common pleas to order the witness to answer or produce the information, notwithstanding his claim of privilege;

"(2) The court of common pleas informs the witness that by answering, or producing the information he will receive immunity under division (B) of this section.

"(B) If, but for this section, the witness would have been privileged to withhold an answer or any information given in any

Exhibit 10: *North Eastern Reporter* decision (Continued).

STATE, EX REL. LEIS v. OUTCALT
Cite as, Ohio, 438 N.E.2d 443

II.

[8, 9] No plain and adequate remedy in the ordinary course of law is available to appellant. In a criminal case, there must be a judgment or final order before there is a basis for appeal. *State v. Chamberlain* (1964), 177 Ohio St. 104, 202 N.E.2d 695 [33 O.O.2d 465]. A final order is one which amounts to a disposition of the cause and which affects "a substantial right in an action which in effect determines the action and prevents a judgment." R.C. 2505.02. Appellee's decision granting immunity is clearly not a final order which would provide appellant with a basis for appeal.

[10] Appellee contends appellant had an adequate remedy at law at the time appellee granted the witness immunity. At that time, appellee argues, appellant should have requested a continuance for purposes of obtaining injunctive relief as to appellee regarding the question of immunity. Assuming, *arguendo*, appellee's suggested procedure would have been appropriate at that point in the trial, it is well-settled an injunction does not constitute a plain and adequate remedy in the ordinary course of law; rather, it is an extraordinary remedy equitable in nature. *State, ex rel. Pressley, v. Indus. Comm.* (1967), 11 Ohio St.2d 141, 228 N.E.2d 631 [40 O.O.2d 141].

[11] Appellee also contends appellant had an adequate remedy at law by way of appeal after the defendant, Schultz, was acquitted upon a jury determination of not guilty. It is noted the witness was not a party to the original criminal proceedings in which the parties were the state and Schultz, and the case was styled *State v. Schultz*. We are at a loss to find a basis of appeal for the state in a criminal case from a decision affecting a non-party when the defendant has already been acquitted.

Thus, appellant's hands were tied—with no basis for appeal at the time appellee granted immunity and no basis for appeal once the defendant was acquitted, appellant's only remedy lay in a complaint for writ of mandamus.

In the case *sub judice*, appellee was under a clear legal duty to vacate his unlawful decision; appellant had a clear legal right to have the decision set aside; appellant had no plain and adequate remedy at law; the Court of Appeals, therefore, erred in granting appellee's motion to dismiss.

The judgment of the Court of Appeals is therefore reversed, and appellee is ordered to vacate his journal entry granting Hope immunity.

Judgment reversed and writ allowed.

SWEENEY, LOCHER, HOLMES and CLIFFORD F. BROWN, JJ., concur.

FRANK D. CELEBREZZE, C. J., and WILLIAM B. BROWN, J., dissent.

WILLIAM B. BROWN, Justice, dissenting.

While the trial court's decision granting Hope immunity may well have been erroneous, I must nonetheless dissent for, in my opinion, the issuance of a writ of mandamus is not an appropriate remedy in this action.

In order to be entitled to a writ of mandamus, the relator must show that he "'* * * has a clear legal right to the relief prayed for, that respondent is under a clear legal duty to perform the requested act, and that relator has no plain and adequate remedy at law.'" *State, ex rel. Meshel, v. Keip* (1981), 66 Ohio St.2d 379, 381, 423 N.E.2d 60 [20 O.O.3d 338].

And in *State, ex rel. Pressley, v. Indus. Comm.* (1967), 11 Ohio St.2d 141, 161, 228 N.E.2d 631 [40 O.O.2d 141], this court stated:

"'The court in the exercise of its discretion may and should take into consideration a wide variety of circumstances in determining whether the writ should issue. It may and should consider the facts of the particular case, the exigency which calls for the exercise of its discretion, the consequences of granting the writ, and the nature and extent of the wrong or injury which would follow a refusal of the writ. The court is not bound to allow the writ merely because applicant shows a clear legal right for which mandamus would be an

Discussions of Several Numbered Headnotes

Decision

Judges Concurring in Majority Opinion

Dissenting Judges

Judge Writing Dissent

Dissenting Opinion

Exhibit 10: *North Eastern Reporter* decision (Continued).

Similarly by examining the opening pages of a typical West advance sheet one can observe the following features which make these reporters so useful in legal research: (See Exhibits 11 to 15.)

Judicial highlights (appear monthly).

Cumulative table of cases reported (in that volume).

Cumulative table of statutes construed or cited (in that volume).

Cumulative Words and Phrases (in cases in that volume).

Key Number Digest (for cases in that issue).

Current Decisions of Interest

November 1983

PHYSICIANS AND SURGEONS—Life Support. The California Court of Appeal for the Second District has held that medical doctors' omission to continue life support treatments of a terminally ill, comatose patient, although intentional and with knowledge that the patient would die, was not an unlawful failure to perform a legal duty, even though the patient was not "dead" by either statutory or historical standards at the time. The patient had suffered severe brain damage, leaving him in a vegetative state which was likely to be permanent and the patient's family had requested cessation of treatment. Barber v. Superior Court of the State of California, County of Los Angeles, Oct. 12, 1983 (opinion by Associate Justice Lynn D. Compton).

SELF DEFENSE—Fetus. A Texas statute permits a person to use deadly force in defense of a third person. An unborn fetus of five months was not a person within the statute, according to the Texas Court of Appeals. Ogas v. State, 655 S.W.2d 322 (opinion by Justice John T. Boyd).

PROFESSIONAL LIABILITY INSURANCE—Coverage. The Pennsylvania Superior Court has recognized an obligation on the part of a

A Special Copyrighted Feature of West Publishing Co. Reporters

1

Exhibit 11: *Judicial Highlights,* summaries of recent federal and state decisions in a *North Eastern Reporter* advance sheet.

CUMULATIVE CASES REPORTED

NEW YORK (Continued)

	Page
People v. Kirby (Mem.)—N.Y.	150
People v. Moorhead—N.Y.	144
People v. Perry—N.Y.	143
People v. Swanchak (Mem.)—N.Y.	150
Rodriguez v. Baker (Mem.)—N.Y.	149
Romano, Matter of (Mem.)—N.Y.	151
Salmon v. Flacke—N.Y.	123
Scivoletti v. Marsala—N.Y.	126
Sims, Matter of—N.Y.	370
Stoganovic v. DiNolfo (Mem.)—N.Y.	149
Tongue v. Tongue—N.Y.	127
Tri-City Elec. Co., Inc. v. People (Mem.) —N.Y.	151
Weinberg v. Transamerica Ins. Co. (Mem.)—N.Y.	151

OHIO

(Cases in this issue, pp. 381–466)

	Page
Akron Standard Div. of Eagle-Picher Industries, Inc. v. Lindley—Ohio	419
Armstrong v. Lindley—Ohio App.	451
Auto-Owners Mut. Ins. Co. v. Lewis —Ohio	396
Avon Lake, City of, v. Anderson—Ohio App.	188
City of Avon Lake v. Anderson—Ohio App.	188
City of Dayton v. Strausbaugh—Ohio Mun.	462
City of Wadsworth v. Slanker—Ohio App.	191
Cohen v. Lamko, Inc.—Ohio	407
Columbia Gas of Ohio, Inc. v. Public Utilities Com'n of Ohio—Ohio	166
Dayton, City of, v. Strausbaugh—Ohio Mun.	462
Dempsey v. Chicago Title Ins. Co.—Ohio App.	184
Donofrio v. B.G.R. Inv. Corp.—Ohio Mun.	193
Jones v. Connor—Ohio App.	186
Jurcisin, State ex rel., v. Cotner—Ohio	381
Karabin v. State Auto. Mut. Ins. Co. —Ohio	403
MacMillian v. Unemployment Compensation Bd. of Review—Ohio App.	177
Meeks, State ex rel., v. Ohio Brass Co. —Ohio	389
Nolan v. Nolan—Ohio	410
Reamsnyder v. Jaskolski—Ohio	392
Richardson v. Car Lot Co.—Ohio Mun.	459
Rinehart, In re—Ohio App.	448
Roseborough v. N.L. Industries—Ohio	384
Scholler v. Scholler—Ohio	158
State v. Clark—Ohio App.	436
State v. Dickard—Ohio App.	180
State v. Gates—Ohio App.	425
State v. Green—Ohio Co.	466
State v. McKnight—Ohio App.	441
State v. Vaughn—Ohio App.	444
State v. Wolfe—Ohio App.	455
State v. Woodruff—Ohio App.	457
State v. Wymbs—Ohio Mun.	195
State ex rel. Jurcisin v. Cotner—Ohio	381
State ex rel. Meeks v. Ohio Brass Co. —Ohio	389
Strauch v. Gross—Ohio App.	433
Suver v. Personal Service Ins. Co. —Ohio	415
Wadsworth, City of, v. Slanker—Ohio App.	191
Weber v. General Acc. Fire & Life Assur. Corp.—Ohio App.	422
Young v. Pal Entities—Ohio App.	174

Exhibit 12: Table of "Cases Reported" in *North Eastern Reporter* advance sheet (cases listed in bold face appear in that advance sheet).

CUMULATIVE STATUTES

NEW YORK—Cont'd

Court of Claims Act

Sec.
8—453 N.E.2d 1241

Labor Law

Sec.
241—453 N.E.2d 1247

Mental Hygiene Law

Sec.
1.03—453 N.E.2d 1085
7.11(b)—453 N.E.2d 1085
7.17—453 N.E.2d 1085

Military Law

Sec.
242—569 F.Supp. 858

Penal Law

Sec.
10.00, subd. 13—453 N.E.2d 515
265.01(2)—453 N.E.2d 515
265.05—453 N.E.2d 515

Public Health Law

Sec.
2810—453 N.E.2d 506
2810, subd. 2, par. a—453 N.E.2d 506

Real Property Tax Law

Sec.
420-a—453 N.E.2d 1094
420-a, subd. 1—453 N.E.2d 1094

Social Services Law

Sec.
392—453 N.E.2d 480
392, subd. 7(a)—453 N.E.2d 480
392, subd. 7(d)—453 N.E.2d 480

State Administrative Procedure Act

Sec.
301, subd. 1—453 N.E.2d 533
306, subd. 1—453 N.E.2d 528

Vehicle and Traffic Law

Sec.
205, subd. 1—453 N.E.2d 531
388—570 F.Supp. 39
1192, subd. 3—453 N.E.2d 533
1194—453 N.E.2d 533

Workers' Compensation Law

Sec.
1 et seq.—453 N.E.2d 1089
29, subd. 6—453 N.E.2d 1247

Commercial Code

Sec.
9–103(2)(a)—717 F.2d 25
9–103(3)(b)—717 F.2d 25
9–103(3)(c)—717 F.2d 25

Court Rules

Sec.
500.2(b)—453 N.E.2d 1076
500.2(b)—453 N.E.2d 1245

Unconsolidated Laws

City Rent and Eviction Regulations

Sec.
2, subd. f(11)—453 N.E.2d 1245

Laws

1937, ch. 617—453 N.E.2d 531
1975, ch. 649—453 N.E.2d 506
1977, ch. 396, § 2—453 N.E.2d 506
1980, ch. 784—453 N.E.2d 1080
1981, ch. 919—453 N.E.2d 1094
1983, ch. 281—453 N.E.2d 531

OHIO

Revised Code

Sec.
319.36—453 N.E.2d 661
319.37—453 N.E.2d 661
723.01—453 N.E.2d 604
1311.011—453 N.E.2d 656
1311.011(A)(3)—453 N.E.2d 656
1311.011(B)(4)—453 N.E.2d 656
2317.42—453 N.E.2d 1270
2505.02—453 N.E.2d 653
2703.14—453 N.E.2d 632
2703.14(L)—453 N.E.2d 632
2705.01–2705.08—453 N.E.2d 1292
2711.06—453 N.E.2d 1109
2721.01 et seq.—453 N.E.2d 661
2723.01 et seq.—453 N.E.2d 661
2723.03—453 N.E.2d 661
2723.01—453 N.E.2d 661
2743.01 et seq.—453 N.E.2d 676
2743.51(M)—453 N.E.2d 1309
2743.60(A–D)—453 N.E.2d 1309
2743.60(D)—453 N.E.2d 1309
2743.65(A)—453 N.E.2d 1309
2901.05—453 N.E.2d 1304
2901.05(A)—716 F.2d 396
2901.12—453 N.E.2d 716
2901.12(A)—453 N.E.2d 715
2901.12(G)—453 N.E.2d 716
2901.12(H)—453 N.E.2d 716
2901.21—716 F.2d 396
2901.21(A)—716 F.2d 396
2901.21(C)—716 F.2d 396
2901.22—716 F.2d 396
2901.22(C)—453 N.E.2d 1124
2903.02—453 N.E.2d 595
2903.04—453 N.E.2d 595
2903.06—453 N.E.2d 1124

453–454 N.E.2d XX

Exhibit 13: Cumulative table of statutes construed or cited in *North Eastern Reporter* advance sheet.

CUMULATIVE WORDS AND PHRASES

For other definitions of Words and Phrases listed below, see publication WORDS AND PHRASES, comprising judicial definitions of Words and Phrases by the Courts, State and Federal, in paragraph form.

453 N.E.2d

(Words and Phrases marked ▲ appear in this issue)

ACTUAL MALICE,
Wachs v. Winter, D.C.N.Y., 569 F.Supp. 1438, 1444.

ADEQUATE ASSURANCE,
In re Evelyn Byrnes, Inc., Bkrtcy.N.Y., 32 B.R. 825, 829.

ADMINISTRATIVELY NECESSARY DAYS,
Addison Gilbert Hosp. v. Rate Setting Com'n, Mass., 453 N.E.2d 424, 426.

ALIMONY,
In re Wellman, Bkrtcy.Ill., 32 B.R. 974, 977.

CLASS OF PURCHASERS,
Reynolds Industries, Inc. v. Mobil Oil Corp., D.C.Mass., 569 F.Supp. 716, 720.

COLLATERAL ESTOPPEL,
People v. One 1974 Chevrolet Corvette Vin #1Z37J4S400951, Ill.App. 2 Dist., 453 N.E.2d 890, 891.

CRIMINAL CONTEMPT,
Harvey v. Carponelli, Ill.App. 1 Dist., 453 N.E.2d 820, 824.

CUTTING MILL,
U. S. v. Soto, C.A.N.Y., 716 F.2d 989, 990.

DANGEROUS KNIFE,
Matter of Jamie D., N.Y.App., 453 N.E.2d 515, 517.

DEADLY WEAPON,
Murphy v. State, Ind.App., 453 N.E.2d 1026, 1027.

DECISION ON THE MERITS,
State v. One 1974 Chevrolet Corvette Vin #1Z37J4S400951, Ill.App. 2 Dist., 453 N.E.2d 890, 891.

DEPRECIATION RESERVE,
Office of Consumers' Counsel v. Public Utilities Com'n of Ohio, Ohio, 453 N.E.2d 584, 587.

DIMINUTION OF RENTAL VALUE,
American Nat. Bank and Trust Co. of Chicago v. K-Mart Corp., C.A.Ill., 717 F.2d 394, 399.

EQUITABLE FUND DOCTRINE,
Insurance Co. of North America v. Norton, C.A.Ill., 716 F.2d 1112, 1115.

EXPENSE OF THE FAMILY,
Lyman v. Harbaugh, Ill.App. 4 Dist., 453 N.E.2d 906, 907.

FAIR CASH VALUE,
Donlon v. Board of Assessors of Holliston, Mass., 453 N.E.2d 395, 402.

FINAL ORDER,
State ex rel. Celebrezze v. K & S Circuits, Inc., Ohio, 453 N.E.2d 653, 654.
People v. One 1974 Chevrolet Corvette Vin #1Z37J4S400951, Ill.App. 2 Dist., 453 N.E.2d 890, 891.

GIFTS,
▲In re Marriage of Cook, Ill.App. 1 Dist., 453 N.E.2d 1357, 1361.

GROCERY STORE,
Best v. New York State Liquor Authority, N.Y., 453 N.E.2d 518, 519.

IMPLEMENTS,
In re Yoder, Bkrtcy.N.Y., 32 B.R. 777, 781.

INSURED,
Connell v. American Underwriters, Inc., Ind.App. 3 Dist., 453 N.E.2d 1028, 1029.

LACK OF DILIGENCE,
Harris v. Beynon, D.C.Ill., 570 F.Supp. 690, 692.

453–454 N.E.2d XXVII

Exhibit 14: Cumulative table of Words and Phrases construed in *North Eastern Reporter* advance sheet.

KEY NUMBER DIGEST

ADMINISTRATIVE LAW AND PROCEDURE

⚷=305. —— Statutory basis and limitation.

Ill.App. 2 Dist. 1983. Failure to comply with a mandatory provision of a statute will render void the proceeding to which the provision relates, but strict observance of a directory provision of a statute is not essential to the validity of the proceedings thereunder.—Village of Mundelein v. Hartnett, 454 N.E.2d 29.

⚷=382. Nature and scope.

Ill.App. 1 Dist. 1983. Not every interpretation by agency has status of a rule or regulation.—Tyska by Tyska v. Board of Educ. Tp. High School Dist. 214, Cook County, 453 N.E.2d 1344.

⚷=405. —— Statement of purpose.

Ill.App. 1 Dist. 1983. No statement or finding that public benefit will be served is required where legislative function is being performed by administrative agency.—Tyska by Tyska v. Board of Educ. Tp. High School Dist. 214, Cook County, 453 N.E.2d 1344.

⚷=485. —— Necessity and purpose.

Ill.App. 1 Dist. 1983. Where administrative decision is not subject to judicial review, there is no substantial reason for requiring written findings in absence of legislative requirement.—Tyska by Tyska v. Board of Educ. Tp. High School Dist. 214, Cook County, 453 N.E.2d 1344.

In absence of statute or rule requiring administrative board to make detailed findings of fact, none are required.—Id.

⚷=744. Trial de novo.

Ill.App. 1 Dist. 1982. A court may not, upon administrative review, hear further evidence or conduct a hearing de novo.—Tri-America Oil Co. v. Dept. of Revenue, 454 N.E.2d 1.

APPEAL AND ERROR

⚷=173(10). Time of bringing suit, limitations, and laches.

Ohio App. 1982. Administrator's claim that statute of limitations did not begin to run, on counterclaim against state for overpayments to state for costs of decedent's daughter's care at state hospital, on date assumed by Court of Appeals, but rather, counterclaim accrued at later date, so that counterclaim was filed within limitation period could not be raised for first time on appeal.—State, Dept. of Mental Health v. Reynolds, 454 N.E.2d 154, 7 Ohio App.3d 59.

⚷=713(1). In general.

Mass.App. 1983. Although several hundred pages of transcript of hearings before a master, as well as exhibits introduced in those proceedings, were reproduced in defendant's record appendix, Appeals Court would decline to look at material, since order of reference provided that evidence was not to be reported, and there was no indication in record that judge subsequently ordered evidence to be reported.—Frank D. Wayne Associates, Inc. v. Lussier, 454 N.E.2d 109.

Filing of transcript by agreement of parties with clerk of trial court did not change status of transcript in absence of change in order of reference providing that transcript was not to be reported on appeal.—Id.

Allowance by trial judge of defendant's motion to include transcript in record on appeal did not enhance its status, in absence of change in order of reference providing that transcript was not to be reported on appeal.—Id.

⚷=757(1). In general.

Ind.App. 4 Dist. 1983. Merits of appeal from grant of summary judgment in favor of contractor in action alleging breach of express and implied warranties, negligence and fraud would be addressed, even though parties' briefs failed to include verbatim statement of judgment as required by rules. Rules App.Proc., Rule 8.3(A)(4), (B).—Grimm v. F.D. Borkholder Co., Inc., 454 N.E.2d 84.

⚷=784. —— Defects in proceedings for review.

Ind.App. 4 Dist. 1983. Court of Appeals will waive issues or dismiss appeals when parties commit flagrant violations of rules of appellate procedure, but will reach merits where violations are comparatively minor. Rules App.Proc., Rule 8.3(A)(4), (B).—Grimm v. F.D. Borkholder Co., Inc., 454 N.E.2d 84.

⚷=848(1). In general.

Mass.App. 1983. Order of reference providing that evidence attending master's report was not to be reported, provided "facts final," and thus under applicable rule of civil procedure only questions of law arising upon the report would be considered. Rules Civ.Proc., Rule 53(e)(4), 43A M.G.L.A.—Frank D. Wayne Associates, Inc. v. Lussier, 454 N.E.2d 109.

⚷=852. —— Scope and theory of case.

Ind.App. 3 Dist. 1983. Judgment of trial court will be upheld if sustainable on any theory, and findings of fact will not be disturbed unless found to be "clearly erroneous," which is when there are no facts or inferences to be drawn therefrom which support the finding.—Kimbrell v. City of Lafayette, 454 N.E.2d 73.

⚷=927(7). Effect of evidence and inferences therefrom on direction of verdict.

Ill.App. 1 Dist. 1983. In passing on propriety of directed verdict for plaintiff, courts of review must consider defendant's evidence in its most

For Earlier Cases, See Same Topic and Key Number in Any West Key Number Digest

XXXI

Exhibit 15: Key Number Digest for cases appearing in a *North Eastern Reporter* advance sheet.

Official State Reports. Once one is familiar with case reporting in the National Reporter System, there is little more that can be learned from the official reports, despite their continuing importance. However, it should be noted that the National Reporter System was created in the late nineteenth century. Therefore, *only* the *official* report may exist for earlier state cases. To facilitate access to these reports, Trans-Media Publishing Company has issued a microfilm edition of the official state reports which antedate the National Reporter System.

For all decisions which appear in an official report, that official report is the authoritative text and must be cited in briefs or memoranda. It is customary to give the official report before the unofficial in citing the case, for example, *State ex rel. Leis v. Outcault,* et al., 1 Ohio St.3d 147, 438 N.E.2d 443 (1982). The citation to the official Ohio State Reports precedes the unofficial *North Eastern Reporter.* Note that the official and unofficial reporters in this citation are in their third and second series, respectively.

Because of the success of the West system and for reasons of economy, a number of states have abandoned their official reporters and many of these have adopted the West reporter as official. In addition to their standard reporters for California, Illinois and New York, West issues separate editions of the decisions of over thirty other states by reproducing the pages of these decisions as they appear in the West regional reporter and cumulating them into bound volumes with their original page numbering. Many of these offprinted reporters and the West regional reporter from which they come have now been designated as the official reporter for that state. Appendix C gives fuller information on the current status of court reporting in each state, but bear in mind that these designations are subject to change.

Most official reporters include only the reports of the high court for that state, usually called the supreme court. Several states (e.g. California, Illinois, New York and Pennsylvania) issue more than one series of official reports, in order to cover adequately the decisions of their intermediate appellate courts and in some instances important decisions from their trial courts. In New York there are three official series of reports (*New York Reports,* covering the Court of Appeals; *Appellate Division Reports* covering the Appellate Divisions of the Supreme Court; and *Miscellaneous Reports* covering a selection of the decisions of the various lower courts). One single West series, *New York Supplement,* publishes as many cases as those three official reporters. In addition, the *North Eastern Reporter* also publishes the decisions of the N.Y. Court of Appeals, that state's highest court.

Official slip decisions and advance sheets are published for the courts of some states, but not for every state.

Annotated Reports. While West purports to publish virtually all of the high court decisions from the various states, the Lawyers Co-operative Publishing Company approaches case reporting from a different point of view. Its series, *American Law Reports,* is based on the annotated reporting of a small selection of significant cases. *A.L.R.*, as it is called, includes the full text of approximately 250 carefully chosen state court decisions annually, each of which is annotated with an editorial discussion of the law of that case. Before 1969, A.L.R. also included some annotated federal decisions, but since 1969, these appear in a separate, parallel series called *A.L.R. Federal. A.L.R. Federal* includes approximately 150 decisions each year.

The *A.L.R.* annotation includes past developments, the *current* law in most states on that problem, and probable future trends. The annotations in both series are prepared by editorial writers employed by the publisher. These annotated reports are favored by many legal researchers for the exhaustive coverage of their annotations, which range in length from several paragraphs to over a hundred pages. Even though the leading decision may be from another state, its annotation provides a survey of the law in all states, indexed by specific subtopics and by jurisdictions (by state in *A.L.R.* and by federal circuit in *A.L.R. Federal*). By focusing on those decisions which significantly affect legal development or facilitate the detailed editorial development of an important area of law, the *A.L.R.* annotation frequently offers quicker access to the leading cases than other tools. In addition, cross references are provided to (and from) the Lawyers Co-op encyclopedia, *American Jurisprudence 2d,* and other research publications in its "Total Client-Service Library".

It should be noted that advance sheets are not issued for *A.L.R.*, since the annotations require time for preparation and there would be little value in issuing a temporary edition of the decisions alone.

Before *A.L.R.* was developed in its present form, various predecessors were published with annotations of varying frequency and quality. These included the following: (1) Trinity series (*American Decisions, American Reports* and *American State Reports*), 1760–1911; (2) *American and English Annotated Cases,* 1906–1911; (3) *American Annotated Cases,* 1912–1918; and (4) *Lawyers Reports Annotated,* 1888–1918. *American Law Reports* includes the following series: 1st series: 1918–1947; 2d series: 1948–1965; 3d series: 1965–1980; and 4th series: 1980–date.

The tools of access to the decisions and annotations of *A.L.R.* have changed from series to series. *A.L.R.* and *A.L.R.2d* were originally accessible by digests (similar to the West digests), by word indexes and by tables of cases. Now, the primary finding tools for all four series of *A.L.R.* and for *A.L.R. Federal* are *Quick Indexes.*

In addition, supplemental services for *A.L.R.* and *A.L.R.2d,* and pocket parts in each volume of *A.L.R.3d, A.L.R.4th* and *A.L.R. Federal,* provide access to later decisions and annotations and permit the reseacher to update any relevant decisions or annotations with later citations. These methods of access and supplementation are explained more fully in Chapter III below, at pages 78–83.

Special Subject or Topical Reporters. There is another significant type of unofficial court reporting, which brings together cases in a particular subject area. Examples of such series are the *American Maritime Cases, Public Utilities Reports Annotated,* and *U.S. Patents Quarterly.* Some of these, like CCH's *Labor Cases* and Prentice-Hall's *American Federal Tax Reports,* are published as adjuncts to looseleaf services on those topics. Some of these reporters also contain decisions of administrative agencies in the same field, such as *Federal Carrier Cases* which includes Interstate Commerce Commission decisions on the regulation of carriers.

LOCATING PARALLEL CITATIONS OF CASE REPORTS

Since there are several reporting systems publishing decisions simultaneously, the same decision often appears both in the official reports and in the National Reporter System. Occasionally it may also be published, with an annotation, in the *American Law Reports.* Frequently the researcher will have a citation to only one of these reports and will want to obtain citations to the others, either to complete the citation in a brief, or to examine the other report.

For that purpose parallel citation tables, such as the following, are used:

1. Case Name. If the case name is known, the Table of Cases volume of the West digest for the appropriate jurisdiction or period will include both the official and unofficial citation. Note the *Roe v. Wade* citations (with digest topics and key numbers) appearing in the following exhibit from the West *U.S. Supreme Court Digest:*

Rockton & R R R v. Walling, SC, 65 SCt 1026, 324 US 880, 89 LEd 1431, den'g cert 146 F2d 111.
Rockwell Mfg Co v. Stanley Works, Pa, 74 SCt 30, 346 US 818, 98 LEd 345, den'g cert Stanley Works v. Rockwell Mfg Co, 203 F2d 846.
Rodgers v. U S, Tenn, 67 SCt 1309, 331 US 799, 91 LEd 1824. Mem.
Rodgers v. U S, Tenn, 68 SCt 5, 332 US 371, 92 LEd 3—Agric 1; Interest 1.
Rodney v. Paramount Pictures, NY, 71 SCt 572, 340 US 953, 95 LEd 687, den'g cert, Paramount Pictures v. Rodney, 186 F2d 111.
Rodrigue v. Aetna Cas & Sur Co, La, 89 SCt 1835, 395 US 352, 23 LEd2d 360—Adm 1.10, 1.20(1), 21, 22.
Rodriquez v. U S, Cal, 89 SCt 1715, 395 US 327, 23 LEd2d 340—Crim Law 997.5, 1004, 1072, 1077.3, 1188.
Roe v. Wade, Tex, 93 SCt 705, 410 US 113, 35 LEd2d 147, reh den 93 SCt 1409, 410 US 959, 35 LEd2d 694—Abort 1; Action 6; Const Law 42.1(3), 46(1), 82, 210, 252, 258(3); Courts 383(1), 385(1, 7), 508(7); Fed Civ Proc 321, 331; Statut 64(6).
Roebling v. C I R 65 SCt 131, 323 US 773, 89 LEd 618, den'g cert 143 F2d 810.
Rogalski, People of State of New York ex rel v. Martin, NY, 64 SCt 53, 320 US 767, 88 LEd 458, reh den 64 SCt 258, 320 US 814, 88 L Ed 492. Mem.
Rogers v. Squier, Wash, 67 SCt 1346, 331 US 866, 91 LEd 1870. Mem.
Rogers v. State of Conn, Conn, 76 US 809, 100 LEd 726, rev'g Rogers, 143 Conn 167, 120 A2d 409.
Rogers v. Teets, Cal, 76 SCt 98, 350 US 809, 100 LEd 726, rev'g Rogers, Application of, 229 F2d 754.
Rogers v. U S, Colo, 70 SCt 978, 339 US 956, 94 LEd 1368, gr'g cert Rogers v. U S, 179 F2d 559.
Rogers v. U S, Colo, 70 SCt 979, 339 US 958, 94 LEd 1369, den'g cert Rogers v. U S, 180 F2d 103.
Rogers v. U S, Colo, 71 SCt 438, 340 US 367, 95 LEd 344, 19 ALR2d 378, reh den 71 SCt 619, 341 US 912, 95 LEd 1348—Consp 24, 47(1); Insurrect 2; Witn 297(1, 12), 298, 305(1), 306, 307, 308.
Rogers' Estate v. C I R 65 SCt 269, 323 US 780, 89 LEd 623, den'g cert 143 F2d 695, 156 ALR 1239.
Rogers' Estate v. Helvering, US, 64 SCt 172, 320 US 410, 88 LEd 134—Int Rev 20.2, 992, 1004.
Rogers v. U S, USLa, 95 SCt 2091, on remand 519 F2d 1084—Courts 383(8); Crim Law 636(1), 641.12(2), 863(1), 885, 1174(1).
Rogoff v. U S, NY, 65 SCt 553, 323 US 799, 89 LEd 638, den'g cert 145 F2d 82.
Rohde v. O'Donnell, Ill, 70 SCt 1015, 339 US 990, 94 LEd 1390, den'g cert People v. Rohde, 403 Ill 41, 85 NE 2d 24.

Exhibit 16: Table of cases in the *U.S. Supreme Court Digest*, showing the listing for *Roe v. Wade.*

2. **Popular Name.** Many cases acquire through common usage a "popular name". Such cases can be traced through that name in a *popular name table* published by Shepard's. This table also lists many *statutes* by their popular names and is entitled *Shepard's Acts and Cases by Popular Names—Federal and State.* Currently, it consists of one bound volume (issued in 1979) and is updated periodically by pamphlet supplements. The following exhibit shows en-

tries in the case section of that volume, including the popular name listing of Roe v. Wade:

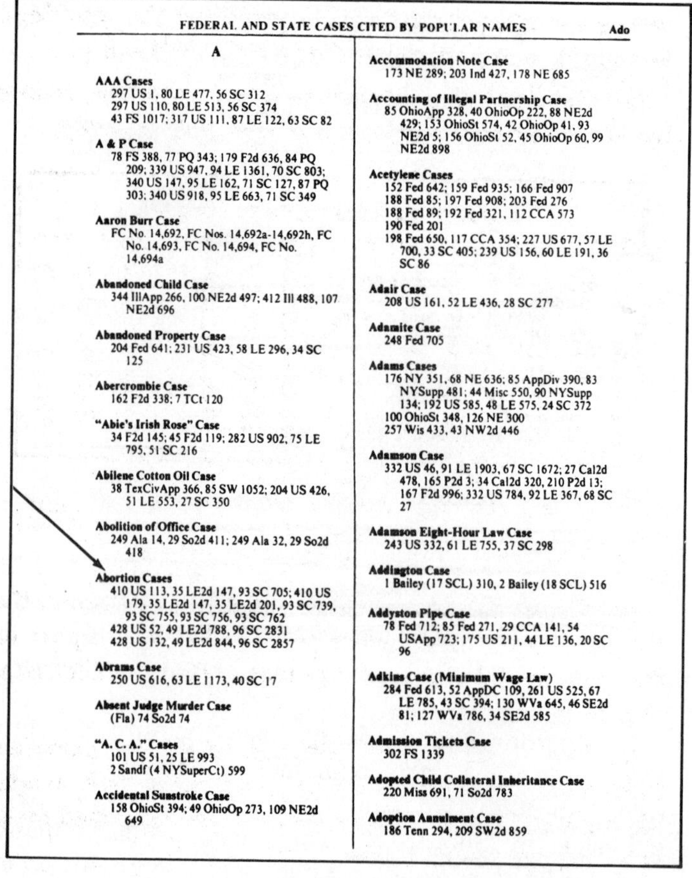

FEDERAL AND STATE CASES CITED BY POPULAR NAMES Ado

A

AAA Cases
297 US 1, 80 LE 477, 56 SC 312
297 US 110, 80 LE 513, 56 SC 374
43 FS 1017; 317 US 111, 87 LE 122, 63 SC 82

A & P Case
78 FS 388, 77 PQ 343; 179 F2d 636, 84 PQ 209; 339 US 947, 94 LE 1361, 70 SC 803; 340 US 147, 95 LE 162, 71 SC 127, 87 PQ 303; 340 US 918, 95 LE 663, 71 SC 349

Aaron Burr Case
FC No. 14,692, FC Nos. 14,692a-14,692h, FC No. 14,693, FC No. 14,694, FC No. 14,694a

Abandoned Child Case
344 IllApp 266, 100 NE2d 497; 412 Ill 488, 107 NE2d 696

Abandoned Property Case
204 Fed 641; 231 US 423, 58 LE 296, 34 SC 125

Abercrombie Case
162 F2d 338; 7 TCt 120

"Abie's Irish Rose" Case
34 F2d 145; 45 F2d 119; 282 US 902, 75 LE 795, 51 SC 216

Abilene Cotton Oil Case
38 TexCivApp 366, 85 SW 1052; 204 US 426, 51 LE 553, 27 SC 350

Abolition of Office Case
249 Ala 14, 29 So2d 411; 249 Ala 32, 29 So2d 418

Abortion Cases
410 US 113, 35 LE2d 147, 93 SC 705; 410 US 179, 35 LE2d 147, 35 LE2d 201, 93 SC 739, 93 SC 755, 93 SC 756, 93 SC 762
428 US 52, 49 LE2d 788, 96 SC 2831
428 US 132, 49 LE2d 844, 96 SC 2857

Abrams Case
250 US 616, 63 LE 1173, 40 SC 17

Absent Judge Murder Case
(Fla) 74 So2d 74

"A. C. A." Cases
101 US 51, 25 LE 993
2 Sandf (4 NYSuperCt) 599

Accidental Sunstroke Case
158 OhioSt 394; 49 OhioOp 273, 109 NE2d 649

Accommodation Note Case
173 NE 289; 203 Ind 427, 178 NE 685

Accounting of Illegal Partnership Case
85 OhioApp 328, 40 OhioOp 222, 88 NE2d 429; 153 OhioSt 574, 42 OhioOp 41, 93 NE2d 5; 156 OhioSt 52, 45 OhioOp 60, 99 NE2d 898

Acetylene Cases
152 Fed 642; 159 Fed 935; 166 Fed 907
188 Fed 85; 197 Fed 908; 203 Fed 276
188 Fed 89; 192 Fed 321, 112 CCA 573
190 Fed 201
198 Fed 650, 117 CCA 354; 227 US 677, 57 LE 700, 33 SC 405; 239 US 156, 60 LE 191, 36 SC 86

Adair Case
208 US 161, 52 LE 436, 28 SC 277

Adamite Case
248 Fed 705

Adams Cases
176 NY 351, 68 NE 636; 85 AppDiv 390, 83 NYSupp 481; 44 Misc 550, 90 NYSupp 134; 192 US 585, 48 LE 575, 24 SC 372
100 OhioSt 348, 126 NE 300
257 Wis 433, 43 NW2d 446

Adamson Case
332 US 46, 91 LE 1903, 67 SC 1672; 27 Cal2d 478, 165 P2d 3; 34 Cal2d 320, 210 P2d 13; 167 F2d 996; 332 US 784, 92 LE 367, 68 SC 27

Adamson Eight-Hour Law Case
243 US 332, 61 LE 755, 37 SC 298

Addington Case
1 Bailey (17 SCL) 310, 2 Bailey (18 SCL) 516

Addyston Pipe Case
78 Fed 712; 85 Fed 271, 29 CCA 141, 54 USApp 723; 175 US 211, 44 LE 136, 20 SC 96

Adkins Case (Minimum Wage Law)
284 Fed 613, 52 AppDC 109, 261 US 525, 67 LE 785, 43 SC 394; 130 WVa 645, 46 SE2d 81; 127 WVa 786, 34 SE2d 585

Admission Tickets Case
302 FS 1339

Adopted Child Collateral Inheritance Case
220 Miss 691, 71 So2d 783

Adoption Annulment Case
186 Tenn 294, 209 SW2d 859

Exhibit 17: The case table in *Shepard's Acts and Cases by Popular Names—Federal and State.*

Popular names of cases are also listed separately in the main table of cases of many digests.

3. **From Official to Unofficial Report,** that is, where the official citation is known and the unofficial is sought, one can use either of the following:

(a) *National Reporter Blue Book* which is issued by West for this purpose and updated annually:

1 OHIO STATE REPORTS, THIRD SERIES

Ohio St. 3d	N.E.2d		Ohio St. 3d	N.E.2d		Ohio St. 3d	N.E.2d		Ohio St. 3d	N.E.2d	
Pg.	Vol.	Pg.	Pg.	Vol.	Pg.	Pg.	Vol.	Pg.	Pg.	Vol.	Pg.
1	437	289	48	438	406	110	438	428	192	438	897
3	437	291	54	437	1174	114	438	431	205	438	1149
6	437	295	57	437	1176	118	438	105	212	438	907
10	437	298	64	437	1182	125	438	111	217	438	910
13	437	300	69	437	1186	129	438	434	221	438	1155
15	437	302	79	437	1194	140	438	114	231	439	417
22	437	586	83	437	1197	143	438	117	238	438	1162
26	437	589	85	438	410	147	438	443	244	438	1167
27	437	591	89	437	1199	151	438	120	255	438	1175
31	437	594	93	438	414	162	438	448	263	438	1181
33	437	596	94	438	415	167	438	128	269	439	888
36	437	598	101	438	420	173	438	881	272	439	891
40	437	601	103	438	422	182	438	888	275	439	893
44	437	605	107	438	425	184	438	890			

Exhibit 18: Part of an entry in the *National Reporter Blue Book,* showing reference from official to unofficial citation of the Ohio case previously noted.

(b) Shepard's state citations—the first citation in the listing of each case refers to the alternate report of the case in the regional reporter. That parallel citation is in parentheses.

(c) Two computerized citation checking services: *Auto-Cite,* available on LEXIS, and *Insta-Cite,* available on WESTLAW. These services are described more fully on pp. 91–92 below.

4. **From Unofficial to Official Report:**

(a) State Blue and White books, issued by West for twenty-four states to provide parallel citations from the official reports to the *National Reporter System.*

Vol. 1 **OHIO STATE REPORTS, 3rd Series**

Vol. 1 **– 1 –** (437NE289) (1OBR28) **– 3 –** (437NE291) (1OBR29) **– 6 –** (437NE295) (1OBR32) 6OS84 6OBR124	**– 44 –** (437NE605) (1OBR77) **– 48 –** (438NE406) (1OBR92) 1OS56 5OS208 1OBR98 5OBR423 **– 54 –** (437NE1174) (1OBR96)	j6OBR185 **– 101 –** (438NE420) (1OBR135) j1OS106 4OS196 5OS76 6OS451 j1OBR140 4OBR516 5OBR130 6OBR493 **– 103 –** (438NE422)	**– 147 –** (438NE443) (1OBR181) **– 151 –** (438NE120) (1OBR185) 3OA191 3OBR217 3OBR[2]217 **– 162 –** (438NE448) (1OBR194) d2OS84 d2OBR638	**– 217 –** (438NE910) (1OBR240) 5OA184 5OBR369 **– 221 –** (438NE1155) (1OBR244) j4OS65 j4OBR154 **– 231 –** (439NE417) (1OBR253) d6OS[1]255	**– 17 –** (442NE452) (2OBR504) **– 19 –** (442NE454) (2OBR506) **– 24 –** (442NE747) (2OBR570) **– 26 –** (442NE749) (2OBR572) e2OS72	**– 62 –** (442NE1288) (2OBR619) **– 69 –** (442NE1295) (2OBR625) 5OS[1]140 6OS[1]35 6OS181 6OS294 5OBR[1]272 6OBR[1]56 6OBR238 6OBR356 83AG28	**– 122 –** (443NE497) (2OBR671) **– 126 –** (443NE501) (2OBR675) **– 131 –** (443NE504) (2OBR678) **– 136 –** (443NE176) (2OBR683)

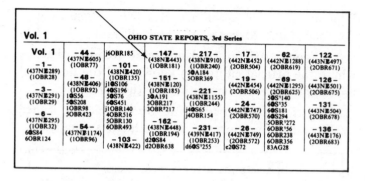

Exhibit 19: Parallel citation to *North Eastern Reporter* for case appearing in *Shepard's Ohio Citations.*

White pages also carry citation tables from the unofficial to the official report. These books are available to law libraries only for the state in which they are located. Their arrangement is similar to that in the *National Reporter Blue Book.* (Exhibit 18).

(b) Shepard's regional reporter citations—the first entry, in parentheses, is to the *official* report (Exhibit 20).

(c) The official citation may also be supplied at the beginning of the case in the regional reporter, *if* it is available at the time of printing.

(d) *Auto-Cite* and *Insta-Cite,* as in paragraph 3(c) above.

In addition to their value as legal precedent and their importance in legal research, the law reports

NORTHEASTERN REPORTER, 2d SERIES **Vol. 438**

-1253- (107IIA516) (63IID331) 548FS69 **-1258-** (107IIA418) (63IID336) **-1261-** (107IIA647) (63IID339) **-1265-** (107IIA686) (63IID343) **-1268-** (107IIA679) (63IID346)	**-1381-** 441NE[11]974 441NE[12]974 441NE[9]975 442NE717 j443NE74 **Vol. 438** **-1-** s431NE132 **-6-** s380NE1285 s424NE166 **-16-** e439NE[8]733 j439NE735	443NE[1]440 455S2d657 j455S2d659 456S2d[2]703 456S2d[3]703 457S2d[1]192 **-99-** Case 1 (56NY830) (452S2d566) s443S2d417 f456S2d372 **-99-** Case 2 (56NY832) (452S2d566) s441S2d826	**-111-** (1OS125) (1OBR163) **-114-** (1OS140) (1OBR175) **-117-** (1OS143) (1OBR178) **-120-** (1OS151) (1OBR185) **-128-** (1OS167) (1OBR199)	**-187-** (91Il2d413) (63IID449) **-198-** (91Il2d326) (63IID460) s103SC336 442NE[2]173 **-203-** (107IIA755) (63IID465) **-211-** (107IIA125) (63IID473) **-213-** (107IIA729)	**-308-** s433NE405 **-327-** (386Mas826) **-329-** (386Mas848) **-334-** (386Mas834) 440NE[3]1183 **-343-** (386Mas868) **-348-** (386Mas885) **-351-**	453S2d598 d453S2d953 454S2d166 j454S2d981 455S2d200 **-402-** (56NY469) (452S2d869) **-406-** (1OS48) (1OBR92) 437NE[1]1175 **-410-** (1OS85) (1OBR122) 442NE[4]759	**-466-** (107IIA848) (63IID535) **-471-** (107IIA992) (63IID540) **-482-** (107IIA810) (63IID551) **-490-** (107IIA772) (63IID559) **-495-** (107IIA780) (63IID564) 441NE91
US App Pndg **-1300-** (107IIA711) (63IID378) **-1307*-** (107IIA721) (63IID385) **-1314*-** (107IIA668) (63IID392) **-1318-** 438NE[16]1054	**-71-** (386Mas831) **-73-** (386Mas 1009) s425NE781 440NE41 **-76-** (14MaA152) s440NE1177 **-82-** (14MaA215)	**-103-** Case 4 (56NY823) (452S2d570) s440S2d115 **-104-** Case 1 (56NY824) (452S2d571) **-104-** Case 2 (56NY826) (452S2d571)	[illegible] (91Il2d295) (63IID421) s410NE341 **-168-** (91Il2d316) (63IID430) 442NE[1]209 442NE[2]209 **-173-** (91Il2d438) (63IID435) 441NE[2]1337	[illegible] (107IIA748) (63IID507) **-250*-** (107IIA742) (63IID512) **-254-** (107IIA902) (63IID516) **-275-** 440NE[4]463 442NE377	**-375-** (14MaA268) s440NE1177 **-382-** (14MaA281) s440NE1177 439NE853 442NE[1]743 **-385-** (14MaA291) **-388-** (14MaA963)	[illegible] (1OS114) (1OBR147) **-434-** (1OS129) (1OBR166) **-443-** (1OS147) (1OBR181) **-448-** (1OS162) (1OBR194) d443NE[1]146	[illegible] (63IID594) **-530-** (107IIA803) (63IID599) **-535*-** (107IIA1062) (63IID604) 439NE121 **-540-** (107IIA1011) (63IID609)

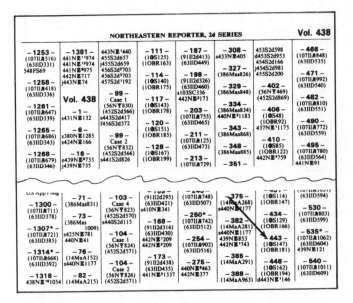

Exhibit 20: Parallel citation to *Ohio State Reports 3rd Series* for case appearing in *Shepard's Northeastern Reporter Citations.*

constitute a literary form with other values as well. They describe human problems and predicaments—domestic crises, moral failings, economic troubles. They reflect the larger social, political and economic trends and conditions of life in particular periods and places. And they frequently have a unique literary quality which adds to the tone and body of the prose of their time. Whether brilliant or dull in style, legal writing has always been an influential part of general literature.

CHAPTER III

CASE–FINDING

Under the modern view of law as a dynamic process rather than a mechanical application of fixed rules, any material which persuades or influences a tribunal has some degree of authority. Thus, primary sources of law may be more authoritative than secondary materials, but the difference is not absolute. Legal research can be seen as a wide-ranging and creative inquiry, but still must begin with the primary rules found in appellate decisions and statutes.

The doctrine of precedent can operate effectively only if judicial decisions are made easily available, so that they can be cited by lawyers and used by courts in deciding later cases. In order to discover what is the applicable law, lawyers must have some means of locating "cases in point," that is, earlier decisions which are factually and legally relevant to the cases on which they are working. They must be able to locate precedents with which they can support their positions and persuade a court to accept their arguments. However, as we have seen, judicial decisions are published in chronological order, both in their official and unofficial reports. This body of law, consisting of over 3,000,000 decisions to which are added 50,000 new decisions every year, could hardly be searched for relevant precedents unless there were some means of subject access.

Such access is provided by various finding tools, such as case digests, encyclopedias, citators, annotated law reports, statutory codes, looseleaf services, legal treatises, periodicals, and computerized search services. Of these, the traditional beginning point and certainly the one most specifically designed as a case finder has been the case digest. Bear in mind, however, that for some searches one of the other case finders may be preferred, and that individual preference can always lead you to another tool.

A digest to judicial decisions superimposes a subject classification upon chronologically published cases. The classification scheme consists of an alphabetically arranged scheme of legal topics and subtopics which can be approached through a detailed index. Brief abstracts of the points of law in decided cases are classified by subject and set out in the digests under appropriate topical headings. The cases are then located and retrieved by the researcher from the citations in the digest.

As soon as comprehensive case reporting began to develop in England, finding tools were published to provide a topical approach. Initially this function was performed by texts, but then abridgments and digests were soon devised to enable lawyers to find relevant prior cases on particular topics. One of the earliest of these was Statham's Abridgment, printed around 1490. Later important abridgments were made by Fitzherbert (1514); Brooke (1568); Rolle (1668); Jacobs (1713); Bacon (1736); and Viner (1742). The early abridgments and digests were prototypes of the modern digests, but used only a few broad topics and included a relatively small number of decisions. Gradually these finding tools grew more intensive, employing finer internal subdivisions, and more extensive, covering more areas of law and a larger number of cases.

WEST DIGESTS

Today the digests of the West Publishing Company constitute the most comprehensive subject approach to case law, although computerized search systems are rapidly developing more effective approaches. The basic unit of the West digest system is the "squib" or one sentence summary of each principle of law dealt with in each of the cases found in the West reporters. As shown in Exhibit 21, the digest as a whole consists of a series of squibs, arranged by topic name and key number (here *Abortion* 1, relating to *Roe v. Wade*) derived from West's key number classification scheme.

⚷1 ABORTION 1 FPD2d—30

For later cases see same Topic and Key Number in Pocket Part

U.S.Tex. 1973. Prior to approximately the end of the first trimester of pregnancy the attending physician in consultation with his patient is free to determine, without regulation by state, that in his medical judgment the patient's pregnancy should be terminated, and if that decision is reached such judgment may be effectuated by an abortion without interference by the state.

Roe v. Wade, 93 S.Ct. 705, 410 U.S. 113, 35 L.Ed.2d 147, rehearing denied 93 S.Ct. 1409, 410 U.S. 959, 35 L.Ed.2d 694.

From and after approximately the end of the first trimester of pregnancy a state may regulate abortion procedure to extent that the regulation reasonably relates to preservation and protection of maternal health.

Roe v. Wade, 93 S.Ct. 705, 410 U.S. 113, 35 L.Ed.2d 147, rehearing denied 93 S.Ct. 1409, 410 U.S. 959, 35 L.Ed.2d 694.

If state is interested in protecting fetal life after viability it may go so far as to proscribe abortion during that period except when necessary to preserve the life or the health of the mother.

Roe v. Wade, 93 S.Ct. 705, 410 U.S. 113, 35 L.Ed.2d 147, rehearing denied 93 S.Ct. 1409, 410 U.S. 959, 35 L.Ed.2d 694.

State criminal abortion laws like Texas statutes making it a crime to procure or attempt an abortion except an abortion on medical advice for purpose of saving life of the mother regardless of stage of pregnancy violate due process clause of Fourteenth Amendment protecting right to privacy against state action. U.S.C.A.Const. Amend. 14; Vernon's Ann.Tex.P.C. arts. 1191–1194, 1196.

Roe v. Wade, 93 S.Ct. 705, 410 U.S. 113, 35 L.Ed.2d 147, rehearing denied 93 S.Ct. 1409, 410 U.S. 959, 35 L.Ed.2d 694.

State in regulating abortion procedures may define "physician" as a physician currently licensed by State and may proscribe any abortion by a person who is not a physician as so defined.

Roe v. Wade, 93 S.Ct. 705, 410 U.S. 113, 35 L.Ed.2d 147, rehearing denied 93 S.Ct. 1409, 410 U.S. 959, 35 L.Ed.2d 694.

C.A.Fla. 1975. The fundamental right to an abortion applies to minors as well as adults. U.S.C.A.Const. Amends. 1, 14.

Poe v. Gerstein, 517 F.2d 787.

Portion of Florida abortion statute requiring consent of parent, custodian or legal guardian if pregnant woman is under 18 years of age and unmarried could not be justified by state interests in preventing illicit sexual conduct among minors, protecting minors from their own improvidence, fostering parental control, and supporting the family as a social unit, and thus such consent requirement was unconstitutional. West's F.S.A. §§ 381.382, 458.22(3), 744.13, 827.06; U.S.C.A.Const. Amends. 1, 14.

Poe v. Gerstein, 517 F.2d 787.

Fundamental right to abortion could not be abridged on the basis of compelling state interests, where, inter alia, the statute in question was not "necessary" to achievement of such interests or was unlikely to achieve them. West's F.S.A. § 458.22(3).

Poe v. Gerstein, 517 F.2d 787.

State's societal interest in marriage relationship was not sufficiently "compelling" to justify Florida statute precluding abortion without the written consent of husband if pregnant woman was married, unless husband was voluntarily living apart from his wife. West's F.S.A. § 458.22(3).

Poe v. Gerstein, 517 F.2d 787.

Florida statute precluding abortion without consent of husband if pregnant woman was married and husband was not voluntarily living apart from her could not be justified by state's interest in protecting the husband's rights with respect to the fetus and with respect to the procreation potential of his marriage, and said statute was unconstitutional as infringement on woman's fundamental right to abortion. West's F.S.A. § 458.22(3).

Poe v. Gerstein, 517 F.2d 787.

C.A.Ill. 1974. It is not until from and after the first trimester of pregnancy that a state may regulate abortions by regulations reasonably related to the preservation and protection of maternal health.

Friendship Medical Center, Ltd. v. Chicago Bd. of Health, 505 F.2d 1141, certiorari denied 95 S.Ct. 1438.

Any general health regulations which would apply to first trimester abortions must be limited so as to give effect to a woman's fundamental right of privacy.

Friendship Medical Center, Ltd. v. Chicago Bd. of Health, 505 F.2d 1141, certiorari denied 95 S.Ct. 1438.

C.A.Minn. 1974. Absent compelling circumstances of state interest, regulation of certain fundamental rights, including abortion, is unconstitutional.

Nyberg v. City of Virginia, 495 F.2d 1342, certiorari denied 95 S.Ct. 169, 419 U.S. 891, 42 L.Ed.2d 136.

Where state fails to take cognizance of separate trimesters of pregnancy in its regulation of abortion procedures, the regulation is overbroad and invalid.

Nyberg v. City of Virginia, 495 F.2d 1342, certiorari denied 95 S.Ct. 169, 419 U.S. 891, 42 L.Ed.2d 136.

For cited U.S.C.A. sections and legislative history

Exhibit 21: A page from *Federal Practice Digest 2d*, showing *Roe v. Wade* under key number Abortion 1. This topic is now called *Abortion and Birth Control* in current digests.

As illustrated in Exhibits 22 to 24, this key number system consists of over 400 digest topics. Within each West digest, the 400 topics are arranged alphabetically from "Abandoned and Lost Property" to "Zoning and Planning." Each topic acts as a chapter in the digest, covering generally the legal issues to be found within that chapter. The topic is further divided into subtopics, each of which bears the name of the broader topic and a key number designating its specific subdivision. Some short topics like *Lotteries* or *Obscenity* employ relatively few subdivisions and key numbers, while broader ones such as *Constitutional Law* or *Criminal Law* may have thousands. See Exhibit 25 for an analysis of *Abortion and Birth Control,* a relatively small topic.

LIST OF DIGEST TOPICS

The digest topics used in this digest conform to the American Digest System

---

Abandoned and Lost Property
Abatement and Revival
Abduction
Abortion and Birth Control
Absentees
Abstracts of Title
Accession
Accord and Satisfaction
Account
Account, Action on
Account Stated
Accountants
Acknowledgment
Action
Action on the Case
Adjoining Landowners
Administrative Law and Procedure
Admiralty
Adoption
Adulteration
Adultery
Adverse Possession
Affidavits
Affray
Agriculture
Aliens
Alteration of Instruments
Ambassadors and Consuls
Amicus Curiae
Animals
Annuities
Appeal and Error
Appearance
Arbitration
Armed Services
Arrest
Arson
Assault and Battery
Assignments
Assistance, Writ of
Associations
Assumpsit, Action of
Asylums
Attachment
Attorney and Client
Attorney General
Auctions and Auctioneers
Audita Querela
Automobiles
Aviation
Bail
Bailment
Bankruptcy
Banks and Banking
Beneficial Associations
Bigamy
Bills and Notes
Blasphemy
Bonds
Boundaries
Bounties
Breach of Marriage Promise
Breach of the Peace
Bribery
Bridges
Brokers
Building and Loan Associations
Burglary
Canals
Cancellation of Instruments
Carriers
Cemeteries
Census
Certiorari
Champerty and Maintenance
Charities
Chattel Mortgages
Chemical Dependents
Citizens
Civil Rights
Clerks of Courts
Clubs
Colleges and Universities
Collision
Commerce
Common Lands
Common Law
Common Scold
Compounding Offenses
Compromise and Settlement
Condominium
Confusion of Goods
Conspiracy
Constitutional Law
Consumer Credit
Consumer Protection
Contempt
Contracts
Contribution
Conversion
Convicts
Copyrights and Intellectual Property
Coroners
Corporations
Costs
Counterfeiting
Counties
Court Commissioners
Courts
Covenant, Action of
Covenants
Credit Reporting Agencies
Criminal Law
Crops
Customs and Usages
Customs Duties
Damages
Dead Bodies
Death
Debt, Action of
Debtor and Creditor
Declaratory Judgment
Dedication
Deeds
Deposits and Escrows
Deposits in Court
Descent and Distribution
Detectives
Detinue
Disorderly Conduct
Disorderly House

31-9th Dec. Pt. 1 VI 1—7

Exhibit 22: List of digest topics used in West's key number classification system, arranged alphabetically.

LIST OF DIGEST TOPICS

District and Prosecuting Attorneys
District of Columbia
Disturbance of Public Assemblage
Divorce
Domicile
Dower and Curtesy
Drains
Drugs and Narcotics
Dueling
Easements
Ejectment
Election of Remedies
Elections
Electricity
Embezzlement
Embracery
Eminent Domain
Employers' Liability
Entry, Writ of
Equity
Escape
Escheat
Estates in Property
Estoppel
Evidence
Exceptions, Bill of
Exchange of Property
Exchanges
Execution
Executors and Administrators
Exemptions
Explosives
Extortion and Threats
Extradition and Detainers
Factors
False Imprisonment
False Personation
False Pretenses
Federal Civil Procedure
Federal Courts
Fences
Ferries
Fines
Fires
Fish
Fixtures
Food
Forcible Entry and Detainer
Forfeitures
Forgery
Fornication
Franchises
Fraud
Frauds, Statute of
Fraudulent Conveyances
Game
Gaming
Garnishment
Gas
Gifts
Good Will
Grand Jury
Guaranty
Guardian and Ward
Habeas Corpus
Hawkers and Peddlers
Health and Environment
Highways
Holidays
Homestead
Homicide
Hospitals
Husband and Wife
Illegitimate Children
Implied and Constructive Contracts
Improvements
Incest
Indemnity
Indians
Indictment and Information
Infants
Injunction
Innkeepers
Inspection
Insurance
Insurrection and Sedition
Interest
Internal Revenue
International Law
Interpleader
Intoxicating Liquors
Joint Adventures
Joint-Stock Companies and Business Trusts
Joint Tenancy
Judges
Judgment
Judicial Sales
Jury
Justices of the Peace
Kidnapping
Labor Relations
Landlord and Tenant
Larceny
Levees and Flood Control
Lewdness
Libel and Slander
Licenses
Liens
Life Estates
Limitation of Actions
Lis Pendens
Logs and Logging
Lost Instruments
Lotteries
Malicious Mischief
Malicious Prosecution
Mandamus
Manufactures
Maritime Liens
Marriage
Master and Servant
Mayhem
Mechanics' Liens
Mental Health
Military Justice
Militia
Mines and Minerals
Miscegenation
Monopolies
Mortgages
Motions
Municipal Corporations
Names
Navigable Waters
Ne Exeat
Negligence
Neutrality Laws
Newspapers
New Trial
Notaries
Notice
Novation
Nuisance
Oath
Obscenity
Obstructing Justice
Officers and Public Employees
Pardon and Parole
Parent and Child
Parliamentary Law
Parties

VII 1—8

Exhibit 23: Continuation of list of West's digest topics.

LIST OF DIGEST TOPICS

Partition
Partnership
Party Walls
Patents
Paupers
Payment
Penalties
Pensions
Perjury
Perpetuities
Physicians and Surgeons
Pilots
Piracy
Pleading
Pledges
Poisons
Possessory Warrant
Post Office
Powers
Pretrial Procedure
Principal and Agent
Principal and Surety
Prisons
Private Roads
Prize Fighting
Process
Products Liability
Prohibition
Property
Prostitution
Public Contracts
Public Lands
Public Utilities
Quieting Title
Quo Warranto
Railroads
Rape
Real Actions
Receivers
Receiving Stolen Goods
Recognizances
Records
Reference
Reformation of Instruments
Reformatories
Registers of Deeds
Release
Religious Societies
Remainders
Removal of Cases
Replevin
Reports
Rescue
Reversions
Review
Rewards
Riot
Robbery
Sales
Salvage
Schools
Scire Facias
Seals
Seamen
Searches and Seizures
Secured Transactions
Securities Regulation
Seduction
Sequestration
Set-Off and Counterclaim
Sheriffs and Constables
Shipping
Signatures
Slaves
Social Security and Public Welfare
Sodomy
Specific Performance
Spendthrifts
States
Statutes
Steam
Stipulations
Submission of Controversy
Subrogation
Subscriptions
Suicide
Sunday
Supersedeas
Taxation
Telecommunications
Tenancy in Common
Tender
Territories
Theaters and Shows
Time
Torts
Towage
Towns
Trade Regulation
Treason
Treaties
Trespass
Trepass to Try Title
Trial
Trover and Conversion
Trusts
Turnpikes and Toll Roads
Undertakings
United States
United States Magistrates
United States Marshals
Unlawful Assembly
Urban Railroads
Usury
Vagrancy
Vendor and Purchaser
Venue
War and National Emergency
Warehousemen
Waste
Waters and Water Courses
Weapons
Weights and Measures
Wharves
Wills
Witnesses
Woods and Forests
Workers' Compensation
Zoning and Planning

Exhibit 24: Conclusion of list of West's digest topics.

ABORTION AND BIRTH CONTROL

SUBJECTS INCLUDED

Causing or procuring miscarriage or premature delivery of a pregnant woman, and acts done for or in aid of such purpose

Right to abortion, and limitations thereon

Contraception and birth control

Nature and extent of criminal responsibility therefor, and grounds of defense

Prosecution and punishment of such acts as public offenses

Civil liability therefor

SUBJECTS EXCLUDED AND COVERED BY OTHER TOPICS

Death, civil liability for causing, see DEATH

Homicide committed in attempting to procure abortion, see HOMICIDE

Malpractice, civil liability for, see PHYSICIANS AND SURGEONS

Public funds, expenditure for abortion, see SOCIAL SECURITY AND PUBLIC WELFARE

For detailed references to other topics, see Descriptive-Word Index

---

Analysis

⇐.50. Right to abortion and regulation thereof.
1. Nature and elements of offenses.
1.10. Contraceptives and birth control.
1.20. Constitutional and statutory provisions.
1.30. —— Validity of statute.
2. Defenses.
3. Persons liable.
4. Indictment and information.
5. —— Requisites and sufficiency.
6. —— Issues, proof, and variance.
7. Evidence.
8. —— Presumptions and burden of proof.
9. —— Admissibility in general.
10. —— Dying declarations.
11. —— Weight and sufficiency.
12. Trial.
13. —— Instructions.
14. —— Verdict.
15. Sentence and punishment.
16. Civil liability.

Exhibit 25: Scope-Note and Analysis of the topic *Abortion and Birth Control* in a West digest.

Use of this key number classification system begins early in the West reporting process. As mentioned previously, editors at West create squibs or abstracts for every significant point of law discussed in each case appearing in the West reporters. Each squib is assigned a topic name and key number which designates its subject content. These squibs first appear as headnotes preceding the text of the opinion in the West reporter advance sheet. (See Exhibit 10, at p. 39). All headnotes within each advance sheet are also arranged by topic and key number in the Key Number Digest which appears in the front of the advance sheet, and then at the end of the bound reporter. (See Exhibit 15, at p. 47). By bringing together all headnotes bearing the same topic and key number, the digest provides in one place summaries and citations to all cases in that advance sheet or volume which deal with the same legal principle.

The squibs from the Key Number Digests in all West advance sheets are collected and published in cumulative volumes which constitute the *General Digest,* the most current component of West's comprehensive digest, the American Digest System.

The American Digest System covers all decisions published in all of West's reporters. Thus the coverage is primarily of appellate court decisions, though selected trial court opinions from some jurisdictions are also included (e.g., those reported in *Federal Supplement* and *New York Supplement*). Since the accumulation into one set of all appellate decisions in the history of the United States would be unmanageable and would require frequent revision, the system is divided into separate units, each of which covers a ten year period. These ten year units are called *decennial digests,* such as the *Eighth Decennial,* which includes cases decided between 1966 and 1976. Due to the increase in the number of cases being reported in recent years, West now cumulates these digests every *five* years, instead of every ten years. The Ninth Decennial Digest will appear therefore in two parts, each a complete five year unit. The first part covers the years 1976–1981. The second part will cover 1981–

1986, when the current Sixth Series of the General Digest is cumulated.

The first unit of the American Digest System, called the *Century Digest*, covers 1658 to 1896, when the volume of litigation was, of course, relatively small. The following are the various units of the American Digest System:

Years	Digest Unit
1658 to 1896	Century Digest
1897 to 1906	First Decennial
1907 to 1916	Second Decennial
1916 to 1926	Third Decennial
1926 to 1936	Fourth Decennial
1936 to 1946	Fifth Decennial
1946 to 1956	Sixth Decennial
1956 to 1966	Seventh Decennial
1966 to 1976	Eighth Decennial
1976 to 1981	Ninth Decennial, Part I
1981 +	General Digest, Sixth Series

The topics and key numbers used for points of law and types of cases are basically the same in each of the component parts of the digest system, from the most recent all the way back to the *First Decennial* covering 1897–1906. The original unit, the *Century Digest* (1658–1896), employs a slightly different numbering system, but a table in volume 21 of the *First Decennial* bridges this discrepancy by providing references from the *Century Digest* key numbers to those in the *First Decennial.* In order to go back from the numbers of the *First Decennial* to those of the *Century Digest,* reverse cross references appear under each key number in the volumes of the *First* and *Second Decennials.* Thus research under the same topic may turn up cases from the seventeenth century down to those decided a few weeks ago.

Each of the American Digest System units includes cases appearing in all of West's reporters—in the National Reporter System, the various federal reporters, and West's individual state reporters. In addition, West also publishes smaller digests which cover in a single set (or sometimes in two or three) all of the decisions of smaller geographical or jurisdictional units. For example, there are such digests for each of the regional reporter series except the *South Western Reporter* and the *North Eastern Reporter*, the latter having been discontinued in 1972.

For each state, except Delaware, Nevada and Utah, West publishes individual digests. Although they are the publisher of these digests, in some instances West retained the name of the former publisher or compiler of the digest, such as the *Vale Pennsylvania Digest* or *Abbott's New York Digest.* Beginning in 1981 with the third series of the New York Digest, however, Abbott's name has been dropped, and the series is now called *West's New York Digest 3d.* Each state digest is devoted to only one state except for the *Dakota Digest* and the *Virginia-West Virginia Digest.* These digests include references to all cases decided in the state's courts which are reported in the National Reporter System, as well as references to federal cases which began in or were appealed from the state. (Only the digest for New York *excludes* references to federal cases.) The state digests contain some features that make them especially beneficial to practitioners and researchers in the particular state, such as references to opinions of that state's attorney general as well as to important legal periodicals and bar association journals published in that state.

For the federal courts, there is also a separate digest. This digest, originally called the *Federal Digest,* has been supplemented by three additional series, and now consists of the following successive units:

Digest Unit	**Years Covered**
Federal Digest	1754–1939
Modern Federal Practice Digest	1939–1961
Federal Practice Digest 2d	1961–1975
Federal Practice Digest 3d	1975–date

Each of these units abstracts cases appearing in the *Supreme Court Reporter, Federal Reporter, Federal Supplement,* and *Federal Rules Decisions.*

In addition, cases reported in West's *Bankruptcy Reporter* are accessible through West's *Bankruptcy Digest,* as well as in *Federal Practice Digest 3d.* Other specialized federal digests include West's *Military Justice Digest,* covering decisions of the U.S. Court of Military Appeals and the Courts of Military Review for the Air Force, Army, Navy and Coast Guard, and *U.S. Claims Court Digest.*

Finally, the decisions of the Supreme Court of the United States are covered by a West digest devoted solely to its decisions, the *United States Supreme Court Digest.* (Note that Lawyers Co-op also has a digest for the Supreme Court with a similar name, *United States Supreme Court Digest, Lawyers' Edition.*)

All of the cases which are digested in these publications also appear in West's all-inclusive American Digest System. The same key numbers and topics are used in the local digests as are used in the main one, and the researcher can move between them easily.

Despite its unquestioned value as a case finder, the digest has the following shortcomings:

It contains no explanatory text or comment, but merely a series of separate unevaluated case abstracts.

It does not conveniently indicate change in the law, whether by statute or later decision.

It reflects much dicta, and over-abstracts many cases, so that the researcher may have to wade through irrelevant material in order to get citations to significant authorities. It does not contain the texts of primary authority, but only provides the means of finding such authority.

It does not introduce contemporary terminology for its topics or establish separate headings for burgeoning areas of the law as fast as the need is felt by researchers. However, West attempts to stay abreast of new developments by revising and expanding old topics and establishing new topics as the need arises. When new topics are introduced, they are accompanied by a scope-note and analysis similar to that shown for the topic *Abortion and Birth Control* in Exhibit 25 at p. 66. The new section includes all cases on the subject under the new key number despite the fact that they have appeared in earlier digests under other key numbers. Tables provide a means of converting previously used topics and key numbers into those newly adopted and vice versa. See Exhibits 26 and 27, below, showing those tables provided for the new topic, *Consumer Credit.*

TABLE 1

KEY NUMBER TRANSLATION TABLE

PAWNBROKERS AND MONEY LENDERS TO CONSUMER CREDIT

The topic PAWNBROKERS AND MONEY LENDERS has been discontinued and now, together with scattered paragraphs from other topics, makes up the topic CONSUMER CREDIT. This table lists the key numbers in the former topic together with the key numbers in the topic CONSUMER CREDIT where cases are now digested.

For the present classification of particular case, see the Table of Cases.

Pawnbrokers and Money Lenders Key Number	Consumer Credit Key Number	Pawnbrokers and Money Lenders Key Number	Consumer Credit Key Number
1	1 et seq.	6.5	14
2	2	6.6	15
3	5	6.7	3 et seq.
4	3 et seq.	6.8	16, 50 et seq.
5	7	6.9	17, 60–63
6	3 et seq.	7.8	7
6.1	3 et seq.	9	18, 64–67
6.2	11, 12	10	19, 61 et seq.
6.3	12	11	20, 68
6.4	12, 13		

Exhibit 26: Conversion table for new topic, *Consumer Credit,* from the old topic, *Pawnbrokers and Money Lenders,* in the 9th Decennial Digest, Part I.

CONSUMER CREDIT

TABLE 2

KEY NUMBER TRANSLATION TABLE

CONSUMER CREDIT TO PAWNBROKERS AND MONEY LENDERS

Listing the key numbers in the topic CONSUMER CREDIT together with the key numbers in the topic PAWNBROKERS AND MONEY LENDERS or other topics where cases were formerly digested.

Consumer Credit Key Number	Pawnbrokers and Money Lenders Key Number	Consumer Credit Key Number	Pawnbrokers and Money Lenders Key Number
1	1	15	6.6
2	2	16	6.1, 6.8
3, 4	1, 4, 6.1, 6.7	17	4, 6.9
5	3	18	9
6	1, 4, 6.1	19	10
7	5, 7, 8	20	11
8, 9	6.1; Sales ⚿55	30–38	6.1
10	6, 6.1, 6.4	39	6.1–6.7
11	6.2, 6.4	50–57	6.1, 6.8
12	6.3, 6.4	60–63	6.9, 10
13	6.4	64–67	9
14	6.5	68	11

Exhibit 27: Conversion table from the new topic, *Consumer Credit,* to the old topic, *Pawnbrokers and Money Lenders.*

Occasionally the squibs do not accurately state the points of law they purport to contain. Thus, the researcher using a digest for case finding must locate the relevant line of cases for study. One must then read the apparently relevant cases and synthesize those which appear *most* relevant, to arrive at an understanding or statement of the applicable law. Finally, the search must be updated and the current status and authority of the cases determined, by using the appropriate volumes of Shepard's citators, which are discussed below at pp. 92–101.

The researcher who wants to use the digest must identify the topic and key number relevant to the problem being researched. Such access to the digest is obtained through one of the following approaches: (1) by the name of a particular case which is known to be in point (or through its headnotes); (2) by the relevant legal concept; or (3) by an analysis of the factual make-up of the problem.

1. Via Tables of Cases or Case Headnotes. If the researcher already knows of a case in point, its citation and the key numbers assigned to it can be located by using the table of cases volume or volumes for the appropriate unit of the West digest system. Every unit of the system, except the *Century Digest* and the *First Decennial*, has its own table of cases volume. A combined table of cases for the *Century Digest* and *First Decennial* is contained in volumes 21–25 of the *First Decennial.*

Even if the researcher knows only the name of the defendant in the case, it is still possible to use the table of cases approach since the *U.S. Supreme Court Digest*, the *Federal Digest* series, and all of the state digests have tables of cases arranged by defendant as well as by plaintiff. However, those in the American Digest System and regional digests are listed by plaintiff only.

If the jurisdiction in which the case was decided is known, one can go to the local digest for that state or region. Otherwise, it is necessary to know in which decennial digest the case appears, since there is no overall table of cases for the entire American Digest System. From that decennial's table a direct reference to the appropriate key numbers under which the points of law of that case have been indexed can be obtained. With the relevant key numbers, it is easy to locate other earlier or later cases on the same topic in the body of the digest. If the table of cases does not contain those references, the report of the case can be located by its citation in the table of cases. The headnotes in the reported decision can then be examined, and the appropriate key numbers for further search obtained from them.

If the complete citation of a case known to be relevant is already in hand, one can of course go directly to its report and obtain the relevant key numbers from its headnotes. By using the table of cases, however, one can also obtain parallel citations to the official report of the same case, the later history of the case (whether it was affirmed, reversed, or modified), and possibly a reference to an *A.L.R.* or *A.L.R.-Federal* annotated report. Exhibit 16, at page 53 above, illustrates a typical case name table in a West digest. It is difficult, however, to use the table of cases approach to the digest unless one knows the jurisdiction or approximate date of the case in question, since there is no single table of cases covering the entire digest system.

2. Topic Approach. This method requires the researcher to select the legal topic used in the West digests which is most relevant to the problem at hand. There is a list of these topics in front of each volume of the digest system and the searcher can run through the list, select the appropriate topic, turn to it in the digest and, by inspecting the detailed table of contents at the beginning of each particular topic (as in Exhibit 25 at page 66 above), find the appropriate key number. With that key number, one can then proceed to locate other cases in point in the digest itself. This method is often less effective and obviously less desirable than the factual approach described below. It is also inefficient to search through the list of topics and then to examine the content analysis of the chosen topic in order to obtain the appropriate key number. A great deal of time and effort can be wasted through the use of this method, particularly where the relevant topic is a broad one like *Constitutional Law* or *Criminal Law.*

3. Descriptive Word Method. The most efficient procedure for case finding in the digest relies on the use of specific factual catch words derived from an analysis of the problem in question. This approach allows common words rather than more difficult legal concepts to be used as access points. These words are searched in the Descriptive Word Indexes of the West digests in order to find the appropriate key number and topic for that problem. Exhibit 28 below illustrates such an index in the *Federal Practice Digest 2d* covering the subject matter of *Roe v. Wade.*

It is usually much faster to use these alphabetical indexes, which contain tens of thousands of legally significant catchwords and phrases, rather than the less precise conceptual approach.

There is a Descriptive Word Index for the General Digest, each decennial digest and for each state and regional digest. West recommends that in using this

88 F P D 2d—7

ABORTION

References are to Digest Topics and Key Numbers

Exhibit 28: A page from the Descriptive Word Index in *Federal Practice Digest 2d.*

method the researcher select relevant search words by breaking down the problem into these components: (a) Parties; (b) Places and things; (c) Basis of action or issue; (d) Defenses; and (e) Relief sought. A sample case used by West involves a professional wrestling match in which the referee was thrown from the ring in such a way that he struck and injured plaintiff who was a front row spectator. West offers the following analysis of that problem to provide appropriate search words for the index:

(a) Parties—Spectator, Patron, Arena Owner, Wrestler, Referee, Promoter

(b) Places and Things—Wrestling Match, Amusement Place, Theater, Show

(c) Basis of Action or Issue—Negligence, Personal Injury to Spectator, Liability

(d) Defense—Assumption of Risk

(e) Relief Sought—Damages

With that analysis, the researcher can look up the most specific words and phrases in the Descriptive Word Index and thereby locate relevant key numbers and cases covering the problem.

CASE–FINDING IN ANNOTATED REPORTS

American Law Reports and its companion, *American Law Reports-Federal,* provide subject access to their chronologically published reports and annotations by a variety of digests and indexes.

A.L.R.1st and *2d* each have a separate multi-volume digest which gives references to cases in much the same way as the West digests, though using a different classification scheme. Both series also have Word Indexes, similar to West's Descriptive Word Index.

With *A.L.R.3d* and *4th,* and *A.L.R. Federal,* a new method of access, the Quick Index, was developed. This index combines both the digest approach and the factual word approach in one alphabet. It is now the standard means of access to the annotations in the entire *A.L.R.* system, and contains cross references to other Lawyers Co-op publications, such as *Am.Jur.2d.* The *A.L.R.3d & 4th Quick Index* also covers *A.L.R. Federal.* A separate *Federal Quick Index* covers annotations in *Lawyers' Edition,* as well as *A.L.R. Federal,* in addition to several other Lawyers Co-op aids for federal law research. Exhibits 29 and 30 illustrate these two *A.L.R.* indexes.

A.L.R. also provides access to cases reported in full by means of a table of cases in the digests for *A.L.R. 1st* and *2d* and in the back of the *A.L.R.3d & 4th Quick Index.*

A.L.R. annotations are kept up to date by collecting all the cases in point which have been decided *since* the annotation was written. The later cases for each annotation in *A.L.R.1st* are found in a six volume set entitled *A.L.R.1st Blue Book of Supplemental Decisions.* For *A.L.R.2d,* the supplementing service is *A.L.R. Later Case Service. A.L.R.3d, A.L.R.4th,* and *A.L.R. Federal* are kept current by cumulative pocket supplements in each volume. The *A.L.R.3d & 4th Quick Index* contains pocket supplements, which are located inside the *front* cover.

QUICK INDEX **Abrasions**

Terroristic threat: validity and construction of "terroristic threat" statutes, 58 ALR3d 533

Uniform Child Custody Jurisdiction Act: validity, construction, and application of Uniform Child Custody Jurisdiction Act, 96 ALR3d 968

Venue in rape cases where crime is committed partly in one place and partly in another, 100 ALR3d 1174

What is "harm" within provisions of statutes increasing penalty for kidnapping where victim suffers harm, 11 ALR3d 1053

ABILITY

As to disability, see **Disability**

Annulment: incapacity for sexual intercourse as ground for annulment, 52 ALR3d 589

Assured clear distance ahead: sudden emergency as exception to rule requiring motorist to maintain ability to stop within assured clear distance ahead, 75 ALR3d 327

Driver's license: validity of statute or regulation authorizing revocation or suspension of driver's license for reason unrelated to use of or ability to operate motor vehicle, 86 ALR3d 1251

Lease: inability to obtain license, permit, or charter required for tenant's business as defense to enforcement of lease, 89 ALR3d 329

Mental Capacity (this index)

Probation or suspended sentence: ability to pay as necessary consideration in conditioning probation or suspended sentence upon reparation or restitution, 73 ALR3d 1240

Summary judgment: sufficiency of showing, under Rule 56(f) of Federal Rules of Civil Procedure, of inability to present by affidavit facts justifying opposition to motion for summary judgment, 47 ALR Fed 206

Testamentary capacity. **Wills** (this index)

Visas: construction and application of 203(a)(3) of Immigration and Nationality Act of 1952 (8 USCS 1153(a)(3)) as amended giving preference visas to professionals or persons having ability in arts and sciences, 18 ALR Fed 287

Wages: employer's inability to pay as defense to wage order under Fair Labor Standards Act, 24 ALR Fed 920

ABILITY TO PAY

Financial Condition (this index)

ABILITY TO WORK

Insurance

- heart or vascular condition as constituting total or permanent disability within insurance coverage, 21 ALR3d 1383
- "total disability" or the like as referring to inability to work in usual occupation or in other occupations, 21 ALR3d 1155

Validity of individual employment contract for specific term which contains provision that employee will perform if physically able, if health permits, or the like, 7 ALR3d 898

ABODE

Domicil or Residence (this index)

ABOLITION OF PUBLIC OFFICE

Public Officers and Employees (this index)

ABORTION ←

Accomplices: woman upon whom abortion is committed or attempted as accomplice for purposes of rule requiring corroboration of accomplice testimony, 34 ALR3d 858

Applicability in criminal proceedings of privilege as to communications between physician and patient, 7 ALR3d 1458

Consent

- minor's right to have abortion performed without parental consent, 42 ALR3d 1406
- right of action for injury to or death of woman who consented to illegal abortion, 36 ALR3d 630
- woman's right to have abortion without consent of, or against objections of, child's father, 62 ALR3d 1097

Diagnosis: physician's failure to diagnose pregnancy, 7 Am Jur POF 2d, pp 579–603

Former jeopardy: earlier prosecution for offense during which homicide was committed as bar to prosecution for homicide, 11 ALR3d 834

Homicide based on killing of unborn child, 40 ALR3d 444

Proof: abortion and miscarriage, 1 Am Jur POF, pp 15–26

Tort liability for wrongfully causing one to be born, 83 ALR3d 15

ABRASIONS

Proof: abrasions, 1 Am Jur POF, pp 27–32

Consult POCKET PART for later annotations 3

Exhibit 29: A sample page from the *A.L.R.3d & 4th Quick Index.*

QUICK INDEX | ABSENCE AND PRESENCE

5

Exhibit 30: A sample page from the *A.L.R. Federal Quick Index.* (3d ed., 1980).

When the effect of later cases is to change substantially the existing law on a particular subject, a new annotation may be written that will supplement or completely supersede a previous annotation. To determine the existence of a supplementing or superseding annotation in *A.L.R.2d, 3d, 4th* or *Fed,* one should check the Annotation History Tables located at the end of the *A.L.R.3d & 4th Quick Index* and at the end of its pocket part. The latest volume of the *A.L.R.1st Blue Book* lists annotations supplementing or superseding those in the first series. Exhibit 29 of a similar table appearing in the *Index to Annotations in Lawyers' Edition,* shows that the annotation on abortion at 28 L.Ed.2d 1053 has been superseded by a new annotation at 35 L.Ed.2d 735.

History Table

9 L Ed 2d 998–1067
Supplemented 20 L Ed 2d 1528

9 L Ed 2d 1138–1159
Superseded 59 L Ed 2d 810

10 L Ed 2d 1243–1306
Superseded 22 ALR Fed 556

11 L Ed 2d 1057–1070
§ 7 Superseded 59 L Ed 2d 852

11 L Ed 2d 1116–1175
§ 18.5 Superseded 56 L Ed 2d 841

15 L Ed 2d 941–951
Superseded 56 L Ed 2d 813

16 L Ed 2d 1053–1076
§ 18.5 Superseded 56 L Ed 2d 841
§ 21.5 Superseded 67 L Ed 2d 859 & 71 L Ed 2d 1000

17 L Ed 2d 929–944
§ 3 superseded 43 ALR Fed 424

17 L Ed 2d 1008–1022
Superseded 59 L Ed 2d 959

17 L Ed 2d 1026–1058
Superseded 67 L Ed 2d 906

19 L Ed 2d 1361–1391
Superseded 60 L Ed 2d 1107

20 L Ed 2d 1623–1660
Superseded 58 L Ed 2d 862

21 L Ed 2d 905–912
Superseded 71 L Ed 2d 983

21 L Ed 2d 928–935
Superseded 37 L Ed 2d 1147

21 L Ed 2d 976–1015
§ 18.5 Superseded 56 L Ed 2d 843
§ 16(c) Superseded 69 L Ed 2d 1110

§ 21.5 Superseded 67 L Ed 2d 859 & 71 L Ed 2d 1000

22 L Ed 2d 821–858
Superseded 65 L Ed 2d 1219

23 L Ed 2d 782–805
§ 7 Superseded 59 L Ed 2d 852

23 L Ed 2d 915–927
Superseded in part 60 L Ed 2d 1166

25 L Ed 2d 968–978
Superseded 67 L Ed 2d 831

25 L Ed 2d 1025–1060
Superseded in part 50 L Ed 2d 876

26 L Ed 2d 893–911
Superseded 66 L Ed 2d 882

27 L Ed 2d 885
§ 8[b] Superseded 70 L Ed 2d 915

27 L Ed 2d 935
Superseded in part 60 L Ed 2d 1188

27 L Ed 2d 953–970
Superseded 56 L Ed 2d 841

28 L Ed 2d 885–904
Superseded in part 61 L Ed 2d 975

28 L Ed 2d 1053–1087 ← Later Annotation Superseding Original Annotation to Roe v. Wade
Superseded 35 L Ed 2d 735

30 L Ed 2d 938–948
Superseded 63 L Ed 2d 832

33 L Ed 2d 865–926
§ 14 Superseded 67 L Ed 2d 859

33 L Ed 2d 932–964
§ 9 Superseded in 51 L Ed 2d 886

37 L Ed 2d 1147–1221
Superseded in part 63 L Ed 2d 804

245

Exhibit 31: Annotation History Table, appearing in the *Index to Annotations* for *Lawyers' Edition.*

ENCYCLOPEDIAS

Conditioned by the use of scholarly general encyclopedias, one tends to expect American legal encyclopedias to be equally scholarly reference works. However, legal encyclopedias are generally less highly reputed, particularly in academic circles, and really function best as case-finders. Since the leading encyclopedias do not cover statutes to any significant extent, they tend to give a somewhat distorted view of the law in many areas. In addition they have a tendency to over-simplify and over-generalize which often does not accurately reflect the complexity of our changing law. Their pocket part supplementation, although useful for references to later cases, does not completely cure this shortcoming.

The two major encyclopedias of national scope are *Corpus Juris Secundum*, published by West, and *American Jurisprudence 2d*, published by Lawyers Co-op. Since the voluminous footnotes to the articles in *Corpus Juris Secundum* and *American Jurisprudence 2d* contain thousands of case references, they can be used directly as finding tools for that purpose. Each has general index volumes, as well as separate topical indexes, to help the researcher locate relevant articles and the most applicable sections thereof. The encyclopedias do not, however, contain tables of cases, presumably because of the large number of cases cited. Not surprisingly, West's *C.J.S.* purports to carry in its footnotes virtually all of the decisions listed in the various West digests, while Lawyers Co-op's *Am.Jur.2d* provides similar access to the relevant annotations of *A.L.R.* and *A.L.R. Federal.*

Illustrating these encyclopedias are pages from *Corpus Juris Secundum* and its pocket part in Exhibits 32 and 33, and pages from *American Jurisprudence 2d* and its pocket part in Exhibits 34 and 35.

1 C.J.S. *ABORTION* § 4

§ 2. Statutory Provisions

Abortion is a statutory crime in practically all jurisdictions under statutes that vary to some extent in their respective provisions.

Although abortion has been made a crime by statute in practically all jurisdictions, the statutes vary to some extent, and hence reference should be made to the statute of particular jurisdiction in which the crime is alleged to have been committed.[8] Where the crime of abortion is defined by statute, it has been held that decisions from courts of last resort in other states whose statutes are different from those of the forum cannot control the construction of the statute,[9] and the legislative intent as expressed in the statute of the forum furnishes the only rule and guide.[10] The power to penalize or to legalize the act of producing an abortion is a matter for the states, and not for congress.[11]

§ 3. Nature and Elements in General

The material element of the crime of abortion is an overt act to use means with the necessary intent to procure an unlawful expulsion of the fetus.

nothing to do with the guilt or innocence of the person prosecuted as an accessory to such abortion.[15] A statute making it a crime to "counsel any person" to procure a miscarriage has been held to mean some person other than the pregnant woman.[16]

Overt act. A mere guilty intention to procure an abortion is not sufficient to constitute the crime; there must be an overt act tending to the perpetration of the crime.[17] Under a statute making it a crime to advise a woman to take a noxious thing with intent to cause a miscarriage, it has been held that the giving of the advice is the only overt act necessary for the completion of the crime, and it is immaterial whether the advice be followed or not.[18]

Trap to catch accused. Where accused was not a passive instrument in the hands of the trapping parties and where he did the act with which he was charged voluntarily, with full knowledge of the subject, the mere fact that he was detected by means of a trap set for him is not a defense to the crime.[19]

Assault. The procuring of an unlawful abortion

crimes of abortion resulting in death and attempts to procure a miscarriage, but simple abortion is a common law offense in this state.—Commonwealth v. Kelsea, 157 A. 42, 103 Pa.Super. 399.

In Texas Pen.Code (1895) arts. 641,

mother's life, to remove the unborn fœtus. To such highly honorable and proper acts, in accord with the highest ethics of the medical profession, the dictates of humanity, and all legal precepts, the statute has, and can have, no application. But to the destruction of unborn life for reasons,

20. State v. Farnam, 161 P. 417, 82 Or. 211.

21. In Pennsylvania the Act of May 12, 1897 (P.L. p 63), has been held to prohibit the use of drugs which will cause a miscarriage, regardless of the intent accompanying the same.

313

Exhibit 32: A sample page from *Corpus Juris Secundum*, showing its treatment of abortion in the bound volume.

§ 2 ABORTION

Page 313

1 CJS 66

State, in promoting its interest in the potentiality of human life, may, if it chooses, regulate, and even proscribe, abortion except where it is necessary, in appropriate medical judgment, for the preservation of the life or health of the mother.[11.55]

11.50 U.S.—Doe v. Bolton, Ga., 93 S.Ct. 739, 410 U.S. 179, 35 L.Ed.2d 201, reh. den. 93 S.Ct. 1410, 410 U.S. 959, 35 L.Ed.2d 694—Nyberg v. City of Virginia, C.A.Minn., 495 F.2d 1342, cert. den. 95 S.Ct. 169, 419 U.S. 891, 42 L.Ed.2d 136—Word v. Poelker, C.A.Mo., 495 F.2d 1349.
N.J.—State v. Norflett, 337 A.2d 609, 67 N.J. 268.

Interest of husband
U.S.—Roe v. Rampton, D.C.Utah, 394 F. Supp. 677, affd., C.A., 535 F.2d 1219.

State financing for nontherapeutic abortions
Mass.—Framingham Clinic, Inc. v. Board of Selectmen of Southborough, 367 N.E.2d 606, 373 Mass. 279.

Parental or judicial consent
U.S.—Wynn v. Scott, D.C.Ill., 448 F. Supp. 997, affd., C.A., 582 F.2d 1375—Planned Parenthood League of Massachusetts v. Bellotti, C.A.Mass., 641 F.2d 1006.
Mass.—Matter of Moe, App., 423 N.E.2d 1038.

Spousal notice requirement, as written, invalid
U.S.—Doe v. Deschamps, D.C.Mont., 461 F.Supp. 682.

Fundamental right
U.S.—Charles v. Carey, C.A.Ill., 627 F.2d 772.

11.55 U.S.—Roe v. Wade, Tex., 93 S.Ct. 705, 410 U.S. 113, 35 L.Ed.2d 147, reh. den. 93 S.Ct. 1409, 410 U.S. 959, 35 L.Ed.2d 694—Hodgson v. Anderson, D.C.Minn., 378 F.Supp. 1008, app. dism., 95 S.Ct. 819, 420 U.S. 903, 42 L.Ed.2d 833, affd. in part, revd. in part on oth. grds., C.A., 542 F.2d 1350—Foe v. Vanderhoof, D.C. Colo., 389 F.Supp. 947—Harris v. McRae, N.Y., 100 S.Ct. 2671, 448 U.S. 297, 65 L.Ed.2d 784, reh. den. 101 S.Ct. 39, 448 U.S. 917, 65 L.Ed.2d 1180.
Ill.—Village of Oak Lawn v. Marcowitz, 427 N.E.2d 36, 55 Ill.Dec. 916, 86 Ill. 2d 406.
Ind.—Razo v. State, App., 431 N.E.2d 550.
Mass.—Framingham Clinic, Inc. v. Board of Selectmen of Southborough, 367 N.E.2d 606, 373 Mass. 279.
Mich.—People v. Nixon, 212 N.W.2d 797, 50 Mich.App. 38.
N.J.—Doe v. Bridgeton Hospital Ass'n, Inc., 366 A.2d 641, 71 N.J. 478, stay den. 97 S.Ct. 1095, 429 U.S. 1086, 51 L.Ed.2d 533, cert. den. 97 S.Ct. 2987, 433 U.S. 914, 53 L.Ed.2d 1100, on remand 389 A.2d 526, 160 N.J.Super. 266.
Pa.—Com. v. Jackson, 312 A.2d 13, 454 Pa. 429.
Tex.—Brady v. Doe, Civ.App., 598 S.W. 2d 338, cert. den. 101 S.Ct. 864, 449 U.S. 1081, 66 L.Ed.2d 805, reh. den. 101 S.Ct. 1421, 450 U.S. 960, 67 L. Ed.2d 386.

Regulation invalid for first trimester
U.S.—Doe v. Bolton, Ga., 93 S.Ct. 739, 410 U.S. 179, 35 L.Ed.2d 201, reh. den. 93 S.Ct. 1410, 410 U.S. 959, 35 L.Ed.2d 694—Wolfe v. Schroering, D.C.Ky., 388 F.Supp. 631, affd. in part, revd. in part on oth. grds. 541 F.2d 523.
Ind.—Indiana Hospital Licensing Council v. Women's Pavilion of South Bend, Inc., App., 420 N.E.2d 1301, corrected 424 N.E.2d 461.

Statute invalid for being applicable to any trimester
U.S.—Doe v. Rampton, D.C.Utah, 366 F.Supp. 189.

Exempt from licensing requirements
U.S.—Hallmark Clinic v. North Carolina Dept. of Human Resources, D.C.N.C., 380 F.Supp. 1153, affd., C.A., 519 F.2d 1315.

After second trimester abortion may be completely proscribed
N.J.—State v. Norflett, 337 A.2d 609, 67 N.J. 268.

Statute unconstitutional
U.S.—Planned Parenthood of Central Missouri v. Danforth, Mo., 96 S.Ct. 2831, 428 U.S. 52, 49 L.Ed.2d 788—Planned Parenthood Ass'n of Kansas City, Mo., Inc. v. Ashcroft, C.A.Mo., 664 F.2d 687, cert. gr. 102 S.Ct. 2267.

Definition of viability constitutional
U.S.—Connecticut v. Menillo, 96 S.Ct. 170, 423 U.S. 9, 46 L.Ed.2d 152.

State intervention on behalf of husband not permitted until fetus becomes "viable"
U.S.—Doe v. Zimmerman, D.C.Pa., 405 F.Supp. 534.

Definition of "viable" vague
U.S.—Doe v. Zimmerman, D.C.Pa., 405 F.Supp. 534.

Portion of statute constitutional
U.S.—Spears v. Circuit Court, Ninth Judicial Dist., Warren County, State of Miss., C.A.Miss., 517 F.2d 360.
N.J.—Livingston v. New Jersey State Bd. of Medical Examiners, 402 A.2d 967, 168 N.J.Super. 259.

Woman less than 24 weeks pregnant entitled to abortion under statute
N.Y.—Chapman v. Schultz, 383 N.Y.S. 2d 512, 86 Misc.2d 543.

Prohibiting saline method after first trimester invalid
U.S.—Wolfe v. Schroering, C.A.Ky., 541 F.2d 523.

Ordinance void
U.S.—Mobile Women's Medical Clinic, Inc. v. Board of Com'rs of City of Mobile, D.C.Ala., 426 F.Supp. 331.

Requirement as to hospital use invalid
U.S.—Arnold v. Sendak, D.C.Ind., 416 F. Supp. 22, affd. 97 S.Ct. 476, 429 U.S. 968, 50 L.Ed.2d 579.

Overriding right to terminate pregnancy during first two trimesters
R.I.—Constitutional Right to Life Committee v. Cannon, 363 A.2d 215, 117 R.I. 52.

Right of parents
U.S.—Gildiner v. Thomas Jefferson University Hospital, D.C.Pa., 451 F.Supp. 692—H. L. v. Matheson, Utah, 101 S.Ct. 1164, 450 U.S. 398, 67 L.Ed.2d 388.

In regulating abortion procedures, a state may proscribe any abortion by a physician not currently licensed by the state,[11.60] and may preserve the right of hospitals to refuse to admit a patient for an abortion and the right of physicians and other employees to refrain from participating in abortion procedures on moral or religious grounds.[11.65]

11.60 U.S.—Roe v. Wade, Tex., 93 S.Ct. 705, 410 U.S. 113, 35 L.Ed.2d 147, reh. den. 93 S.Ct. 1409, 410 U.S. 959, 35 L.Ed.2d 694—Spears v. Ellis, D.C. Miss., 386 F.Supp. 653, affd. 96 S.Ct. 9, 423 U.S. 802, 46 L.Ed.2d 23.

Nonmedically trained person subject to conviction
N.J.—State v. Norflett, 337 A.2d 609, 67 N.J. 268.

Midwife not authorized
U.S.—Spears v. Circuit Court, Ninth Judicial Dist., Warren County, State of Miss., C.A.Miss., 517 F.2d 360.

Constitutionality considered
Fla.—Wright v. State, 351 So.2d 708.

Provision constitutionally permissible
U.S.—Wynn v. Scott, D.C.Ill., 448 F. Supp. 997, affd., C.A., 582 F.2d 1375.

11.65 U.S.—Doe v. Bolton, Ga., 93 S.Ct. 739, 410 U.S. 179, 35 L.Ed.2d 201, reh. den. 93 S.Ct. 1410, 410 U.S. 959, 35 L.Ed.2d 694.

Residency requirements for patients seeking abortions are invalid, where they are not based on a policy of preserving state supported facilities for residents of the state.[11.70]

11.70 U.S.—Doe v. Bolton, Ga., 93 S.Ct. 739, 410 U.S. 179, 35 L.Ed.2d 201, reh. den. 93 S.Ct. 1410, 410 U.S. 959, 35 L.Ed.2d 694.

Procedural requirements not reasonably related to the purpose of an abortion statute are invalid.[11.75]

11.75 U.S.—Florida Women's Medical Clinic, Inc. v. Smith, D.C.Fla., 536 F.Supp. 1048.

Accreditation of hospital
U.S.—Doe v. Bolton, Ga., 93 S.Ct. 739, 410 U.S. 179, 35 L.Ed.2d 201, reh. den. 93 S.Ct. 1410, 410 U.S. 959, 35 L.Ed.2d 694.

Approval by hospital abortion committee
U.S.—Doe v. Bolton, Ga., 93 S.Ct. 739, 410 U.S. 179, 35 L.Ed.2d 201, reh. den. 93 S.Ct. 1410, 410 U.S. 959, 35 L.Ed.2d 694.

Regulation beyond similar surgical procedures
U.S.—Hodgson v. Lawson, C.A.Minn., 542 F.2d 1350.

The point of viability may differ with each pregnancy, accordingly, neither the legislature or the courts may proclaim one of the elements entering into the ascertainment of viability as the determinant of when the state has a compelling interest in the life or health of the fetus, for purposes of regulating abortion.[11.80] Viability is reached when, in the judgment of the attending physician on the particular facts of the case before him, there is a reasonable likelihood of the fetus' sustained survival outside the womb, with or without artificial support.[11.85] There is no justification to restrict the ability of a competent doctor to perform legal first trimester abortions by requiring him or her to have hospital privileges.[11.90]

11.80 U.S.—Colautti v. Franklin, Pa., 99 S.Ct. 675, 439 U.S. 379, 58 L.Ed.2d 596.

11.85 **Effect of regulation on physician's determination**
U.S.—Colautti v. Franklin, Pa., 99 S.Ct. 675, 439 U.S. 379, 58 L.Ed.2d 596.

11.90 U.S.—Women's Medical Ctr. of Providence, Inc. v. Cannon, D.C.R.I., 463 F.Supp. 531.

§ 3. Nature and Elements in General

Library References

Abortion and Birth Control 🔑1.

12. Va.—Coffman v. Com., supra, n. 2.
13. Cal.—People v. Root, 55 Cal.Rptr. 89, 246 C.A.2d 600.

Exhibit 33: A sample page from the pocket part of vol. 1 of *Corpus Juris Secundum,* showing reference to Roe v. Wade.

I. CRIMINAL LIABILITY

A. In General

§ 1. Definition, nature, and elements of offense generally.

From a medical standpoint, abortion includes all cases wherein pregnancy is terminated before the time that a living child may possibly be anticipated. After the 28th week, the process is spoken of as premature labor. Miscarriage is the term more properly limited to the time between the 16th and 28th week.[1] In law, however, "abortion" and "miscarriage" are practically synonymous.[2] Abortion is the expulsion of the fetus at so early a period of uterogestation that it has not acquired the power of sustaining an independent life.[3] "Abortion" does not necessarily connote a criminal act,[4] for the act may be necessary to save the woman's life.[5] The crime of abortion is the wilful bringing about of an abortion without justification or excuse.[6] At common law this was a misdemeanor only.[7]

The gravamen of the charge of abortion under the usual statute is the intent with which the drugs, instruments, or other means of producing an abortion are used.[8] Thus, under a statute providing for punishment of any person who uses any means with an intent to produce an abortion or miscarriage, and produces

1. Gray, Attorney's Textbook of Medicine 3rd ed p 596.

2. State v Harris, 90 **Kan** 807, 136 P 264; Wells v New England Mut. L. Ins. Co. 191 **Pa** 207, 43 A 126; Anderson v Commonwealth, 19 **Va** 665, 58 SE2d 72, 16 ALR2d 942.

3. People v Heisler, 300 **Ill** 98, 132 NE 802; State v Harris, 90 **Kan** 807, 136 P 264; State v Grissom, 35 **NM** 323, 298 P 666; Coffman v Commonwealth, 188 **Va** 553, 50 SE2d 431; Lubcke v Teckam, 179 **Wis** 543, 191 NW 968.

4. Abrams v Foshee, 3 **Iowa** 274; People v Aiken, 66 **Mich** 460, 33 NW 821; State v Fitzgerald (**Mo**) 174 SW2d 211.

5. § 9, infra.

6. Mississippi State Bd. of Health v Johnson, 197 **Miss** 417, 19 So2d 445, 827.

7. Smith v State, 33 **Me** 48; Worthington v State, 92 **Md** 222, 48 A 355; State v Cooper, 22 NJL 52.

8. People v Cummings, 141 **Cal** App 2d 193, 296 P2d 610; State v Fitzgerald (**Mo**) 174 SW2d 211.

188

Exhibit 34: A sample page from *American Jurisprudence 2d*, showing its treatment of abortion in the bound volume.

ABORTION **§ 1.5**

limited and related to the preservation and protection of maternal health.[10] However, from and after the point the fetus becomes viable, a state may prohibit abortions altogether; and during the entire term of pregnancy, a state may legitimately require that all abortions be performed by licensed physicians.[11] A state may nevertheless not unduly restrict the availability of abortions, and thus it may not require, during the first trimester, that abortions be performed in hospitals, nor may it require that they be performed only in hospitals accredited by the Joint Commission on Accreditation of Hospitals.[12] Furthermore, a state may not require that a hospital committee approve all abortions, nor may it require the concurrence of two physicians other than the attending physician that an abortion is necessary, for to permit such is to allow an unwarranted interference with a physician's right to practice medicine.[13]

n 1—

Annotation: 28 L Ed 2d 1053, 1056, § 2.

n 2—

Annotation: 28 L Ed 2d 1053, 1067, § 3[b].

See People v Belous, 71 **Cal** 2d 954, 80 Cal Rptr 354, 458 P2d 194, cert den 397 **US** 915, 25 L Ed 2d 96, 90 S Ct 920, holding that abortion statute which punished one performing abortion "unless the same is necessary to preserve . . . life" was unconstitutionally vague as constituting an invalid abridgment of pregnant woman's constitutional rights, and that the statute as framed put an impossible burden on a physician that would pressure him to decide against abortion. The court referred to a new statute (not involved in the case) that authorized abortion under certain circumstances where there was substantial risk that continuation of pregnancy would gravely impair physical or mental health of the mother.

The requirement in an abortion act that the continuance of pregnancy would gravely impair the prospective abortee's health, as one ground for an abortion, is impermissibly vague. People v Barksdale, 8 **Cal** 3d 320, 105 Cal Rptr 1, 503 P2d 257 (upholding the constitutionality of other severable portions of the act).

See State v Barquet **(Fla)** 262 So 2d 431, holding that statutes prohibiting an abortion unless it is necessary to preserve the life of the mother were so vague as to violate the federal and state constitutions.

n 3—

Annotation: 28 L Ed 2d 1053, 1061, § 3[a].

A statute which makes criminal the performance or attempted performance of an abortion "unless done under the direction of a licensed physician as necessary for the preservation of the mother's life or health," is to be construed as permitting abortions for both physical and mental health reasons, whether or not the patients had a previous history of mental defects; so construed, the statute is not unconstitutionally vague in violation of the due process clause of the Constitution. United States v Vuitch, 402 **US** 62, 28 L Ed 2d 601, 91 S Ct 1294.

A statute which, following modification of its terms by a United States District Court, permits a physician to perform an abortion only after, using his best clinical judgment, he concludes that an abortion is necessary, is not unconstitutionally vague. Doe v Bolton, 410 **(US)** 179, 35 L Ed 2d 201, 93 S Ct 739, reh den 410 **US** 959, 35 L Ed 2d 694, 93 S Ct 1410.

n 4—

Annotation: 28 L Ed 2d 1053, 1070, § 4[a].

n 5—

Annotation: 28 L Ed 2d 1053, 1073, § 4[b].

n 6—

Annotation: 28 L Ed 2d 1053, 1076, § 5[a].

n 7—

Annotation: 28 L Ed 2d 1053, 1078, § 5[b]. Roe v Wade, 410 **US** 113, 35 L Ed 2d 147, 93 S Ct 705, reh den 410 **US** 959, 35 L Ed 2d 694, 93 S Ct 1409. ←

n 8—Doe v Bolton, 410 **US** 179, 35 L Ed 2d 201, 93 S Ct 739, reh den 410 **US** 959, 35 L Ed 2d 694, 93 S Ct 1410.

n 9—Roe v Wade, 410 **US** 113, 35 L Ed 2d 147, 93 S Ct 705, reh den 410 **US** 959, 35 L Ed 2d 694, 93 S Ct 1409; Doe v Bolton, 410 **US** 179, 35 L Ed 2d 201, 93 S Ct 739, reh den 410 **US** 959, 35 L Ed 2d 694, 93 S Ct 1410.

n 10—Roe v Wade, 410 **US** 113, 35 L Ed 2d 147, 93 S Ct 705, reh den 410 **US** 959, 35 L Ed 2d 694, 93 S Ct 1409.

n 11—Roe v Wade, 410 **US** 113, 35 L Ed 2d 147, 93 S Ct 705, reh den 410 **US** 959, 35 L Ed 2d 694, 93 S Ct 1409.

n 12—Doe v Bolton, 410 **US** 179, 35 L Ed 2d 201, 93 S Ct 739, reh den 410 **US** 959, 35 L Ed 2d 694, 93 S Ct 1410.

n 13—Doe v Bolton, 410 **US** 179, 35 L Ed 2d 201, 93 S Ct 739, reh den 410 **US** 959, 35 L Ed 2d 694, 93 S Ct 1410.

Generally, as to woman's right to have abortion without consent of child's father, see § 37.5, infra.

Case authorities:

A state statute providing that it shall be unlawful to terminate the pregnancy of a human being unless the pregnancy is terminated by a physician is constitutional. Wright v State (1977, Fla) 351 So 2d 708.

A state statute which provides that it shall be unlawful to terminate the pregnancy of a human being unless the pregnancy is terminated in an approved facility (defined as a licensed hospital or medical facility) by a physician who

[1 Am Jur 2d Supp] **83**

Exhibit 35: A sample page from the pocket part of vol. 1 of *American Jurisprudence 2d,* showing references to Roe v. Wade.

WORDS AND PHRASES

Another useful case-finding tool is *Words and Phrases,* an encyclopedia of definitions and interpretations of legally significant words and phrases, published in forty-six volumes by West. This set consists of an alphabetical arrangement of thousands of words and phrases followed by abstracts of judicial decisions which have interpreted, defined or construed them. The abstracts are in the same form as the West digest squibs, containing a one sentence summary of the legal interpretation and the citation to the decision from which it is taken. A typical page looks like the sample in Exhibit 36 below.

Words and Phrases is supplemented by annual pocket parts inserted in the back of each volume and by tables of words and phrases which appear in every West advance sheet and bound reporter for the cases therein. *Words and Phrases* entries also appear in the various West digests.

32 W & P—37

PERSON

Civil Rights Act and thus was not liable to suit thereunder. Educational Equality League v. Tate, C.A.Pa., 472 F.2d 612, 614.

Term "person" as used in statute prohibiting person from denying an individual the full and equal enjoyment of facilities of a place of public accommodation because of race, color, religion or national origin includes every legal, commercial and governmental entity. Oklahoma Human Rights Commission v. Hotie, Inc., Okl., 505 P.2d 1320, 1322.

Even those who have been convicted remained "persons" under Constitution and a fortiori that is true of persons in county jails most of whom are awaiting trial and presumed to be innocent. U. S. ex rel. Manicone v. Corso, D.C.N.Y., 365 F.Supp. 576, 577.

Unborn child is a "person" for purpose of remedies given for personal injuries, and child may sue after his birth. Weaks v. Mounter, Nev., 493 P.2d 1307, 1309.

"Person" is defined as a human being. Bale v. Ryder, Me., 290 A.2d 359, 360.

Word "person" as used in the Fourteenth Amendment does not include the unborn. Roe v. Wade, U.S.Tex., 93 S.Ct. 705, 729, 410 U.S. 113, 35 L.Ed.2d 147.

An unborn child is not a "person" within meaning of wrongful death statute. Bayer v. Suttle, 100 Cal.Rptr. 212, 214, 23 C.A.3d 361.

Federal courts sit not to supervise prisons but to enforce constitutional rights of all "persons," which includes prisoners. Cruz v. Beto, U.S.Tex., 92 S.Ct. 1079, 1081, 405 U.S. 319, 31 L.Ed.2d 263.

A housing authority is a "person" within Fourteenth Amendment and therefore has standing to challenge constitutionality of state statute under due process and equal protection clauses. Housing Authority of City of Woonsocket v. Fetzik, R.I., 289 A.2d 658, 662.

Political subdivision is not a "person" within the meaning of the Civil Rights Act when pecuniary damages are sought. Reed v. Nebraska School Activities Ass'n, D.C.Neb., 341 F. Supp. 258, 260.

Sale of a security to a husband and wife so denominated is a sale made to one "person" within meaning of Securities Law provision exempting seller from registration so long as total number of holders does not exceed 25 and during a period of 12 consecutive months, sales are made to not more than an additional 15 "persons". Cann v. M & B Drilling Co., Mo.App., 480 S.W.2d 81, 85.

Legislature, in enacting Administrative Procedure and Review Act section providing that any "person" who is aggrieved by a final decision shall be entitled to judicial review, intended that such right be available to any person, party or not, who can show himself to be aggrieved by the decision. State ex rel. Pruitt-Igoe Dist. Community Corp. v. Burks, Mo.App., 482 S.W.2d 75, 77.

If a foetus is born alive it becomes a "person" with at least theoretical possibility of survival and of enduring consequences of prenatal injury throughout its life but a foetus not born alive incurs no such risk of continuing injury and is not a "person" within meaning of the wrongful death statute. Leccese v. McDonough, Mass., 279 N.E.2d 339, 341.

Viable fetus born dead as result of prenatal injuries is not "person" within Wrongful Death Act, and no cause of action therefore existed for death of fetus, notwithstanding fetus would have been able to maintain cause of action for his injuries incurred prior to birth had he survived to be born alive. Chrisafogeorgis v. Brandenberg, 279 N.E.2d 440, 442, 3 Ill.App.3d 422.

A "person" is generally understood as denoting a natural person and word ordinarily will be taken in that sense unless, from statutory context or elsewhere, it appears that artificial persons are intended to be embraced. People v. McGreal, 278 N.E.2d 504, 510, 4 Ill. App.3d 312.

Where suit under 1871 civil rights statute sought no damages but only equitable relief and where University of Alaska by Alaskan statute had power to sue and be sued in its own name, university, its president and Board of Regents were "persons" within the statute. Wolfe v. O'Neill, D.C.Alaska, 336 F.Supp. 1255, 1258.

A fetus is not a "person" or "citizen" within contemplation of the Fourteenth Amendment and the Civil Rights Act. McGarvey v. Magee-Womens Hospital, D.C.Pa., 340 F.Supp. 751, 754; Abele v. Markle, D.C.Conn., 351 F. Supp. 224, 228.

A viable fetus is a "person" within statute governing actions for wrongful death. Rice v. Rizk, Ky., 453 S.W.2d 732, 735.

Where signatures on check gave no indication that check was signed in representative capacity, fact that check, underneath date, contained statement "Food for Love Acc't" did not indicate a "person" so as to alert payee to any representational capacity in which signature was executed. Star Dairy, Inc. v. Roberts, 326 N.Y.S.2d 85, 87, 37 A.D.2d 1038.

Employer who borrowed truck for use by his employee was a "person" under statute which provides that no person shall operate any motor truck after dark unless truck is equipped with flares or other warning devices and the employer's failure to so equip a ¾ ton pickup truck constituted independent actionable negligence as to motorist and passenger injured in a collision after dark with the unlighted truck. Taylor v. Purifoy, 445 S.W. 2d 485, 487, 247 Ark. 368.

Unborn viable child was not a "person" within meaning of wrongful death statutes. Lawrence v. Craven Tire Co., 169 S.E.2d 440, 442, 210 Va. 138.

Viable fetus is "person" within intendment of West Virginia's Wrongful Death Statute. Panagopoulous v. Martin, D.C.W.Va., 295 F. Supp. 220, 226.

Viable unborn child is entity in meaning of general word "person" within wrongful death statute. City of Louisville v. Stuckenborg, Ky., 438 S.W.2d 94, 95.

"Person" liable for withholding, F.I.C.A., and other taxes includes but is not restricted to persons designated by statute. Lawrence v. U. S., D.C.Tex., 299 F.Supp. 187, 190.

Stillborn child is not "person" under Massachusetts Wrongful Death statute, and action is not maintainable for wrongful death based upon injury-caused stillbirths of viable fetuses. Henry v. Jones, D.C.Mass., 306 F.Supp. 726, 727.

In sense intended by legislature in enacting statute limiting crime of vehicular homicide to death of a "person", quoted word means a living individual, and a seven-month, viable, unborn child could be considered such a "person". State v. Dickinson, Ohio Com.Pl., 248 N.E.2d 458, 461, 18 Ohio Misc. 151.

Once the stage of viability is reached the fetus is regarded as a legal "person" with separate existence of its own, as respects issue whether there is a cause of action on behalf of unborn fetus for tort injury. Orange v. State Farm Mut. Auto. Ins. Co., Ky., 443 S.W. 2d 650, 651, 652.

A viable unborn child of insured was a legal "person" with a separate existence of its own, and, hence, was member of class excluded from coverage by a "family" or "household" exclusion clause of automobile liability policy. Id.

Word "person" has no fixed and rigid signification. U. S. v. Merchants Mut. Bonding Co., D.C.Iowa., 220 F.Supp. 163, 182.

Exhibit 36: A sample page from *Words and Phrases*, showing definition of "person" in Roe v. Wade.

CASE–FINDING BY COMPUTER

In recent years, computerized legal research has developed as an important supplement to traditional case-finding tools and has now achieved wide acceptance among lawyers and others doing legal research. Two systems, LEXIS (owned by Mead Data Central) and WESTLAW (a West Publishing Company service), now offer access to a broad range of federal and state cases in a variety of data bases and formats. Although a full description of the contents and search procedures for these systems is not possible here, each provides instructional manuals for that purpose.

Both LEXIS and WESTLAW permit searching for relevant court decisions by the use of words or combinations of words selected by the user from the facts or issues of the problem being researched. These are typed into the keyboard of the terminal and the decisions which contain those words in the specified combinations are retrieved by the computer and displayed on its screen. The decisions can be seen by citation only, by the relevant portion of the text containing the words, or by the full text of the decision. An attached printer enables the user to obtain a paper copy of that information, in any of those forms.

LEXIS includes some decisions which will never be published in the regular reports, while both LEXIS and WESTLAW make available many decisions before they are published even in advance sheets. WESTLAW also provides for searching of words in combination with the topics and key numbers of the West digest system, and for the searching of West syllabi and headnotes, thereby narrowing the search at the outset and saving time and expensive computer charges.

In addition to searching within a specific time period, or a single court or jurisdiction, both services include a variety of specialized data bases or "libraries" for particular subject fields (e.g., taxation, labor law, trade regulation, securities law, etc.). The use of these features, either singly or in combination, can help reduce costly searching time.

Shepard's Citations are available on LEXIS and WESTLAW, and each service also provides an alternative abbreviated citation checking capability for quicker verification of the current authority and status of case citations. These options are called *Auto-Cite* in LEXIS and *Insta-Cite* in WESTLAW. *Auto-Cite* is owned by, and also available directly from, the Lawyers Co-operative Publishing Company.

Both systems include many research sources beyond judicial decisions. Some of these (statutes, administrative law, legal periodicals, etc.) will be discussed in later chapters. Computer searching is expensive, however, and does not yet reach many early decisions and other relevant material. One cannot usually rely on computer searching alone, but must integrate the computer search, when it is available, with other traditional case-finding techniques.

CASE CITATORS

Citators can be used as case-finders, and also provide access to the judicial history and interpretation of reported decisions. Shepard's Citations, Inc., publisher of the most comprehensive system of case citators in the United States, accomplishes this function by listing in separate sets virtually every published case by citation, in both its official and unofficial reporter, and then by listing under that citation every subsequent case that has cited the case in question.

Thus, the use of Shepard's citators aids a lawyer in accomplishing the following three purposes:

1. Tracing the judicial history of each case appearing in an official or West reporter, by providing parallel citations to that case in the other reporter (as shown above in Exhibits 19 and 20 at pages 56–57) and citations to other proceedings in that same case.

2. Verifying the current status of each case in order to establish whether it is still effective law, or has been reversed, overruled, or its authority otherwise diminished.

3. Finding later cases which have cited the main case, as well as providing research leads to periodical articles, attorney general opinions, *A.L.R.* annotations, etc.

Shepard's citators exist for the reports of every state, the District of Columbia and Puerto Rico, every region of the National Reporter System, the lower federal courts, the Supreme Court, and some administrative agencies. The formats for each series of citators are similar. However, the types of citing materials included for the cited cases may vary among the series. Therefore, to be certain that one is obtaining all available citations to a particular case, it is wise to consult the fuller explanations of each set of citators in *How to Use Shepard's Citations,* a teaching pamphlet issued by Shepard's and available in most law school libraries. The preliminary pages in each citator will list the cited material and the citing sources contained in that citator.

For an example of the variations in citing material, note the differences between *Shepard's North Western Citations* and *Shepard's Wisconsin Citations.* Both citators provide the parallel citation to the case in the other reporter, the judicial history of the case, and citations to other Wisconsin cases which have cited the case. However, citations to the case by *other* state courts can be found only in *Shepard's North Western Citations,* while references to the case in the opinions of the attorney general of Wisconsin and in local law reviews can be found only in the Wisconsin Shepard's.

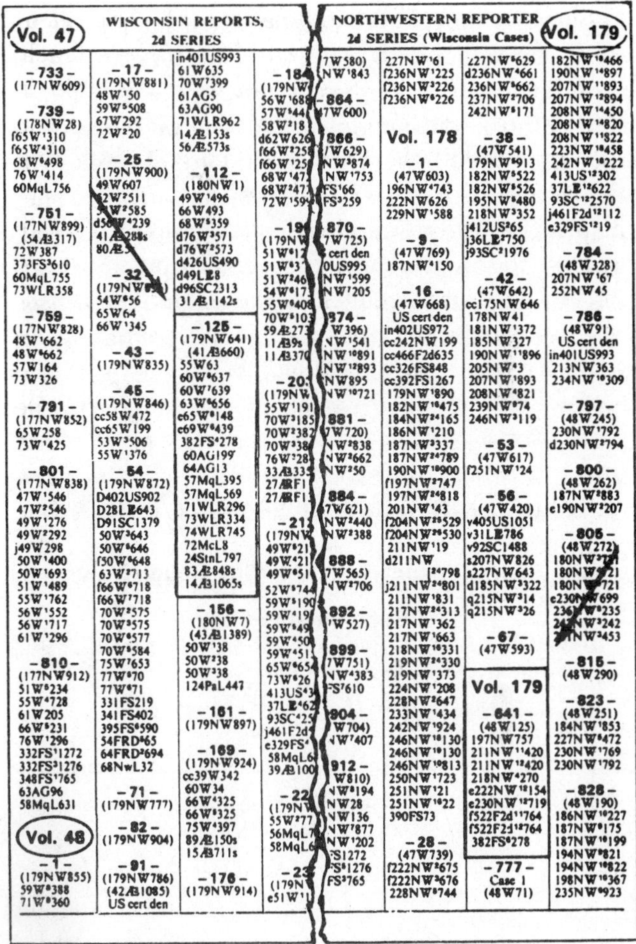

Vol. 47 — WISCONSIN REPORTS, 2d SERIES

- 733 -
(177NW609)

- 739 -
(178NW28)
f65W[1]310
f65W[4]310
68W[6]498
76W[1]414
60MqL756

- 751 -
(177NW899)
(54A3317)
72W387
373FS[3]610
60MqL755
73WLR358

- 759 -
(177NW828)
48W[1]662
48W[6]662
57W164
73W326

- 791 -
(177NW852)
65W258
73W[1]425

- 801 -
(177NW838)
47W[1]546
47W[2]546
49W[1]276
49W[2]292
j49W298
50W[1]400
50W[1]693
51W[1]489
55W[1]762
56W[1]552
56W[1]717
61W[1]296

- 810 -
(177NW912)
51W[5]234
55W[4]728
61W205
66W[5]231
76W[1]296
332FS[1]1272
332FS[3]1276
348FS[1]765
63AG96
58MqL631

Vol. 48

- 1 -
(179NW855)
59W[8]388
71W[8]360

- 17 -
(179NW881)
48W[1]50
59W[5]508
67W292
72W[2]20

- 25 -
(179NW900)
49W607
52W[2]511
54W[2]585
d56W[4]239
41A2288s
80A2[illegible]

- 32 -
(179NW[illegible])
54W[6]56
65W64
66W[1]345

- 43 -
(179NW835)

- 45 -
(179NW846)
cc58W472
cc65W199
53W[3]506
55W[1]376

- 54 -
(179NW872)
D402US902
D28LE643
D91SC1379
50W[3]643
50W[6]646
f50W[6]648
63W[2]713
f66W[6]718
f66W[7]718
70W[2]575
70W[3]575
70W[6]577
70W[5]584
75W[7]653
77W[8]70
77W[8]71
331FS219
341FS402
395FS[6]590
54FRD[6]65
64FRD[2]694
68NwL32

- 71 -
(179NW777)

- 82 -
(179NW904)

- 91 -
(179NW786)
(42A31085)
US cert den

in401US993
61W635
70W[7]399
61AG5
63AG90
71WLR962
14A2153s
56A2573s

- 112 -
(180NW1)
49W[1]496
66W493
68W[5]359
d76W[3]571
d76W[2]573
d426US490
d49LE8
d96SC2313
31A21142s

- 125 -
(179NW641)
(41A3660)
55W63
60W[6]637
60W[7]639
63W[6]656
e65W[8]148
e69W[6]439
382FS[4]278
60AG199
64AG13
57MqL395
57MqL569
71WLR296
73WLR334
74WLR745
72McL8
24StnL797
83A2848s
14A31065s

- 156 -
(180NW7)
(43A31389)
50W[1]38
50W[2]38
50W[3]38
124PaL447

- 161 -
(179NW897)

- 169 -
(179NW924)
cc39W342
60W34
66W[4]325
66W[5]325
75W[4]397
89A2150s
15A3711s

- 176 -
(179NW914)

- 184 -
(179NW[illegible]
56W[1]688
57W[5]44[illegible]
58W[2]18
d62W626
f66W[2]258
f66W[1]25[illegible]
68W[1]47[illegible]
68W[2]47[illegible]
72W[1]59[illegible]

- 19[illegible]
(179NW[illegible]
51W[6]12[illegible]
51W[6]3[illegible]
51W[2]46[illegible]
54W[6]17[illegible]
55W[6]408
70W[5]103
59A2273
11A39s
11A3370

- 20[illegible]
(179NW[illegible]
55W[1]191
70W[3]185
70W[2]382
70W[3]38[illegible]
76W[2]28[illegible]
33A3335
27ARF1
27ARF1[illegible]

- 21[illegible]
(179NW[illegible]
49W[6]21[illegible]
49W[4]21[illegible]
49W[6]51[illegible]
52W[5]74[illegible]
59W[5]190
59W[4]19[illegible]
59W[5]49[illegible]
59W[4]50[illegible]
59W[4]51[illegible]
65W[6]65[illegible]
73W[6]26
413US[4]3[illegible]
37LE[4]62[illegible]
93SC[4]25[illegible]
j461F2d[illegible]
e329FS[4]
58MqL6[illegible]
39A3100

- 22[illegible]
(179NW[illegible]
55W[2]77
56MqL7[illegible]
58MqL6[illegible]

- 23[illegible]
(179N[illegible]
e51W[1][illegible]

NORTHWESTERN REPORTER 2d SERIES (Wisconsin Cases) — Vol. 179

[illegible]7W580)
[illegible]NW[1]843

- 864 -
[illegible]7W600)

- 866 -
[illegible]W629)
[illegible]NW[3]874
[illegible]NW[1]753
[illegible]FS[1]66
[illegible]FS[3]259

- 870 -
[illegible]7W725)
[illegible] cert den
[illegible]0US995
[illegible]NW[1]599
[illegible]NW[7]205

- 874 -
[illegible]W396)
[illegible]NW[1]541
[illegible]NW[10]891
[illegible]NW[12]893
[illegible]NW895
[illegible]NW[10]721

- 881 -
[illegible]W720)
[illegible]NW[2]838
[illegible]NW[2]662
[illegible]NW[2]50

- 884 -
[illegible]7W621)
[illegible]NW[2]440
[illegible]NW[2]388

- 888 -
[illegible]7W565)
[illegible]NW[2]706

- 892 -
[illegible]W527)

- 899 -
[illegible]7W751)
[illegible]NW[4]383
[illegible]FS[7]610

- 904 -
[illegible]W704)
[illegible]NW[7]407

- 912 -
[illegible]W810)
[illegible]NW[8]194
[illegible]NW28
[illegible]NW136
[illegible]NW[7]877
[illegible]NW[1]202
[illegible]FS1272
[illegible]FS[8]1276
[illegible]FS[3]765

227NW[1]61
f236NW[1]225
f236NW[3]226
f236NW[6]226

Vol. 178

- 1 -
(47W603)
196NW[4]743
222NW626
229NW[1]588

- 9 -
(47W769)
187NW[4]150

- 16 -
(47W668)
US cert den
in402US972
cc242NW199
cc466F2d635
cc326FS848
cc392FS1267
179NW[1]890
182NW[10]475
184NW[24]165
186NW[1]210
187NW[3]337
187NW[24]789
190NW[10]900
f197NW[2]747
197NW[24]818
201NW[1]43
f204NW[25]529
f204NW[25]530
211NW[1]19
d211NW[24]798
j211NW[24]801
211NW[1]831
217NW[24]313
217NW[1]362
217NW[1]663
218NW[10]331
219NW[24]330
219NW[1]373
224NW[1]208
228NW[2]647
233NW[1]434
242NW[1]924
246NW[18]130
246NW[10]130
246NW[10]813
250NW[1]723
251NW[1]21
251NW[10]22
390FS73

- 28 -
(47W739)
f222NW[2]675
f222NW[3]676
228NW[8]744

227NW[5]629
d236NW[4]661
236NW[5]662
237NW[2]706
242NW[5]171

- 38 -
(47W541)
179NW[5]913
182NW[5]522
182NW[5]526
195NW[5]480
218NW[3]352
j412US[2]65
j36LE[2]750
j93SC[2]1976

- 42 -
(47W642)
cc175NW646
178NW41
181NW[1]372
185NW327
190NW[11]896
205NW[4]3
207NW[1]893
208NW[4]821
239NW[9]74
246NW[3]119

- 53 -
(47W617)
f251NW[1]24

- 56 -
(47W420)
v405US1051
v31LE786
v92SC1488
s207NW826
s227NW643
d185NW[3]322
q215NW[3]14
q215NW[3]26

- 67 -
(47W593)

Vol. 179

- 641 -
(48W125)
197NW757
211NW[11]420
211NW[12]420
218NW[4]270
e222NW[12]154
e230NW[12]719
f522F2d[11]764
f522F2d[12]764
382FS[6]278

- 777 -
Case 1
(48W71)

182NW[10]466
190NW[14]897
207NW[11]893
207NW[12]894
208NW[14]450
208NW[14]820
208NW[11]822
223NW[10]458
242NW[10]222
413US[12]302
37LE[12]622
93SC[12]2570
j461F2d[12]112
e329FS[12]19

- 784 -
(48W328)
207NW[1]67
252NW45

- 786 -
(48W91)
US cert den
in401US993
213NW363
234NW[10]309

- 797 -
(48W245)
230NW[1]792
d230NW[2]794

- 800 -
(48W262)
187NW[2]883
e190NW[2]207

- 805 -
(48W272)
180NW[3]721
180NW[4]721
180NW[5]721
e230NW[illegible]699
236NW[6]235
24[illegible]NW[3]242
2[illegible]NW[3]453

- 815 -
(48W290)

- 823 -
(48W251)
184NW[1]853
227NW[6]472
230NW[1]769
230NW[1]792

- 828 -
(48W190)
186NW[10]227
187NW[8]175
187NW[10]199
194NW[8]821
194NW[10]822
198NW[10]367
235NW[6]923

Exhibit 37: Sample page from Shepard's instructional pamphlet, *How to Use Shepard's Citations*, showing parallel citations in *Shepard's North Western Citations* and *Shepard's Wisconsin Citations*.

To give the most up-to-date information on the status of a particular case, Shepard's citators are supplemented frequently. For each citator there is usually one or more bound volumes, and one or more of the following: a gold paperback annual supplement, a red paperback supplement, and a newsprint advance sheet. To insure that the researcher has at hand all the parts necessary to *Shepardize* a specific case, Shepard's prints in a box on the cover of the pamphlets a list of all the issues needed for a complete search in that particular citator. See Exhibit 38.

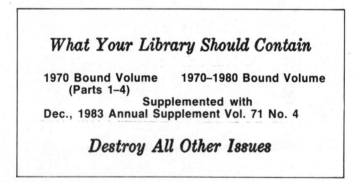

What Your Library Should Contain

1970 Bound Volume (Parts 1–4) **1970–1980 Bound Volume**

Supplemented with

Dec., 1983 Annual Supplement Vol. 71 No. 4

Destroy All Other Issues

Exhibit 38: Listing on the face of a Shepard's advance sheet of all issues of a particular citator.

As an example of how a Shepard's citator functions, let us refer to its treatment of *Roe v. Wade,* 410 U.S. 113 (1973).

To clarify the following explanations, Exhibit 39 below has been marked with numbers to illustrate the various ways in which a cited case is treated. These different treatments include the following:

(1) When the case is *first* listed in *Shepard's U.S. Citations,* parallel citations are given to the alternative unofficial reports of *Roe v. Wade* in the *Supreme Court Reporter* and *Lawyers' Edition.* These citations appear in parentheses.

(2) Next are listed the citations of the case in the U.S. Supreme Court and the lower federal courts with appropriate symbols to show the history of *Roe v. Wade* in its earlier stages.

UNITED STATES SUPREME COURT REPORTS **Vol. 410**

h64FRD[1]3
e65FRD[1]451
68FRD[2]381
64TCt200
41FC€181
42CA3d654
8C3d937
Ariz
540P2d664
Calif
106CaR635
114CaR731
117CaR112
506P2d1011
NH
337A2d790
60ABA551

– 113 –
(35LE147)
(93SC705)
US reh den
in410US959
s314FS1217
cc402US941
cc410US179
cc319FS1048
f410US[1]949
f410US950
f410US951
e410US991
411US34
j411US100
412US[1]761
f412US902
f412US926
413US[2]14
413US[3]65
j413US[1]109
f413US909
414US640
j414US659
j414US1150
415US[1]457
e415US[2]459
j416US[2]10
j416US[3]16
j416US86
416US[5]121
416US[2]126
416US[2]319
416US[2]818
417US[1]279
417US[2]282
418US[2]34
j418US[2]67
c419US1098
421US813
d422US[2]401
422US505
j422US[3]1018
f473F2d1371
474F2d898
474F2d1247
475F2d704
f475F2d[3]706
476F2d[3]96
e476F2d191
476F2d[3]405
477F2d352
477F2d878
478F2d[3]525
478F2d[2]696
j478F2d698
478F2d[3]1338
Continued

369FS463
369FS519
369FS791
369FS[3]808
f369FS[2]809
f369FS[3]974
371FS[3]33
371FS[3]170
371FS[3]979
371FS[3]980
j371FS[3]983
f371FS1382
372FS1160
372FS1201
e373FS[1]423
377FS[4]678
377FS1333
f377FS[3]1342
378FS[3]725
378FS[2]734
378FS[3]735
f378FS1012
f378FS[3]1015
379FS323
379FS[1]512
d380FS[2]1144
380FS1145
380FS[3]1146
380FS[5]1146
380FS1155
380FS[3]1157
j380FS[3]1160
381FS329
f381FS[2]356
383FS[3]547
383FS560
e383FS[3]1145
384FS[2]8
384FS[3]9
f385FS256
f385FS[3]258
f385FS[4]259
388FS[3]96
388FS[2]253
f388FS634
f388FS[3]635
f389FS388
f389FS[3]389
389FS396

389FS[2]745
389FS[2]746
389FS[2]844
f389FS[3]949
e390FS[2]381
f390FS749
f390FS[3]751
391FS[2]1132
392FS[3]1367
j392FS[3]1374
393FS[1]47
393FS[2]47
393FS629
d393FS[2]850
j393FS[3]857
f398FS[3]760
398FS[2]967
e399FS[3]1214
f399FS[2]1228
400FS[2]1008
401FS[3]126
401FS559
f401FS[3]562
f401FS[4]562
j401FS[3]585
67FRD[3]431
291Ala444
293Ala99
293Ala654
54A1A105
41Ap2d714
42Ap2d560
44Ap2d483
44Ap2d518
45Ap2d233
46Ap2d317
22AzA553
23AzA478
23AzA482
31CA3d535
38CA3d645
53CA3d574
9C3d203

181Col49
165Ct557
96Ida714
10IlA534
29IlA31
54Il2d29
55Il2d380
57Il2d537
50McA39
54McA499
56McA403
389Mch527
389Mch536
391Mch366
272Md397
5Msc2d842
6Msc2d567
65NJ271
66NJ221
67NJ272
68NJ303
84NM672
84NM673
33NY167
33NY585
268Or266
18OrA626
51Pa316
51Pa335
51Pa337
53Pa87
54Pa142
261SoC20
122Su422
124Su477
128Su288
129Su491
130Su242
130Su419
135Su52
136Su75
137Su264
214Va341
69Wis2d775
84W2d231
84W2d903
84W2d917
84W2d918
Ala
282So2d270
300So2d357
305So2d379
309So2d432
Alk
515P2d718

525P2d527
536P2d813
537P2d497
537P2d514
537P2d515
537P2d516
Ariz
505P2d590
509P2d246
511P2d198
528P2d1264
529P2d707
534P2d286
534P2d290
542P2d1151
542P2d1153
Ark
492SW888
492SW890
502SW656
Calif
107CaR139
107CaR463
113CaR524
126CaR162
507P2d1347
Colo
507P2d863
535P2d246
Conn
339A2d62
Del
318A2d632
319A2d32
320A2d767
344A2d262
DC
315A2d574
342A2d49
Fla
278So2d341
291So2d571
Haw
535P2d1401
Idaho
Ill
304NE94
315NE22
329NE423
338NE580
Ind
321NE588
329NE74
329NE585
329NE599
337NE561
337NE564
Iowa
211NW336
232NW550
Ky
497SW220
497SW714
La
313So2d802
Me
303A2d796
339A2d517
Md
308A2d225

313A2d542
325A2d415
329A2d41
336A2d104
Mass
294NE869
314NE130
314NE133
314NE135
318NE480
327NE667
327NE889
331NE921
334NE616
339NE678
339NE702
Mich
208NW174
208NW177
212NW798
216NW912
221NW169
223NW752
Minn
204NW198
204NW199
210NW223
Miss
278So2d444
Mo
518SW290
NJ
300A2d602
307A2d645
319A2d781
321A2d233
324A2d93
326A2d88
344A2d770
348A2d821
NM
506P2d1219
506P2d1220
539P2d210
540P2d218
NY
301NE435
305NE906
341S2d242
345S2d562
346S2d921
347S2d453
348S2d910
350S2d894
351S2d90
353S2d21
355S2d782
357S2d269
362S2d596
362S2d918
363S2d487
365S2d112
373S2d737
Ohio
295NE916
Okla
509P2d481
Ore
518P2d640

526P2d596
Pa
302A2d836
303A2d217
303A2d218
306A2d292
309A2d808
311A2d641
311A2d648
312A2d13
312A2d14
320A2d364
323A2d766
329A2d893
331A2d472
RI
301A2d580
304A2d351
So C
198SE254
SD
229NW88
Tex
493SW793
496SW128
507SW290
519SW847
519SW851
526SW217
Utah
526P2d1191
Va
200SE680
Wash
525P2d258
530P2d262
530P2d270
Wis
59ABA1016
59ABA1265
60ABA432
61ABA830

– 179 –
(35LE147)
(35LE201)
(93SC739)
(93SC755)
(93SC756)
(93SC762)
US reh den
in410US959
s410US113
s319FS1048
cc402US936
cc402US941
f410US949
f410US950
f410US951
e410US991
f412US902
Continued

1 Same case reported in Lawyers' Edition and Supreme Court Reporter

2 Judicial history of Roe v. Wade and companion case

3a Cited in other Supreme Court decisions

3b Cited by lower federal court

4 Distinguished with reference to paragraph three of the Syllabus

5 Cited in all units of the National Reporter System with state of citing case shown

6 Cited in American Bar Association Journal

See note on first page of this division

751

Exhibit 39: *Roe v. Wade* as it appears in *Shepard's U.S. Citations.*

(3) Then follow citations to other decisions in federal tribunals: (a) U.S. Supreme Court and (b) lower federal courts. Symbols, such as "e" for explained, "d" for distinguished, or "f" for followed, indicate the nature of the citing court's treatment of *Roe v. Wade.* Explanation of all the symbols so used are set forth in Exhibit 40.

ABBREVIATIONS – ANALYSIS

History of Case	
a (affirmed)	Same case affirmed on rehearing.
cc (connected case)	Different case from case cited but arising out of same subject matter or intimately connected therewith.
m (modified)	Same case modified on rehearing.
r (reversed)	Same case reversed on rehearing.
s (same case)	Same case as case cited.
S (superseded)	Substitution for former opinion.
v (vacated)	Same case vacated.
US reh den	Rehearing denied by U. S. Supreme Court.
US reh dis	Rehearing dismissed by U.S. Supreme Court.
Treatment of Case	
c (criticised)	Soundness of decision or reasoning in cited case criticised for reasons given.
d (distinguished)	Case at bar different either in law or fact from case cited for reasons given.
e (explained)	Statement of import of decision in cited case. Not merely a restatement of the facts.
f (followed)	Cited as controlling.
h (harmonized)	Apparent inconsistency explained and shown not to exist.
j (dissenting opinion)	Citation in dissenting opinion.
L (limited)	Refusal to extend decision of cited case beyond precise issues involved.
o (overruled)	Ruling in cited case expressly overruled.
p (parallel)	Citing case substantially alike or on all fours with cited case in its law or facts.
q (questioned)	Soundness of decision or reasoning in cited case questioned.

Exhibit 40: Shepard's case symbols with explanatory notes.

(4) Small raised numbers to the left of the page numbers of the citing cases correspond to the number of the paragraph of the syllabus or headnote of *Roe v. Wade* which states the legal principle involved in the citing case. The symbols and superior numbers can

be used to reduce the number of citing cases to be consulted by focusing on those dealing specifically with the aspect of *Roe v. Wade* in which the lawyer or researcher is interested.

(5) Next are lists of citations to decisions in state reporters and units of the National Reporter System.

(6) We find here that *Roe v. Wade* has been cited in a periodical article in the *American Bar Association Journal.*

In using any of the above citations in Shepard's, it should be remembered that each reference to a citing case is to the *page* of that case on which the cited case is found, rather than to the beginning page of the citing decision.

OTHER CASE–FINDING TOOLS

There are a variety of other research tools which are frequently used as case-finders. Although each of these will be discussed in more detail in a later chapter, they are mentioned briefly here because of their relevance to case-finding.

Annotated Statutes. The annotated editions of the United States Code and of the statutory compilations for every state include, following each statutory section, abstracts of judicial decision which have applied, interpreted or construed that section. These abstracts appear in the same form as digest abstracts. Whenever there are more than a few abstracts under a statutory section, an index to the abstracts is provided. If one's research involves a statute, the annotated statutory code is a convenient means of access to cases on that problem. Having found the relevant statute, the researcher can at the same time locate the relevant cases under that statute in the same source. (See Chapter IV for further details.)

Looseleaf Services. Another research tool which brings together several types of legal material, including cases, is the looseleaf service. These services are devoted to specific subject fields (e.g., taxation, labor law, criminal law, etc.), and most of them are updated by *weekly* supplements. Looseleaf services include new judicial decisions in their fields of coverage, either in full text or in an abstracted form. Their detailed indexing, prompt supplementation, and inclusion of varied legal sources (decisions, statutes, regulations, rulings, etc.) make them invaluable for research in the areas on which they report. (See Chapter VII for further details.)

Treatises and Periodicals. Although legal treatises and periodical articles are primarily of interest for their text discussions, they also provide references to decisions which make them useful for case-finding. Having found a relevant text passage in a treatise or journal article, one can use the footnotes or other supporting citations to find cases on that problem, as in the encyclopedias discussed earlier. (See Chapter IX for more detail on these sources.)

Restatements. The American Law Institute has published *Restatements of the Law* on a number of subjects. Since these commentaries are frequently cited and discussed by the courts, annotations have been published which list the judicial decisions citing particular sections of the *Restatements.* Such decisions are also accessible through *Shepard's Citations.* Where a section of a Restatement is relevant to one's research, any one of several publications can be used to locate cases citing, and perhaps discussing, that section. (See Chapter IX for further treatment of the *Restatements.*)

CONCLUSION

No single case-finder can be designated as the best for all purposes. Selection of the most useful case-finder for any particular search will depend upon the nature of the problem at hand. The availability of a computer search service, like LEXIS or WESTLAW, will certainly suggest its use. A problem involving the definition of a word might lead one to *Words and Phrases,* while a problem requiring general background knowledge of a topic could begin in an encyclopedia. If the problem deals with federal administrative or regulatory law, a looseleaf service will not only be useful for case-finding, but will also bring together other relevant primary sources.

Each research problem must be analyzed separately, the available tools evaluated, and the most appropriate approach chosen. Inevitably personal preference will play a part when two or more tools seem equally useful as case-finders. Experimentation and the development of skill in the use of all of these approaches enable the researcher to make the most effective choices for each problem encountered.

CHAPTER IV

STATUTES

Statutory material appeared very early in recorded history, as evidenced by the legal codes of the ancient Near East, many of which are well known to us today (e.g., those of the Assyrians, Babylonians, Hittites, and particularly the Hebrew codes of the Bible). Legal codes have been used throughout the ages to formulate new rules of kings or priests, as well as to codify existing custom and judicial pronouncements. There are fundamental differences between the decisional material of case law and the directive texts of statutory enactments: differences of purpose and source, of language and style, and of bibliographic form and reference.

There are also very significant differences between the statutory forms of different ages and legal systems. In modern times, Anglo-American laws have developed very differently from the Napoleonic codes in Europe. The Continental codes legislate in general terms, using provisions which are quite broad and yet concise and simple in language. American statutes, on the other hand, have sought to meet every future situation specifically, using many words and considerable detail to do so. The multiplicity of American statutes is in part due to our optimistic striving for a solution of all social and economic problems by legislation; the prolixity results from our desire to anticipate every conceivable violation. Although our compilations are often called codes, they are as different from the European codes as the Penal Law of New York is from the Ten Commandments.

American statutes are published in three forms. The first published official text of a statute is the *slip law.* In that form each law is issued as a pamphlet with separate pagination, or as a single sheet. Slip laws of the U.S. Congress are available shortly after enactment, but on the state level are often quite difficult to obtain.

Next are the *session laws,* chronologically arranged collections of statutes which are published in separate volumes for each year or session of the legislature. Within each volume, the statutes are arranged by date of passage, with an index at the end. *Statutes at Large* is the name of the session laws of the U.S. Congress. Examples of state session laws are the *Laws of New York* and *Acts and Resolves of Massachusetts.* All states issue official editions of their session laws, the titles varying from state to state, and a few also have commercial editions.

Access to laws on a specific subject is very difficult through this chronological form of publication. Subject access is required by the lawyer or researcher who must find *all* of the statutes which are currently applicable to a particular problem. Such access is provided by statutory compilations known generally as *codes.* They collect those statutes of a jurisdiction which have general application and are in force, and arrange them by broad subject topics. Each topic is given a descriptive title and frequently a title number. The statutes collected under each title are arranged in numbered sections. Frequently a single law, as enacted in the session laws, will be broken up and listed under several different titles, or in different sections of the same title of the code. A more or less detailed index enables the researcher to find the sections dealing with particular problems or topics. Many editions of codes, particularly the *unofficial* editions, also include annotations to relevant court decisions from the same jurisdiction, which interpret, construe, or apply each statutory section. Such annotations consist of a brief squib of the applicable legal principle and a citation to the case from which it was taken, similar to the West reporter headnote and digest abstracts.

Codes or statutory compilations must be updated promptly to include the output of the latest legislative session. Because of the numerous changes which are made in statutory law every time a legislature meets and because of the frequency of legislative sessions in this country (by 1983, thirty-nine state legislatures were meeting annually and eleven biennially), it is necessary to provide some form of prompt and convenient supplementation. Failure to do so would render a legislative compilation virtually useless. Supplementation is usually provided by pocket parts in the back of the bound volumes or by looseleaf additions. Some official editions of the codes are updated only by the publication of revised editions every few years.

With statutes, as with case law, there are both official and unofficial editions. The *unofficial* texts usually provide additional research material which make them more useful than the official edition. For example, most of the *annotated* codes are published unofficially by commercial publishers. These usually provide faster and more convenient supplementation than the official editions, fuller editorial notes, historical comments, analyses of statutes, other interpretative material, and cross references to other relevant publications. The *U.S. Code* is the official edition of the federal statutory code, and there are also two unofficial, annotated editions—*U.S. Code Annotated* and *U.S. Code Service.* These three editions will be discussed below, beginning at page 115.

The official text is, as always, the authoritative one and must be cited in every legal reference. The citation problem for statutes is also somewhat complicated by the fact that there may be *two* official sources: the *chronologically* published session laws and a *subject* compilation or code of statutes in force. Usually only one of these forms is the *authoritative* text, which should always be cited, although both may be official. While the session law is generally the authoritative text, the researcher may have difficulty in determining this. In a few states, unofficial codes have been recognized as authoritative to some extent, because of the absence of convenient official editions.

There are also jurisdictional problems of statutory coverage and authority which arise in part from our federal system and in part from the multiplicity of state laws. We have both a federal legislature and fifty state legislatures. Sometimes a conflict between enactments of the United States Congress and those of the states may create uncertainty as to which law applies in a particular situation. There are also problems of interpretation and application arising from the variety of laws on the same subject in the fifty states.

These problems have given rise to a movement for uniform state laws, which is reflected in the work of the National Conference of Commissioners on Uniform State Laws. The publication of these laws is described below at pages 134–135.

It is also relevant to note that legislation comes not only from traditional legislative bodies like the Congress and the state legislatures, but also from subordinate legislative units. These lawmaking bodies, generally operating under a statutory delegation of authority from the legislature, include administrative agencies and executive departments; courts which issue their own rules; and towns, municipalities and other local units of government.

The nature of legal authority assigned to legislation is different from that of case law. Statutes have binding or mandatory authority in the jurisdiction in which they are enacted or promulgated. Outside of that jurisdiction they have no effect and are not even persuasive authority, except of course as evidence of the law of the state which enacted them. If, however, a state is contemplating the adoption of a law already passed by another state, the latter's experience under that law may be persuasive to the deliberating legislature or to later courts which may have to construe the statute.

Finally, it should be pointed out that statutes are often marked by ambiguities or vagueness which give rise to legal controversy by making their interpretation and application difficult. Such controversies frequently require lawyers to ascertain the lawmakers' intent through the collection and study of documents of legislative history. This statutory ambiguity may stem from linguistic uncertainty or poor draftsmanship, but frequently is the inevitable result of negotiation and compromise in the legislative process. Research in legislative history is discussed in Chapter V below.

TYPES OF LEGISLATION

Legislative materials can be divided in the following ways:

1. Conventional legislation and subordinate or delegated legislation.
2. Federal and state legislation.
3. Statutory compilations and session laws.
4. Official and unofficial publications.
5. Authoritative and non-authoritative texts.
6. Annotated and unannotated editions.

There are other descriptive categories of legislation which should be mentioned. Among them are the following forms which legislation can take in this country:

1. Constitutions are the organic laws of particular jurisdictions. They define political relationships, enumerate the rights and liberties of citizens, and create the necessary governmental framework. Constitutions are published in the statutory code of each jurisdiction, as well as in separate editions. Research in constitutional sources is discussed below at pages 127–128.

2. Resolutions (joint, concurrent and simple) and **Acts** are the forms by which a legislature carries on its work and promulgates laws. In the United States Congress, laws are passed by either a *joint resolution* or an *act.* Simple and concurrent resolutions are used for expressing the sentiment or intent of Congress or for performing housekeeping functions short of actual legislation. A simple resolution is the action of one house of Congress, while a concurrent resolution stems from both houses.

3. Treaties are the instruments by which sovereign nations can agree to act with other nations. Treaties are considered a legislative form, but are discussed separately in Chapter VIII below.

4. Interstate Compacts are agreements between two or more states, which are legislative in nature and somewhat like treaties in form and effect. Compacts require the consent of Congress before the states can enter into them, so they often appear in both federal and state legislative publications.

5. Reorganization Plans are presidential proposals to reorganize executive agencies below the departmental level which are submitted to Congress pursuant to a general authorizing statute. If Congress does not veto the plan, it becomes law automatically in a reversal of the usual legislative process—that is, enactment by the President, subject to veto by the Congress, instead of vice versa.

6. Executive Legislation includes presidential proclamations, orders and messages, all of which belong more properly in the area of administrative law and will be discussed in Chapter VI below.

7. **Administrative Regulations** (substantive and procedural) consist of rules adopted by executive and regulatory agencies, pursuant to congressional authorization. These will also be discussed in detail in Chapter VI below.

8. **Court Rules** are enactments for the regulation of proceedings in the courts. They are promulgated by the courts themselves, or by conferences of judges, usually under authority specifically granted by statute.

9. **Local Laws and Ordinances** are delegated legislation in that the power to legislate has been delegated by the state legislature to some lawmaking agency of local government. Publication is generally very poor in this area, although a tremendous number of such laws are enacted regularly by municipalities and counties.

In addition to the foregoing legislative categories, the distinction between *public laws* and *private laws* must also be mentioned. Public laws are those which are designed to affect the general public, as distinguished from private laws which are passed to meet a special need of an individual or small group. In some cases, the distinction is hard to justify, as when a special interest group promotes legislation, which, although general in tone, actually affects very few people. Both types are passed in the same way and both usually appear in the session law publication, but only *public* laws become part of the statutory code.

FEDERAL STATUTORY FORMS

1. The Quick Text. Many laws take effect upon enactment or soon thereafter and, whether immediately effective or not, lawyers and researchers need the text of such new laws as soon as possible. Although new laws can be obtained from Congress itself, the best source for the text of new laws immediately after enactment is generally a looseleaf service, if one is published on that subject.

As we have seen, the first *official* text is the *slip law,* which can be requested from the appropriate congressional clerk or an individual legislator, or ordered from the U.S. Government Printing Office, on an individual basis or by subscription. There is often, however, a frustrating time lag between enactment and distribution of slip laws to subscribers.

Commercially published looseleaf services provide a quick text of federal enactments in particular subject fields. Since these publications are usually supplemented on a weekly basis, they are an excellent source for new legislation. Such services are commonly published in public law fields like taxation, labor law, trade regulation, etc., and will be discussed below in Chapter VII. Their publishers will also supply copies of individual new laws at the request of subscribers, when the law does not appear in full in the service itself.

One of the most popular sources of new federal *public* laws is the *U.S. Code Congressional and Administrative News,* published fortnightly by West during the congressional session and monthly when

Congress is not in session. It appears initially in an advance sheet edition containing the complete text of all public laws. The bound volumes, at the end of each session, contain selective documents of legislative history (in the form of committee reports) on the more important enactments. *U.S.C.C.A.N.* also contains congressional news notes, selected administrative regulations, executive documents, and useful tables and indexes.

2. **Session Law Form.** At the end of each session of Congress, the public and private slip laws are accumulated and corrected. Together with Presidential proclamations, reorganization plans, and proposed and ratified Constitutional amendments, they are then issued in bound volumes as the official *Statutes at Large* for that session. These are cited by volume and page, for example, 84 Stat. 1590 (referring to volume 84 of the *Statutes at Large*, page 1590). The *Statutes at Large* supersede the slip laws as the authoritative text of federal laws and remain the authoritative text for all but those twenty-one titles of the *U.S. Code* which have been reenacted as positive law. The *Statutes at Large* contain an index for each session, but since these indexes do not cumulate, the researcher must use the *U.S. Code* and *its* general index in order to locate the current law on a particular subject.

There are also two unofficial session law texts of public laws. *U.S. Code Congressional and Administrative News,* mentioned above, is published by the West Publishing Company and can be used as a supplement to its *United States Code Annotated. U.S. C.C.A.N.* cumulates at the end of each session into

1590 PUBLIC LAW 91-596–DEC. 29, 1970 [84 STAT.

Public Law 91-596

December 29, 1970
[S. 2193]

AN ACT

To assure safe and healthful working conditions for working men and women; by authorizing enforcement of the standards developed under the Act; by assisting and encouraging the States in their efforts to assure safe and healthful working conditions; by providing for research, information, education, and training in the field of occupational safety and health; and for other purposes.

Occupational Safety and Health Act of 1970.

Be it enacted by the Senate and House of Representatives of the United States of America in Congress assembled, That this Act may be cited as the "Occupational Safety and Health Act of 1970".

CONGRESSIONAL FINDINGS AND PURPOSE

SEC. (2) The Congress finds that personal injuries and illnesses arising out of work situations impose a substantial burden upon, and are a hindrance to, interstate commerce in terms of lost production, wage loss, medical expenses, and disability compensation payments.

DUTIES

SEC. 5. (a) Each employer—

(1) shall furnish to each of his employees employment and a place of employment which are free from recognized hazards that are causing or are likely to cause death or serious physical harm to his employees;

(2) shall comply with occupational safety and health standards promulgated under this Act.

(b) Each employee shall comply with occupational safety and health standards and all rules, regulations, and orders issued pursuant to this Act which are applicable to his own actions and conduct.

APPROPRIATIONS

SEC. 33. There are authorized to be appropriated to carry out this Act for each fiscal year such sums as the Congress shall deem necessary.

EFFECTIVE DATE

SEC. 34. This Act shall take effect one hundred and twenty days after the date of its enactment.

Approved December 29, 1970.

Exhibit 41: The beginning, a middle section, and the end of a statute from the *U.S. Statutes at Large*, the Occupational Safety and Health Act of 1970. This act will be the focus of most of the exhibits in this chapter and in chapters V and VI.

bound volumes which provide a permanent record of public legislation, with a selection of congressional committee reports.

U.S. Code Service, published by Lawyers Co-op, is another subject compilation of federal statutes. It is supplemented by a monthly advance sheet service, called *U.S.C.S. Advance,* which provides the texts of public laws, summaries of the legislative history of each public law, texts of new court rules, executive orders and Presidential proclamations. *U.S.C.S. Advance* issues do not cumulate into bound volumes. These monthly advance sheets provide subscribers to the *U.S.C.S.* with a session law service similar to that of *U.S.C.C.A.N.,* but without the actual documents of legislative history. Neither *U.S.C.C.A.N.* nor *U.S.C.S. Advance* include *private* laws; these are only available in the official *Statutes at Large.*

3. **Subject compilations.** The first official compilations of federal statutes designed to provide subject access were the *U.S. Revised Statutes* of 1873 and its second edition of 1878. These one volume compilations arranged all *public, general* and *permanent* federal statutes into some seventy-five titles or subject categories with consecutive section numbering and a general index. The *Revised Statutes* of 1873 were more than just a subject compilation, however. It actually reenacted as positive law the statutes it contained and expressly repealed their original *Statutes at Large* texts. Therefore, for those public laws which predate 1873 and are included in the *Revised Statutes,* that compilation is their authoritative text. The second edition, however, did not have that status, although little distinction is made between them today.

Although it soon became apparent that the *Revised Statutes* were not adequate to provide a convenient subject arrangement of current federal statutes, no other official compilation was prepared for almost fifty years. Then in 1926, the first edition of the *United States Code* was published, arranging the public, general, permanent laws by subject into some *fifty* titles. The *Code* is published in a completely revised edition every six years with bound cumulative supplements in the intervening years. As previously noted, the statutes contained in approximately one-third of the titles of the *Code* have been reenacted and for them the *Code* has become the authoritative text. For the others, the *Statutes at Large* retain that status. The congressional plan of reenactment is described in the preface of the 1982 edition of the *Code* as follows:

> "Because many of the general and permanent laws that are required to be incorporated in the Code are inconsistent, redundant, and obsolete, the Office of the Law Revision Counsel of the House of Representatives has been engaged in a continuing, comprehensive project authorized by law to revise and codify, for enactment into positive law, each title of the Code. When this project is completed, all the titles of the Code will be legal evidence of the general and permanent laws and recourse to the numerous volumes of the United States Statutes at Large for this purpose will no longer be necessary. Titles 1, 3, 4, 5, 9, 10, 11, 13, 14, 17, 18, 23, 28, 31, 32, 35, 37, 38, 39, 44, and 49 have been revised, codified

and enacted into positive law and the text thereof is legal evidence of the laws therein contained. The matter contained in the other titles of the Code is prima facie evidence of the laws."

Note that title 6 was enacted and then later repealed, and that title 34 was eliminated by the enactment of title 10.

Citations to the *Code* refer to title and section, rather than to volume and page, as in the *Statutes at Large.* For example, 18 U.S.C. § 1621 describes Title 18 of the *U.S. Code,* section 1621. If the title is one of those reenacted into positive law, it is technically unnecessary to cite its *Statutes at Large* source, but many writers include both forms in their statutory citations.

In addition to the actual text of statutes, the *Code* also includes historical and editorial notes, parallel tables and other research aids. Each section of the *Code* is followed by a citation to the *Statutes at Large* provision which originally enacted it. These alternative citations are particularly important where the *Statutes at Large* is still the authoritative source and must be cited. In recent editions of the *U.S. Code,* cross references are provided at the beginning of each re-enacted title to citations of sections in that title made elsewhere in the *Code.*

(4) Nothing in this chapter shall be construed to supersede or in any manner affect any workmen's compensation law or to enlarge or diminish or affect in any other manner the common law or statutory rights, duties, or liabilities of employers and employees under any law with respect to injuries, diseases, or death of employees arising out of, or in the course of, employment. (Pub. L. 91–596, § 4, Dec. 29, 1970, 84 Stat. 1592.)

REFERENCES IN TEXT

The Outer Continental Shelf Lands Act, referred to in subsec. (a), is classified to section 1331 et seq. of Title 43, Public Lands.

The Act of June 30, 1936, commonly known as the Walsh-Healey Act, referred to in subsec. (b)(2), is classified to sections 35 to 45 of Title 41, Public Contracts.

The Service Contract Act of 1965, referred to in subsec. (b)(2), is classified to chapter 6 of Title 41.

Public Law 91–54, Act of August 9, 1969, referred to in subsec. (b)(2), is classified to section 333 of Title 40, Public Buildings, Property, and Works.

Public Law 85–742, Act of August 23, 1958, referred to in subsec. (b)(2), is classified to section 941 of Title 33, Navigation and Navigable Waters.

The National Foundation on Arts and Humanities Act, referred to in subsec. (b)(2), is classified to section 951 et seq. of Title 20, Education.

The effective date of this chapter, referred to in subsec. (b)(2), (3), is the effective date of Pub. L. 91–596, which is 120 days after Dec. 29, 1970.

EFFECTIVE DATE

Section effective 120 days after Dec. 29, 1970, see section 34 of Pub. L. 91–596, set out as a note under section 651 of this title.

SECTION REFERRED TO IN OTHER SECTIONS

This section is referred to in section 673 of this title.

§ 654. Duties of employers and employees.

(a) Each employer—

(1) shall furnish to each of his employees employment and a place of employment which are free from recognized hazards that are causing or are likely to cause death or serious physical harm to his employees;

(2) shall comply with occupational safety and health standards promulgated under this chapter.

(b) Each employee shall comply with occupational safety and health standards and all rules, regulations, and orders issued pursuant to this chapter which are applicable to his own actions and conduct. (Pub. L. 91–596, § 5, Dec. 29, 1970, 84 Stat. 1593.)

EFFECTIVE DATE

Section effective 120 days after Dec. 29, 1970, see section 34 of Pub. L. 91–596, set out as a note under section 651 of this title.

SECTION REFERRED TO IN OTHER SECTIONS

This section is referred to in sections 658, 666 of this title.

§ 655. Standards.

(a) Promulgation by Secretary of national consensus standards and established Federal standards; time for promulgation; conflicting standards.

Without regard to chapter 5 of Title 5 or to the other subsections of this section, the Secretary shall, as soon as practicable during the period beginning with the effective date of this chapter and ending two years after such date, by rule promulgate as an occupational safety or health standard any national consensus standard, and any established Federal standard, unless he determines that the promulgation of such a standard would not result in improved safety or health for specifically designated employees. In the event of conflict among any such standards, the Secretary shall promulgate the standard which assures the greatest protection of the safety or health of the affected employees.

(b) Procedure for promulgation, modification, or revocation of standards.

The Secretary may by rule promulgate, modify, or revoke any occupational safety or health standard in the following manner:

(1) Whenever the Secretary, upon the basis of information submitted to him in writing by an interested person, a representative of any organization of employers or employees, a nationally recognized standards-producing organization, the Secretary of Health, Education, and Welfare, the National Institute for Occupational Safety and Health, or a State or political subdivision, or on the basis of information developed by the Secretary or otherwise available to him, determines that a rule should be promulgated in order to serve the objectives of this chapter, the Secretary may request the recommendations of an advisory committee appointed under section 656 of this title. The Secretary shall provide such an advisory committee with any proposals of his own or of the Secretary of Health, Education, and Welfare, together with all pertinent factual information developed by the Secretary or the Secretary of Health, Education, and Welfare, or otherwise available, including the results of research, demonstrations, and experiments. An advisory committee shall submit to the Secretary its recommendations regarding the rule to be promulgated within ninety days from the date of its appointment or within such longer or shorter period as may be prescribed by the Secretary, but in no event for a period which is longer than two hundred and seventy days.

(2) The Secretary shall publish a proposed rule promulgating, modifying, or revoking an occupational safety or health standard in the Federal Register and shall afford interested persons a period of thirty days after publication to submit written data or comments. Where an advisory committee is appointed and the Secretary determines that a rule should be issued, he shall publish the proposed rule within sixty days after the submission of the advisory committee's recommendations or the expiration of the period prescribed by the Secretary for such submission.

(3) On on before the last day of the period provided for the submission of written data or comments under paragraph (2), any interested person may file with the Secretary written objections to the proposed rule, stating the grounds therefore and requesting a public hearing on such objections. Within thirty days after the last day for filing such objections, the Secretary shall publish in the Federal Register a notice specifying the occupational safety or health standard to which objections have been filed and a hearing requested, and specifying a time and place for such hearing.

(4) Within sixty days after the expiration of the period provided for the submission of written data

Exhibit 42: A page from the *U.S. Code,* showing the codification of part of the Occupational Safety and Health Act of 1970.

In order to get from the *Statutes at Large* citation to the *Code* citation, tables are provided at the end of the *U.S. Code* itself, which give such parallel references. The form of these tables, as revised in the 1970 edition of the *Code,* is shown in Exhibit 43. Similar tables also appear in the two unofficial editions of the *Code.*

STATUTES AT LARGE — Page 13448

91st Cong. 84 Stat.	Pub. L.	Section	Page	U.S.C. Title	U.S.C. Section	Status
1970—Dec. 24	91-588	10	1585	38	521 nt	
	91-589	1	1586	2	168	
		2	1586	2	168a	
		3	1586	2	168b	
		4	1587	2	168c	
		5	1587	2	168d	
28	91-590	1	1587	49	903	
		2	1587	49	903 nt	
	91-591	2	1588	7	2264	
		3	1588	7	2265	
29	91-596	1	1590	29	651 nt	
		2	1590	29	651	
		3	1591	29	652	
		4	1592	29	653	
		5	1593	29	654	
		6	1593	29	655	

Exhibit 43: A parallel reference table in the 1970 edition of *U.S. Code,* showing the codification of the Occupational Safety and Health Act of 1970.

4. Annotated Subject Compilations. In addition to the *U.S. Code,* which is the official subject compilation, there are also two privately published, annotated editions of the *Code.* As noted above, these are the *U.S. Code Annotated (U.S.C.A.),* published by West, and the *U.S. Code Service (U.S.C.S.),* published by Lawyers Co-op. Both compilations follow the same title and section numbering as the official edition and contain the same statutory text, but add the following features:

(a) Annotations of court decisions interpreting, construing, and applying code sections.

(b) Editorial notes and analytical discussions on particular statutes or provisions.

(c) References to attorney general opinions, administrative regulations, various secondary sources, and legislative history.

(d) Supplementation by annual pocket parts, quarterly pamphlets, and revised volumes as necessary.

U.S.C.S. also contains annotations of uncodified laws and treaties, and preserves the original *Statutes at Large* text in which the law was enacted. Both the *U.S.C.* and *U.S.C.A.*, on the other hand, may make minor changes in integrating particular provisions into the *Code* format.

Their special research aids have made the annotated statutes very popular and they are used widely in preference to the official text. Exhibit 44 shows the *U.S.C.A.* version of the same section of Title 29 as was shown in Exhibit 42, Exhibit 45 shows a page of annotations to court decisions following that section in *U.S.C.A.;* it also illustrates the summary indexing of such annotations. Exhibits 46 to 48 show the corresponding section, index to annotations, and annotations in *U.S.C.S.* Note the Research Guide in that edition, citing to relevant secondary sources, and the list of related sections in the *Code of Federal Regulations.*

ly to make a new statute applicable to Puerto Rico. Caribtow Corp. v. Occupational Safety and Health Review Commission, C.A.1, 1974, 493 F.2d 1064.

2. Workmen's compensation laws

Since intestate's death, which resulted from injuries sustained in accident arising out of and in the course of his employment with defendant, was covered under the North Carolina Workmen's Compensation Act, subsec. (b)(4) of this section providing that nothing in this chapter should be construed to supersede any workmen's compensation law or to enlarge or diminish liability of employer precluded a private remedy, and plaintiff was not entitled to recover from employer for alleged negligence in violation of this chapter. Byrd v. Fieldcrest Mills, Inc., C.A.N.C.1974, 496 F.2d 1323.

3. Common law or statutory rights, duties or liabilities

Federal safety and health regulations did not enlarge responsibility of the property owner who hired prime contractor or of the prime contractor who hired independent sewer line subcontractor whose employee was killed during excavation of sewer line trench in view of provision in this section stating that this chapter does not enlarge or diminish the common law or statutory rights, duties, or liabilities of employers and employees with respect to injuries, diseases or death of employees arising out of employment. Hare v. Federal Compress & Warehouse Co., D.C.Miss.1973, 359 F.Supp. 214.

This chapter was not applicable in situation where employee was injured while voluntarily complying with his employer's request during a two man repair job on a farm roof, inasmuch as its provisions do not enlarge or diminish or affect in any other manner the common law or statutory rights, duties, or liabilities of employers and employees under the law with respect to injuries, diseases, or death of employees arising out of, or in course of, employment. Dekle v. Todd, Ga.App.1974, 207 S.E.2d 654.

§ 654. Duties of employers and employees

(a) Each employer—

(1) shall furnish to each of his employees employment and a place of employment which are free from recognized hazards that are causing or are likely to cause death or serious physical harm to his employees;

(2) shall comply with occupational safety and health standards promulgated under this chapter.

(b) Each employee shall comply with occupational safety and health standards and all rules, regulations, and orders issued pursuant to this chapter which are applicable to his own actions and conduct.

Pub.L. 91–596, § 5, Dec. 29, 1970, 84 Stat. 1593.

Historical Note

Effective Date. Section effective 120 days after Dec. 29, 1970, see section 34 of Pub.L. 91–596, set out as a note under section 651 of this title.

Legislative History. For legislative history and purpose of Pub.L. 91–596, see 1970 U.S.Code Cong. and Adm.News, p. 5177.

Notes of Decisions

569

Exhibit 44: The *U.S.C.A.* version of 29 *U.S.C.* § 654.

---

1. Employees to whom duty is owed

Employer does not owe a lesser duty of care to its supervisory personnel under this section than is owed to the rank-and-file employees. National Realty & Const. Co., Inc. v. Occupational Safety and Health Review Commission, 1973, 489 F.2d 1257, 160 U.S.App.D.C. 133.

2. Places of employment where duty is owed

Fact that circuit breaker power room was not open to all employees but only to certain authorized personnel did not render it immune from coverage of this chapter. REA Exp., Inc. v. Brennan, C.A.2, 1974, 495 F.2d 822.

3. Recognized hazards—Generally

Within this section, a "recognized hazard" is not limited to one which can be recognized directly by human senses without assistance of any technical instruments. American Smelting & Refining Co. v. Occupational Safety and Health Review Commission, C.A.8, 1974, 501 F.2d 504.

4. —— Knowledge of employer

Employer's obligation under this section is to maintain a work place free from "recognized hazards" which are causing or likely to cause death or serious physical harm to employees; a "recognized hazard" is a condition that is known to be hazardous, and is known not necessarily by each and every individual employer, but is known by taking into account the standard of knowledge in the industry. Brennan v. Occupational Safety and Health Review Commission, C.A.7, 1974, 501 F.2d 1196.

This section requires that, for a serious violation citation to be sustained, danger must be one of which employer knew or, with reasonable diligence, could have known. Id.

A hazard is "recognized" for purposes of this section, if an employer has actual knowledge of a hazard. Brennan v. Occupational Safety and Health Review Commission, C.A.8, 1974, 494 F.2d 460.

5. —— Unpreventable hazards

This section does not impose an absolute liability on the employer, since it may be that some hazards are unpreventable, particularly if employee's conduct is wilfully reckless or so unusual that employer cannot reasonably prevent the existence of the hazard which such behavior creates. REA Exp. Inc. v. Brennan, C.A.2, 1974, 495 F.2d 822.

Standard imposed by this section is not intended to impose strict liability but to require elimination only of preventable hazards, and unpreventable hazards are not to be considered "recognized" under this section. National Realty & Const. Co., Inc. v. Occupational Safety and Health Review Commission, 1973, 489 F.2d 1257, 160 U.S.App.D.C. 133.

6. Likelihood of hazard to cause death or injury

Although act of employee in cutting band which held packaged railroad ties together prior to time unloader was in place gave rise to a substantial probability that death or serious physical harm would result, a serious violation of this section did not occur in respect to employee's death, where instruction given employee to stay away from trucks because the unloader did all the unloading was sufficient to satisfy employer's duty, and employer, using reasonable diligence, would not have foreseen danger. Brennan v. Occupational Safety and Health Review Commission, C.A.7, 1974, 501 F.2d 1196.

Where it was reasonably foreseeable that awkward and uncomfortable respirators would not be properly worn by employees, furnishing of such respirators could not be relied on by employer to establish that its protective measures prevented the likelihood of harm to employees from airborne lead, for purposes of this section. American Smelting and Refining Co. v. Occupational Safety and Health Review Commission, C.A.8, 1974, 501 F.2d 504.

No mathematical test as to probability of serious mishap is proper in construing the "likely to cause death or serious physical harm" element of this section. National Realty & Const. Co., Inc. v. Occupational Safety and Health Review Commission, 1973, 489 F.2d 1257, 160 U.S. App.D.C. 133.

570

Exhibit 45: Annotations under 29 *U.S.C.A.* § 654.

LABOR **29 USCS § 653.**

§ 654. Duties of employers and employees

(a) Each employer—

(1) shall furnish to each of his employees employment and a place of employment which are free from recognized hazards that are causing or are likely to cause death or serious physical harm to his employees;

(2) shall comply with occupational safety and health standards promulgated under this Act.

(b) Each employee shall comply with occupational safety and health standards and all rules, regulations, and orders issued pursuant to this Act which are applicable to his own actions and conduct.

(Dec. 29, 1970, P. L. 91-596, § 5, 84 Stat. 1593.)

HISTORY; ANCILLARY LAWS AND DIRECTIVES

References in text:

"This Act", referred to in this section, is Act Dec. 29, 1970, P. L. 91-596, 84 Stat. 1590, popularly known as the Occupational Safety and Health Act of 1970, which appears generally as 29 USCS §§ 651 et seq For full classification of this Act, consult USCS Tables volumes.

Effective date of section:

For the effective date of this section, see the Other provisions note to 29 USCS § 651.

CODE OF FEDERAL REGULATIONS

Coordinated enforcement, 29 CFR Part 42.

Inspections, citations and proposed penalties, 29 CFR Part 1903.

Administrative requirements governing all grants and agreements by which Department of Labor agencies award funds to State and local governments, Indian and native American entities, public and private institutions of higher

410

Exhibit 46: The *U.S. Code Service* version of 29 *U.S.C.* § 654, with *Code of Federal Regulations* citations.

education and hospitals and other quasi-public and private nonprofit organizations, 41 CFR Parts 29-70.

CROSS REFERENCES

USCS Administrative Rules, OSHRC, 29 CFR Part 2200.

RESEARCH GUIDE

Am Jur:

61 Am Jur 2d, Plant and Job Safety—OSHA and State Laws §§ 1–3, 9, 21, 25, 26, 31, 34–38, 40, 43, 57, 58, 67, 78, 82, 88, 101, 102, 106, 112, 124.

Forms:

10 Federal Procedural Forms L Ed, Health, Education, and Welfare §§ 37:211, 37:213.

Federal Regulations of Employment Service:

FRES, Introduction and Scope § 9:4.

FRES, Job Safety and Health §§ 10:1–10:3, 10:4, 10:6, 10:16, 10:28, 10:29, 10:100.

FRES, Enforcement § 11:20.

Annotations:

What is "recognized hazard" within meaning of general duty clause of Occupational Safety and Health Act (29 USCS § 654(a)(1)). 50 ALR Fed 742.

When is "greater hazard" defense available to employer cited for violation of Occupational Safety and Health Act (29 USCS §§ 651 et seq.). 47 ALR Fed 348.

Validity, construction, and application of OSHA General Industry Standards for scaffolding (29 CFR § 1910.28). 47 ALR Fed 809.

Validity, construction, and application of OSHA general industry standard regulating exposure to occupational noise (29 CFR § 1910.95). 43 ALR Fed 159.

Validity, construction, and application of personal protective equipment subpart of OSHA general industry standards (29 CFR §§ 1910.132–1910.140. 39 ALR Fed 141

Machinery and machine guarding OSHA General Industry Standards (29 CFR §§ 1910.211–1910.222). 38 ALR Fed 507

OSHA violation by employer or third party as providing cause of action for employee. 35 ALR Fed 461.

Who is "Employer" for purposes of Occupational Safety and Health Act (29 USCS §§ 651 et seq.). 27 ALR Fed 943.

Law Review Articles:

Rader, Smotherman, and Ehlke, How to Handle an OSHA Case: An Employer's Rights and Options. 33 Baylor L Rev 493, Summer, 1981.

Morey, The General Duty Clause of the Occupational Safety and Health Act. 88 Harvard L Rev 988 (1973).

411

Exhibit 46 (continued): Research Guide, following § 654 of title 29 in *U.S. Code Service.*

Fluegel, The Right of an Employee Under OSHA to Refuse to Work in the Face of Imminent Danger. 64 Minnesota L Rev 115, November, 1979.

State Plans and the General Duty Clause in the Occupational Safety and Health Act of 1970. 34 Ohio State LJ 599 (1973).

Mahoney, Kendall, OSHA's Medical Surveillance and Removal Programs: Implications and Validity. 42 University of Pittsburgh L Rev 779, Summer, 1981.

INTERPRETIVE NOTES AND DECISIONS

412

Exhibit 47: Index to annotations, following § 654 of title 29 in *U.S. Code Service.*

I. IN GENERAL

1. Promulgation of standards

Promulgation of specific safety standard by Secretary of Labor, pursuant to 29 USCS § 655, unambiguously forecloses discretion in employer to decide that failure to comply with such standard would not be dangerous in particular situation. F. X. Messina Constr. Corp. v Occupational Safety & Health Review Com. (1974, CA1) 505 F2d 701.

Standards promulgated under Occupational Safety & Health Act (29 USCS §§ 651–678) have force of law by virtue of 29 USCS § 654, imposing upon every employer duty to comply with occupational safety and health standards promulgated thereunder or face civil and criminal penalties. Florida Peach Growers Asso. v United States Dept. of Labor (1974, CA5) 489 F2d 120.

OSHA imposed duties upon employees, as well as on employers, to comply with standards, rules, regulations and orders. Buhler v Marriott Hotels, Inc. (1974, ED La) 390 F Supp 999.

2. Reservation of place for additional regulations

Missing regulations marked "Reserved" do not create exceptions by silence to existing regulations, since content of those reserved titles are unknown, and furthermore, 29 USCS § 654(a)(2) provides that each employer shall comply with Occupational Safety and Health Standards promulgated. Delmarva Power & Light Co. (1974) OSHRC Docket No. 1416, 1973–1974 CCH OSHD ¶ 17904.

3. Construction of standards

Because violation of OSHA regulation involves penal sanction, coverage of agency regulation should be no broader than what is encompassed within its terms. Dravo Corp. v Occupational Safety & Health Review Com. (1980, CA3) 613 F2d 1227.

Although titles and topic headings in OSHA standards are merely tools of statutory interpretation which cannot limit plain meaning of text, they clearly do indicate or characterize subject matter of standard. Everglades Sugar Refinery, Inc. (1979) OSHRC Docket No. 76-2643.

Standard at 29 CFR § 1926.550(a)(17), which incorporates by reference advisory standard of power crane and shovel association is advisory rather than mandatory, where although § 1926.550(a)(17) says that employers "shall" comply with association standard, use in association standard of "should" signifies advisory nature of standard in accordance with distinction between advisory and mandatory standards set out in definitions of "should" and "shall" in 29 CFR §§ 1926.32(p) and (q). Brown & Root, Inc. (1980) OSHRC Docket No. 76-2938.

4. Application of standards

Since Congress' intent, as expressed in 29 USCS § 651(b), was to protect working men and women from hazards at place of employment, standard [29 CFR § 1910.28(a)(17)] which provides that scaffolds shall be provided with screen between toe board and guardrail, where persons are required to work or pass under scaffolds, cannot be extended to provide protection for pedestrians or other nonemployees. City Wide Tuckpointing Service Co. (1973) OSHRC Docket No. 247, 1971–1973 CCH OSHD ¶ 15769.

Effective date provision in Subpart X of 29 CFR Part 1926 applies only to operation of Part 1926 under Construction Safety Act (40 USCS § 327 et seq.) and has no application under Occupational Safety and Health Act (29 USCS § 651 et seq.); under OSHA, effective date provision for construction industry standards is found at 29 CFR § 1910.17. Mayfair Constr. Co. (1977) OSHRC Docket No. 2171.

Agricultural operations are exempted from general industry standards by virtue of 29 CFR § 1928.21(b); employer's activities, as far as they entailed employees' climbing of ladders to unload feed into farmers' feed bins, which was performed on farmers' land and was integrally related to farmers' agricultural operations, were

Exhibit 48: Annotations to § 654 of title 29 in *U.S. Code Service.*

5. Constitutional Texts and Sources. The United States Constitution appears in numerous publications ranging from simple pamphlets to large annotated texts with full scholarly apparatus. It is also included in most subject compilations of federal and state statutes. The best separate edition had been that edited by Edward Corwin and published by the Library of Congress in 1953. Revised editions of this work by Lester Jayson were published in 1964 and 1973 with the title: *The Constitution of the United States of America, Analysis and Interpretation.* It includes the text of the Constitution along with case annotations and detailed discussions of each provision, its history and interpretation. Although pocket part supplementation is provided in the current edition, it is not sufficiently frequent. Recourse to other updating services is therefore essential.

The Constitution appears in the *U.S. Code*, the *U.S.C.A.* and the *U.S.C.S.*, although it is not an integral part of the *Code* itself. The *U.S.C.A.* and *U.S.C.S.* versions are, of course, heavily annotated with thousands of case abstracts, in the typical format of those code editions.

There is also a great historical literature concerning the original drafting, adoption and ratification of the Constitution. Among the most useful of these publications are the following collections:

J. Elliot, *The Debates, Resolutions and Other Proceedings, in Convention, on the Adoption of the Federal Constitution,* . . . , 4 volumes (Washington, 1827–1830).

Documentary History of the Constitution of the United States of America, 1786–1870, 5 volumes (Washington, U.S. Government Printing Office, 1894–1905).

Documents Illustrative of the Formation of the Union of the American States, by C.C. Tansill (Washington, U.S. Government Printing Office, 1927).

M. Farrand, *The Records of the Federal Convention of 1787,* 4 volumes (Yale University Press, 1937; reprinted in paperback, 1967).

M. Jensen, *Documentary History of the Ratification of the Constitution,* in progress, 5 volumes to date (State Historical Society of Wisconsin, 1976–).

W.F. Swindler, *Sources and Documents of U.S. Constitutions,* 11 volumes (Oceana Publications, 1973–date). Second Series in progress, *National Documents* (1982–date), which includes the Federal Constitution.

6. Looseleaf Services. A variety of looseleaf publications collect legal materials in specific subject areas and many of them, particularly those published by Bureau of National Affairs, Commerce Clearing House and Prentice-Hall, are kept up to date by weekly supplementation. Such looseleaf services invariably include statutes and offer one of the fastest means of access to new legislation. Since the statutes are usually annotated with abstracts of judicial and administrative decisions, and are accompanied by relevant administrative regulations and explanatory text, they are convenient sources for integrated research. Detailed and varied indexing enhances their usefulness. Looseleaf services are described more fully in Chapter VII below.

7. Subject Collections of Statutes. Another source of statutes in particular fields of interest is the subject compilations of laws published by various public and private agencies and groups. These include government departments, Congress itself, trade associations, public interest organizations, and commercial publishers. Such collections are particularly helpful to researchers in fields not covered by looseleaf services. However, they are not up-dated with the same frequency as looseleaf services and many in fact are never supplemented at all. Therefore, these publications must be used with caution and supplemented by other means. A convenient index to those collections which contain *state* laws is *Subject Compilations of State Laws, Research Guide and Annotated Bibliography,* by L. Foster and C. Boast (Greenwood Press, 1981).

STATE STATUTES

Most of the forms of publication of federal statutes, described above, also appear in the statutory law of the various states. There are slip laws; official editions of state session laws; state constitutions; and annotated and/or unannotated texts of the state codes. There are also the universal problems of providing for subject access to chronologically published laws and keeping up-to-date an ever-changing mass of legislation. In fact, the publication of state laws reproduces many of the achievements and difficulties of federal statutory publications. The finding aids and special features in the annotated codes for *some* of the states, however, are less well developed than those in the two annotated editions of the *U.S. Code.*

1. State Constitutions. State constitutions have developed a bibliography of their own because of their variety and legal importance. There is a looseleaf compilation of state constitutions called *Constitutions of the U.S.: National and State* (Oceana, 2d ed., 1974–75). Since 1980, this set has been augmented by a series of looseleaf indexes, with the collective title, *Index to Constitutions of the United States: National and State.* The first of these indexes is called *Fundamental Liberties and Rights: A Fifty State Index,* by B.F. Sachs, a sample page of which is shown in Exhibit 49.

The best sources for individual state constitutions, however, are still the annotated statutes of the individual states, where one can usually find the latest text of the constitution, along with annotations of court decisions interpreting and construing it. Popular pamphlet texts are also available in many states. Shepard's citators for the various states are useful in developing both legislative and judicial histories of state constitutions, as well as providing citations from the courts of each state to the United States Constitution.

LABOR

BLACKLISTING
Freedom to Obtain Employment, *see also, this title, below,* RIGHT TO WORK
ND I 23

BONDAGE
Vt I 1

COLLECTIVE BARGAINING
Fla I 6
Mo I 29
NJ I 19
NY I 17

COMMODITY
NY I 17

GENERAL DECLARATIONS
Freedom to obtain employment, *see this title, above,* BLACKLISTING; *see this title, below,* RIGHT TO WORK
W Va III 11
Wyo I 22

HEALTH AND SAFETY
NY I 18

Exhibit 49: Sample entries from *Index to Constitutions of the United States, National and State:* Release #1, *Fundamental Liberties and Rights.*

2. State Session Laws. Slip laws are issued in many of the states, but are rarely distributed to the public. However, every state has a session law publication which arranges chronologically the laws enacted at each sitting of its legislature, usually with a non-cumulative index for each volume or session. These chronological collections are similar to the *U.S. Statutes at Large* in form and purpose. They are initially the authoritative text of each state's laws and in most states never lose that status, since only rarely does the subject compilation acquire positive law status. In citing session laws, one must always include the year of the session. Without the year, the citation is meaningless. The session law volumes for all of the states are now also available on microfiche.

There is a considerable time lag in the publication of most state session laws and they are often delayed until long after the end of the session. In some states, the commercial publisher of the statutory compilation provides a "session law service" which gives access to new laws while the legislature is still sitting, very much as the *U.S. Code Congressional and Administrative News* and *U.S.C.S. Advance* do for congressional enactments.

3. State Codes. Since the indexes to state session laws do not cumulate, there is need for some means of subject access to relevant laws in force. All states now have subject compilations of their statutes, similar to the *U.S. Code,* which serve that function. These are usually commercially published, unofficial collections, which typically include annotations of court decisions on those statutes. For a few states, there is no unofficial edition and the state itself publishes an official subject compilation. A few other states have both an official and an unofficial edition of the code. As one might suspect, the better edited and more useful unofficial editions are gradually driving out the less elaborate (but usually less expensive) official sets. The *Bluebook* contains a useful table of the current codes for each state, with session law information as well.

The authority of the unofficial editions varies from state to state. These editions are usually accepted as at least *prima facie* evidence of the statutory law. They are rarely considered the "positive law" or authoritative text of statutes, but that distinction is becoming increasingly a matter of form rather than substance. One can usually determine the status of a subject compilation by looking for a certificate which indicates its authority in the front of each volume. Sometimes such information is supplied in the preface.

State statutes are annotated and supplemented in much the same way as federal statutes. The West Publishing Company's state codes are usually similar to *U.S.C.A.* in format and coverage. The best of them contain analytical notes, reference to historical sources, parallel tables, citations to attorney general opinions, cross references to relevant secondary materials, and other useful research material, in addition to the usual judicial annotations. Supplementation is generally by pocket part or looseleaf insertions, although West also provides quarterly pamphlet supplements and session law services for most of its codes.

4. Uniform Laws. As noted above, there has been a movement in this country for some years to secure enactment by the states of various uniform laws. It has been felt that in many fields there is unnecessary confusion and conflict because of widely different state statutes on the same subject. Sometimes this is a necessary reflection of the peculiar history, customs, economics or geography of the region, but in many cases there is no reasonable justification for these differences. The National Conference of Commissioners on the Uniform State Laws, founded in 1912, is a quasi-official body with representatives from every state, which meets annually to propose, draft, and promote uniform legislation. Over two hundred uniform laws have been approved by the National Conference, and now over one hundred of those acts have been passed by at least one state. Among the most widely known is the *Uniform Commercial Code* which has been adopted by virtually every state.

All of the uniform laws are compiled and published by West in one annotated set called *Uniform Laws Annotated* (Master edition, 1965–1975). Not only does this set contain every uniform law adopted by at least one state, along with the Commissioners' notes on these laws, but it also includes annotations to the court decisions of *every* state which has adopted and then litigated each law. These annotations are particularly useful in giving enacting states the benefit of the case law developed in those states having the same uniform law. The *U.L.A.* also contains tables indicating which states have adopted each law, variations in their adoptions, and other useful information. The set is kept up-to-date annually by pocket parts and is supplemented by the annual *Handbook of the National Conference of Commissioners on Uniform State Laws* which provides current information about new laws, discussions of pending and proposed laws, and recent adoptions.

The text of each uniform law can, of course, also be found in the statutes of each state which has adopted that law, usually with annotations on the law from the courts of that particular state. This source is particularly valuable since the uniform laws are frequently enacted in a form different from that proposed by the Commissioners.

5. Procedural Legislation and Court Rules. There are legal and bibliographic distinctions between procedural and substantive legislation. Procedural laws describe the procedures to be followed in the courts in effectuating one's legal rights and remedies. They concern the forms of action and defense, motion practice, time limitations, service of papers, hearing and trial arrangements, and all of the thousands of other details relating to the administration of legal business. These procedural requirements are frequently statutory in form, as in civil practice acts; many appear as non-statutory rules promulgated by the judiciary. In virtually all states, the procedural law is a combination of both statutes and rules.

Most statutory subject compilations include both substantive and procedural law, but in many states the procedural law is also separately published in unofficial services or manuals. These are typically annotated with court decisions and sometimes with sample forms to guide the practicing attorney. Such practice manuals are generally well supplemented or frequently revised.

Every state also has court rules which govern the operation of its courts. These tend to be even more specific than the civil practice acts or rules, including such things as hours of court, make-up of court calendars, place and times for filing legal papers, etc. Court rules are published in the following forms: (a) as issued, in the official state reports (sometimes indicated by a notation on the spine of the particular volume that it contains new rules); (b) in the state statutory compilations; and (c) in separate pamphlets issued by the particular court or by commercial publishers.

6. Local Law Sources. As we have seen, our legal system encompasses many different levels of jurisdiction—federal, state, county, town, city. Legislation is enacted by all of these units and there is a large literature of local ordinances, charters, and codes, which is usually poorly published, rarely annotated and infrequently supplemented.

Many of the larger cities in the United States now publish collections of their ordinances with some attempt at supplementation (e.g. *Philadelphia Code of Ordinances, New York City Charter and Administrative Code,* etc.). In a few states (e.g., Connecticut and New York), there has been a commendable improvement in the publication of municipal ordinances of smaller cities by specialized legal publishers. On the whole, however, the situation is still very bad and in many cities there is no accessible, up-to-date compilation of ordinances.

Generally, individual ordinances may be obtained at the county, city or town clerk's office, which may also be the only depository for all of the ordinances of that jurisdiction. The astute lawyer must become familiar with what is generally available in the area and then take steps to locate sources of further information. With the increasing importance of local law in many fields, such as environmental protection, welfare, housing, transportation, etc., better access to these sources is badly needed. The unavailability of local ordinances is a serious impediment to the proper administration of justice.

FINDING TOOLS FOR STATUTES

In addition to the subject compilations of statutes, there are other aids to statutory research. Among these are indexes of various kinds, which provide a direct topical approach to statutes, and tables which permit the researcher to convert citations from one form to another.

1. **Indexes to Federal Statutes.** Among the older retrospective indexes to federal laws are Beaman and MacNamara, *Index Analysis of the Federal Statutes, 1789–1873* and McClenon and Gilbert, *Index to the Federal Statutes, 1874–1931.* These cover only public, general laws, and are now useful only for historical research. The indexes to the *Revised Statutes* (1873 and 1878 editions) and to the various editions of the *U.S. Code* are necessary for searching those compilations.

There are indexes to statutes by legislative session in the volumes of the *Statutes at Large* and its unofficial editions, *U.S.C.C.A.N.* and *U.S.C.S. Advance,* described above. Indexes for the entire body of currently effective, public, general and permanent federal statutes can be found in the *U.S. Code, U.S. Code Annotated* and *U.S. Code Service.* These are probably the most frequently used of all statutory indexes, since most research is done in the latest subject compilations. The page of the *U.S. Code* index shown in Exhibit 50 below is typical of this group.

The *U.S. Code* can now also be searched by computer in either the LEXIS or WESTLAW data bases.

Exhibit 50: A page from the index to the official edition of the *U.S. Code.*

For federal statutes which have become commonly known by a popular name, there are popular name tables (similar to those described above for cases) which provide citations to their actual text. Such tables can be found in the *Shepard's Acts and Cases by Popular Names–Federal and State,* and in the designated volumes of the *U.S.C., U.S.C.A.* and *U.S. C.S.* Exhibit 51 illustrates the Shepard's table:

Occ FEDERAL AND STATE ACTS CITED BY POPULAR NAMES

Occupational Health Act
Mont. Rev. Code 1947, 69-4206 et seq.
Okla. Stat. 1971, Title 63, §691 et seq.

Occupational License Tax Act
Fla. Stat. 1977, 205.013 et seq.
La. Rev. Stat. 1950, 47:341 et seq.
N. C. Gen. Stat. 1943, §105-33 et seq.

Occupational Safety and Health Act of 1970
U. S. Code 1976 Title 29, §651 et seq.
Dec. 29, 1970, P. L. 91-596, 84 Stat. 1590

Occupational Safety and Health Act
Az. Rev. Stat. 1956, §23-401 et seq.
Cal. Labor Code §6300 et seq.
Colo. Rev. Stat. 1973, 8-11-100.1 et seq.
Haw. Rev. Stat. 1976, §396-1 et seq.
Ind. Code 1976, 22-8-1.1-1 et seq.
Md. Anno. Code 1957, Art. 89, §28 et seq.
Mich. Comp. Laws 1970, 408.1001 et seq.
Min. Stat. 1976, 182.65 et seq.
N. C. Gen. Stat. 1943, §95-126 et seq.
Nev. Rev. Stat. 1973 Reprint, 618.005 et seq.
N. M. Stat. Anno. 1953, 59-14-1 et seq.
Okla. Stat. 1971, Title 40, §401 et seq.
P. R. Laws Anno. 1954, Title 29, §361 et seq.
Ten. Code Anno. 1955, 50-501 et seq.
Utah Code Anno. 1953, 35-9-1 et seq.
Wyo. Stat. 1957, §27-274 et seq.

Occupational Tax Wagering Stamp Act
U. S. Code 1976 Title 26, §4411 et seq.
Aug. 16, 1954, c. 736, 68A Stat. 1

Occupational Therapy Licensing Act
Ga. Code 1933, 84-7101 et seq.

Occupying Claimants Act
U. S., June 1, 1874, c. 200, 18 Stat. 50
Ill. Rev. Stat. 1977, Ch. 45, §56
Ind. Code 1976, 34-1-49-1 et seq.
Iowa Code 1977, 560.1 et seq.
Kan. Stat. Anno. 60-1004, 60-1005
Ky. Rev. Stat. 1971, 381.460 et seq.
Min. Stat. 1976, 559.10 et seq.
Mo. Rev. Stat. 1969, 524.160
Neb. Rev. Stat. 1943, 76-301 et seq.
Ohio Rev. Code 1953, 5303.07 et seq.
Okla. Stat. 1971, Title 12, §1481 et seq.
Pa. Purdons Stat., Title 72, §5875
Utah Code Anno. 1953, 57-6-1 et seq.

Ocean County Oyster Act of 1886
N. J. Laws 1886, p. 343

Ocean Exposition Appropriations Authorization Act of 1973
U. S., Jan. 8, 1974, P. L. 93-304, 88 Stat. 194

Ocean Mail Act
U. S., Mar. 3, 1891, c. 519, 26 Stat. 830
U. S., May 22, 1928, c. 675, 45 Stat. 689, §§401 to 414

Ocean Science Center Act
Ga. Code 1933, 43-1301 et seq.

Oceanographic Commission Act
N. H. Rev. Stat. 1955, 12-C:1 et seq.

Oceans and Atmosphere Advisory Committee Act
U. S. Code 1976 Title 33, §857-13 et seq.
July 5, 1977, P. L. 95-63, 91 Stat. 265

Exhibit 51: Shepard's *Acts and Cases by Popular Names—Federal and State.*

2. Parallel Conversion and Transfer Tables. In view of the varied forms which statutes take, it is necessary to provide parallel reference tables from one form or stage of a law to another form or a later stage of the same law. The following is a list of the most commonly used tables or aids and where they can be found:

(a) **Bill number to public law number:**

(1) In legislative status tables which include enactments (e.g., CCH *Congressional Index, Congressional Calendars, Digest of Public General Bills, Congressional Monitor, Congressional Information Service/Index,* and *Congressional Record*).

(2) *U.S.C.C.A.N.:* Table of Enacted Bills.

(3) *Statutes at Large:* List of Bills Enacted into Public Law (beginning with 88th Congress, 1st Sess., 1963).

(b) **Public law number to bill number:**

(1) Slip laws and *Statutes at Large* at the head of the text.

(2) Public Law Table of *Digest of Public General Bills.*

(3) *Daily Digest* of *Congressional Record:* History of Bills Enacted into Public Law (see Exhibit 64 below).

(4) *U.S.C.C.A.N.:* Table of Public Laws.

(5) CCH *Congressional Index:* Table of Enactments.

(6) *Congressional Information Service/Index.*

(c) **Bill number or public law number to Statutes at Large:**

(1) Text of Slip Law (since 1951).

(2) *Statutes at Large:* List of Public Laws.

(3) *U.S.C.C.A.N.:* Slip Law and Table of Public Laws.

(4) *U.S. Code: Statutes at Large* table (see Exhibit 43 above).

(d) **Bill number or public law number to Code:**

(1) *U.S.C.C.A.N.:* Table of Classifications.

(2) *U.S. Code: Statutes at Large* table, which also lists statutes by their public law number (Exhibit 43 above at page 119.

(e) ***U.S. Code* sections to *Statutes at Large*:** Use parenthetical references following text of *Code* section.

3. State Statutory Finding Tools. Research in state statutes involves very much the same techniques as in federal statutes, although the indexes, tables and other research aids are frequently less sophisticated in state materials.

State statutes can be searched in the following ways:

(a) By subject—via the general index of the various annotated codes and by the annual indexes in the session law volumes;

(b) By retrospective, cumulative statutory indexes which have been published from time to time in a few of the states;

(c) By popular name tables which are provided by Shepard's *Acts and Cases by Popular Names . . .*, and in the annotated codes of some states.

Cross references for state statutes, similar to those for federal, are provided in the following ways:

(a) **From session law citation to code:** in the tables of the annotated codes.

(b) **From code to session law:** usually following the text of the code section in a footnote or parenthetical reference.

(c) **From an earlier code edition to a later revision or vice-versa:** by parallel conversion tables in the tables volume or individual title volumes of the annotated codes.

4. **Supplementation and Updating of Statutes.** As we have noted, laws are passed by Congress every year and by the various state legislatures in annual or biennial sessions. Hence there is need for constant supplementation to be sure that the statutory texts reflect the latest changes. A compilation of statutes which does not have internal supplementation is almost useless, unless it can be easily updated by some other means. Statutory supplementation is ordinarily provided by pocket parts inserted annually in the back of each volume; by pamphlets, such as the quarterly supplements to the *U.S.C.A.;* or by looseleaf, as in those few states which issue their codes in that form (e.g. Alaska and Nevada). Statutes of some of the states are also updated by *session law services* which

provide advance sheet pamphlets while the legislature is in session.

Shepard's state citators enable the researcher to determine whether there have been any changes in a statutory text, thereby updating the statute, but, of course, not providing the actual text of any changes recorded therein.

5. Methods of Access to Statutory Material. Judicial decisions, as noted previously, can be located by their case name, by the legal concept involved or by descriptive factual catchwords. Statutes can be approached in the same three ways, that is (a) by a citation table or popular name table; (b) through the relevant legal concept, by selecting the apparently pertinent title of the code and using its analytical breakdowns to find the appropriate section; or (c) using the statutory word indexes to get directly to the relevant sections. The subject indexes to the federal and state statutory codes are in fact the most commonly used means of access to statutes. The circuitous approach (b) suffers from the same disadvantage as approaching a case digest by its broad legal divisions rather than through the descriptive word index. It is almost always faster to use method (c) based on indexes which provide quick reference to relevant sections by specific catchwords and phrases.

The two computerized legal research services, LEXIS and WESTLAW, have added an important new dimension to research in federal statutes. For state statutes, however, their effect has been minimal. The *U.S. Code* can now be rapidly searched by computer through both of these services by using specific combinations of words or phrases to formulate a search inquiry. Both LEXIS and WESTLAW also facilitate searching of federal statutes through their specialized data bases in fields such as federal taxation, labor law, and securities regulation.

With regard to state statutes, the computer capability is less promising. LEXIS has offered searching of statutes for four states, but now seems to be diminishing rather than increasing that coverage. WESTLAW has not yet added state statutes to its data bases and is still uncertain about doing so.

A new Commerce Clearing House computer service, *Electronic Legislative Search System,* offers searching of both federal and state enactments and legislative history, but only on a current basis.

CITATORS FOR STATUTORY MATERIALS

Shepard's publishes statutory citators which perform much the same function as their case citators, although the former are somewhat more difficult to use because of the different statutory forms. There is a statutory citator for every state and for federal laws, with the usual advance sheet supplementation.

On the federal level, *Shepard's United States Citations* includes entries for *U.S. Code* sections and for provisions in the *Statutes at Large* which have not been incorporated into the *Code.* Exhibits 52 and 53 explain those two types of coverage.

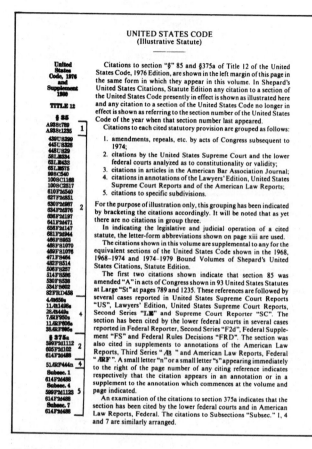

UNITED STATES CODE
(Illustrative Statute)

United States Code, 1976 and Supplement 1980

TITLE 12

§ 85

1
A93St789
A93St1235

2
439US299
445US328
448US29
58LE534
63LE433
65LE575
99SC540
100SC1168
100SC2517
610F2d540
627F2d851
630F2d987
634F2d376
636F2d197
641F2d471
656F2d147
681F2d944
466FS953
468FS1070
469FS1076
471FS464
482FS514
506FS257
514FS586
530FS538
534FS602
82FRD458

4
4A3650s
11A31498s
28A3449s
7ARF950s
11ARF608s
38ARF895s

§ 375a

2
599F2d1112
605F2d102
614F2d488

4
51ARF444n

5
Subsec. 1
614F2d488
Subsec. 4
599F2d1123
614F2d488
Subsec. 7
614F2d488

Citations to section "§" 85 and §375a of Title 12 of the United States Code, 1976 Edition, are shown in the left margin of this page in the same form in which they appear in this volume. In Shepard's United States Citations, Statute Edition any citation to a section of the United States Code presently in effect is shown as illustrated here and any citation to a section of the United States Code no longer in effect is shown as referring to the section number of the United States Code of the year when that section number last appeared.

Citations to each cited statutory provision are grouped as follows:

1. amendments, repeals, etc. by acts of Congress subsequent to 1974;
2. citations by the United States Supreme Court and the lower federal courts analyzed as to constitutionality or validity;
3. citations in articles in the American Bar Association Journal;
4. citations in annotations of the Lawyers' Edition, United States Supreme Court Reports and of the American Law Reports;
5. citations to specific subdivisions.

For the purpose of illustration only, this grouping has been indicated by bracketing the citations accordingly. It will be noted that as yet there are no citations in group three.

In indicating the legislative and judicial operation of a cited statute, the letter-form abbreviations shown on page xiii are used.

The citations shown in this volume are supplemental to any for the equivalent sections of the United States Code shown in the 1968, 1968–1974 and 1974–1979 Bound Volumes of Shepard's United States Citations, Statute Edition.

The first two citations shown indicate that section 85 was amended "A" in acts of Congress shown in 93 United States Statutes at Large "St" at pages 789 and 1235. These references are followed by several cases reported in United States Supreme Court Reports "US", Lawyers' Edition, United States Supreme Court Reports, Second Series "LE" and Supreme Court Reporter "SC". The section has been cited by the lower federal courts in several cases reported in Federal Reporter, Second Series "F2d", Federal Supplement "FS" and Federal Rules Decisions "FRD". The section was also cited in supplements to annotations of the American Law Reports, Third Series "A3" and American Law Reports, Federal "ARF". A small letter "n" or a small letter "s" appearing immediately to the right of the page number of any citing reference indicates respectively that the citation appears in an annotation or in a supplement to the annotation which commences at the volume and page indicated.

An examination of the citations to section 375a indicates that the section has been cited by the lower federal courts and in American Law Reports, Federal. The citations to Subsections "Subsec." 1, 4 and 7 are similarly arranged.

Exhibit 52: Explanation in Shepard's *United States Citations*, for Shepardizing the *U.S. Code*.

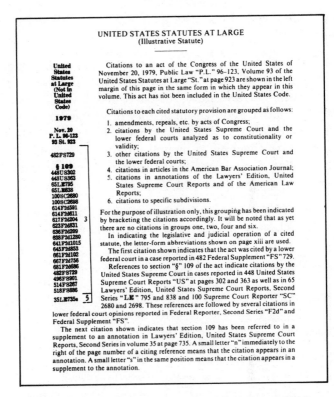

UNITED STATES STATUTES AT LARGE
(Illustrative Statute)

United States Statutes at Large (Not in United States Code)

1979

Nov. 20
P. L. 96-123
93 St. 923

482FS729

§ 109
448US302
448US363
65LE795
65LE838
100SC2680
100SC2698
614F2d591
614F2d611
617F2d204 3
623F2d831
636F2d209
638F2d1280
641F2d1015
645F2d853
661F2d102
667F2d756
681F2d686
482FS729
496FS901
514FS267
518FS886
35LE735s 5

Citations to an act of the Congress of the United States of November 20, 1979, Public Law "P.L." 96-123, Volume 93 of the United States Statutes at Large "St." at page 923 are shown in the left margin of this page in the same form in which they appear in this volume. This act has not been included in the United States Code.

Citations to each cited statutory provision are grouped as follows:

1. amendments, repeals, etc. by acts of Congress;
2. citations by the United States Supreme Court and the lower federal courts analyzed as to constitutionality or validity;
3. other citations by the United States Supreme Court and the lower federal courts;
4. citations in articles in the American Bar Association Journal;
5. citations in annotations of the Lawyers' Edition, United States Supreme Court Reports and of the American Law Reports;
6. citations to specific subdivisions.

For the purpose of illustration only, this grouping has been indicated by bracketing the citations accordingly. It will be noted that as yet there are no citations in groups one, two, four and six.

In indicating the legislative and judicial operation of a cited statute, the letter-form abbreviations shown on page xiii are used.

The first citation shown indicates that the act was cited by a lower federal court in a case reported in 482 Federal Supplement "FS" 729.

References to section "§" 109 of the act indicate citations by the United States Supreme Court in cases reported in 448 United States Supreme Court Reports "US" at pages 302 and 363 as well as in 65 Lawyers' Edition, United States Supreme Court Reports, Second Series "LE" 795 and 838 and 100 Supreme Court Reporter "SC" 2680 and 2698. These references are followed by several citations in lower federal court opinions reported in Federal Reporter, Second Series "F2d" and Federal Supplement "FS".

The next citation shown indicates that section 109 has been referred to in a supplement to an annotation in Lawyers' Edition, United States Supreme Court Reports, Second Series in volume 35 at page 735. A small letter "n" immediately to the right of the page number of a citing reference means that the citation appears in an annotation. A small letter "s" in the same position means that the citation appears in a supplement to the annotation.

Exhibit 53: Explanation in Shepard's *United States Citations*, for Shepardizing the *Statutes at Large.*

In the Shepard's state citators, statutes are usually listed by their citations in the latest code edition. Even if the code is used as the basis of listing, there will still be many statutes not in the code which will be listed in Shepard's by their *session law* citation. Citators for state legislation are similar in format to those for federal statutes, as illustrated in Exhibits 52 and 53 above.

Shepard's statutory citators can be used and, in fact, often *must* be used for the following purposes: to verify the current status of particular laws; to trace the legislative and judicial history of particular laws to determine whether they have been changed or affected by later enactments or judicial interpretations; and to develop further research leads to court decisions, attorney general opinions or legal periodical articles.

Shepard's statutory citators typically cover the following classes of cited and citing materials:

Cited Material	**Citing Material**
Constitutions	Later statutes and legislative changes
Codes	
Session laws	Cases
Treaties	Legal periodicals
Administrative regulations	Opinions of the Attorney General
Municipal charters	*A.L.R.* annotations
Local ordinances	
Court rules	
Jury instructions	

Shepard's uses the following symbols to indicate significant actions which have been taken with respect to a particular statute either by later legislative changes or court decisions:

ABBREVIATIONS—ANALYSIS

Form of Statute

Amend.	Amendment
App.	Appendix
Art.	Article
Ch.	Chapter
Cl.	Clause
Ex. Ord.	Executive Order
H.C.R.	House Concurrent Resolution
No.	Number
¶	Paragraph
P.L.	Public Law
Pr.L.	Private Law
Proc.	Proclamation
Pt.	Part
Res.	Resolution
§	Section
St.	Statutes at Large
Subch.	Subchapter
Subcl.	Subclause
Subd.	Subdivision
Sub ¶	Subparagraph
Subsec.	Subsection
Vet. Reg.	Veterans' Regulations

Operation of Statute

Legislative

A	(amended)	Statute amended.
Ad	(added)	New section added.
E	(extended)	Provisions of an existing statute extended in their application to a later statute, or allowance of additional time for performance of duties required by a statute within a limited time.
L	(limited)	Provisions of an existing statute declared not to be extended in their application to a later statute.
R	(repealed)	Abrogation of an existing statute.
Re-en	(re-enacted)	Statute re-enacted.
Rn	(renumbered)	Renumbering of existing sections.
Rp	(repealed in part)	Abrogation of part of an existing statute.
Rs	(repealed and superseded)	Abrogation of an existing statute and substitution of new legislation therefor.
Rv	(revised)	Statute revised.
S	(superseded)	Substitution of new legislation for an existing statute not expressly abrogated.
Sd	(suspended)	Statute suspended.
Sdp	(suspended in part)	Statute suspended in part.
Sg	(supplementing)	New matter added to an existing statute.
Sp	(superseded in part)	Substitution of new legislation for part of an existing statute not expressly abrogated.
Va	(validated)	

Judicial

C	Constitutional.
U	Unconstitutional.
Up	Unconstitutional in part.
V	Void or invalid.
Va	Valid.
Vp	Void or invalid in part.

NOTES

Absence from any bound volume or cumulative supplement of a reference to a statutory provision indicates that the provision has not been cited within the scope of that volume or cumulative supplement.

A reference enclosed in parentheses immediately following a reference to a statutory provision identifies the act from which the provision originates.

Exhibit 54: Shepard's abbreviations for statutory materials, appearing in its *United States Citations*.

Although Shepard's is the primary and indispensable citator in American legal research, there are other citators which may be useful for limited purposes. Looseleaf services frequently provide a citator of sorts for statutes in their fields. Because of the prompt supplementation of these services, they often inform the subscribers of changes in particular laws more quickly than that information is conveyed by Shepard's. In addition, the looseleaf services provide the text of the statute itself which can not be found in Shepard's. However, looseleaf services exist for only some subjects and even in those areas do not offer as complete coverage of citations to cases and other materials as does Shepard's.

For local ordinances, Shepard's offers its *Ordinance Law Annotations* (1969–1970, 6 vols.), which digests leading American state decisions that interpret or apply city and county ordinances. These annotations are arranged alphabetically by 157 broad topics and then subdivided by more specific subjects. It provides a unique research tool which is closer to a digest than to the usual Shepard's citator and is kept up to date by annual pocket parts. (See Exhibit 55.)

§ 16. Prohibiting Most Businesses

A Sunday closing ordinance prohibiting most businesses from operating on Sunday is not unconstitutional as violating any provision of the 1st Amendment of the U.S. Constitution, or as impinging on freedom of conscience or compelling or denying the observance of any religious duty.

NC State v McGee (1953) 237 NC 633, 75 SE2d 783.

D. INVALID SUNDAY CLOSING

§ 17. When Enabling Statute Is Void

An ordinance restricting or regulating the carrying on of business on Sunday, which derives its legislative grant from an invalid statute, is itself void.

NC High Point Surplus v Pleasants (1965) 264 NC 650, 142 SE2d 697.

§ 18. Discriminatory Closing

An ordinance making it unlawful to carry on certain businesses on Sunday is invalid where it prohibits the exercise of businesses or occupations legitimate and lawful within themselves, which do not carry inherent reasons for special discrimination, while allowing general privileges to similar occupations.

Ariz Elliott v State (1926) 29 Ariz 389, 242 P 340, 46 ALR 284.

An ordinance may prohibit the conducting of businesses or occupations on Sunday, except those of necessity or charity, on the ground that the peace, good order, good government, and welfare of the inhabitants will be promoted. But if such an ordinance is discriminatory or amounts to class or special legislation, it is not authorized.

Colo Allen v Colorado Springs (1937) 101 Colo 498, 75 P2d 141.

An ordinance prohibiting the operation of any business on Sunday, but excepting motels, restaurants, eating places, drug, tobacco and confectionery stores, news dealers, ice dealers, shoe shine parlors, garages, gasoline filling stations, telephone exchanges, telegraph offices, and moving picture theaters, is invalid as arbitrary and discriminatory,

Exhibit 55: Shepard's *Ordinance Law Annotations,* showing cases digested under the topic "Sunday Laws."

Shepard's also provides coverage of local ordinances in two ways in its various state statutory citators. The ordinances of the municipalities of each state are included as cited material in the statutory citator for that state, with judicial citations, legislative references, attorney general opinions and legal periodical articles listed as citing material where appropriate. (See Exhibit 56.) In addition, subject indexes to local ordinances are included in the statutory citators. (See Exhibit 57 below.) These indexes enable the researcher to identify the relevant ordinance, which can then be located in the citator section for ordinances and shepardized there.

Unfortunately, LEXIS and WESTLAW do not yet include Shepard's statutory citators in their services, and AUTO–CITE does not cover statutes either. Such computer coverage would be a valuable addition in the future.

REVISED ORDINANCES OF BOSTON, 1961 (As Amended, 1963) **Ch. 29**

Ch. 1
§ 4
Subd. 11
City Markets
Faneuil Hall Market–Limits
1937C90
Subd. 12
City Markets
General Markets–Limits
342Mas626
174NE670
§ 5
Seal
Official–Form
1965C656 [§7
§ 16
Departments
Creation–Control
191Mas292
77NE888

Ch. 2
§ 1
Mayor
Department Heads–Appointment–Term
303Mas545
22NE190
7AG39

Ch. 3
§ 5
Mayor
Salary
1945C4
§ 12
Officers
Subordinates–Employment–Compensation
303Mas547
22NE191
§ 17
Officers
Tort Lia-

Ch. 6
§ 1
Auditing Department
Powers–Duties
342Mas69
172NE98

Ch. 7
Auditorium
Commission–Created
338Mas246
154NE704

Ch. 14
§ 1
Fire Department
Maintenance–Regulations
101US17
25LE980

Ch. 15
§ 1
Health
Department–Commissioner–Powers–Duties
257Mas580
154NE267
322Mas539
78NE632
§ 2
Health
Department–Divisions–Deputy Commissioners
241Mas406
135NE376
257Mas580
154NE267

Ch. 16
§ 2
City Hospitals

Ch. 19
§ 2
Municipal Corporations
Park Commissioners–Authority–Statutory
321Mas336
73NE241
Park Department
Commissioners–Duties–Powers
204Mas12
90NE360
§ 10
Parks
Frontages–Restrictions
343Mas37
176NE24
Va346Mas [185
Va191NE [129

Ch. 21
§ 1
et seq.
Public Works Department
Commissioner–Qualifications–Duties–Powers
191Mas292
77NE888
228Mas14
116NE969
Refuse–Collection Charge
328Mas270
103NE238
–Disposal
304Mas102
23NE122
§ 4
Streets

§ 9
Public Works Department
Commissioner–Street Work–Permits
323Mas538
83NE174
'50-51AG23
Streets
Obstructions–Excavations–Permits
188Mas57
74NE297
197Mas332
83NE1110
201Mas96
87NE201
249Mas182
143NE902
292Mas215
197NE881
296Mas443
6NE348
300Mas253
15NE227
Opening–Permit
292Mas215
197NE881
296Mas442
6NE348
Subd. 1
et seq.
Streets
Opening–Regulations
182Mas400
65NE835
Subd. 2
Streets
Obstructions–Excavations–Protection of Public
348Mas736
205NE707
§ 10
Drains
Permits–Public Drains
340Mas546
165NE116

Pipes–Permits
'50-51AG23
§ 18
Cellars
Leakage–City Liability
334Mas401
135NE659
Steam Pipes
Under Streets–City Indemnified
260F2d873
§ 20
Public Works Department
Commissioner–Sidewalks–Excavations–Filling
'50-51AG23
§ 22
et seq.
Water Supply
Municipal–Management–Provisions
41F23
§ 22
Water Supply
Board–Powers–Contracts–Procedure–Limitations
41F23
§ 28
Subd. 2
Water Supply
Discontinuance–Liability
264Mas460
163NE82
§ 36
Public Works Department

197Mas200
83NE415

Ch. 29
§ 10
et seq.
Sewage
Disposition–Restrictions
233Mas150
123NE505
§ 14
Refuse
Disposition–Regulation
191Mas292
77NE888
233Mas277
123NE684
328Mas269
103NE238
§ 17
Drainage
Connections–Permit
286Mas416
190NE788
§ 19
Peddling
Regulations
36BUR241
§ 36
Streets
Passage–Obstruction–Loitering
325Mas519
91NE666
43MQ(2)44
§ 37
Advertisements
Placards–Permit
279Mas73
180NE615
308Mas371
32NE684
308Mas592
33NE522
15BUR359
43MQ(2)44
Placards
Carrying
299Mas357
13NE21

314Mas520
50NE776
§ 48
Streets
Use–Throwing of Missiles–Prohibition
197Mas364
83NE868
§ 49
Streets
Snow Removal–Regulations
229Mas300
118NE263
§ 52
Animals
Running at Large–Prohibition
270Mas420
170NE398
Horses
Regulations–Control
288Mas162
192NE503
§ 58
Streets
Vaults–Cellars–Liability of Owner
304Mas18
22NE627
§ 62
Streets
Sidewalks–Obstructions
310Mas92
37NE244
§ 69
Hackneys
Licenses
'56-57AG20
§ 70
et seq.
Street Railways
Operation–Control
263Mas578
161NE609
–Regulations

23NE860
309Mas221
34NE657
§ 71
Street Railways
Operation–Speed–Intersections
215Mas173
102NE330
222Mas271
110NE266
§ 73
Street Railways
Operation–Descending Grades
263Mas577
161NE609
§ 80
Street Railways
Operation–Stopping at Intersections
215Mas173
102NE330
§ 85
et seq.
Public Grounds
Use–Regulations
285Mas323
189NE63
289Mas201
193NE823
321Mas336
73NE241
167US43
42LE71
17SC731
307US514
83LE1436
59SC963
148F522
171F734
100F2d694
9BUR129
56HLR522
34NYL840
§ 86
Permits
Public Speaking
101F2d785
25FS150

Exhibit 56: Local ordinances (of the City of Boston) listed as cited material in *Shepard's Massachusetts Citations,* illustrating such coverage in various state statutory citators.

INDEX TO ORDINANCES A-B

A

Advertisements
Placards
Permit
Boston Rev. Ord. '61, Ch. 29, §37
Restrictions ....Lynn
Restrictions
Streets
Springfield Rev. Ord. '63, §22-66

Ambulances
Municipal
Contract for Service ....Lowell

Animals
Running at Large
Prohibition
Boston Rev. Ord. '61, Ch. 29, §52

Appropriations
Bond Issue
Finance Committee ....Rockland
Validity
Contract—Public Building..Brookline

Assessments
Public Construction
Sewers—Sidewalks—Collection
Cambridge

Assessors
Board
Chairman—Designation .....Waltham
Members—Appointment .....Waltham
Election
Term ....Chicopee

Auditing Department
Powers
Duties..Boston Rev. Ord. '61, Ch. 6, §1

Auditorium
Commission
Created ...Boston Rev. Ord. '61, Ch. 7

Awnings
Erection
Consent of Mayor and Aldermen
Lawrence Rev. Ord. '54, §24-30
License
Erection ....Boston
—Restrictions ....Boston

B

Billboards
Regulations
Consent ....Boston
Lowell
Erection—Permit ....Falmouth
Proximity to Parks—Restriction
Concord
Restrictions ....Concord
Milton
Size—Location ....Concord

Board of Health
Hospitals
Management ....Fall River
Membership ....Fall River

Bond Issue
Order Authorizing .... Quincy

Bowling Alley
License ....Winchester

Bridges
Municipal
Management—Provisions
Boston Rev. Ord '61, Ch. 21, §5

Buildings
Alterations
Application—Notice ....Medford
Permit—Application ....Wakefield
—Application—Conformity to
Ordinances ....Malden
(Continued)

Buildings—(Continued)
Permits ....Milton
Supervision—Regulations .....Boston
Basement
Grade Limitation. ....Cambridge
Board of Appeal
Composition ....Springfield
Creation ....Taunton
Building Line
Establishment ....Pittsfield
Code
Permits ....Duxbury
—Approval ....Brookline
Provisions ....Billerica
Boston
Brookline
Natick
Violations—Use of Building ..Sudbury
Construction
Application—Accompanying
Papers ....Wayland
—Filing ....Brookline
—Form—Contents ....Wayland
Bay Windows—Front Yards.Waltham
—Measurement ....Waltham
—Side Yards................Waltham
Permit ....Somerville
—City Council—Duties ......Medford
—Requirements ....Bedford
—Requirements ....Wayland
Roofcovering ....Somerville
Setback—Requirements ....Dennis
Specifications—Bricks .....Cambridge
Walls—Brick—Thickness . Springfield
Width of Foundations.....Fall River
Definitions
Basement ....Brockton
Cellar ....Brockton
Story ....Brockton
Erection
Permit—First Fire Zone ......Boston
Halls
Stairs—Lighting ....Springfield
Inspector
Duties ....Bedford
Dennis
Lawrence Rev. Ord '54, §6-1 et seq.
Permit
Application ....Springfield
Permits
Application—Contents—Approval
Medford
Milton
—Plans ....Newton
Denial—Appeal ....Belmont
Dennis
—Conditions ....Stockbridge
Expiration ....Chelmsford
Garages ....Newton
Plans and Specifications—Filing
Lowell
Malden
Requirements ....Belmont
Variances—Application .....Billerica
Regulations ....Boston
Springfield
Appeal ....Acton
Enforcement ....Belmont
Violation—Penalty ....Newton
Superintendent
Appointment—Term
Lawrence Rev. Ord. '54, §6-8
Tenement Houses
Restricted Heights.........Somerville

Buses
Fare
Limitation ....Springfield
License
Application
Springfield Rev. Ord. '63, §5-2
Bond ....Springfield
—Surety—Increase ....Springfield
Fee ....Springfield
Necessity
Springfield Rev. Ord. '63, §5-1
Plates—Requirements ....Springfield
Requirements
Springfield Rev. Ord. '63, §5-1 et seq.
Specified Route
Springfield Rev. Ord. '63, §5-3
Temporary ....Springfield
(Continued)

See note on page 633 635

Exhibit 57: Subject index to local ordinances (from *Shepard's Massachusetts Citations*), appearing in Shepard's various state statutory citators.

CONCLUSION

In statutory research, one should be aware of the various forms of published legislation which are available for that jurisdiction (constitutions, session laws, code editions, procedural acts, treaties on the federal level, interstate compacts on the state level, procedural acts, and delegated legislation such as court rules, administrative regulations, and local ordinances). The relative authority of the session laws and the code should be ascertained, and the statutory provisions should be updated through whatever supplementation is available. Cross references should be pursued to be certain that all relevant sections are located, and the results Shepardized.

Finally, extensive aids to interpretation of the statute should be identified and studied. These may include judicial decisions applying or construing the statutes, attorney general opinions on the meaning of the provision, or documents revealing the legislature's intent in enacting the law. Research in legislative history for that last purpose is described in the Chapter that follows.

CHAPTER V

LEGISLATIVE HISTORY

The ambiguities which occur so frequently in the language of our laws require lawyers and scholars to locate legislative documents from which they can learn the intent of Congress or a state legislature. Statutory research also often involves the investigation of the pre-enactment history of an existing statute or the current status of a proposed law which is then under consideration in the legislature. Both of these inquiries require the study of what we call "legislative history". There are thus two main purposes in this area of research: (a) to determine the meaning or intent of a particular *enactment* from the documents of its consideration by the legislature; and (b) to ascertain the status of a pending *bill* during the legislative session, or to follow the steps in its legislative progress.

GUIDES AND REFERENCE AIDS FOR LEGISLATIVE HISTORY

Before describing the actual sources and research tools used in legislative history, it will be helpful to note a few guides and reference aids which can facilitate work in this field.

G.B. Folsom, *Legislative History: Research for the Interpretation of Laws* (University Press of Virginia, 1972; reprinted, Fred B. Rothman, 1979). A detailed introduction to research in legislative history, with specialized chapters on the legislative history of tax laws, constitutional provisions, and treaties.

L.F. Schmeckebier & R.B. Eastin, *Government Publications and Their Use* (Brookings Institution, 2d revised ed., 1969) Ch. 6, "Congressional Publications." Although outdated for current publications, it provides detailed descriptions of the main series of legislative documents used in research for earlier periods.

Monthly Catalog of U.S. Government Publications (U.S. Govt. Printing Office, 1895-date). The *Monthly Catalog* is the most complete listing of documents of the federal government, including *official* sources of legislative history except congressional bills. It is issued monthly, but there is often a substantial time lag between publication and listing, during which the supply of documents may be exhausted. The Monthly Catalog lists some publications which are not for sale, and occasionally omits significant documents. Exhibit 58 below illustrates a page from the *Catalog,* with a hearing on the Occupational Safety and Health Act indicated. Indexing is provided monthly, with annual cumulations, and there are decennial indexes for 1941–50 and 1951–60, five year indexes for 1961–65, 1966–70, and 1971–76, and a five year index for 1976 to 1980 on microfiche.

For information about individuals, offices and the organizational structure of Congress, see the annual *Official Congressional Directory* (U.S. Govt. Printing Office, 1809-date); the unofficial

Congressional Staff Directory (Cong. Staff Directory, 1959-date), annual; the *Congressional Yellow Book* (Washington Monitor), annual; and *Guide to the Congress* (Congressional Quarterly, 3d ed., 1982).

G.P.O., 1981. iv, 132 p. : ill. ; 24 cm. ●Item 1043-A, 1043-B (microfiche) 1. Marihuana — Physiological effect. 2. Drug abuse — United States. I. Title. 82-601252 OCLC 08186037

82-12227

Y 4.L 11/4:L 97

United States. Congress. Senate. Committee on Labor and Human Resources. Subcommittee on Labor.

Black lung benefits and revenue amendments of 1981 : hearing before the Subcommittee on Labor of the Committee on Labor and Human Resources, United States Senate, Ninety-seventh Congress, first session on S. 1922 ... December 14, 1981. — Washington : U.S. G.P.O., 1981 [i.e. 1982] iv, 211 p. ; 24 cm. ●Item 1043-A, 1043-B (microfiche) 1. Coal-miners — Legal status, laws, etc. — United States. 2. Lungs — Dust diseases. 3. Compensation (Law) — United States. I. Title. OCLC 08210881

82-12228

Y 4.L 11/4:M 46

United States. Congress. Senate. Committee on Labor and Human Resources.

Preventive medicine and health promotion, 1981 : hearings before the Committee on Labor and Human Resources, United States Senate, Ninety-seventh Congress, first session, on examination on the most important aspect of medical care, the prevention of poor health and disease, July 16 and 17, 1981. — Washington : U.S. G.P.O., 1981. v, 347 p. : ill. ; 24 cm. Includes bibliographical references. ●Item 1043-A, 1043-B (microfiche) 1. Medicine, Preventive — United States. 2. Health planning — United States. I. Title. 82-601069 OCLC 08223262

82-12229

Y 4.L 11/4:N 72/981-11

United States. Congress. Senate. Committee on Labor and Human Resources.

Nomination : hearing before the Committee on Labor and Human Resources, United States Senate, Ninety-seventh Congress, first session, on Francis S.M. Hodsoll, of Virginia, to be chairman of the National Endowment for the Arts, November 6, 1981. — Washington : U.S. G.P.O., 1981. ii, 41 p. ; 24 cm. ●Item 1043-A, 1043-B (microfiche) 1. Hodsoll, Francis Samuel Monaise. 2. National Endowment for the Arts — Appointments, promotions, salaries, etc. I. Title. 82-601171 OCLC 08185927

82-12230

Y 4.L 11/4:Oc 1/981

United States. Congress. Senate. Committee on Labor and Human Resources. Subcommittee on Investigations and General Oversight.

Oversight on the administration of the Occupational Safety and Health Act, 1981 : joint hearing before the Subcommittee on Investigations and General Oversight and the Subcommittee on Labor of the Committee on Labor and Human Resources, United States Senate, Ninety-seventh Congress, first session, on oversight on the status of policy development and program management and operation of the Occupational Safety and Health Administration, September 23, 1981. — Washington : U.S. G.P.O., 1981 [i.e. 1982] iv, 369 p. : ill. ; 24 cm. Includes bibliographical references. ●Item 1043-A, 1043-B (microfiche) 1. United States. Occupational Safety and Health Administration. 2. Industrial hygiene — United States. 3. Industrial safety — United States. I. United States. Congress. Senate. Committee on Labor and Human Resources. Subcommittee on Labor. II. Title. 82-601486 OCLC 08243365

82-12231

Y 4.L 11/4:P 96

United States. Congress. Senate. Committee on Labor and Human Resources.

A guide to the bound publications of the Committee on Labor and Human Resources, United States Senate for the ... Congress. Washington : U.S. G.P.O., v. ; 24 cm. Biennial 96th- Congress At head of title: 97th Congress, 1st session. Committee print. 96th Congress. ●Item 1043-A, 1043-B (microfiche) Continues: United States. Congress. Senate. Committee on Human Resources. Guide to the bound publications of the Committee on Human Resources, United States Senate 1. United States. Congress. Senate. Committee on Labor and Human Resources — Bibliography — Periodicals. I. Title. OCLC 08253766

MERCHANT MARINE AND FISHERIES, Committee on, House Washington, DC 20515

82-12232

Y 4.M 53:97-B

United States. Congress. House. Committee on Merchant Marine and Fisheries. Subcommittee on Fisheries and Wildlife Conservation and the Environment.

Oversight report on the Magnuson Fishery Conservation and Management Act of 1976 / submitted by John B. Breaux, Subcommittee on Fisheries and Wildlife Conservation and the Environment, Committee on Merchant Marine and Fisheries. — Washington : U.S. G.P.O., 1981. ii, 37 p. ; 24 cm. At head of title: 97th Congress, 1st session. Committee print. "September 1, 1981." Includes bibliographical references. "Serial no. 97-B." ●Item 1021-B, 1021-C (microfiche) 1. Fishery law and legislation — United States. 2. Fishery conservation — United States. 3. Marine resources conservation — Law and legislation — United States. I. Breaux, John B. II. Title. 81-603544 OCLC 08166935

82-12233

Y 4.M 53:97-13

United States. Congress. House. Committee on Merchant Marine and Fisheries. Subcommittee on Merchant Marine.

United States public Health service hospitals and clinics : hearings before the Subcommittee on Merchant Marine of the Committee on Merchant Marine and Fisheries, House of Representatives, Ninety-seventh Congress, first session, on public health service hospitals oversight, March 23, 1981 ... April 3, 1981 ... April 24, 1981 ... Public Health Service Hospitals Closure and Eliminate Merchant Seamen Entitlement—H.R. 3223, April 27, 1981 ... June 9, 1981. — Washington : U.S. G.P.O., 1981 [i.e. 1982] x, 530 p. : ill. ; 24 cm. "Serial no. 97-13." ●Item 1021-B, 1021-C (microfiche) 1. Hospitals, Public — United States. 2. Merchant seamen — Medical care — United States. I. Title. 82-601362 OCLC 08230917

Page 381

Exhibit 58: *Monthly Catalog of U.S. Government Publications,* showing entries for congressional hearings.

SOURCES OF FEDERAL LEGISLATIVE HISTORY

The principal sources in which evidence of congressional intent may be sought are the following:

1. Presidential Messages. Although not legislative in origin, these documents accompany legislation proposed to Congress by the executive and often explain the purpose and intent of the draftsmen. Messages are also frequently issued when the President signs or vetoes proposed legislation. They are printed and indexed in the *Congressional Record*, appear in the *Weekly Compilation of Presidential Documents* and the *House* and *Senate Journals*, and are also issued as *House* and *Senate Documents*. Important messages are reproduced in the advance sheets of the *U.S. Code Congressional and Administrative News*. While only indirect evidence of congressional intent, they provide helpful background information for that purpose. For an example of a presidential message, see Exhibit 59.

2. Congressional Bills. Differences between the several bills leading to a particular enactment may aid in determining legislative intent, since deletions, additions, or other variations in the bill at different stages of the legislative process imply deliberate choices of language by the legislators. The bills of each house are individually numbered in series and retain their identifying number through both sessions of a Congress. At the end of a term, a bill lapses and must be reintroduced and renumbered if it is to be considered. (The term of a Congress is two years, consisting of

WEEKLY COMPILATION OF PRESIDENTIAL DOCUMENTS

OCCUPATIONAL SAFETY AND HEALTH

The President's Message to the Congress. August 6, 1969

To the Congress of the United States:

Technological progress can be a mixed blessing. The same new method or new product which improves our lives can also be the source of unpleasantness and pain. For man's lively capacity to innovate is not always matched by his ability to understand his innovations fully, to use them properly, or to protect himself against the unforeseen consequences of the changes he creates.

The side effects of progress present special dangers in the workplaces of our country. For the working man and woman, the byproducts of change constitute an especially serious threat. Some efforts to protect the safety and health of the American worker have been made in the past both by private industry and by all levels of government. But new technologies have moved even faster to create newer dangers. Today we are asking our workers to perform far different tasks from those they performed five or fifteen or fifty years ago. It is only right that the protection we give them is also up-to-date.

There has been much discussion in recent months about the quality of the environment in which Americans live. It is important to note in this regard that during their working years most American workers spend

Exhibit 59: A presidential message on the subject of occupational safety and health.

two one-year sessions.) The bill number is used in all status tables and on most legislative documents to identify the proposed legislation. It also appears on the law after enactment, both in its slip form and in the bound volumes of the *Statutes at Large.*

Bills are received in many large law libraries in a slip form or on microfiche from the Government Printing Office, and can also be obtained individually from the clerk of the House or Senate, their sponsor, or the appropriate congressional committee, if requested promptly after their introduction. Several commercial publishers are now making bills, as well as other legislative documents available by subscription. Commerce Clearing House (*CCH*) offers two such services, *ELSS* (*Electronic Legislative Search Service*), a computer-based legislative service, and its long-standing *Legislative Reporting Service.* Both cover Congress and the state legislatures. Congressional Information Service (*C.I.S.*), described below, issues bills and resolutions, as well as other congressional documents on microfiche, beginning with the 89th Congress (1965).

The form of a bill is shown in Exhibit 60 below. (Note that the exhibits that follow in this chapter illustrate various stages in the progress of this bill through Congress and its treatment in several legislative guides.)

3. Hearings. These are transcripts of testimony before Senate and House committees on proposed legislation or on a particular subject under congressional investigation. In addition to such testimony, exhibits contributed by interested individuals or groups are also included (e.g. letters, statements, statistical material, newspaper articles, etc.). The purpose of a hearing is to determine the need for new legislation or to bring before Congress information relevant to its preparation and enactment. Hearings are not, however, held for all legislation, nor are all hearings published.

In using hearings to explore the background of a particular piece of legislation, one should keep in mind that the quality of the testimony given at hearings will vary depending on the bias of the testifying witness and his or her degree of expertise on the subject under investigation. Thus, as a source of legislative intent,

91ST CONGRESS
1ST SESSION

S. 2193

IN THE SENATE OF THE UNITED STATES

MAY 16, 1969

Mr. WILLIAMS of New Jersey (for himself, Mr. KENNEDY, Mr. MONDALE, and Mr. YARBOROUGH) introduced the following bill; which was read twice and referred to the Committee on Labor and Public Welfare

A BILL

To authorize the Secretary of Labor to set standards to assure safe and healthful working conditions for working men and women; to assist and encourage States to participate in efforts to assure such working conditions; to provide for research, information, education, and training in the field of occupational safety and health, and for other purposes.

Be it enacted by the Senate and House of Representatives of the United States of America in Congress assembled, That this Act may be cited as the "Occupational Safety and Health Act of 1969".

VII—O

Exhibit 60: A congressional bill on occupational safety and health.

hearings are less authoritative than committee reports and must be used with discrimination.

A search for relevant hearings should not be limited to the session in which the particular law is enacted, since hearings may extend over more than one session and be issued in multiple parts and volumes. There is no uniformity in the numbering of the various series of hearings issued by the committees of Congress, but they are generally identified by the *name of the committee* holding them, the *session* and *Congress* during which they are held, the *title* which appears on the cover, the *bill* on which they are being held, and the *date span* of the testimony. Exhibit 61 below shows the title page of a typical hearing.

Hearings are available from the committee conducting them, from the Government Printing Office, or occasionally from members of the committee. They are listed in the *Monthly Catalog of U.S. Government Publications* by committee and subject, though not by bill number. Since 1970, the difficulty in locating hearings has been eased by *Congressional Information Service/Index,* a finding aid described below, which provides indexing to congressional hearings by subject, bill number, committee, title, and witness. C.I.S. is also currently producing a retrospective index of hearings held from the early 1800's through 1969 (91st Congress), entitled *CIS U.S. Congressional Committee Hearings Index.* To date, the volumes covering 1935 to 1969 have been published, with completion of the index scheduled for 1985. Access is by subject, organization, personal name, title, bill number, Superintendent of Documents number, and report or document number. Full text microfiche copies of each publication listed in the *Index* are available through C.I.S.' *U.S. Congressional Committee Hearings on Microfiche Full Collection.* See Exhibit 62 below.

Another index to hearings entitled, *Cumulative Index of Congressional Committee Hearings,* is published by the U.S. Senate Library. Coverage to date, in several volumes, is from the 41st Congress (1869) to the 95th Congress (1977–78). Access to the hearings is by subject, bill number and committee.

OCCUPATIONAL SAFETY AND HEALTH ACT, 1970

HEARINGS

BEFORE THE

SUBCOMMITTEE ON LABOR

OF THE

COMMITTEE ON LABOR AND PUBLIC WELFARE UNITED STATES SENATE

NINETY-FIRST CONGRESS

FIRST AND SECOND SESSIONS

ON

S. 2193 and S. 2788

BILLS ON OCCUPATIONAL SAFETY AND HEALTH

SEPTEMBER 30, NOVEMBER 4, 21, 24, 26, DECEMBER 9, 15, 16, 1969; MARCH 7, AND APRIL 10, 28, 1970

PART 1

Printed for the use of the Committee on Labor and Public Welfare

U.S. GOVERNMENT PRINTING OFFICE

42-537 O WASHINGTON : 1970

Exhibit 61: Title page of a hearing on various bills related to occupational safety and health.

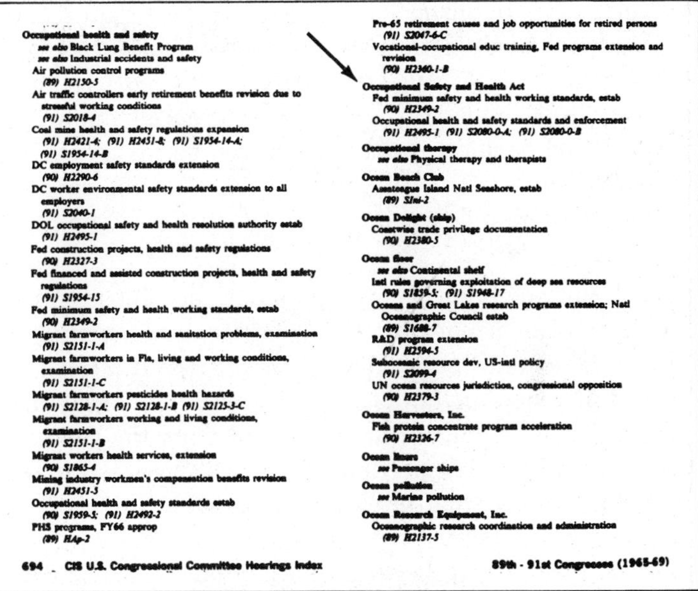

Occupational health and safety
see also Black Lung Benefit Program
see also Industrial accidents and safety
Air pollution control programs
(89) H2150-5
Air traffic controllers early retirement benefits revision due to stressful working conditions
(91) S2018-4
Coal mine health and safety regulations expansion
(91) H2421-4; (91) H2451-8; (91) S1954-14-A; (91) S1954-14-B
DC employment safety standards extension
(90) H2290-6
DC worker environmental safety standards extension to all employers
(91) S2040-1
DOL occupational safety and health resolution authority estab
(91) H2495-1
Fed construction projects, health and safety regulations
(90) H2327-3
Fed financed and assisted construction projects, health and safety regulations
(91) S1954-15
Fed minimum safety and health working standards, estab
(90) H2349-2
Migrant farmworkers health and sanitation problems, examination
(91) S2151-1-A
Migrant farmworkers in Fla, living and working conditions, examination
(91) S2151-1-C
Migrant farmworkers pesticides health hazards
(91) S2128-1-A; (91) S2128-1-B (91) S2125-3-C
Migrant farmworkers working and living conditions, examination
(91) S2151-1-B
Migrant workers health services, extension
(90) S1865-4
Mining industry workmen's compensation benefits revision
(91) H2451-5
Occupational health and safety standards estab
(90) S1959-5; (91) H2492-2
PHS programs, FY66 approp
(89) HAp-2

Pre-65 retirement causes and job opportunities for retired persons
(91) S2047-6-C
Vocational-occupational educ training, Fed programs extension and revision
(90) H2360-1-B

Occupational Safety and Health Act
Fed minimum safety and health working standards, estab
(90) H2349-2
Occupational health and safety standards and enforcement
(91) H2495-1 (91) S2080-0-A; (91) S2080-0-B

Occupational therapy
see also Physical therapy and therapists

Ocean Beach Club
Assateague Island Natl Seashore, estab
(89) SIni-2

Ocean Delight (ship)
Coastwise trade privilege documentation
(90) H2380-5

Ocean floor
see also Continental shelf
Intl rules governing exploitation of deep sea resources
(90) S1859-5; (91) S1948-17
Oceans and Great Lakes research programs extension; Natl Oceanographic Council estab
(89) S1688-7
R&D program extension
(91) H2594-5
Suboceanic resource dev, US-intl policy
(91) S2099-4
UN ocean resources jurisdiction, congressional opposition
(90) H2379-3

Ocean Harvesters, Inc.
Fish protein concentrate program acceleration
(90) H2326-7

Ocean liners
see Passenger ships

Ocean pollution
see Marine pollution

Ocean Research Equipment, Inc.
Oceanographic research coordination and administration
(89) H2137-5

694 CIS U.S. Congressional Committee Hearings Index   89th - 91st Congresses (1965-69)

Exhibit 62: Subject index listing for O.S.H.A. in CIS *U.S. Congressional Committee Hearings Index.*

4. **Committee Reports.** Reports are the most important source of legislative history. They are issued by the congressional committees of both houses (and by conference committees of the two houses) on each bill reported out of committee for action. Reports frequently include the text of the bill, describe its contents and purposes, and give reasons for the committee's recommendations (sometimes including a minority view). They are also issued by committees on various investigations, studies and hearings not related to a particular bill under consideration. Committee

reports are published in a numbered series which indicates house, Congress, and report number, e.g., Senate Report No. 91–1282. A typical report is illustrated in Exhibit 63 below. Conference committee reports are included in the numbered series of House reports. Like other congressional documents, reports are listed and indexed in the *Monthly Catalog* and in the *CIS Index.*

Committee reports are available on subscription from the Government Printing Office, and sometimes from the committee issuing them or from the clerk of the House or Senate, as the case may be. Many are placed on sale and can be purchased from the Government Printing Office. Reports on the most important enactments are also published selectively in the *U.S. Code Congressional and Administrative News* and the *Congressional Record,* and all appear, along with House and Senate Documents, in the bound official compilation called the *Serial Set.* C.I.S. has published a thirty-six volume retrospective index to the *Serial Set,* entitled the *U.S. Serial Set Index,* which covers the period 1789 to 1969.

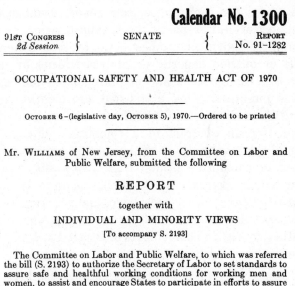

Calendar No. 1300

91st Congress, 2d Session } SENATE { Report No. 91–1282

OCCUPATIONAL SAFETY AND HEALTH ACT OF 1970

October 6–(legislative day, October 5), 1970.—Ordered to be printed

Mr. Williams of New Jersey, from the Committee on Labor and Public Welfare, submitted the following

REPORT

together with

INDIVIDUAL AND MINORITY VIEWS

[To accompany S. 2193]

The Committee on Labor and Public Welfare, to which was referred the bill (S. 2193) to authorize the Secretary of Labor to set standards to assure safe and healthful working conditions for working men and women, to assist and encourage States to participate in efforts to assure such working conditions, to provide for research, information, education, and training in the field of occupational safety and health, and for other purposes, having considered the same, reports favorably thereon with an amendment (in the nature of a substitute) and recommends that the bill (as amended) do pass.

Purpose

The purpose of S. 2193 is to reduce the number and severity of work-related injuries and illnesses which, despite current efforts of employers and government, are resulting in ever-increasing human misery and economic loss.

The bill would achieve its purpose through programs of research, education and training, and through the development and administration, by the Secretary of Labor, of uniformly applied occupational safety and health standards. Such standards would be developed with the assistance of the Secretary of Health, Education and Welfare, and both their promulgation and their enforcement would be judicially reviewable. Encouragement is given to Federal-state cooperation, and financial assistance is authorized to enable states, under approved plans, to take over entirely and administer their own programs for achieving safe and healthful jobsites for the Nation's workers.

48-010—70——1

Exhibit 63: **A congressional report, accompanying the proposed Occupational Safety and Health Act of 1970.**

5. Committee Prints. Issued generally in consecutive series for each house, committee prints usually contain material prepared specifically for the use of a committee, such as studies done by the committee staff or outside experts, or are statements by members of a committee or subcommittee on a pending bill. These publications are also listed and indexed in the *Monthly Catalog* and *CIS/Index.* See Exhibit 64 below for an abstract of a committee print in the annual C.I.S. volume. C.I.S. has issued a retrospective index to committee prints, *CIS U.S. Congressional Committee Prints Index* (1980), comparable to its *Hearings Index* described above, and covering in five volumes committee prints from the middle of the 19th century to 1969. This index is illustrated in Exhibit 65 below.

H341-67.1 Education and Labor

Statements and Discussion: Importance of improved international business education; comparison of H.R. 4526 with related S. 2306, the International Education Programs Act; preference for S. 2306. (p. 13-45)

Support for H.R. 4526; description of education programs for international business; advantages for businessmen of knowing foreign languages and cultures. (p. 45-79)

H342 Prints
EDUCATION AND LABOR Committee, House

H342-1 LEGISLATIVE CALENDAR, No. 2.
Jan. 1980. 96-2.
i+236 p. Oversized. ‡
CIS/MF/(not filmed)
°Y4.Ed8/1:96/cal.2.
MC 80-1704. LC 51-62926.

Cumulative record of committee activities to Jan. 1980.

H342-2 PROBLEMS OF YOUTH UNEMPLOYMENT.
Jan. 1980. 96-2.
vii+497 p. il. † CIS/MF/8
●Item 1015.
°Y4.Ed8/1:Y8/19.
MC 80-11057. LC 80-601207.

CRS compilation of papers, prepared for *Subcom on Elementary, Secondary, and Vocational Education* and *Subcom on Employment Opportunities,* on youth unemployment. Organized as follows:

Root causes, including:

a. National Commission for Employment Policy, "Youth Employment Policies for the 1980s" Sept. 28, 1979 (p. 9-19).

b. Iden, George (CBO), "Black Youth Unemployment and Employment in the 1970's" with tables and graphs (p. 20-38).

c. Hooper, Patricia G. (Amer Personnel and Guidance Assn), "Youth Unemployment" policy paper on guidance and counseling impact on youth unemployment (p. 51-63).

d. Stern, Barry E. (Seattle Public Schools), youth unemployment myths and suggested solutions (p. 77-95).

e. Farkas, George (Abt Assocs); and Stromsdorfer, Ernst W. (Abt Assocs), "Social Policies To Reduce Youth Unemployment: Lessons from Experience and the Potential of Recent Initiatives" rpt partly based on Youth Incentive Entitlement Pilot Projects under Manpower Demonstration Research Corp., Oct. 1, 1979, with tables (p. 96-112).

f. Carter, Lewis J. (NAACP), black youth unemployment causes and proposed solutions Sept. 25, 1979 (p. 113-126).

g. Holmes, Marion B. (Philadelphia School Dist), "Root Causes of High Incidence of Youth Unemployment and Policies for Addressing the Problem" Sept. 28, 1979 (p. 136-150).

Education, including:

a. Hornbeck, David W. (et al.), "Facing the Challenge of Youth Employability and Employment" draft rpt, prepared for Council of Chief State School Officers (p. 158-193).

b. Taylor, Robert E. (Natl Center for Research in Vocational Educ), "Education's Role in Youth Unemployment" Nov. 1979 (p. 194-222).

c. Timpane, P. Michael (Natl Inst of Educ), "Role of Education in Reducing Youth Unemployment" rpt on secondary school role (p. 230-241).

d. Wurzburg, Gregory (Natl Council on Employment Policy), "Enhancing the Role of Local Schools in Reducing Youth Unemployment" rpt on school collaboration with Fed employment and training programs, including CETA (p. 246-256).

e. Shoemaker, Byrl R. (Ohio Dept of Educ), "Vocational Education and Transition of Youth to Work Ages 14-21" (p. 282-291).

f. Parks, Darrell (Ohio Dept of Educ); and Cronin, F. Patrick (Ohio Dept of Educ), "Concept Paper for the Development of Three Human Resource Student Service Centers for Vocational Education" (p. 292-303).

g. Copa, George H. (Univ of Minn), "Improving Vocational Education's Effectiveness in Reducing Youth Unemployment" Sept. 15, 1979 (p. 309-328).

Employment and training systems, including:

a. Law, Charles J., Jr. (NC Bd of Educ); and Latta, E. Michael (NC Advisory Council on Educ), "Improvements Needed in the Employment and Training System: A North Carolina Perspective" Sept. 28, 1979 (p. 358-380).

b. Barlow, Melvin L. (Univ of Calif), "Improvements in the Employment and Training System To Reduce the Extent of Youth Unemployment" Sept. 15, 1979 (p. 393-402).

c. Schiff, Frank W. (Committee for Economic Dev), "Strategies for Dealing with Youth Unemployment" Oct. 1, 1979 (p. 403-413).

Miscellaneous papers

a. Casserly, Michael (Council of Great City Schools); and Siegel, Reva (Council of Great City Schools), "Youth Employment: Its Implications for Federal Policy" (p. 414-425).

b. Boyle, William R. (Oak Ridge Associated Univs), "One Approach to Industrial-Based Training Programs" rpt on CETA-funded model training and technology programs with Union Carbide Corp. and Lockheed-Georgia Corp., June 1979, with tables (p. 426-461).

c. Stevenson, George A., Jr. (Chrysler Learning, Inc), Chrysler employment and training programs for disadvantaged youth rpt on Chrysler Inst programs, Oct. 1, 1979 (p. 462-482).

d. National School Boards Association, "Youth Employment: CETA and Vocational Education" rpts (p. 483-497).

H342-3 STAFF REPORT ON THE OVERSIGHT OF THE OCCUPATIONAL SAFETY AND HEALTH ADMINISTRATION WITH RESPECT TO GRAIN ELEVATOR FIRES AND EXPLOSIONS.
Jan. 1980. 96-2.
v+151 p. il. † CIS/MF/4
●Item 1015.
°Y4.Ed8/1:Sa1/10.
MC 80-13198. LC 80-601779.

Staff report, prepared for full committee by *Subcom on Health and Safety* with the assistance of Maury Aton (CRS), based on 95th Congress *Subcom on Compensation, Health, and Safety* 1978 hearings to examine causes and incidence of explosions and fires inside grain elevators and to determine how the health and safety of grain elevator employees can be protected.

Appendices (p. 39-151) include lists of 1958-78 explosions (p. 40-45), detailed GAO data on six 1977-78 grain dust explosions and fires (p. 46-51) and texts of the Occupational Safety and Health Act of 1980 (p. 51-73) and Federal agencies regulations governing grain elevator safety (p. 73-151 passim).

H342-4 NEEDS OF ELEMENTARY AND SECONDARY EDUCATION IN THE 1980'S. A Compendium of Policy Papers.
Jan. 1980. 96-2. x+693 p.
† CIS/MF/10 ●Item 1015.
°Y4.Ed8/1:Ed8/36/980.
MC 80-15567. LC 80-601572.

Compilation of papers, solicited from members of the educational community by the *Subcom on Elementary, Secondary, and Vocational Education* and organized by K. Forbis Jordan and Dennis L. Little (CRS), on prospects for elementary and secondary education in the 1980s. Materials are grouped in the following categories:

Part 1 - Leadership and governance (p. 1-244). Perspectives on educational quality and costs, administrative challenges, and public expectations, including:

a. Dede, Chris (World Future Soc), "Next Ten Years in Education" (p. 25-42).

b. Howe, Harold, II (Ford Fdn), "Brown Decision, Pluralism, and the Schools in the 1980s" paper presented before Chief State School Officers of the U.S., Aug. 1, 1979 (p. 52-74).

c. Tyler, Ralph W. (Science Research Assocs), "Needs of Elementary and Secondary Education for the 1980's" (p. 75-89).

d. Farr, Roger (Indiana Univ), "Let's Build on the Strengths of our Comprehensive Public School System: A Recommendation to Educational Policy Makers" Nov. 1979 (p. 100-115).

e. Bailey, Stephen K. (Harvard Univ), "Education in the Eighties: The Case for Optimism" (p. 169-185).

f. Jordan, K. Forbis (CRS) "Challenges to Education in the 1980s" (p. 234-244).

Part 2 - Social Change and Demographics (p. 245-371). Assessments of age distribution and school enrollment trends, including:

a. Gappert, G. Michael (Research for Better Schools), "Educational Consequences of Post-Affluence" Nov. 1979 (p. 246-265).

b. Wegmann, Robert G. (Natl Inst of Educ), "Educational Challenges of the 1980's" Aug. 1979 (p. 275-292).

c. Hollis, Phoebe P. (Univ of Nebr, Omaha), "Student of the Future: A Profile" (p. 298-312).

d. Little, Dennis L. (CRS) "Demographic Projections and Educational Policy Issues" Oct. 31, 1979 (p. 321-342).

224 CIS/INDEX JANUARY-DECEMBER 1980

Exhibit 64: Abstract of committee print in annual CIS volume.

Index by Subjects and Names **Occupational health and safety**

Veterans disability benefits eligibility revision, Veterans, Administration report on proposed legislation
(85/1/57) H9621

Nursing homes
see Hospitals and nursing homes

Nutrition
see Hunger and malnutrition
see terms beginning with Food

Nuts
see also Peanuts
Research and related services in the U.S. Department of Agriculture
(81/2/50) H0892
Tariff bill, hearing on H.R. 7456. Schedules 1-15, by individual schedule
(67/1/21) S3283, S3284
Tariff information surveys on individual articles in Tariff Act of 1913, by paragraph
(66/3/21) H3619
Tariff information, 1929, on Tariff Act of 1922, summary of. Schedules 1-15, by schedule [1918-28 data]
(70/2/29) H3224
Tariff revision. Hearings on schedules 1-15, by schedule
(70/2/29) H3189, H3190

Nyasaland
see Federation of Rhodesia and Nyasaland

Oahe Dam
Construction of Oahe and Randall Dams on the Missouri River, acquisition of lands by the U.S. required by reservoirs created by construction of the dams, and for effects on the Indians of the Standing Rock, Lower Brule, and Crow Creek Sioux Reservation in North and South Dakota. Department reports and information relating to bills to provide for
(85/2/58) H4924
Construction of Oahe Dam on the Missouri River, acquisition of lands by the U.S. required for the reservoir created by construction of the Dam, and for rehabilitation of the Indians of the Standing Rock Sioux Reservation in South and North Dakota. Bills to provide for
(85/1/57) H4926, H4931; (85/2/58) H4927
Missouri River, acquisition of lands by the U.S. required for the reservoir created by the construction of Oahe Dam on, and for rehabilitation of the Standing Rock Sioux Reservation in South Dakota and North Dakota, H.R. 5608, bill to provide for, and for other purposes
(84/2/56) H8866

Oak Ridge, Tenn.
Dormitory rental problem, Oak Ridge, Tenn. Report
(81/1/49) J0678
Government-owned communities at Oak Ridge, Tenn., and Richland, Wash., disposal of
(83/2/54) J0064; (84/1/55) J0068
Natural gas pipeline, Oak Ridge, Tenn. Report
(81/1/49) J0677

Oakdale Fuel Co.
Coal mines of Colorado, conditions in
(63/2/14) H3906

Oakland, Calif.
Harbor, Oakland, Calif., reports on. Army Engineers project
(59/2/07) H4010; (68/2/24) H4165; (70/1/28) H4185; (71/2/30) H4245
Poverty, examination of war on: Community Action Program
(90/1/67) S1065
Veterans hospital construction, Veterans Administration report on proposed legislation
(80/2/48) H6788

Oakland County, Mich.
Community action program: Great Lakes. Examination of the war on poverty, staff and consultants reports. Vol. 6
(90/1/67) S2185

Oakland Regional Hospital
Sale of Oakland Regional Hospital and construction of new veterans hospital at Oakland, Calif., Veterans Administration report on proposed legislation
(80/2/48) H6788

Oaks, Dallin H.
Criminal Justice Act in the federal district courts
(90/2/68) S1438

OAS
see Organization of American States

OASDHI
see Old-Age, Survivors, Disability, and Health Insurance

Oaths
Citizenship candidates, bill to permit oath of allegiance to be made with certain reservations. Hearings extract on H.R. 3547
(71/2/30) H3826
Schwimmer, Rosika, and Martha Jane Graber, Supreme Court decisions, citations, comment, etc. in re
(71/2/30) H3830

Oatis, William N.
Arrest and conviction of William N. Oatis by the Czechoslovakian government, expressing indignation at
(82/1/51) H4863, H8168

Oaxaca, Mexico
Mexico-U.S. Interparliamentary Group, House delegation report on conference of
(90/1/67) H1060
Mexico-U.S. Interparliamentary Group, Senate delegation report on conference of
(90/1/67) S1548

O'Brien, George D.
Great Lakes-St. Lawrence Basin. Hearings on improvement of seaway and power project
(77/1/41) H3962

O'Brien, T. C.
Great Lakes-St. Lawrence Basin. Hearings on improvement of seaway and power project
(77/1/41) H3966

Obscenity and pornography
District of Columbia public school situation. Hearing extracts, with comments
(66/2/20) S5376
Juvenile delinquency, obscene and pornographic literature and
(84/2/56) S2171
Obscene matter sent through the mail
(86/1/59) H1666
Postal Revenue and Offensive Intrusion of Sexually Oriented Mail Act of 1969. Recommendations and section-by-section analysis of H.R. 10877
(91/1/69) H1686

O'Callaghan, Jerry A.
Oregon, disposition of the public domain in [history of public land policies and settlement of Oregon]
(86/2/60) S0410

Occupational health and safety
see also Industrial accidents and safety
Coal mines, federal inspection of, hearing before the committee, 77th Congress, 1st session, on H.R. 2082, a bill relating to. Investigations in coal mines
(77/1/41) H8559
Federal Construction Safety Act, legislative history of
(91/1/69) S1964
Longshore and harbor work, safety in [analysis of H.R. 5796 to amend Longshoremen's and Harbor Workers' Compensation Act]
(82/2/52) H1630
Panama Canal skilled labor. Hearings extracts relative to pay, allowances, health, and other conditions, fiscal years 1907-1915
(63/2/14) H7015
Radiation exposure of uranium miners. Summary analysis of hearings
(90/1/67) J0657
Radiation hazards to employees, and workmen's compensation
(86/1/59) J0098, J0618
Radiation protection criteria and standards: Their basis and use. Selected materials on
(86/2/60) J0144

CIS U.S. Congressional Committee Prints Index **903**

Exhibit 65: CIS *U.S. Congressional Committee Prints Index*, showing entries related to occupational health and safety.

6. Debates. The *Congressional Record* is a nearly verbatim transcript of legislative debates and proceedings, published each day that one or both houses are in session. It is subject to revision only by members of Congress who wish to amend their own remarks. In addition, the Appendix to the *Congressional Record* includes extensions of floor remarks, exhibits from legislators, communications on pending legislation and almost any other material a Senator or Representative wishes to get into the *Record.* Beginning with the Eightieth Congress, each issue contains a Daily Digest which summarizes the day's activities, including news of legislation introduced, reported on or passed and actions taken within various committees. There is a fortnightly index, and at the end of the session, a bound edition usually consisting of over thirty volumes. That compilation includes a cumulative index (with entries by subject, title and member of Congress), a cumulation of the Daily Digest, and a complete status table for that session entitled History of Bills and Resolutions. (For a description of this status table, see page 178 below.) Since the Eighty-Third Congress, second session, the Appendix has not been included in the bound set, although the Index still cites to it. It is available on microfilm and microfiche, however. Access to the *Record* is also provided by the *Federal Index* (Capitol Services, Inc.), an unofficial finding tool described below on pages 197–198.

The *Congressional Record* differs from the *House* and *Senate Journals* in that the journals do not include the verbatim debates. The journals merely record the proceedings, indicate whether there was debate, and report the resulting action and votes taken. The *Congressional Record* never contains hearings and only on rare occasions reports. Some bills are read into the *Record,* but it is not to be considered a major source for bills. Its importance is primarily as a report of debates and actions taken. For an excerpt from the *Record,* see Exhibit 66 below.

36508 CONGRESSIONAL RECORD — SENATE *October 13, 1970*

ought not be dispersed throughout the Office of Education, not administered by bureaus which are also responsible for other programs involving greater amounts of grant money.

The Committee believes that the environment education program should have viability and that its Director should have sufficient stature as to have direct access to the Commissioner. Moreover, the administrative unit charged with responsibility for the program ought to be staffed with a sufficient number of specialists. If the environmental education program is placed in one of the present bureaus, its Director would be at least three degrees removed from the office of the Commissioner and would have to compete with other programs for personnel, at a time when adequate staffing and proper administrative direction are difficult problems for the Office of Education.

It is for these reasons that the committee recommends the establishment of the Office of Environmental Education by law. Further, the committee recommends, in section 3(d), language which permits appropriations to be used for the administration of the program.

The intent of Congress to establish an independent office in the Office of the Commissioner is unequivocably clear.

OCCUPATIONAL SAFETY AND HEALTH ACT OF 1970

Mr. MANSFIELD. Mr. President, I ask unanimous consent that the pending

The PRESIDING OFFICER. The bill will be reported.

The assistant legislative clerk read as follows:

A bill (S. 2193) to authorize the Secretary of Labor to set standards to assure safe and healthful working conditions for working men and women; to assist and encourage States to participate in efforts to assure such working conditions; to provide for research, information, education, and training in the field of occupational safety and health; and for other purposes.

The PRESIDING OFFICER. The question is on agreeing to the motion to proceed to the consideration of the bill.

The Senator from New York is recognized.

Mr. JAVITS. Mr. President, a parliamentary inquiry.

The PRESIDING OFFICER. The Senator will state it.

Mr. JAVITS. Mr. President, am I correct in assuming that the motion is debatable?

The PRESIDING OFFICER. The motion is debatable.

Mr. JAVITS. Mr. President, I would like to be recognized, if I may, for a moment. Will the Senator from Montana yield to me?

Mr. MANSFIELD. I yield the floor.

The PRESIDING OFFICER. The Senate will be in order. Senators and staff members will take their seats.

Mr. JAVITS. Mr. President, I am the

deal of difference of opinion on certain matters. Although I have my views—and I tried to work them out on the committee—I think there is some substance to the disagreement. But the fundamental point is that the bill is extremely important and extremely desirable for all the workers.

I doubt very much that the bill could be finished in the 24 or 36 hours we have remaining. The Senator from Colorado (Mr. DOMINICK)—whether he does so by a substitute or by amendment—he has some 19 amendments, I understand. Every one of them is substantive and is not a facade or an effort to delay the matter.

However, Mr. President, I hope the Senate will proceed to the consideration of the bill. At the very least, if we cannot finish it by tomorrow night, it will be the pending business when we return.

We can pass the bill, and it should be passed. It is a critically important piece of legislation.

I hope that Senators will not be confused and believe that the amendments represent management-labor differences. In all honesty, most of them do not.

The bill should be passed.

Mr. President, I think it is important and fair to rebut any idea that any Senators have sought to stall the bill and not come to grips with it. The idea that this should be challenged and debated and that it should have the deliberate consideration of the Senate is only fair.

that feel the same way. That was why objection was made to the unanimous-consent request that had been propounded on two other occasions.

Exhibit 66: An excerpt from the debates on the Occupational Safety and Health Act of 1970, as reported in the *Congressional Record.*

The predecessors of the *Congressional Record,* which began in 1873, are: the *Annals of Congress* (1789–1824); the *Register of Debates* (1824–1837); and the *Congressional Globe* (1833–1873).

7. **House and Senate Documents.** Only occasionally useful as sources of legislative history, House and Senate Documents include reports of some congressional investigations not in the regular committee reports. They also contain presidential messages, special studies or exhibits prepared by or at the request of Congress, and communications to Congress from executive departments or agencies. They are listed in the *Monthly Catalog* and in the *Congressional Information Service/Index,* described below, and are published by the Government Printing Office in a numbered series for each house and Congress. Identification is by house, Congress, and document number, similar to the identification scheme for the Report series. These documents also appear in the official *Serial Set* and are indexed in the *U.S. Serial Set Index* (CIS).

8. **Treaty Documents and Senate Executive Reports.** These are restricted or confidential publications of the Senate forming an essential part of the legislative histories of treaties. Treaty Documents contain the texts of treaties before the Senate for its advice and consent and related correspondence from the President and Secretary of State. Senate Executive Reports are issued by the Foreign Relations Committee after its consideration of individual treaties. Both Documents and Reports are issued in numbered series. Both also require the Congress and session number for identification. Only when released by the Senate are they listed in the *Monthly Catalog* and made available to the public. They are not, however, routinely sent to depository libraries. Non-confiden-

tial Documents and Reports are now available on microfiche from C.I.S.'s *Legislative History Service.*

OUTLINE OF LEGISLATIVE STEPS AND RELEVANT DOCUMENTS

An understanding of the legislative process is essential for one compiling a legislative history. Each of the relevant documents of legislative history can be associated with the stage of law-making at which it is issued. The following are the most significant steps and their related documents:

Action	**Document**
Preliminary Inquiry	Hearings on the general subject of the proposed legislation. (N.B. Relevant hearings may have been held in a previous Congressional session or may run through several sessions.)
Executive Recommendation	Presidential Message proposing an administration bill.
Introduction of Bill	Original text—Slip Bill as introduced.
Referred to Committee	Committee Print of Bill.
Hearings on Bill	Hearings—published transcript and exhibits, sometimes including a Hearing Print of Bill.
Executive Agency Recommendations	House or Senate Document; *Congressional Record Appendix.*
Reported out of Committee	Committee Report including Committee's version or Reported Print of Bill.

Legislative Debates	*Congressional Record,* sometimes including texts of bill in amended forms.
Passage or defeat	Final House or Senate version of bill.
Other House	Generally same procedure and documents as above.
Referred to Conference Committee (if texts passed by each House differ)	Conference Committee version of bill; Conference Committee Report.
Passage by 2nd House	Enrolled Bill signed by Speaker of House or President of Senate and then sent to President (not available to public).
If vetoed	Presidential Veto Message.
If approved by President	Slip law (also *U.S.C.C.A.N.* and *U.S.C.S.* advance sheet). Subsequently bound into *Statutes at Large* and annual volumes of *U.S.C.C.A.N.* Then classified in the appropriate titles of the *U.S. Code* and its unofficial, annotated editions. Presidential Message may also be issued on signing of the law.

FINDING TOOLS

The essential finding tools for locating and tracing congressional bills and their legislative history are status tables, which are published in a variety of forms. Status tables are lists of pending bills and resolutions, with statements of the actions taken thereon and references to the documents which reflect such actions. They are arranged by bill numbers and often include a short digest of each bill. Status tables enable the researcher to trace the history of a bill or locate legislative documents which may aid in ascertaining congressional intent.

Some of these finding tools are in official publications, while others are produced by commercial publishers. The latter are often more useful since they usually include other research aids in addition to status tables, are updated more frequently, and/or contain more comprehensive indexing. The following publications are themselves status tables or contain status tables and additional references to legislative information.

1. **Congressional Record, History of Bills and Resolutions.** Arranged by bill and resolution number, this table includes a brief summary of each bill and resolution, the committee investigating the proposed legislation, and the action taken on the legislation to date, including amendments and passage. It is the best source of page references to debates within the *Record,* and includes House and Senate Report numbers, if any, and public law number if the measure has been enacted.

This table is published fortnightly in the Index to the *Record* and then cumulated for each session in the bound Index volume. The final cumulative table is very useful for retrospective research and is weak only in lacking references to hearings. The fortnightly listing is less helpful since it lists only those bills and resolutions acted upon within the preceding two week period. However, the information supplied on each bill is complete from date of introduction to the present. This table is illustrated in Exhibit 67 below.

2176–2362 **SENATE BILLS**

S.2176—To implement the Convention on Offenses and Certain Other Acts Committed on Board Aircraft, and for other purposes.

From Committee on Commerce, 27879.—Reported (S. Rept. 91–1083), 27879.—Passed Senate, 28643.—Referred to House Committee on Interstate and Foreign Commerce, 28990.—Rules suspended. Passed House (in lieu of 14301), 34808.—Examined and signed, 35398, 35595.—Presented to the President, 35597.—Approved [Public Law 91–449], 37264.

S.2193—To amend the title so as to read: "to assure safe and healthful working conditions for working men and women; by authorizing enforcement of the standards developed under the act; by assisting and encouraging the States in their efforts to assure safe and healthful working conditions; by providing for research, information, education, and training in the field of occupational safety and health; and for other purposes."

Cosponsor, 4266.—Cosponsors added, 14296, 37546.—Reported with amendment (S.Rept. 91–1282), 35087.—Debated, 35968, 36369, 36508, 36511, 36520, 36529, 36534, 37317, 37601, 37605, 37613, 37615.—Amended and passed Senate, 37632.—Amended and passed House (in lieu of H.R. 16785), 38724.—Title amended, 38733.—House insists on its amendments and asks for a conference, 38733.—Conferees appointed, 38733.—Senate disagrees to amendments of House and agrees to a conference, 39193.—Conferees appointed, 39193.—Conference report (H.Rept. 91–1765), submitted in Senate and agreed to 41753.—Conference report (H.Rept. 91–1765) submitted in House and agreed to, 41965, 42199.—Examined and signed, 42666, 43257.—Presented to the President, 43258.—Approved [Public Law 91–596], 44064.

S.2208—To authorize the Secretary of the Interior to study the feasibility and desirability of a national lakeshore on Lake Tahoe in the States of Nevada and California, and for other purposes.

Cosponsor added, 12706.—From Committee on Interior and Insular Affairs, 14816.—

Exhibit 67: History of Bills and Resolutions table in the *Congressional Record*, providing a brief summary of S.2193 and actions taken thereon.

2. **Congressional Record, Daily Digest.** This daily summary of congressional activity is published in each issue of the *Record* and includes a subject index which serves as a status table for bills acted upon that day. The Daily Digest cumulates at the end of each session into a separate bound volume of the *Record* which contains the final History of Bills Enacted into Public Law. This table is a useful one, although it lacks the debate references found in the History of Bills and Resolutions. It is illustrated in Exhibit 68 below.

3. Digest of Public General Bills and Resolutions. This publication of the Congressional Research Service of the Library of Congress is primarily useful for its synopses of all public bills and resolutions introduced in each session of Congress, beginning with the 74th Congress (1936). Each issue of the *Digest* contains three sections, arranged in numerical order by either public law, bill or resolution number, as follows: Part I, dealing with actions taken by Congress during the session, covers "public laws" and "other measures receiving action". Included here are digests of the law, bill or resolution, as well as legislative histories and other useful information about each measure. Part II includes digests of *all* public bills and resolutions in numerical order as introduced in Congress. Part III contains the various indexes to the *Digest:* sponsors or co-sponsors, identical bills, short titles, and subject index.

During each congressional session, the *Digest* is normally issued in two cumulations, with occasional intervening supplements, and a final cumulative edition at the end of the session. This final issue is very valuable for retrospective research.

D 760

CONGRESSIONAL RECORD — DAILY DIGEST

HISTORY OF BILLS ENACTED INTO PUBLIC LAW (91ST CONG., 2D SESS.)

(Cross-reference of bill number to public law number may be found on pp. D741–D742)

Title	Bill No.	Date introduced	Committee		Date reported		Report No.		Page of passage in Congressional Record		Date of passage		Public Law	
			House	Senate	House	Senate	House	Senate	House	Senate	House	Senate	Date approved	No.
Designating the first week in May of each year as National Employ the Older Worker Week.	S.J. Res. 74	Mar. 10 1969	Jud	Jud	....	Sept. 21	....	91–1207	40917	33349	Dec. 10	Sept. 23	Dec. 28	91–593
To authorize the President to proclaim the first full calendar week in May of each year as "Clean Waters for America Week."	S.J. Res. 172	Feb. 10	Jud	Jud	....	Feb. 16	....	91–703	40917	3496	Dec. 10	Feb. 17	Dec. 28	91–594
Authorizing President to designate the third Sunday in June of each year as Father's Day.	S.J. Res. 187	Mar. 25	Jud	Jud	....	Sept. 21	....	91–1209	40916	33350	Dec. 10	Sept. 23	Dec. 28	91–595
To establish comprehensive safety and health standards for the American worker.	S. 2193 (H.R. 16785)	May	EdL	LPW	July 9	Oct. 6	91–1291	91–1282	38724	37632	Nov. 24	Nov. 17	Dec. 29	91–596
Providing for inspection of certain egg products by the Department of Agriculture.	H.R. 19888 S. 2116	Dec. 1	Agr	Agr	Dec. 3	Jan. 28	91–1670	91–639	41116	41338 2089	Dec. 11	Dec. 14 Feb. 2	Dec. 29	91–597
To establish a Federal Broker-Dealer Insurance Corporation.	H.R. 19333 (S. 2348)	Sept. 17	IFC	BC	Oct. 21	Sept. 21	91–1613	91–1218	39370	40907	Dec. 1	Dec. 10	Dec. 30	91–598
To authorize U.S. participation in increases in the resources of certain international financial institutions.	H.R. 18306	July 6	BC	FR	July 14	Sept. 24	91–1300	91–1241	31477	42913	Sept. 14	Dec. 21	Dec. 30	91–599
To extend and improve programs under the Library Services and Construction Act.	S. 3318 (H.R. 19363)	Jan. 21	EdL	LPW	Dec. 3	Sept. 9	91–1659	91–1162	40181	32871	Dec. 7	Sept. 21	Dec. 30	91–600
To authorize the establishment of standards for the child-resistant packaging of hazardous substances.	S. 2162	May 13 1969	IFC	Com	Dec. 1	May 6	91–1642	91–845	40193	14797	Dec. 7	May 11	Dec. 30	91–601
To provide that the President transmit his Economic Report to the Congress not later than Feb. 1, 1971, and that the Joint Economic Committee file its report thereon with the House not later than Mar. 1, 1971.	H.J. Res. 1417	Dec. 15	....	....	....	....	....	....	41480	41765	Dec. 15	Dec. 16	Dec. 31	91–602
To authorize regulations to assist the United Seamen's Service to provide facilities and services to U.S. merchant seamen.	H.R. 15549	Jan. 27	MMF	Com	Aug. 11	Dec. 9	91–1404	91–1424	31441	41166	Sept. 14	Dec. 11	Dec. 31	91–603
Providing establishment of air quality standards	H.R. 17255 (S. 4358)	Apr. 27	IFC	PW	June 3	Sept. 17	91–1146	91–1196	19244	33120	June 10	Sept. 22	Dec. 31	91–604
Federal-Aid Highway Amendments of 1970	H.R. 19504 (S. 4418)	Sept. 29	PW	PW	Oct. 2	Sept. 30	91–1554	91–1254	38997	40095 34753	Nov. 25	Dec. 7 Oct. 2	Dec. 31	91–605
To establish a comprehensive Federal program for disaster relief and assistance.	S. 3619	Mar. 20	PW	PW	Sept. 29	Aug. 31	91–1524	91–1157	34798	31058	Oct. 5	Sept. 9	Dec. 31	91–606
To amend the Bank Holding Company Act of 1956	H.R. 6778	Feb. 17 1969	BC	BC	July 23 1969	Aug. 10	91–387	91–1084	33154	32136	Nov. 5 1969	Sept. 16	Dec. 31	91–607
To name a lock of the Cross-Florida Barge Canal as the "Henry Holland Buckman Lock."	H.R. 956 (S. 4368)	Jan. 3 1969	PW	PW	Dec. 9	Dec. 18	91–1697	91–1497	40921	42773	Dec. 10	Dec. 19	Dec. 31	91–608
Housing and Urban Development Act of 1970	H.R. 19436	Sept. 23	BC	BC	Oct. 5	Sept. 21	91–1556	91–1216	39842	40459	Dec. 3	Dec. 8	Dec. 31	91–609
To extend for 1 year the authorization for various programs under the Vocational Rehabilitation Act.	H.R. 19401	Sept. 22	EdL	LPW	Dec. 3	Dec. 14	91–1660	91–1433	40184	42118	Dec. 7	Dec. 17	Dec. 31	91–610
Omnibus rivers and harbors and flood control authorizations bill.	H.R. 19877 (S. 4572)	Nov. 30	PW	PW	Dec. 3	Dec. 8	91–1665	91–1422	40152	40620	Dec. 7	Dec. 9	Dec. 31	91–611
Private relief bill, and providing 3-year extension of exemption from marine safety standards of the vessel *Delta Queen*.	H.R. 6114	Feb. 4 1969	Jud	Jud	Oct. 1	Oct. 8	91–1550	91–1295	35164	36316	Oct. 6	Oct. 12	Dec. 31	91–612
To revise the definition of "metal bearing ores" in the tariff schedules.	H.R. 6049	Feb. 4 1969	WM	Fin	May 18	Dec. 16	91–1102	91–1465	20626	42354	June 22	Dec. 18	Dec. 31	91–613
Establishing a working capital fund for the Treasury Department, to continue certain excise taxes, and to accelerate the collection of estate and gift taxes.	H.R. 16199	Feb. 26	WM	Fin	May 13	Dec 15	91–1078	91–1444	16131	43891	May 19	Dec. 29	Dec. 31	91–614

Exhibit 68: Daily Digest: History of Bills Enacted into Public Law, recording the steps in the passage of the Occupational Safety and Health Act of 1970.

Exhibit 69 illustrates the synopsis and legislative history of Public Law 91–596, the Occupational Safety and Health Act of 1970.

Considered in House 12/10/70.
Passed House (amend.) 12/10/70.
Senate agreed to House (amend.) 12/15/70.

Authorizes the President to designate the third Sunday in June, 1971 as "Fathers' Day".

Pub. L. 91-596. Approved 12/29/70. S. 2193.
Reported in Senate 10/6/70, S. Rept. 91-1282.
Considered in Senate 10/13/70; 11/16/70-11/17/70.
Passed Senate 11/17/70.
Brought to House floor by unanimous consent 11/24/70.
Considered in House 11/24/70.
Passed House (amend.) 11/24/70.
Senate agreed to Conf. Rept. 12/16/70.
House agreed to Conf. Rept. 12/17/70. H. Rept. 91-1765.

Occupational Safety and Health Act - Makes it a finding of Congress that personal injuries and illnesses arising out of work impose a substantial burden upon interstate commerce; and declares a Congressional policy to assure as far as possible every working man and woman safe and healthful working conditions and to preserve our human resources.

Procedure Act) as an occupational safety or health standard any national consensus standard or any established Federal standard unless he determines promulgation would not result in improved safety or health for specifically designated employees.

Provides that the Secretary may request the recommendations of an advisory committee whenever he determines from information submitted in writing by an interested person, a representative of an employer or employee organization, a nationally recognized standard producing organization, the Secretary of Health, Education, and Welfare, the National Institute of Occupational Health and Safety, a State or political subdivision, or on the basis of his own information, that a rule (standard) should be promulgated.

Requires the Secretary to publish a proposed rule promulgating, modifying or revoking an occupational safety or health standard in the Federal Register and afford interested persons a period of 30 days after publication to submit written comments.

Permits any interested person to file with the Secretary written objections to the proposed rule and requesting a public hearing on or before the last day of the period.

Provides that where the Secretary determines that employees are being exposed to grave dangers from exposure to substances or agents determined to be toxic or physically harmful or from new hazards and that an emergency standard is necessary to

of employment free from recognized hazards so as to provide safe and healthful working conditions; and (2) must comply with occupational health and safety standards and rules, regulations and orders promulgated under this act, except as provided in section 16 (relating to State jurisdiction and State plans).

Directs the Secretary as soon as practicable after the effective date of the act, and until two years from such date, to promulgate (without regard to the rule making provisions of the Administrative

consent of any Federal agency, the services, facilities, or personnel of such Federal agency, with or without reimbursement, or of a State or its political subdivision with reimbursement; and (2) employ experts and consultants.

Provides that each committee is to include one or more designees of the Secretary of Health, Education, and Welfare, and may include employer and employee representatives in equal numbers; representatives of State and local safety agencies,

196

Exhibit 69: Summary and legislative history of the Occupational Safety and Health Act of 1970, as it appears in the *Digest of Public General Bills and Resolutions.*

4. **Legislative Calendars** (for the House, Senate and various committees). Each house and most committees issue calendars of pending business for the use of their members. These calendars, occasionally available in law libraries, contain very useful status

tables, including the House of Representatives' *Numerical Order of Bills and Resolutions Which Have Passed Either or Both Houses, and Bills Now Pending on the Calendar.* This status table is particularly valuable because of its frequency. It appears daily, is cumulative, and includes reported bills of both the House and Senate. The final issue comes out *before* the bound volumes of the *Congressional Record* and includes actions during both sessions of Congress. However, unlike the History of Bills and Resolutions, it does not include all bills introduced, but only those on which action was taken. Note that committee calendars are usually excellent sources of information on hearings.

5. **Congressional Information Service/Index.** This service, begun in 1970, indexes and abstracts nearly all congressional publications, except the *Congressional Record.* Its indexing is extremely detailed, providing access to hearings, reports, and documents, by subject, title (both official and popular), name (corporate and individual), number if any, and, in case of hearings, by witness. See Exhibits 70 and 71. The references are to the abstract portion of the service. Exhibit 72 shows an abstract of a hearing on the administration of the Occupational Safety and Health Act.

Exhibit 70: References in the *CIS/Index* to documents relating to the Occupational Safety and Health Act.

Exhibit 71: Indexing by witnesses before hearings in *CIS/Index*, showing testimony relating to Occupational Safety and Health Act.

S541-19.4: Additional Testimony.

Witnesses: **PEPPER, Claude,** (Rep, D-Fla), p. 3-4.

HAYES, Helen, actress, p. 11-24.

LEVIN, Carl, (Sen, D-Mich), p. 19-20.

JEPSEN, Roger W., (Sen, R-Iowa), p. 71-74.

Statements and Discussion: Need for home health care incentives.

S541-20 **OVERSIGHT ON THE ADMINISTRATION OF THE OCCUPATIONAL SAFETY AND HEALTH ACT, 1981.**
Sept. 23, 1981. 97-1.
iv+369 p. il. † CIS/MF/6
•Item 1043-A; 1043-B.
'Y4.L11/4:Oc1/981.
MC 82-12230. LC 82-601486.

Hearing before the *Subcom on Investigations and General Oversight* and the *Subcom on Labor* to examine Occupational Safety and Health Administration (OSHA) effectiveness in meeting health and safety needs of workers under provisions of the Occupational Safety and Health Act of 1980.

Includes submitted statements and correspondence (p. 251-368).

S541-20.1: Sept. 23, 1981. p. 11-125.

Witness: **AUCHTER, Thorne G.,** Asst Sec, OSHA, DOL.

Statement and Discussion: Overview of OSHA objectives, activities, and responses to criticism of Occupational Safety and Health Act programs implementation; summary of current efforts to increase worker safety and reduce compliance costs; rationale for revised policies and procedures regarding enforcement, standards promulgation and review, State plans approval, and employee training and education.

Merits of OSHA inspection procedures targeted to most hazardous worksites (injury rpt plan, p. 65-71); status of health standards for workplace exposure to hazardous substances; clarification of strategies to encourage industry compliance with safety directives, including labor-management programs.

S541-20.2: Sept. 23, 1981. p. 126-170.

Witness: **THOMPSON, Robert T.,** chm, labor relations committee, Chamber of Commerce of U.S.

Statement and Discussion: Disappointment with OSHA performance, including failure to reduce occupation-related injuries and illnesses, poor management, and high compliance costs; ... workers.

Statements and Discussion: Concerns about recent OSHA policies, procedures, and regulatory proposals (summary, p. 214-215); evidence of reduced OSHA compliance activity and decreased labor involvement in occupational health and safety activities; detailed criticism of OSHA proposed enforcement directives, including revisions in complaint handling and inspection targeting policies; negative implications of proposals for worker participation in abatement of occupational hazards.

S541-20.4: Sept. 23, 1981. p. 223-250.

Witness: **FORDICE, Kirk,** pres, Fordice Construction Co; representing Associated Gen Contractors.

Statement and Discussion: Problems in Occupational Safety and Health Act application to construction industry; recommended legislative and administrative changes in OSHA programs.

S541-21 **NOMINATION (C. Everett Koop).**
Oct. 1, 1981. 97-1.
ii+190 p. † CIS/MF/4
•Item 1043-A; 1043-B.
'Y4.L11/4:N72/981-15.
MC 82-15171. LC 82-601644.

Hearing to consider the nomination of C. Everett Koop (pediatrics prof, Univ of Pa School of Medicine; surgeon-in-chief, Children's Hosp of Philadelphia) to be Surgeon General, PHS.

Includes correspondence and articles (p. 11-27, 189-190).

S541-21.1: Oct. 1, 1981. p. 32-70.

Witness: **KOOP, C. Everett (Dr.),** nominee to be Surg Gen, PHS.

Statement and Discussion: Review of background and qualifications; views on responsibilities and issues involved in designated position.

S541-21.2: Oct. 1, 1981. p. 127-188.

Witnesses: **McBEATH, William H. (Dr.),** exec dir, Amer Public Health Assn.

WELLS-SCHOOLEY, Jane, vp, Natl Organization for Women.

Statements and Discussion: Opposition to Koop nomination; review of nominee's lack of public health service qualifications.

S541-21.3: Nominee Support.

Witnesses: **SPECTER, Arlen,** (Sen, R-Pa), p. 2-3.

Volume 13, Number 1-12 CIS/INDEX 889

Exhibit 72: Abstract of the hearing held on the Occupational Safety and Health Act of 1970 in *Congressional Information Service/Index.*

CIS/Index is published monthly, with quarterly cumulations and annually cumulated bound volumes (*CIS/Annual*). The annual volumes include comprehensive legislative histories of enacted laws, with references to bills, hearings, reports, debates, Presidential documents and all legislative actions. (See Exhibit 73). There are now also three cumulative indexes covering the periods 1970–1974, 1975–1978, and 1979–1982, with further cumulations expected.

Microfiche copies of all publications listed in the *CIS/Index* are available by subscription from C.I.S., as are the documents listed in C.I.S.' retrospective *U.S. Serial Set Index.* System Development Corp. (SDC) has also now made *CIS/Index* available on-line by computer. Microfiche copies of any document included in that data base will also be provided on demand.

Legislative History (H.J. Res. 1413 and related bills):

House Hearings: *See 1971 CIS/Annual: H501-4.*

Senate Hearings: *See 1971 CIS/Annual: S541-2.*

House Reports: H503-69 (No. 91-1686); H503-70 (No. 91-1714, Conference Report).

Senate Report: S543-41 (No. 91-1426).

Congressional Record Vol. 116 (1970):
Dec. 9, considered and passed House; considered and passed Senate, amended, in lieu of S.J. Res. 248.
Dec. 10, House and Senate agreed to conference report.

PL91-548 MINUTE MAN NATIONAL HISTORICAL PARK, boundary revision.
Dec. 14, 1970. 91-2. •
•Item 575. 1 p.
84 STAT. 1436.

"To amend the Act of September 21, 1959 (73 Stat. 590), to authorize the Secretary of the Interior to revise the boundaries of Minute Man National Historical Park, and for other purposes."

Also increases authorization.

Legislative History (H.R. 13934):

Senate Hearings: *See 1971 CIS/Annual: S441-5.*

House Report: H443-60 (No. 91-1398).

Senate Report: S443-97 (No. 91-1390).

Congressional Record Vol. 116 (1970):
Sept. 14, considered and passed House.
Dec. 4, considered and passed Senate.

PL91-554 WILSON'S CREEK BATTLEFIELD NATIONAL PARK, name change.
Dec. 16, 1970. 91-2. •
•Item 575. 1 p.
84 STAT. 1441.

"To amend the Act of April 22, 1960, providing for the establishment of the Wilson's Creek Battlefield National Park."

Legislative History (H.R. 1160 and related bill):

Senate Hearings: *See 1971 CIS/Annual: S441-5.*

House Report: H443-54 (No. 91-1395).

Senate Report: S443-96 (No. 91-1389).

Congressional Record Vol. 116 (1970):
Sept. 14, considered and passed House.
Dec. 4, considered and passed Senate.

Congressional Record Vol. 115 (1969):
Sept. 5, considered and passed Senate.

Congressional Record Vol. 116 (1970):
Dec. 10, considered and passed House.

PL91-574 WILLIAM G. STONE NAVIGATION LOCK, CALIF., designation.
Dec. 24, 1970. 91-2. •
•Item 575. 1 p.
84 STAT. 1508.

"To designate the navigation lock on the Sacramento deepwater ship channel in the State of California as the William G. Stone navigation lock."

Legislative History (S. 3192 and related bill):

House Hearings: *See 1971 CIS/Annual: H641-2.*

House Report: [Public WorksRB (No. 91-1703, accompanying H.R. 15205).

Senate Report: [Public Works] (No. 91-1032).

Congressional Record Vol. 116 (1970):
July 21, considered and passed Senate.
Dec. 10, considered and passed House, in lieu of H.R. 15205.

PL91-576 PICK-SLOAN MISSOURI BASIN PROGRAM, designation.
Dec. 24, 1970. 91-2. •
•Item 575. 1 p.
84 STAT. 1541.

"To designate the comprehensive Missouri River Basin development program as the Pick-Sloan Missouri Basin program."

Legislative History (S. 1100):

House Hearings: *See 1971 CIS/Annual: H641-2.*

House Report: [Public Works] (No. 91-1710).

Senate Report: [Public Works] (No. 91-891).

Congressional Record Vol. 116 (1970):
May 25, considered and passed Senate.
Dec. 10, considered and passed House.

PL91-583 WILLIAM "BILL" DANNELLY RESERVOIR, ALA., designation.
Dec. 24, 1970. 91-2. •
•Item 575. 1 p.
84 STAT. 1574.

PL91-590 INTERSTATE COMMERCE ACT, amendment.
Dec. 28, 1970. 91-2. •
•Item 575. 2 p.
84 STAT. 1587.

"To amend section 308(b) of the Interstate Commerce Act to modernize certain restrictions upon the application and scope of the exemption provided therein, and for other purposes."

Applies to water carriers transporting bulk and non-bulk commodities.

Legislative History (H.R. 8298):

Senate Hearings: *See 1971 CIS/Annual: S261-3.*

House Reports: [Interstate and Foreign Commerce] (No. 91-520); H503-71 (No. 91-1744, Conference Report).

Senate Report: S263-34 (No. 91-1330).

Congressional Record Vol. 116 (1970):
Aug. 12, considered and passed House.
Nov. 23, considered and passed Senate, amended.
Dec. 16, Senate and House agreed to conference report.

PL91-596 OCCUPATIONAL SAFETY AND HEALTH ACT OF 1970.
Dec. 29, 1970. 91-2. •
•Item 575. 31 p.
84 STAT. 1590.

"To assure safe and healthful working conditions for working men and women; by authorizing enforcement of the standards developed under the Act; by assisting and encouraging the States in their efforts to assure safe and healthful working conditions; by providing for research, information, education, and training in the field of occupational safety and health; and for other purposes."

Legislative History (S. 2193 and related bill):

Senate Hearings: S541-43; S541-44.

Senate Committee Print: *See 1971 CIS/Annual: S542-17.*

House Reports: H343-6 (No. 91-1291, accompanying H.R. 16785); H343-18 (No. 91-1765, Conference Report).

Senate Report: S543-37 (No. 91-1282).

Congressional Record Vol. 116 (1970):
Oct. 13, Nov. 16, 17, considered and passed Senate.
Nov. 23, 24, considered and passed House, amended, in lieu of H.R. 16785.
Dec. 16, Senate agreed to conference report.
Dec. 17, House agreed to conference report.

Senate Report: [Public Works] (No. 91-391). Dec. 10, considered and passed House. House Hearings: H561-15.

Volume 2, Number 1-12 **Unless otherwise noted, all accession numbers refer to the 1970 CIS/Annual.** **CIS/INDEX 663**

Exhibit 73: Legislative history of the Occupational Safety and Health Act of 1970, in the *Congressional Information Service/Annual.*

6. Congressional Index (Commerce Clearing House). This commercial service is a very popular guide to current legislative information. Although it does not contain the actual texts of bills, debates or reports, it does provide extensive indexes, including an index of public general bills by subject and author, a digest of each bill and a status table of actions taken thereon. This status table contains references to hearings, a characteristic lacking in many of the research aids described here.

In addition, *Congressional Index* contains an index of enactments and vetoes; a table of companion bills; lists of pending treaties, reorganization plans, and nominations; a table of voting records on each bill and resolution; and a weekly newsletter on the highlights of the week in Congress.

Issued in two volumes for each Congress, the *Index* has a looseleaf format which permits convenient weekly supplementation of all its indexes and tables. Exhibit 74 shows the Current Senate Status Table entry for the Occupational Safety and Health Act of 1970 in this service.

2462 Current Senate Status Table Number 114—130

For digest, see "Senate Bills" Division.
See also Senate Status Table.

2116
Reptd., no amend., S. Rept. 91-639 .. 1/28/70
Amended on S. Floor [Voice] 2/2/70
Passed S., with amend. [Voice] 2/2/70
To H. Agriculture 2/3/70

2143
S. hearing available 3/13/70

★2162
Reptd., with amend., S. Rept. 91-845 ...... 5/6/70
Passed S. as reported [Voice] 5/11/70
To H. Interstate and Foreign Commerce 5/12/70
H. hearing available 9/18/70
Reptd., with amend., H. Rept. 91-1642 ...... 12/1/70
Passed H., without amend., [Voice] 12/7/70
H. appoints conferees 12/8/70
S. appoints conferees 12/10/70
Conf. Rept. submitted to H., H. Rept. 91-1755 ...... 12/15/70
Conf. Rept. agreed to by S. 12/16/70
Conf. Rept. agreed to by H. 12/16/70
Approved [Public Law 91-601] 12/30/70

★2176
S. hearing available 7/7/70
Reptd., no amend., S. Rept. 91-1083 ...... 8/10/70
Passed S., without amend., [Voice] 8/13/70
To H. Interstate and Foreign Commerce 8/14/70
Passed H., without amend., [Voice] 10/5/70
Approved [Public Law 91-449] 10/14/70

★2193
S. hearing available (Parts 1 & 2) 8/13/70
Reptd., with amend., S. Rept. 91-1282 ...... 10/6/70
Amended on S. Floor [Voice] 11/19/70
Amended on S. Floor [Roll-call] 11/19/70
Passed S., with amend., [Roll-call] 11/17/70
Amended on H. Floor [Voice] 11/24/70
Passed H., with amend., in lieu of H. 16785 [Voice] 11/24/70
H. appoints conferees 11/24/70
S. appoints conferees 11/30/70
Conf. Rept. agreed to by S. 12/16/70
Conf. Rept. submitted to H., H. Rept. 91-1765 ...... 12/16/70
Conf. Rept. agreed to by H. 12/17/70
Approved [Public Law 91-596] 12/29/70

2203
Hearing in S. 1/20/70
S. hearing available 6/12/70

★2208
Reptd., with amend., S. Rept. 91-855 ...... 5/11/70
Passed S. as reported [Voice] 5/13/70
To H. Interior and Insular Affairs 5/14/70
Reptd., with amend., H. Rept. 91-1403 ...... 8/10/70
Passed H. as reported [Voice] 9/14/70
H. amend. agreed to by S. 9/16/70
Approved [Public Law 91-425] 9/26/70

2209
Reptd., with amend., S. Rept. 91-936 ...... 6/18/70
Passed S. as reported [Voice] 6/23/70
To H. Interior and Insular Affairs 6/24/70

★2214
Reptd., no amend., H. Rept. 91-802 .. 1/27/70
Passed H., without amend. [Voice] 2/9/70
Approved [Public Law 91-196] 2/20/70

★2224
H. hearing available (Part 1) 2/13/70
Amended on H. Floor [Voice] 9/23/70
Passed H., with amend., in lieu of H. 17333 [Voice] 9/23/70
H. appoints conferees 9/23/70
S. appoints conferees 10/13/70
Conf. Rept. submitted to H., H. Rept. 91-1631 ...... 11/25/70
Conf. Rept. agreed to by S. 11/30/70
Conf. Rept. agreed to by H. 12/1/70
Approved [Public Law 91-547] 12/14/70

2225
S. hearing available 2/13/70

2230
Hearing in S. 3/12/70

2242
S. hearing available 3/11/70

2245
Hearing in S. 5/6/70

2246
S. hearing available (Part 1) 5/27/70

2253
Reptd., no amend., S. Rept. 91-779 ...... 4/23/70
Indefinitely postponed by S. 4/30/70

Exhibit 74: The Current Senate Status Table in the CCH *Congressional Index,* showing action on S. 2193, the Occupational Safety and Health Act of 1970.

7. U.S. Code Congressional and Administrative News (West Publishing Company). The great value of this service, as noted above, is its publication of the *texts* of enacted public laws and of selected congressional committee reports on the more important acts. None of the previously mentioned publications in this section includes the actual texts of the documents. The bi-weekly advance sheets of *U.S.C.C.A.N.* during the congressional session and its cumulative bound volumes at the end of the session also include a legislative history table providing for each public law: the date approved, the *Statutes at Large* citation, the bill and report numbers, the committees that recommended the legislation, and the dates of consideration and passage. No reference is made to hearings.

U.S.C.C.A.N. only includes measures that have been enacted into law and thus cannot be used to determine the status of *pending* legislation.

Exhibit 75 shows the beginning of the Senate Report on the Occupational Safety and Health Act of 1970, as set out in *U.S.C.C.A.N.* Note that the report is preceded by references to steps in the passage of the legislation, including committee reports not set out there. Exhibit 76 illustrates the treatment of the Act in the legislative history table.

OCCUPATIONAL SAFETY AND HEALTH
P.L. 91-596

OCCUPATIONAL SAFETY AND HEALTH ACT OF 1970

P.L. 91-596, see page 1852

Senate Report (Labor and Public Welfare Committee) No. 91-1282, Oct. 6, 1970 [To accompany S. 2193]

House Report (Education and Labor Committee) No. 91-1291, July 9, 1970 [To accompany H.R. 16785]

Conference Report No. 91-1765, Dec. 16, 1970 [To accompany S. 2193]

Cong. Record Vol. 116 (1970)

DATES OF CONSIDERATION AND PASSAGE

Senate November 17, December 16, 1970

House November 24, December 17, 1970

The Senate bill was passed in lieu of the House bill. The Senate Report and the Conference Report are set out.

SENATE REPORT NO. 91-1282

THE Committee on Labor and Public Welfare, to which was referred the bill (S. 2193) to authorize the Secretary of Labor to set standards to assure safe and healthful working conditions for working men and women, to assist and encourage States to participate in efforts to assure such working conditions, to provide for research, information, education, and training in the field of occupational safety and health, and for other purposes, having considered the same, reports favorably thereon with an amendment (in the nature of a substitute) and recommends that the bill (as amended) do pass.

PURPOSE

The purpose of S. 2193 is to reduce the number and severity of work-related injuries and illnesses which, despite current efforts of employers and government, are resulting in ever-increasing human misery and economic loss.

The bill would achieve its purpose through programs of research, education and training, and through the development and administration, by the Secretary of Labor, of uniformly applied occupational safety and health standards. Such standards would be developed with the assistance of the Secretary of Health, Education and Welfare, and both their promulgation and their enforcement would be judicially reviewable. Encouragement is given to Federal-state cooperation, and financial assistance is authorized to enable states, under approved plans, to take over entirely and administer their own programs for achieving safe and healthful jobsites for the Nation's workers.

5177

Exhibit 75: Senate Report No. 91-1282 on the Occupational Safety and Health Act, as set out in *United States Code Congressional and Administrative News.*

TABLE 4—LEGISLATIVE HISTORY

Public Law				Report No. 91-		Comm. Reporting **		Cong.Rec.Vol. 116 (1970) Dates of Consideration and Passage	
No.91-	Date App.	84 Stat. Page	Bill No.	House	Senate	House	Senate	House	Senate
572	Dec. 24	1504	S. 2108	1472 1667	1004	IFC (H.R. 19318)	LPW	Nov. 16 Dec. 8	July 14 Dec. 10
573	Dec. 24	1508	S. 1499	1711	391	PW	PW	Dec. 10	Sept. 5
574	Dec. 24	1508	S. 3192	1703	1032	PW (H.R. 15205)	PW	Dec. 10	July 21
575	Dec. 24	1509	S. 1079	1643	1333	J	J	Dec. 7	Oct. 14
576	Dec. 24	1541	S. 1100	1701	891	PW	PW	Dec. 10	May 25
577	Dec. 24	1542	S. 3070	1605	1138 1246	Agr	AgrF J	Dec. 8	Oct. 2 Dec. 9
578	Dec. 24	1559	S. 3479	1399	867	IIA (H.R. 15978)	IIA	Sept. 14 Dec. 9	May 18 Sept. 29
579	Dec. 24	1560	H.R. 19846	1651	none	Agr	none	Dec. 7	Dec. 8
580	Dec. 24	1565	S. 4557	1677	1414	AE (H.R. 19908)	AE	Dec. 10	Dec. 9
581	Dec. 24	1566	S. 368	1544	1160	IIA	IIA	Oct. 5 Dec. 9	Sept. 16 Dec. 4, 10
582	Dec. 24	1574	H.R. 8663	1138	1417	AS	AS	June 15	Dec. 10
583	Dec. 24	1574	S. 528	1709	889	PW	PW	Dec. 10	May 22
584	Dec. 24	1575	S. 3785	1232	1606	VA	LPW	Nov. 16 Dec. 10	Sept. 25 Dec. 8
585	Dec. 24	1578	S. 1500	1712	892	PW	PW	Dec. 10	May 25
586	Dec. 24	1578	H.R. 18012	1468	1420	FA	FR	Dec. 7	Dec. 10
587	Dec. 24	1579	S. 4083	1658	1070	EL	LPW	Dec. 7	Aug. 11 Dec. 8
588	Dec. 24	1580	H.R. 15911	1448	1439	VA	F	Sept. 21	Dec. 17
589	Dec. 24	1585	S.J.Res. 236	1598	1229	HA	RA	Dec. 15	Sept. 25
590	Dec. 28	1587	H.R. 8298	520 1744	1330	IFC	C	Aug. 12 Dec. 16	Nov. 23 Dec. 16
591	Dec. 28	1588	H.R. 19402	1615	1440	Agr	AgrF	Dec. 7	Dec. 17
592	Dec. 28	1588	S.J.Res. 226	none	1213	none	J	Dec. 10	Sept. 23 Dec. 15
593	Dec. 28	1589	S.J.Res. 74	none	1207	none	J	Dec. 10	Sept. 23 Dec. 15
594	Dec. 28	1589	S.J.Res. 172	none	703	none	J	Dec. 10	Feb. 17 Dec. 15
595	Dec. 28	1589	S.J.Res. 187	none	1209	none	J	Dec. 10	Sept. 23 Dec. 15
596	Dec. 29	1590	S. 2193	1291 1765	1282	EL (H.R. 16785)	LPW	Nov. 24 Dec. 17	Nov. 17 Dec. 16

** For key to Committee abbreviations see end of Table.

Exhibit 76: The legislative history table in *U.S.C.C.A.N.*, showing its treatment of the Occupational Safety and Health Act of 1970.

8. **Congressional Quarterly Weekly Report.** This weekly commercial publication summarizes congressional activity on major pieces of legislation. The weekly issue is most useful for its coverage of new developments and background discussion of pending legislation. Its status table (Exhibit 77) covers only selected pending proposals and its legislative history table for measures enacted into public law is less comprehensive than that found in other services. The tables of House and Senate votes, however, are thorough and easy to use.

The *Congressional Quarterly Almanac,* "a compendium of legislation for one session of Congress," is published annually. It cumulates many of the tables in the Weekly Report and contains pertinent background material of permanent value relating to congressional activities. The enactment of the Occupational Safety and Health Act is summarized in Exhibit 78.

MAJOR CURRENT LEGISLATION IN 91st CONGRESS

Compiled by Congressional Quarterly as of Dec. 30, 1970

	House	Senate
Democrats	243	58
Republicans	190	42
Vacancies	2	0

HS—Hearings Scheduled OR—Ordered Reported NA—No Action Required
HB—Hearings Begun R—Reported P—Passed
HC—Hearings Completed DB—Debate Begun C—In Conference

BILL	Most Recent Page Reference	HOUSE		SENATE		FINAL
Bank Holding Companies. Federal regulation of one-bank holding companies. **(HR 6778)**	2641	R 7/23/69	P 11/5/69	R 8/10/70	P 9/16/70	Cleared 12/18/70
Broker-Dealer Insurance. Protect investors from broker insolvency. **(HR 19333)**	2939	R 10/21/70	P 12/1/70	R 9/21/70	P 12/10/70	11/30/70 PL 91-598
Congressional Reform. Revises committee and floor procedures. **(HR 17654)**	2321	R 6/17/70	P 9/17/70	R 5/23/69	P 10/6/70	10/26/70 PL 91-510
Consumer Agency. Creates agency to represent consumers in Government proceedings. **(HR 18214)**	3002	R 7/30/70		R 10/12/70	P 12/1/70	
Consumer Relief. Permits class actions in deceptive consumer practices. **(S 3201)**	2640	HC		R 8/14/70		
Credit Reporting. Disclosure of consumer credit reporting. **(Attached to HR 15073)**	2613	HC	P 10/13/70	R 11/5/69	P 11/6/69	10/26/70 PL 91-508
Defense Procurement. Authorizes procurement, research funds for Defense Department. **(HR 17123)**	2471	R 4/24/70	P 5/6/70	R 7/14/70	P 9/1/70	10/7/70 PL 91-441
Drug Control. Revises Federal narcotics and drug laws. **(HR 18583)**	2724	R 9/10/70	P 9/24/70	R 12/16/69	P 1/28/70	10/27/70 PL 91-513
Electoral Reform. Constitutional amendment for direct election of President. **(S J Res 1, H J Res 681)**	2645	R 5/16/69	P 9/18/69	R 8/14/70	DB 9/8/70	
Emergency Home Financing. Emergency funds for home mortgage market. **(S 3685)**	1894	R 5/28/70	P 6/25/70	R 4/7/70	P 4/16/70	7/24/70 PL 91-351
Food Stamp Reform. Free stamps for the neediest of the poor. **(HR 18582, S 2547)**	2900	R 8/10/70	P 12/16/70	R 7/7/69	P 9/24/69	
Foreign Bank Accounts. Curbs evasion of U.S. laws and taxes. **(HR 15073)**	2613	R 3/28/70	P 5/25/70	R 8/24/70	P 9/18/70	10/26/70 PL 91-508
Foreign Trade. Establishes import quotas and extends authority to cut tariffs. **(HR 18970)**	2948	R 8/21/70	P 11/19/70	R 12/11/70	DB 12/16/70	
Higher Education. Extends Federal aid programs for higher education. **(Misc. bills)**	2727	HC		HC		
Impact Aid. Revises per-pupil funding in Federally affected areas. **(HR 16307)**	2642	HC		HC		
Mass Transit. Long-term financing for urban public transportation programs. **(S 3154, HR 18185)**	2391	R 6/30/70	P 9/29/70	R 12/22/69	P 2/3/70	10/15/70 PL 91-453
Military Sales. Extends foreign credit sales 2 years; Indochina amendments. **(HR 15628)**	2643	R 3/5/70	P 3/24/70	R 5/12/70	P 6/30/70	C
Mutual Funds. Tighten regulation of mutual funds. **(S 2224, HR 17333)**	2893	R 8/7/70	P 9/23/70	R 5/21/69	P 5/26/69	12/14/70 PL 91-547
Newspaper Preservation. Exempts from antitrust laws certain operating plans. **(S 1520)**	1784	R 6/15/70	P 7/8/70	R 11/18/69	P 1/30/70	7/24/70 PL 91-353
Occupational Safety. Protect health and safety of employees. **(S 2193)**	2889	R 7/9/70	P 11/24/70	R 10/6/70	P 11/17/70	12/29/70 PL 91-596
Omnibus Farm Bill. Price supports, production controls for major commodities. **(HR 18546)**	2812	R 7/23/70	P 8/5/70	R 8/28/70	P 9/15/70	11/30/70 PL 91-524

Exhibit 77: A summary of the Occupational Safety and Health Act of 1970 in the *Congressional Quarterly Weekly Report.*

MAJOR CONGRESSIONAL ACTION

PASSAGE OF JOB SAFETY BILL ENDS THREE-YEAR DISPUTE

Congress in 1970 completed action on a bill (S 2193—PL 91-596), the Occupational Safety and Health Act, establishing a comprehensive on-the-job safety program for about 55 million industrial, farm and construction workers employed by firms engaged in interstate commerce.

Final action came when the House Dec. 17 by a 309-60 roll-call vote adopted a conference report on the bill. The Senate had adopted the report Dec. 16 by voice vote. *(Vote 242, p. 84-H)*

The legislation gave the Secretary of Labor authority to set safety and health standards for the protection of workers and created a three-member commission to enforce regulations.

Final passage marked the end of a three-year dispute between labor and business forces over how the Federal Government should adopt and enforce safety standards.

Organized labor and most liberal Democrats had wanted the Secretary to set and enforce safety standards while business interests backed by Republicans and the Administration had requested that two Presidentially appointed boards be created, one to set standards and the other to enforce them.

Labor groups contended that independent boards could become captives of the industries they were supposed to regulate. Business interests argued that due process would be violated if the Secretary were allowed to set, monitor and enforce safety rules.

The Senate Nov. 17 passed a bill which provided a compromise by giving the Secretary standards-setting authority and a three-member commission enforcement power.

The House, however, Nov. 24 adopted the Administration- and business-backed approach by establishing two independent boards.

House-Senate conferees followed the Senate version, giving the Secretary the rule-making responsibilities.

But on another key provision, conferees deleted a Senate provision allowing the Secretary to close a plant if an "imminent danger" threatened the lives of workers. House conferees insisted that the Secretary should obtain a court order before a plant could be closed.

Although the conference version drew mixed reactions from labor and business interests, final passage was assured when the Labor Department as well as some business and labor groups endorsed the bill.

Provisions

As cleared by Congress, S 2193:

Duties of Employers

- Required employers to furnish a work place free from recognized hazards that had caused or were likely to cause death or serious physical harm to employees.

Safety and Health Standards

- Required the Secretary of Labor within two years after enactment to promulgate national consensus safety standards and established Federal safety standards.
- Provided that when the Secretary of Labor wished to promulgate, revise or revoke an occupational safety and health standard, he could appoint an ad hoc advisory committee to submit recommendations within three to nine months, but not after that period.
- Required the Secretary of Labor to schedule a hearing on objections to a proposed standard within 30 days after the last day for filing recommendations.
- Authorized the Secretary of Labor to promulgate, revise or revoke a standard within 60 days after the completion of hearings or within 60 days after the last day for filing comments.
- Provided for exemption from standards for any employer who applies to the Secretary of Labor and meets certain requirements.
- Required posting of labels or warnings to apprise employers of safety and health standards to which they are exposed.
- Provided that the Secretary of Labor should establish emergency standards when employees were exposed to grave dangers from toxic materials or new hazards.
- Permitted any person to file for judicial review of a standard within 60 days after it was promulgated.

Advisory Committee

- Established a National Advisory Committee on Occupational Safety and Health consisting of 12 members representing management, labor and occupational safety and

Occupational Accident Facts

"The on-the-job health and safety crisis is the worst problem confronting American workers," reported the House Committee on Education and Labor in October 1970.

The following annual statistics compiled by the Bureau of Labor Statistics (BLS) were cited by the Committee for the nation's 80 million workers:

- 14,500 killed, an average of 55 per day during a five-day work week.
- 2.2 million injured.
- 390,000 cases of occupational diseases (lung cancer, asbestosis, heart disease and others).
- 250 million man days of work lost, 10 times as many as from strikes.
- More than $1.5 billion lost in wages.
- More than an $8 billion loss to the Gross National Product.

A report submitted on contract to the Labor Department Sept. 20 by the Delphic Systems and Research Corporation concluded that the annual BLS survey of work-related accidents was "seriously restricted" by survey-sampling and data-collection procedures at state levels.

The Delphic validation of work injuries reported to the BLS by the state of California—a state with rigorous accident reporting procedures—revealed that more than 36 percent of firms reporting "no injuries" actually had employee accidents. On a national basis, the report projected approximately 200,000 disabling work injuries beyond the 2.2 million reported in 1969.

1970 CQ ALMANAC—675

Exhibit 78: A summary of the Occupational Safety and Health Act of 1970 in the *Congressional Quarterly Almanac.*

9. Congressional Monitor. Similar to the official *Daily Digest*, this *daily* congressional legislative service includes summaries of each day's scheduled activity in the committees and the actions concluded the previous day on the floor. In addition, it contains forecasts of expected activity, brief excerpts of important congressional documents, a weekly list of printed hearings, reports and other legislative documents, and a weekly status table of active bills arranged by broad subject categories. It is not as complete a status table as those discussed previously, and is therefore most useful for quick daily information on major legislative activity.

10. Federal Index (Capitol Services, Inc.). This monthly index, with annual cumulative volumes, provides another means of access to legislative documents, to the *Congressional Record* and to various Presidential documents. In addition, the *Federal Register*, the *Code of Federal Regulations* and other administrative documents and government-related publications are indexed. Access to this service is either by the name of the government agency involved, by specific governmental functions, or by the names of the industries, individuals, institutions, or countries affected by the documents being indexed. (See Exhibit 79 for an illustrative sample.)

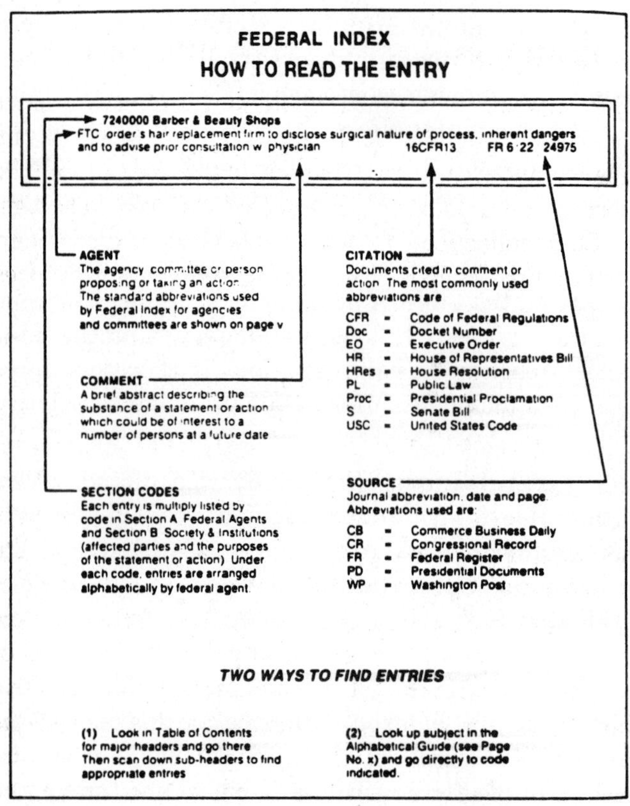

FEDERAL INDEX

HOW TO READ THE ENTRY

7240000 Barber & Beauty Shops
FTC order's hair replacement firm to disclose surgical nature of process, inherent dangers and to advise prior consultation w physician 16CFR13 FR 6 22 24975

AGENT
The agency, committee or person proposing or taking an action. The standard abbreviations used by Federal Index for agencies and committees are shown on page v

COMMENT
A brief abstract describing the substance of a statement or action which could be of interest to a number of persons at a future date

SECTION CODES
Each entry is multiply listed by code in Section A Federal Agents and Section B Society & Institutions (affected parties and the purposes of the statement or action). Under each code, entries are arranged alphabetically by federal agent.

CITATION
Documents cited in comment or action. The most commonly used abbreviations are

CFR = Code of Federal Regulations
Doc = Docket Number
EO = Executive Order
HR = House of Representatives Bill
HRes = House Resolution
PL = Public Law
Proc = Presidential Proclamation
S = Senate Bill
USC = United States Code

SOURCE
Journal abbreviation, date and page. Abbreviations used are:

CB = Commerce Business Daily
CR = Congressional Record
FR = Federal Register
PD = Presidential Documents
WP = Washington Post

TWO WAYS TO FIND ENTRIES

(1) Look in Table of Contents for major headers and go there. Then scan down sub-headers to find appropriate entries

(2) Look up subject in the Alphabetical Guide (see Page No. x) and go directly to code indicated.

Exhibit 79: Sample entry and instructions appearing in each issue of the *Federal Index.*

COMPILED LEGISLATIVE HISTORIES

The legislative histories of a few important laws have been compiled and published in book form. These compilations may include some or all of the important bills, debates, committee reports, hearings, etc. Such collections save the researcher the considerable time and trouble of compiling relevant references and documents. Among those issued commercially are a six volume *Legislative History of the 1909 Copyright Act* (Rothman, 1976), Resnick & Wypyski's seventeen volume *Bankruptcy Reform Act of 1978* (Hein, 1979) and Earl Kintner's *Legislative History of the Federal Antitrust Laws and Related Statutes* (Chelsea House, 1978—in progress). Others are published by government agencies, e.g., the National Labor Relations Board's excellent two volume histories of the Wagner Act, the Taft-Hartley Act, and the Labor-Management Reporting and Disclosure Act of 1959. For an example of a recent compiled legislative history, see Exhibit 80, the *Legislative History of the Occupational Safety and Health Act of 1970*, prepared by the Subcommittee on Labor of the Committee on Labor and Public Welfare of the U.S. Senate.

92d Congress }
1st Session }

COMMITTEE PRINT

LEGISLATIVE HISTORY OF THE OCCUPATIONAL SAFETY AND HEALTH ACT OF 1970

(S. 2193, P.L. 91–596)

PREPARED BY THE

SUBCOMMITTEE ON LABOR

OF THE

COMMITTEE ON LABOR AND PUBLIC WELFARE
UNITED STATES SENATE

JUNE 1971

Printed for the use of the Committee on Labor and Public Welfare

Exhibit 80: The title page of a compiled legislative history of the Occupational Safety and Health Act of 1970.

Compiled legislative histories are now also available in various microformats issued by several commercial publishers. C.I.S., through its *Legislative History Service,* offers on microfiche full documentation on all major acts beginning with the 97th Congress (1981). Available with this service is the loose-leaf, *Annotated Directories,* summarizing each major law and providing citations to and abstracts of the documents included in the history. The accompanying *List of Laws Covered* identifies laws enacted to date within the session and indicates whether each is covered by the *Service.* Similar retrospective coverage was formerly provided by Information Handling Service's *Legislative Histories Microfiche Program,* but this has now been discontinued. That *Program* covered general acts and internal revenue acts for the 82nd Congress (1951) to the 95th Congress (1980), and internal revenue acts only, for the 61st Congress (1909) to the 81st Congress (1950).

Commerce Clearing House's service, *Public Laws—Legislative Histories on Microfiche,* provides documents beginning with enactments of the 96th Congress (1981). Paper indexes accompany the service, including one showing the complete legislative history of each public law. Selective legislative histories are also published from time to time by the American Enterprise Institute, the Congressional Research Library of the Library of Congress, and the U.S. General Accounting Office.

LEXIS provides full-text legislative histories for two of its files: Federal Tax Library and Securities Law Library. The Tax Library includes all public laws beginning with the 1954 *Internal Revenue Code*, all revenue bills reported out of committee, and house, senate and conference reports. The Securities Library includes House & Senate and conference reports relating to the Securities Act of 1933, the Securities Exchange Act of 1934, and all subsequent amendments.

Until 1979 the means for identification and location of compiled legislative histories was quite limited. Now Nancy Johnson's *Sources of Compiled Legislative Histories* (Rothman, 1979, with 1981 supplement) covers laws from the 1st to the 96th Congresses, and this long-neglected area is now well served. The volume is composed of two parts, plus indexes. Part I lists major compilations arranged by publisher, looseleaf services, on-line services, and subject collections according to topic. Part II lists the sources of compiled legislative histories in public law number sequence, with indication of the types of materials available. See Exhibit 81, below, for a sample page.

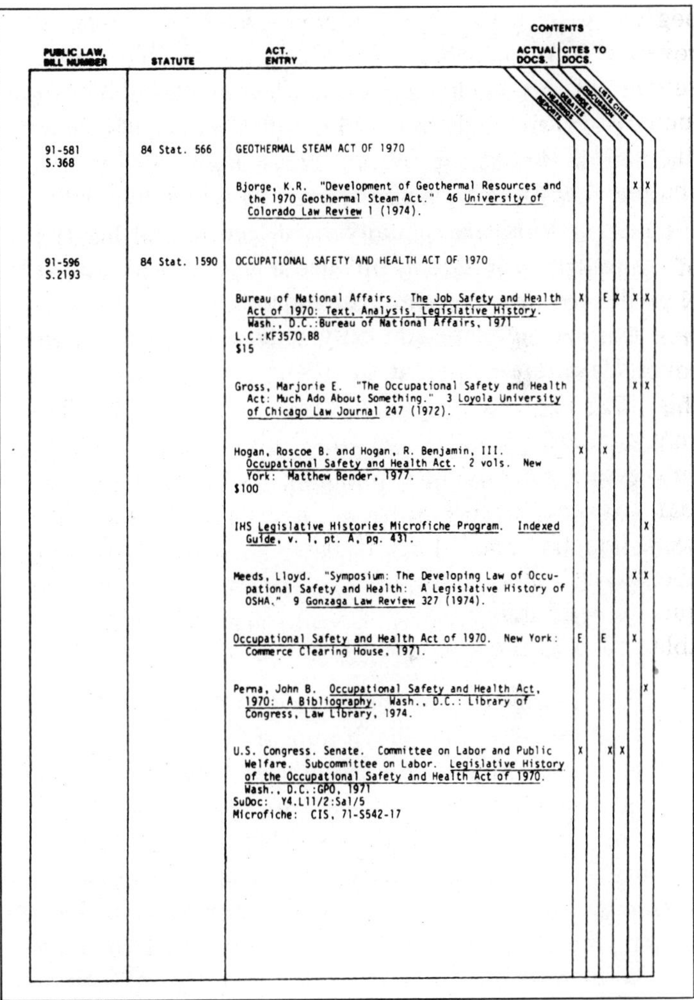

PUBLIC LAW, BILL NUMBER	STATUTE	ACT. ENTRY	CONTENTS: ACTUAL DOCS. REPORTS	HEARINGS	DEBATES	INDEX	CITES TO DOCS. DISCUSSION	LISTS CITES
91-581 S.368	84 Stat. 566	GEOTHERMAL STEAM ACT OF 1970						
		Bjorge, K.R. "Development of Geothermal Resources and the 1970 Geothermal Steam Act." 46 University of Colorado Law Review 1 (1974).					X	X
91-596 S.2193	84 Stat. 1590	OCCUPATIONAL SAFETY AND HEALTH ACT OF 1970						
		Bureau of National Affairs. The Job Safety and Health Act of 1970: Text, Analysis, Legislative History. Wash., D.C.:Bureau of National Affairs, 1971 L.C.:KF3570.B8 $15	X		E	X	X	X
		Gross, Marjorie E. "The Occupational Safety and Health Act: Much Ado About Something." 3 Loyola University of Chicago Law Journal 247 (1972).					X	X
		Hogan, Roscoe B. and Hogan, R. Benjamin, III. Occupational Safety and Health Act. 2 vols. New York: Matthew Bender, 1977. $100	X		X			
		IHS Legislative Histories Microfiche Program. Indexed Guide, v. 1, pt. A, pg. 431.						X
		Meeds, Lloyd. "Symposium: The Developing Law of Occupational Safety and Health: A Legislative History of OSHA." 9 Gonzaga Law Review 327 (1974).					X	X
		Occupational Safety and Health Act of 1970. New York: Commerce Clearing House, 1971.	E		E		X	
		Perna, John B. Occupational Safety and Health Act, 1970: A Bibliography. Wash., D.C.: Library of Congress, Law Library, 1974.						X
		U.S. Congress. Senate. Committee on Labor and Public Welfare. Subcommittee on Labor. Legislative History of the Occupational Safety and Health Act of 1970. Wash., D.C.:GPO, 1971 SuDoc: Y4.L11/2:Sa1/5 Microfiche: CIS, 71-S542-17	X		X	X		

Exhibit 81: Some entries for the Occupational Safety & Health Act, in N. Johnson, *Sources of Compiled Legislative Histories.*

STATE LEGISLATIVE HISTORY

The search for legislative history on the state level is a very difficult and frequently impossible task. Although almost every state has a legislative journal, only a few of these actually include transcripts of the debates. Bills are usually available from the state legislatures on request, but are not widely distributed and hence hard to locate after enactment. Committee reports are published in only a few states and hearings even more rarely.

There are status tables or digests of current bills published in a number of states, either officially by the state or by a private publisher. One of the best sources of legislative history are the session law services published in connection with some of the annotated statutory codes. Some looseleaf services also provide coverage of current state legislation in their subject areas.

Official agencies for the recommendation and drafting of new legislation have appeared in many states. These may be independent agencies (such as some of the law revision commissions); or be attached to the judiciary (such as judicial councils); or may function as branches of the legislatures (like the legislative councils). Such groups recommend new rules or legislation and prepare drafts of bills designed to implement their proposals. Their studies are, of course, persuasive with the legislatures and their recommendations are often enacted into law. In such a case the published report of the commission or council may provide an invaluable source of legislative history of the resultant enactment. Citations to such studies and reports can often be found in the *State Government Research Checklist* (formerly the *Legislative Research Checklist*), issued bi-monthly by the Council of State Governments.

Mary Fisher's *Guide to State Legislative Materials* (Rothman, rev. ed., 1983) is an extremely useful tool for identifying what legislative and administrative documents are available for each state, and from whom these documents can be obtained. This work also identifies and describes the services of several commercial firms which monitor legislative and regulatory activity within the states. Among such services are *ELSS, State Legislative Reporting Service* and *Advanced Session Laws Reports,* all provided by Commerce Clearing House; *Public Affairs Information* of Falls Church, Virginia, and *S.&F.A. Reporting Services* of Washington, D.C., both of which monitor legislative and regulatory activity in all states for clients on a subscription basis.

Since the available materials and tools for research in legislative history vary widely from state to state, one should become familiar with the sources that exist in the states of particular interest. Frequently the state law library or legislative reference library offers useful assistance in this area. Appendix A, below, contains a list of legal research guides for a number of states. Most of these guides include information on the state's legislative materials.

For directory information on state legislatures, their members, staffs, committees and organization, official state manuals (sometimes called *Blue Books* or *Red*

Books) are published annually or biennially by most states. A list of these is available from the Council of State Governments, *State Blue Books and Reference Publications* (1972). The Council's biennial *Book of the States* is a useful source of varied information on state legislation and legislative trends and developments. The *Monthly Checklist of State Publications* (Library of Congress, 1910-date) lists most publications, including legislative documents, issued by each state. It is not complete, however, and is somewhat slow in its coverage.

CHAPTER VI

ADMINISTRATIVE LAW

Although administrative and executive agencies have existed since the creation of our country, their real growth began with the Industrial Revolution in the late nineteenth century. At that time, the increasingly complex problems of society and economy led to an expansion of the traditional functions of executive departments and to the creation of many new administrative agencies. In this century, two World Wars and an economic depression hastened this development and brought about a tremendous proliferation of documentary output, much of which is of legal significance.

The regulatory agencies were created by Congress to carry out new economic legislation when it became apparent that Congress and the courts lacked the flexibility, expertise, time and personnel to handle this task. The agencies were given the power to promulgate regulations in order to perform their statutory functions and, when it appeared that these regulations had been violated, to hold quasi-judicial hearings. Their orders, regulations and decisions have the force of law, and form an important segment of legal bibliography.

Administrative agencies exist on all levels of our political system: in the federal government, where access to regulations and decisions is relatively good; in the states, where such administrative materials are often difficult to locate; and on the local level, where published texts of regulations and agency decisions are virtually non-existent.

UNITED STATES GOVERNMENT MANUAL

Research in administrative law frequently requires a preliminary understanding of the functions and structure of the agency under consideration. The most comprehensive single source for such information is the *United States Government Manual,* an annual directory of general information about the federal government, with primary emphasis upon the executive branch and regulatory agencies. (It also contains some information about Congress and the judiciary.) Each executive department and agency is described with the following coverage:

1. Citations to statutes creating and affecting the agency.
2. Descriptions of the functions and authority of the agency.
3. Information about subsidiary units, bureaus, and predecessor agencies.
4. Names and functions of major officials.
5. Organizational charts.
6. Sources of information available from the agency.

The *Manual* is one of the most important reference books of the federal government and is a major publication of the Federal Register System. It can often save a researcher considerable time by providing quick answers to questions which might otherwise require extensive research.

For a description of the Occupational Safety and Health Review Commission in the *Manual,* see Exhibit 82.

The *Federal Regulatory Directory* (Congressional Quarterly, Inc., 1979-date, annual) is another useful source of similar information on federal agencies, their activities and personnel.

OCCUPATIONAL SAFETY AND HEALTH REVIEW COMMISSION

1825 K Street NW., Washington, D.C. 20006
Phone, 202–634–7943

Robert A. Rowland	*Chairman*
	Commissioners:
Timothy F. Cleary	
Bertram Robert Cottine	
Paul A. Tenney (Chief Judge)	*Administrative Law Judge*
	Executive Staff:
Robert A. Rowland	*Chairman*
James R. Meadows, Jr.	*Executive Director*
Paul A. Tenney	*Chief Judge*
E. Ross Buckley	*General Counsel*
Ray H. Darling, Jr.	*Executive Secretary*
Linda A. Smith	*Public Information Specialist*

The Occupational Safety and Health Review Commission is an independent quasi-judicial agency established by the Occupational Safety and Health Act of 1970 (84 Stat. 1590; 29 U.S.C. 651–678).

The Occupational Safety and Health Review Commission (OSHRC) is charged with ruling on cases forwarded to it by the Department of Labor when disagreements arise over the results of safety and health inspections performed by the Department's Occupational Safety and Health Administration (OSHA). Employers have the right to dispute any alleged job safety or health violation found during the inspection by OSHA, the penalties proposed by OSHA, and the time given by OSHA to correct any hazardous situation. Employees and representatives of employees may initiate a case by challenging the propriety of the time OSHA has allowed for correction of any violative condition.

The Occupational Safety and Health Act covers virtually every employer in the country. Enforced by the Secretary of Labor, the act is an effort to reduce the incidence of personal injuries, illness, and deaths among working men and women in the United States which result from their employment. It requires each employer to furnish to each of his employees, employment and a place of employment which are free from recognized hazards that are causing or likely to cause death or serious physical harm to his employees and to comply with occupational safety and health standards promulgated under the act.

Functions

The Review Commission was created to adjudicate enforcement actions initiated under the act when they are contested by employers, employees, or representatives of employees. A case arises when a citation is issued against an employer as the result of an OSHA inspection and it is contested within 15 working days.

The Commission is more of a court system than a simple tribunal, for within the Review Commission there are two levels of adjudication. All cases which require a hearing are assigned to a Review Commission Administrative Law Judge (ALJ) who decides the case. Ordinarily the hearing is held in the community where the alleged violation occurred or as close as possible. At the hearing, the Secretary of Labor will generally have the burden of proving the case. After the hearing, the judge must issue a decision, based on finding of fact and conclusion of law. A substantial number of the decisions of the judges become final orders of the Commission. However, each ALJ decision is subject to

Exhibit 82: Description of the Occupational Safety and Health Review Commission in the *United States Government Manual.*

discretionary review by the three members of the Review Commission upon the direction of any one of the three, if done within 30 days of the filing of the decision. When that occurs, the Commission issues its own decision.

Once a case is decided, any person adversely affected or aggrieved, thereby may obtain a review of the decision in the United States Court of Appeals.

The principal office of the Review Commission is in Washington, D.C. There are also seven regional offices where Review Commission Judges are stationed:

Review Commission Judges—Occupational Safety Review Commission

Address	Phone
Atlanta, Ga. 30309	
1365 Peachtree St. NE	404-881-4086
Boston, Mass. 02110	
John W. McCormack Post Office and Courthouse	617-223-3757
Chicago, Ill. 60603	
55 E. Monroe St.	312-353-2564
Dallas, Tex. 75242	
1100 Commerce St.	214-767-5271
Denver, Colo. 80265	
1050 17th St.	303-837-2281
New York, N.Y. 10036	
1515 Broadway	212-944-3455
St. Louis, Mo. 63101	
1114 Market St.	314-425-5071

Sources of Information

To give the public and persons appearing before the Commission a better understanding of the act, and the Commission's procedures and decisions, members and officials participate as speakers or panel members before bar associations, safety councils, labor organizations, management associations, and educational, civic, and other groups. Requests for speakers, panelists, or any publications may be made to the Commission's Washington office.

For further information, contact the Public Information Speciali.t, Occupational Safety and Health Review Commission, 1825 K Street NW., Washington, D.C. 20006. Phone, 202-634-7943.

Approved.

Robert A. Rowland,
Chairman.

Exhibit 82: Cont'd

FEDERAL ADMINISTRATIVE REGULATIONS

1. Federal Register. As more and more executive and administrative orders and regulations were promulgated in the early New Deal period it became increasingly difficult to locate them and to know which were in effect at any particular time. There was no requirement that regulations be centrally filed, nor that they be published either as issued or in a compiled form. Public indignation arose over the confusion, uncertainty, and inaccessibility of these legal sources.

Two important cases reached the U.S. Supreme Court where it was discovered that the administrative regulations on which they were based no longer were in effect. Newspapers throughout the country and opponents of the government criticized it for prosecuting people under non-existent laws.

This furor led in 1935 to the enactment of the Federal Register Act which established the *Federal Register* as a daily gazette for executive and administrative promulgations. Executive orders and administrative regulations must be published in the *Federal Register* if they are to be legally effective. A 1937 amendment to the Act created the *Code of Federal Regulations,* which arranged the effective regulations in an indexed subject compilation with provision for supplementation.

The *Federal Register,* pursuant to its authorizing legislation, contains the following documents:

(a) Presidential proclamations and executive orders of general applicability and legal effect;

(b) Such other documents as the President may determine from time to time have general applicability and legal effect;

(c) Such documents as may be required to be published by Act of Congress;

(d) Other documents selected by the director of the *Federal Register.*

For the purpose of inclusion in the *Register*:

"Document includes any Presidential proclamation or Executive order, and any rule, regulation, order, certificate, code of fair competition, license, notice, or similar instrument issued, prescribed, or promulgated by an agency;

" 'Document having general applicability and legal effect' means any document issued under proper authority prescribing a penalty or course of conduct, conferring a right, privilege, authority, or immunity, or imposing an obligation, and relevant or applicable to the general public, members of a class, or persons in a locality, as distinguished from named individuals or organizations; . . ." (1 *C.F.R.* § 1.1, 1984).

In addition to such executive and administrative documents, every federal agency must publish in the *Federal Register* proposed rules that it plans to adopt, and must afford to interested parties an opportunity to be heard on the proposed rules. Federal agencies frequently formulate and adopt *policies* governing the way they conduct agency business of various kinds. If such policies are formally adopted for general use, they must be published in the *Federal Register.* A policy adopted for a particular adjudication, however, does not have to be published.

For an example of a regulation published in the *Federal Register,* see Exhibit 83.

The arrangement of material in the *Federal Register* has changed from time to time. Presently, the documents in each issue of the *Register* appear in the following order:

(1) List of selected subjects covered in the issue.

(2) Contents table.

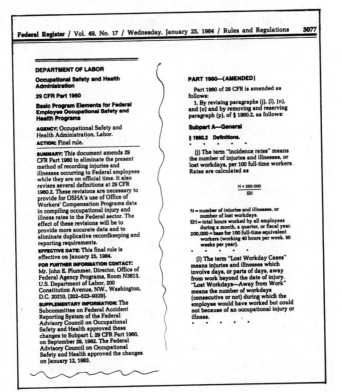

Federal Register / Vol. 49, No. 17 / Wednesday, January 25, 1984 / Rules and Regulations 3077

DEPARTMENT OF LABOR

Occupational Safety and Health Administration

29 CFR Part 1960

Basic Program Elements for Federal Employee Occupational Safety and Health Programs

AGENCY: Occupational Safety and Health Administration, Labor.

ACTION: Final rule.

SUMMARY: This document amends 29 CFR Part 1960 to eliminate the present method of recording injuries and illnesses occurring to Federal employees while they are on official time. It also revises several definitions at 29 CFR 1960.2. These revisions are necessary to provide for OSHA's use of Office of Workers' Compensation Programs data in compiling occupational injury and illness rates in the Federal sector. The effect of these revisions will be to provide more accurate data and to eliminate duplicative recordkeeping and reporting requirements.

EFFECTIVE DATE: This final rule is effective on January 25, 1984.

FOR FURTHER INFORMATION CONTACT: Mr. John E. Plummer, Director, Office of Federal Agency Programs, Room N3613, U.S. Department of Labor, 200 Constitution Avenue, NW., Washington, D.C. 20210, (202-523-9329).

SUPPLEMENTARY INFORMATION: The Subcommittee on Federal Accident Reporting System of the Federal Advisory Council on Occupational Safety and Health approved these changes to Subpart I, 29 CFR Part 1960, on September 29, 1982. The Federal Advisory Council on Occupational Safety and Health approved the changes on January 12, 1983.

PART 1960—[AMENDED]

Part 1960 of 29 CFR is amended as follows:

1. By revising paragraphs (j), (l), (n), and (o) and by removing and reserving paragraph (p), of § 1960.2, as follows:

Subpart A—General

§ 1960.2 Definitions.

* * * * *

(j) The term "incidence rates" means the number of injuries and illnesses, or lost workdays, per 100 full-time workers. Rates are calculated as

$$\frac{N \times 200.000}{EH}$$

N = number of injuries and illnesses, or number of lost workdays.
EH = total hours worked by all employees during a month, a quarter, or fiscal year.
200,000 = base for 100 full-time equivalent workers (working 40 hours per week, 50 weeks per year).

* * * * *

(l) The term "Lost Workday Cases" means injuries and illnesses which involve days, or parts of days, away from work beyond the date of injury. "Lost Workdays—Away from Work" means the number of workdays (consecutive or not) during which the employee would have worked but could not because of an occupational injury or illness.

* * * * *

Exhibit 83: A new rule appearing in the *Federal Register*, amending 29 *C.F.R.* with respect to occupational safety and health.

(3) List of CFR Parts Affected in the issue.

(4) Presidential Documents.

(5) Rules and Regulations.

(6) Proposed Rules.

(7) Notices.

(8) List of Sunshine Act Meetings.

(9) Readers' Aids, which include:

(a) Telephone numbers for information and assistance.

(b) A listing of *Federal Register* pages and dates for the month.

(c) Cumulative list of *C.F.R.* parts affected in that month's issues.

(d) A list of agencies which have agreed to publish their documents on designated days of the week.

(e) A list of public bills which have been enacted into law.

The *Federal Register* has been published continuously since March 14, 1936 and provides a chronological source, similar to a session law text, for administrative documents. Indexing has improved over the years until now each daily issue contains its own table of contents as well as two guides noting which regulations have been changed in that issue (List of C.F.R. Parts Affected in this Issue) and which have been changed since the beginning of the month (Cumulative List of C.F.R. Parts Affected During ______). In addition, at the end of each month, a monthly index is published along with a separate pamphlet entitled *List of C.F.R. Sections Affected* which cumulates references to all changes since the last revision of the titles in the *Code of Federal Regulations.* These lists, which are the basic finding tool for locating changes in the *Register,* are based on the titles and sections of the *Code of Federal Regulations* into which they will be codified. Exhibit 84 shows a portion of such a list in the February 17, 1984, issue of the *Register.*

Federal Register / Vol. 49, No. 34 / Friday, February 17, 1984 / Contents

CFR PARTS AFFECTED IN THIS ISSUE

A cumulative list of the parts affected this month can be found in the Reader Aids section at the end of this issue.

3 CFR
Administrative Orders:
Presidential Determinations:
No. 84-3 of December 10, 1983.......... 6071
No. 84-4 of January 18, 1984.......... 6073

7 CFR
271.......... 6292
272.......... 6292
273.......... 6292
275.......... 6292
277.......... 6292
301.......... 6075
620.......... 6075
622.......... 6075
623.......... 6075
910.......... 6080
Proposed Rules:
810.......... 6103

9 CFR
201.......... 6080
203.......... 6080

13 CFR
Proposed Rules:
124.......... 6103

14 CFR
39 (2 documents).... 6085, 6086
71 (2 documents).... 6087, 6088
Proposed Rules:
71 (3 documents).... 6103, 6112

16 CFR
2.......... 6089

21 CFR
430.......... 6090
436.......... 6090
440.......... 6090
450.......... 6090
455.......... 6090
555.......... 6090
Proposed Rules:
176.......... 6113

29 CFR
Proposed Rules:
1926.......... 6280

30 CFR
250.......... 6095

32 CFR
1-39.......... 6262

39 CFR
111.......... 6095

40 CFR
35 (2 documents).... 6224, 6254
Proposed Rules:
35.......... 6113

43 CFR
426.......... 6096

47 CFR
95.......... 6098
Proposed Rules:
81.......... 6116
83 (2 documents).... 6114, 6116

49 CFR
Proposed Rules:
1002.......... 6118
1011.......... 6118
1152.......... 6118
1177.......... 6118
1180.......... 6118
1182.......... 6118

50 CFR
17.......... 6099

Exhibit 84: List of C.F.R. Parts Affected in a daily issue (February 17, 1984) of the *Federal Register.*

The text of material in the *Federal Register* is *prima facie* evidence of its filing. If a regulation is not published therein, it is not binding unless one can be shown to have had *actual and timely* notice of the regulation. Such proof is, of course, quite difficult and the requirement effectively deters non-publication.

Because of the great bulk of the *Register* and because of the poor quality of paper used, more and more libraries are purchasing a microfilm or microfiche edition of the *Register* and keeping only the annual index and *List of C.F.R. Sections Affected* in their original form as finding tools for the microfacsimile. The *Federal Register* has a permanent reference value and consequently should be accessible in some form. That importance is enhanced by the *Register's* inclusion of some material which never appears in its companion publication, the *Code of Federal Regulations.* It provides the only complete history of regulations with the text of all changes, and includes the following documents which may not be carried over to the *Code:* descriptions of agency organization and reorganization, proposed rules, policy statements relating to the adoption of new rules, and rules which have been repealed.

There is a detailed description of the *Federal Register,* with explanations for its use, in the Office of the Federal Register's publication, *The Federal Register: What it is and How to Use it; a Guide for the User of the Federal Register, Code of Federal Regulations* (U.S.G.P.O., 1980).

2. Code of Federal Regulations. In 1937, realizing the limitations of chronological publication and the need for a permanent subject compilation of current regulations, Congress established the *Code of Federal Regulations.* The regulations in the *Code* are collected from the *Federal Register* and are arranged in a subject scheme that comprises fifty titles, most of which carry the names of the titles of the *U.S. Code* to which they relate. Each title is divided into chapters, parts, and sections, and the citation form is to title and section, e.g., 29 *C.F.R.* § 1910 (Title 29, Section 1910). The *Code* includes an annually revised "Index and Finding Aids" volume which provides access to the *Code's* contents by agency name and subject.

The *Code* is kept up to date by a process of perpetual revision. Each year, the set is completely revised by the issuance of new pamphlets, containing all the regulations in force at the time of publication. The revisions of the various titles are issued on a quarterly basis—Titles 1–16 as of January 1; titles 17–27 as of April 1; titles 28–41 as of July 1; and titles 42–50 as of October 1.

Each volume contains, at the back, a list of C.F.R. Sections Affected, cumulating all changes back to January 1, 1973. Changes from 1949 to 1973 have been cumulated and published in a three separate volume set for the whole Code, called *List of C.F.R. Sections Affected, 1949–1963,* and *1964–1972.*

The *C.F.R.* pamphlets may not reflect all of the changes made during the year if sections were then modified again. As noted above, the *Federal Register* therefore remains the only source for obtaining *all* of the different versions which may have been in effect, even briefly, during the year. Sample pages of the *Code* are reproduced in Exhibit 85.

Chapter XVII—Occupational Safety and Health Administration **Part 1910**

§ 1908.10 Exclusions.

An agreement under this part will not restrict in any manner the authority and responsibility of the Assistant Secretary under sections 8, 9, 10, 13, and 17 of the Act, or any corresponding State authority.

PART 1910—OCCUPATIONAL SAFETY AND HEALTH STANDARDS

73

Exhibit 85: The beginning of Part 1910 of Title 29, *Code of Federal Regulations*, concerning occupational safety and health standards.

Subpart A—General

§ 1910.1 Purpose and scope.

(a) Section 6(a) of the Williams-Steiger Occupational Safety and Health Act of 1970 (84 Stat. 1593) provides that "without regard to chapter 5 of title 5, United States Code, or to the other subsections of this section, the Secretary shall, as soon as practicable during the period beginning with the effective date of this Act and ending 2 years after such date, by rule promulgate as an occupational safety or health standard any national consensus standard, and any established Federal standard, unless he determines that the promulgation of such a standard would not result in improved safety or health for specifically designated employees." The legislative purpose of this provision is to establish, as rapidly as possible and without regard to the rule-making provisions of the Administrative Procedure Act, standards with which industries are generally familiar, and on whose adoption interested and affected persons have already had an opportunity to express their views. Such standards are either (1) national concensus standards on whose adoption affected persons have reached substantial agreement, or (2) Federal standards already established by Federal statutes or regulations.

(b) This part carries out the directive to the Secretary of Labor under section 6(a) of the Act. It contains occupational safety and health standards which have been found to be national consensus standards or established Federal standards.

§ 1910.2 Definitions.

As used in this part, unless the context clearly requires otherwise:

(a) "Act" means the Williams-Steiger Occupational Safety and Health Act of 1970 (84 Stat. 1590).

(b) "Assistant Secretary of Labor" means the Assistant Secretary of Labor for Occupational Safety and Health;

(c) "Employer" means a person engaged in a business affecting commerce who has employees, but does not include the United States or any State or political subdivision of a State;

(d) "Employee" means an employee of an employer who is employed in a business of his employer which affects commerce;

(e) "Commerce" means trade, traffic, commerce, transportation, or communication among the several States, or between a State and any place outside thereof, or within the District of Columbia, or a possession of the United States (other than the Trust Territory of the Pacific Islands), or between points in the same State but through a point outside thereof;

(f) "Standard" means a standard which requires conditions, or the adoption or use of one or more practices, means, methods, operations, or processes, reasonably necessary or appropriate to provide safe or healthful employment and places of employment;

(g) "National consensus standard" means any standard or modification thereof which (1) has been adopted and promulgated by a nationally recognized standards-producing organization under procedures whereby it can be determined by the Secretary of Labor or by the Assistant Secretary of Labor that persons interested and affected by the scope or provisions of the standard have reached substantial agreement on its adoption, (2) was formulated in a manner which afforded an opportunity for diverse views to be considered, and (3) has been designated as such a standard by the Secretary or the Assistant Secretary, after consultation with other appropriate Federal agencies; and

(h) "Established Federal standard" means any operative standard established by any agency of the United States and in effect on April 28, 1971, or contained in any Act of Congress in force on the date of enactment of the Williams-Steiger Occupational Safety and Health Act.

§ 1910.3 Petitions for the issuance, amendment, or repeal of a standard.

(a) Any interested person may petition in writing the Assistant Secretary of Labor to promulgate, modify, or revoke a standard. The petition should set forth the terms or the substance of the rule desired, the effects thereof if

Exhibit 85 (continued): the text of 29 *C.F.R.* § 1910 (1983 revision).

RESEARCH IN FEDERAL REGULATIONS

The basic finding aids for the *Federal Register* are the indexes and *Lists of CFR Sections Affected,* described above. For the *Code of Federal Regulations,* research usually begins with a reference found in the *Federal Register,* in an annotated edition of the *U.S. Code,* or in a looseleaf service. If one's research actually starts in the *C.F.R.,* the initial step is to check the index section of the "Index and Finding Aids" volume to locate the relevant title and part of the *Code* for the problem at hand. Exhibit 86 shows sample entries from that index.

Congressional Information Service (CIS) publishes a multi-volume *Index to the Code of Federal Regulations* which offers very detailed indexing of the *C.F.R.* by subject and by geographic locations affected by the *C.F.R.* regulations. See Exhibit 87 for an illustration of this index. Both LEXIS and WESTLAW offer data bases containing the *Federal Register* and *Code of Federal Regulations,* and, as this coverage expands, computer searching of federal regulations may replace many of the traditional indexes.

Two commercial services, the *Federal Index* (Capitol Services, Inc.) and *Federal Regulatory Week* (Prentice-Hall), are also useful for research involving federal regulations. *Federal Index* provides monthly indexing of both the *Federal Register* and *Code of Federal Regulations* (see Exhibit 79 at page 198 above for a sample entry). *Federal Regulatory Week* summarizes major regulations proposed, considered, adopted or rescinded during the previous week. Both are really current awareness services for following recent developments rather than systematic aids for thorough research.

CFR Index — Occupational Safety and Health Administration

455

Exhibit 86: Sample entries from the *C.F.R.* Index in its "Index and Finding Aids" volume, showing entries under O.S.H.A.

CFR INDEX, 1981
SUBJECT INDEX

OCCUPATIONAL

OCCUPATIONAL SAFETY AND HEALTH
SEE ALSO:
(RT) EMPLOYEE SAFETY, HAZARDOUS OCCUPATIONS; INDUSTRIAL HYGIENE; LABOR CONDITIONS; OCCUPATIONAL INJURIES; OCCUPATIONAL SAFETY AND HEALTH PROGRAMS

Occupational Safety and Health Research and Related Activities
T42 Ch1-G 42PH1981: Pg 100

ACCOUNTING — GRANTS
Occupational Safety and Health Training Grants
T42 Ch1-G Pt86-B 42PH1981: Pg 112
Grantee Accountability
T42 Ch1-G Pt87-D 42PH1981: Pg 124

DEMONSTRATION PROGRAMS
Grants for Research and Demonstrations Relating to Occupational Safety and Health
T42 Ch1-G Pt87 42PH1981: Pg 119

FELLOWSHIPS
Occupational Safety and Health Direct Traineeships
T42 Ch1-G Pt86-C 42PH1981: Pg 118

GRANTS — ACCOUNTING
Occupational Safety and Health Training Grants
T42 Ch1-G Pt86-B 42PH1981: Pg 112
Grantee Accountability
T42 Ch1-G Pt87-D 42PH1981: Pg 124

GRANTS — TRAINING PROGRAMS
Grants for Education Programs in Occupational Safety and Health
T42 Ch1-G Pt86 42PH1981: Pg 111

PROGRAM PLANNING — HIGHER EDUCATION
Special Project Grants for Graduate Programs in Public Health
T42 Ch1-D Pt58-B 42PH1981: Pg 532

RESEARCH GRANTS
Grants for Research and Demonstrations Relating to Occupational Safety and Health
T42 Ch1-G Pt87 42PH1981 Pg 119

RESEARCH GRANTS — ELIGIBILITY
Eligibility Award and Termination
T42 Ch1-G Pt87-B 42PH1981 Pg 120

TRAINING PROGRAMS
Administrative Functions Practices and Procedures
T42 Ch1-G Pt80 42PH1981 Pg 100

TRAINING PROGRAMS — GRANTS
Grants for Education Programs in Occupational Safety and Health
T42 Ch1-G Pt86 42PH1981 Pg 111

OCCUPATIONAL SAFETY AND HEALTH ACT OF 1970
USED FOR: WILLIAMS-STEIGER OCCUPATIONAL SAFETY AND HEALTH ACT OF 1970

Executive Order 12196 Occupational Safety and Health Programs for Federal Employees
T3 3PR1981 Pg 145
General Contract Requirements
T25 Ch1-Y Pt273-E 25IN1981: Pg 701
T25 Ch1-Y Pt274-C 25IN1981: Pg 712
General Contract Requirements [Descriptive heading omitted in text for the Subpart]
T25 Ch1-Y Pt277-C 25IN1981: Pg 747
Coordinated Enforcement
T29A Pt42 29LB1981: Pg 238
Occupational Safety and Health Administration, Department of Labor
T29B Ch17 29LB1981: Pg 3
Rules of Procedure
T29B Ch20 Pt2200 29LB1981 Pg 416
Environmental Noise Abatement [Bibliography]
T32A Ch5-K Pt650-G 32ND1981 Pg 912
State Cemetery Grants
T38 Ch1 Pt39 38PR1981 Pg 356
Requirements and Recommended Procedures
T40 Ch1-I Pt240-B 40PF1981 Pg 269
T40 Ch1-I Pt241-B 40PF1981 Pg 277
Williams Steiger Occupational Safety and Health Act of 1970
T41A Ch1 Pt1-12 41PM1981 Pg 61
Labor Relations
T41A Ch9 Pt50-12 41PM1981 Pg 489
Williams Steiger Occupational Safety and Health Act of 1970
T41A Ch29 Pt12-12 41PM1981 Pg 201
Administrative Requirements Governing All Grants and Agreements by Which Department of Labor Agencies Award Funds to State and Local Governments, Indian and Native American Entities, Public and Private Institutions of Higher Education and Hospitals, and Other Quasi-Public and Private Nonprofit Organizations
T41A Ch29 Pt70 41PM1981 Pg 214
Safety and Health Standards for Federal Supply Contracts
T41B Ch50 Pt204 41PM1981 Pg 398
Building Operations Maintenance Protection and Alterations

OCCUPATIONAL SAFETY AND HEALTH ADMINISTRATION (continued)

ADMINISTRATIVE LAW PROCEDURE
Rules of Practice for Variances, Limitations, Variations, Tolerances, and Exemptions Under the Williams-Steiger Occupational Safety and Health Act of 1970
T29B Ch17 Pt1905 29LB1981: Pg 44
Rules of Procedure for Promulgating, Modifying, or Revoking Occupational Safety or Health Standards
T29B Ch17 Pt1911 29LB1981: Pg 4
Rules of Practice in Enforcement Proceedings Under Section 41 of the Longshoremen's and Harbor Workers' Compensation Act
T29B Ch17 Pt1921 29LB1981: Pg 5

ADVISORY BODIES
Advisory Committees on Standards
T29B Ch17 Pt1912 29LB1981: Pg 9

CARCINOGENS — CLASSIFICATIONS
Identification, Classification, and Regulation of Potential Occupational Carcinogens [Forms, Tables]
T29B Ch17 Pt1990 29LB1981: Pg 388

CARCINOGENS — EMPLOYEE SAFETY
Identification, Classification, and Regulation of Potential Occupational Carcinogens [Forms, Tables]
T29B Ch17 Pt1990 29LB1981: Pg 388

CARCINOGENS — REVIEW COMMITTEES
Identification, Classification, and Regulation of Potential Occupational Carcinogens [Forms, Tables]
T29B Ch17 Pt1990 29LB1981: Pg 388

CARCINOGENS — RULE MAKING
Identification, Classification, and Regulation of Potential Occupational Carcinogens [Forms, Tables]
T29B Ch17 Pt1990 29LB1981: Pg 388

CARGO HANDLING EQUIPMENT — INSPECTOR CERTIFICATION
Procedure Governing Accreditation
T29B Ch17 Pt1919-B 29LB1981: Pg 213
Accreditation to Certificate Shore-Based Equipment
T29B Ch17 Pt1919-F 29LB1981: Pg 224

CONSULTANTS — SERVICE CONTRACTS
On-Site Consultation Agreements
T29B Ch17 Pt1908 29LB1981: Pg 64

DISCRIMINATION INVESTIGATIONS — OCCUPATIONAL SAFETY AND HEALTH STANDARDS
Discrimination Against Employees Exercising Rights Under the Williams-Steiger Occupational Safety and Health Act of 1970
T29B Ch17 Pt1977 29LB1981: Pg 383

EMPLOYEE SAFETY — CARCINOGENS
Identification, Classification, and Regulation of Potential Occupational Carcinogens [Forms, Tables]
T29B Ch17 Pt1990 29LB1981: Pg 388

ENVIRONMENTAL IMPACT STATEMENTS
Department of Labor National Environmental Policy Act (NEPA) Compliance Procedures
T29A Pt11 29LB1981: Pg 111

FACILITY CERTIFICATION — SAFETY TESTING LABORATORIES
Accreditation of Testing Laboratories
T29B Ch17 Pt1907 29LB1981: Pg 56

FACILITY INSPECTION — SAFETY TESTING LABORATORIES
Accreditation
T29B Ch17 Pt1907-B 29LB1981: Pg 57

INDUSTRIAL ACCIDENTS — HEARINGS
Investigational Hearings Under Section 41 of the Longshoremen's and Harbor Workers' Compensation Act
T29B Ch17 Pt1922 29LB1981: Pg 11

INFORMATION ACCESS
Special Rules Applicable to Certain Specific Records
T29A Pt70-C 29LB1981: Pg 293

INFORMATION ACCESS — MEDICAL RECORDS
Rules of Agency Practice and Procedure Concerning OSHA Access to Employee Medical Records
T29B Ch17 Pt1913 29LB1981: Pg 19

INSPECTOR CERTIFICATION — CARGO HANDLING EQUIPMENT
Procedure Governing Accreditation
T29B Ch17 Pt1919-B 29LB1981: Pg 213
Accreditation to Certificate Shore-Based Equipment
T29B Ch17 Pt1919-F 29LB1981: Pg 224

INSPECTORS — SECURITY CLEARANCE
Inspections Citations and Proposed Penalties
T29B Ch17 Pt1903 29LB1981: Pg 27

MEDICAL RECORDS — INFORMATION ACCESS
Rules of Agency Practice and Procedure Concerning OSHA Access to Employee Medical

Exhibit 87: Sample entries in the Subject Index if the CIS *Index to the Code of Federal Regulations* (1981-82 edition).

The "Index and Finding Aids" volume of the *Code of Federal Regulations* contains many parallel reference tables which enable the researcher to convert from one legal form to another. The following parallel references can be obtained in that volume or other sources as indicated:

(a) **U.S. Code to C.F.R.:** This table lists those sections of the *U.S. Code* which have been cited as the authority for the rules of an administrative agency. Rules issued by the agency pursuant to that authority appear in the column headed "CFR". See Exhibit 88 below. *U.S.C.A.* and *U.S.C.S.* also provide cross references to the *C.F.R.* under specific code sections.

(b) **C.F.R. to U.S. Code or Statutes at Large:** This information is provided not by a table, but by an "Authority" note at the end of each section of the *C.F.R.*, or at the beginning of a group of similar sections in the *Code.*

(c) **Proclamation, executive order, or reorganization plan to C.F.R.:** These tables, last revised in 1976 and found in the 1976 "Finding Aids" volume of *C.F.R.*, give parallel references from presidential documents to those sections of the *Code* which cite or utilize them. Exhibit 89 below provides cross references from Executive Orders to their related *C.F.R.* citations.

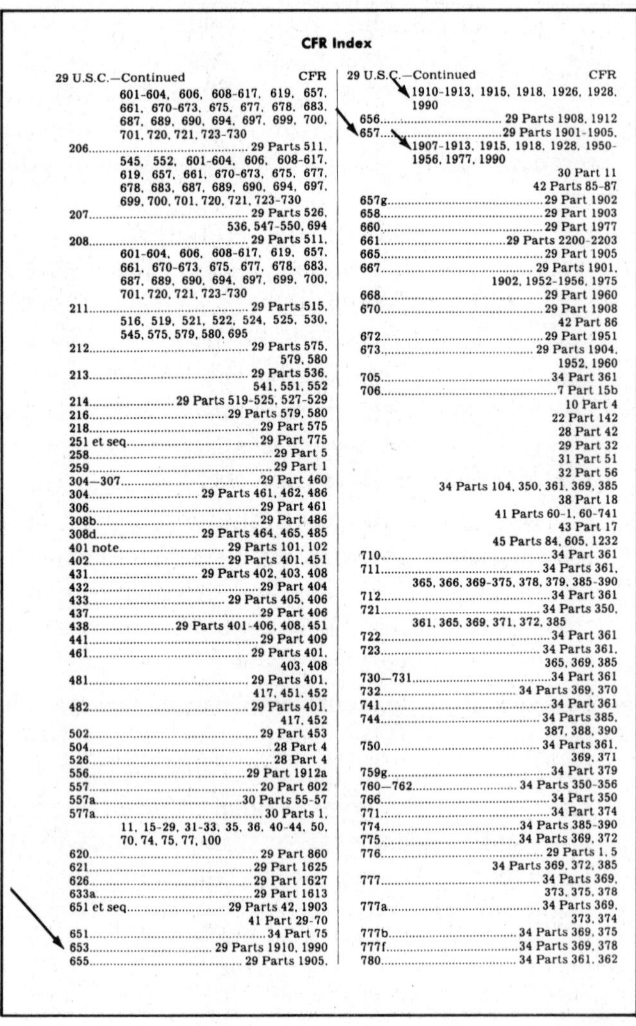

CFR Index

29 U.S.C.—Continued CFR
601-604, 606, 608-617, 619, 657, 661, 670-673, 675, 677, 678, 683, 687, 689, 690, 694, 697, 699, 700, 701, 720, 721, 723-730
206 .... 29 Parts 511, 545, 552, 601-604, 606, 608-617, 619, 657, 661, 670-673, 675, 677, 678, 683, 687, 689, 690, 694, 697, 699, 700, 701, 720, 721, 723-730
207 .... 29 Parts 526, 536, 547-550, 694
208 .... 29 Parts 511, 601-604, 606, 608-617, 619, 657, 661, 670-673, 675, 677, 678, 683, 687, 689, 690, 694, 697, 699, 700, 701, 720, 721, 723-730
211 .... 29 Parts 515, 516, 519, 521, 522, 524, 525, 530, 545, 575, 579, 580, 695
212 .... 29 Parts 575, 579, 580
213 .... 29 Parts 536, 541, 551, 552
214 .... 29 Parts 519-525, 527-529
216 .... 29 Parts 579, 580
218 .... 29 Part 575
251 et seq .... 29 Part 775
258 .... 29 Part 5
259 .... 29 Part 1
304—307 .... 29 Part 460
304 .... 29 Parts 461, 462, 486
306 .... 29 Part 461
308b .... 29 Part 486
308d .... 29 Parts 464, 465, 485
401 note .... 29 Parts 101, 102
402 .... 29 Parts 401, 451
431 .... 29 Parts 402, 403, 408
432 .... 29 Part 404
433 .... 29 Parts 405, 406
437 .... 29 Part 406
438 .... 29 Parts 401-406, 408, 451
441 .... 29 Part 409
461 .... 29 Parts 401, 403, 408
481 .... 29 Parts 401, 417, 451, 452
482 .... 29 Parts 401, 417, 452
502 .... 29 Part 453
504 .... 28 Part 4
526 .... 28 Part 4
556 .... 29 Part 1912a
557 .... 20 Part 602
557a .... 30 Parts 55-57
577a .... 30 Parts 1, 11, 15-29, 31-33, 35, 36, 40-44, 50, 70, 74, 75, 77, 100
620 .... 29 Part 860
621 .... 29 Part 1625
626 .... 29 Part 1627
633a .... 29 Part 1613
651 et seq .... 29 Parts 42, 1903
41 Part 29-70
651 .... 34 Part 75
653 .... 29 Parts 1910, 1990
655 .... 29 Parts 1905, 1910-1913, 1915, 1918, 1926, 1928, 1990

29 U.S.C.—Continued CFR
656 .... 29 Parts 1908, 1912
657 .... 29 Parts 1901-1905, 1907-1913, 1915, 1918, 1928, 1950-1956, 1977, 1990
30 Part 11
42 Parts 85-87
657g .... 29 Part 1902
658 .... 29 Part 1903
660 .... 29 Part 1977
661 .... 29 Parts 2200-2203
665 .... 29 Part 1905
667 .... 29 Parts 1901, 1902, 1952-1956, 1975
668 .... 29 Part 1960
670 .... 29 Part 1908
42 Part 86
672 .... 29 Part 1951
673 .... 29 Parts 1904, 1952, 1960
705 .... 34 Part 361
706 .... 7 Part 15b
10 Part 4
22 Part 142
28 Part 42
29 Part 32
31 Part 51
32 Part 56
34 Parts 104, 350, 361, 369, 385
38 Part 18
41 Parts 60-1, 60-741
43 Part 17
45 Parts 84, 605, 1232
710 .... 34 Part 361
711 .... 34 Parts 361, 365, 366, 369-375, 378, 379, 385-390
712 .... 34 Part 361
721 .... 34 Parts 350, 361, 365, 369, 371, 372, 385
722 .... 34 Part 361
723 .... 34 Parts 361, 365, 369, 385
730—731 .... 34 Part 361
732 .... 34 Parts 369, 370
741 .... 34 Part 361
744 .... 34 Parts 385, 387, 388, 390
750 .... 34 Parts 361, 369, 371
759g .... 34 Part 379
760—762 .... 34 Parts 350-356
766 .... 34 Part 350
771 .... 34 Part 374
774 .... 34 Parts 385-390
775 .... 34 Parts 369, 372
776 .... 29 Parts 1, 5
34 Parts 369, 372, 385
777 .... 34 Parts 369, 373, 375, 378
777a .... 34 Parts 369, 373, 374
777b .... 34 Parts 369, 375
777f .... 34 Parts 369, 378
780 .... 34 Parts 361, 362

Exhibit 88: Table in the "Index and Finding Aids" volume of the *C.F.R.* listing section of the *U.S. Code* which is authority for the regulations at 29 *C.F.R.* § 1910.

Table I—Authorities

Executive Orders—Continued	CFR
	60-2, 60-4, 60-20, 60-30, 60-40, 60-50, 60-60
12091	10 Part 1008
12101	22 Part 151
12105	5 Part 581
12106	29 Part 1613
12107	5 Parts 5, 293, 315, 2400
	12 Part 409
12109	5 Part 595
12114	7 Part 3100
	12 Part 409
	14 Part 1216
	32 Parts 197, 651
	40 Part 6
12123	33 Part 135
	46 Part 544
12125	5 Part 315
12127	44 Parts 1, 2, 5, 6, 9-12, 55-57, 59-62, 64-68, 70, 75-77, 80-83, 150, 151, 200, 201, 205, 300-310, 351, 360
12137	5 Parts 315, 316
	45 Part 1225
12138	36 Part 906
	41 Part 4-1
	49 Part 23
12142	10 Parts 1500, 1502, 1506, 1530
12143	5 Part 352
12144	29 Part 1620
12148	32 Part 185
	44 Parts 1, 2, 9, 12, 200, 201, 205, 300-304, 306-312, 320-333, 351, 360
12155	41 Part 101-14
	44 Part 328
12170	31 Part 535
12173	35 Parts 3, 9, 51, 61, 67, 251, 253
12183	14 Part 91
	15 Parts 368, 370, 386
12185	13 Parts 301, 305-308, 311, 314
	14 Part 152
	23 Parts 420, 450, 630, 1204
	34 Parts 75, 76
	49 Parts 258, 260, 266, 622
12188	7 Parts 2, 16
	15 Parts 359, 2009
12196	29 Part 1960
12205	31 Part 535
12211	22 Part 51
	31 Part 535
12214	15 Parts 368-379, 385-390, 399
12215	35 Parts 70, 101, 103, 105, 107, 109, 111, 113, 115, 117, 119, 123, 125, 133, 135
12224	15 Part 2011
12234	46 Parts 33, 50, 54, 56, 58, 61, 73-75, 94, 163
12241	44 Part 351
12250	7 Part 15b
	28 Parts 41, 42
	32 Part 56

Executive Orders—Continued	CFR
	43 Part 17
12276	31 Part 535
12278—12284	31 Part 535
12291	32 Part 56
	44 Part 1
12294	31 Part 535
12300	5 Part 6
12316	40 Part 300
12341	45 Part 401
12353	5 Part 950
12356	8 Parts 103, 242
	12 Part 403
	14 Part 1203
	17 Part 200
	22 Part 9
	32 Part 2001
	45 Part 601
	50 Part 540
12362	5 Parts 315, 316
12364	5 Part 315
Directives:	
May 17, 1972	5 Part 1301
	7 Part 10
	18 Part 3a
	29 Part 14
	35 Part 60
	40 Part 11
Dec. 7, 1979	44 Part 351
Memorandums:	
Aug. 21, 1963	47 Parts 212, 213
Oct. 10, 1963	7 Part 19
Reorganization Plans:	
1939 Plan No. 1	34 Part 621
1939 Plan No. 2	50 Part 290
1940 Plan No. 4	7 Part 612
1946 Plan No. 2	20 Parts 25, 501
	42 Part 3
1946 Plan No. 3	15 Parts 7a-7c, 9, 10, 16, 17a
	43 Parts 1870, 3100, 3500
1947 Plan No. 3	12 Parts 500, 501, 505-505c, 506, 506a, 508-512, 521-529, 531-534, 541, 543-552, 555, 556, 561-563, 563b-572, 583, 584, 588, 589
1950 Plan No. 2	8 Parts 2, 3
	28 Parts 3, 42, 45
1950 Plan No. 3	25 Parts 84-86, 150, 249, 250
	41 Part 14R-9
	43 Parts 6, 1780
1950 Plan No. 5	15 Parts 4, 4b, 15, 15a, 17a, 30, 807
1950 Plan No. 6	20 Parts 1, 10, 701-704, 718, 725, 727, 801, 802
	29 Parts 2, 70, 526, 541, 579, 580, 689, 697
	41 Parts 29-50, 29-60
1950 Plan No. 10	17 Part 200
1950 Plan No. 14	29 Parts 1, 3, 5-7, 29, 30
1950 Plan No. 17	24 Part 490
1950 Plan No. 19	20 Parts 25, 61, 62, 501

13-046 O—83——46

Exhibit 89: Parallel reference Table in *C.F.R.* "Index and Finding Aids" volume, providing references from Executive orders to *C.F.R.* citations.

(d) **U.S. Code to Presidential Documents:**

The cumulative volumes of Title 3 of *C.F.R.* (except from 1971 to 1973) contain a table of statutory authorities for executive orders and proclamations which cite the *U.S. Code* as authority.

(e) **Presidential Documents to U.S. Code:**

These tables, illustrated in Exhibit 90, are not found in *C.F.R.*, but in the Tables volumes of the *U.S. Code* and its two unofficial versions, *U.S.C.A.* and *U.S.C.S.* They list each executive publication by date and indicate its statutory source in the *U.S. Code.*

(f) **Statutes at Large to C.F.R.:**

These tables, appearing in the "Index and Finding Aids" volume of *C.F.R.*, list the statutes which give an agency the authority to promulgate regulations. An example is shown below in Exhibit 91.

(g) **Public Laws to C.F.R.:**

These tables list the citation to the Public Law which gives each agency the authority to promulgate regulations.

Page 1397

TABLE VI—EXECUTIVE ORDERS

Exec. Ord. Date		Exec. Ord. No.	U.S.C. Title	U.S.C. Sec.	U.S.C. Status
1978					
Jan.	10	12033	22	288 nt	
		12034	42	4992 nt	
	20	12035	5	5317 nt	Elim.
	24	12036	50	401 nt	
Feb.	3	12038	15	717, 717b, 761 nts	
			19	1862 nt	
			31	16 nt	
			42	1962b, 6201, 7151 nts	
			50 App.	2153, 2251 nts	
	24	12039	42	6601 nt	
		12040	42	5910 nt	
	25	12041	19	1202	
				2462 nt	
Mar.	7	12043	5	3301 nt	
	23	12044	5	553 nt	Elim.
	27	12045	3	nt prec. 101	
		12046	47	305 nt	
			50 App.	2251, 2271 nts	
		12047	22	2459 nt	
		12048	22	1461 nt	
		12049	10	131 nt	
Apr.	4	12050	42	2000e nt	
	7	12051	19	2432 nt	
		12052	15	nt prec. 1	
	27	12055	42	2155 nt	
May	8	12057	42	2000e nt	
	11	12058	22	3201 nt	
		12059	28	44 nt	Elim.
	15	12060	5	5317 nt	Elim.
	18	12061	15	631 nt	Elim.
June	5	12063	10	867 nt	Elim.
		12064	26	7443 nt	Elim.
	28	12065	50	401 nt	
	29	12066	22	2382 nt	Elim.
	30	12067	42	2000e nt	
		12068	42	2000e-6 nt	
		12069	5	5317 nt	Elim.
		12070	5	5941 nt	
July	12	12071	29	1001 nt	
Aug.	16	12072	40	490 nt	
		12073	41	401 nt	
		12074	31	16 nt	
		12075	42	1450 nt	
	18	12076	5	5317 nt	Elim.
Sept.	18	12079	49	1723 nt	
		12080	44	1505 nt	
		12081	8	1440 nt	
	19	12082	10	5707 nt	Elim.
	27	12083	42	7101 nt	
		12084	28	133 nt	Elim.
Oct.	5	12086	42	2000e nt	
	7	12087	5	5332 nt	Elim.
	13	12088	42	4321 nt	
	23	12089	15	2401 nt	Elim.
Nov.	1	12091	15	631 nt	
		12092	41	401 nt	Elim.
		12094	37	301 nt	
	2	12096	15	1511 nt	Elim.
	8	12097	28	44, 133 nts	
	17	12099	5	5317 nt	
		12101	22	254c nt	
		12102	19	2111 nt	
Dec.	15	12104	19	2462 nt	
	19	12105	42	661 nt	
	28	12106	29	791 nts	
			42	2000e, 2000e-4, 3001 nts	
		12107	5	1101 nt	
		12108	29	1001 nt	
		12109	5	5948 nt	
		12110	5 App.	14 nt	Elim.
1979					
Jan.	2	12111	5	5317 nt	
		12113	42	1962 nt	
		12114	42	4321 nt	
	19	12115	36	132 nt	
		12116	7	202 nt	

Exec. Ord. Date		Exec. Ord. No.	U.S.C. Title	U.S.C. Sec.	U.S.C. Status
1979					
Feb.	6	12117	22	2151 nt	
		12118	22	2381nt, 2751 nt	
	14	12119	5	5317 nt	
	26	12121	42	7101 nt	
		12122	3	nt prec. 101	
		12123	43	1811 nt	
	28	12124	19	1202, 2462 nt	
Mar.	15	12125	5	3301 nt	
	29	12126	5	1101 nt	
	31	12127	15	2201 nt	
Apr.	4	12128	5	1101 nt	
			22	801 nt	
	5	12129	42	2235 nt	
	11	12130	42	5848 nt	Elim.
May	4	12131	50 App.	2401 nt	
	9	12133	3	nt prec. 101	
		12134	3	nt prec. 101	
		12135	43	2000e nt	
	15	12136	5	4103 nt	
	16	12137	22	2501 nt	
	18	12138	15	631 nt	
	23	12139	50	401 nt, 1802 nt	
	29	12140	15	754 nt	
June	5	12141	42	1962 nt	
	21	12142	15	719e nt	
	22	12143	22	3301 nt	
		12144	42	2000e-4 nt	
July	18	12145	22	1065 nt	Elim.
		12146	28	509 nt	
	19	12147	22	2381 nt	
	20	12148	5	3301 nt	
			41	10d nt	
			42	1450 nt, 1062b nts, 4321 nt, 6201 nt, 7101 nt	
			47	305 nt	
			50	401 nt, 404 nt, 1431 nt	
			50 App.	2153 nts, 2251 nts	
		12149	31	16 nt	
	23	12150	22	2348 nt	
Aug.	14	12152	3	301 nt	
	17	12153	15	757 nt	
Sept.	4	12154	5	5317 nt	
	10	12155	50	98 nt	
			50 App.	2251 nt	
		12156	42	7151 nt	
			50 App.	2251 nt	
	14	12157	5	1101 nt	Elim.
	26	12160	20	2981 nt	
	28	12161	41	401 nt	
		12162	15	754 nt	
	29	12163	7	1691 nt	
			19	2111 nt	
			22	2191 nt, 2381 nt, 2393 nt, 2751 nt	
			50	401 nt	
		12164	22	286b nt	
Oct.	9	12165	5	5332 nt	
	19	12166	12	635 nt	
	23	12167	19	2432 nt	
Nov.	14	12170	50	1701 nt	
	19	12171	5	7103 nt	
	26	12172	8	1185 nt	
	29	12173	22	3831 nt	
	30	12174	5	552 nt	Elim.
Dec.	7	12175	19	2171 nt	
	10	12177	31	68a nt	
		12178	22	2393 nt	
	11	12180	19	1202, 2462 nt	
		12181	19	1202, 2462 nt	
	16	12183	22	287c	
	17	12184	4[illegible]	300v nt	
		12185	42	8373 nt	
	21	12186	15	757 nt	
	29	12187	15	757 nt	

Exhibit 90: Table in the *U.S. Code* (1981 suppl. to 1976 edition) indicating statutory authority for Executive Orders.

Table I—Authorities

83 Stat.	CFR
108	45 Part 1209
124	14 Part 1221
141	34 Part 682
210	32 Part 166
281	50 Part 10
536	26 Part 1
542	26 Part 1
587	26 Part 1
592	26 Part 1
792	20 Part 718
852	33 Part 236
853—854	18 Part 2
854	40 Part 6
1280	15 Part 933
84 Stat.	
55	29 Part 870
204	36 Parts 800, 805
220—233	14 Part 154
234—235	14 Part 139
413	8 Part 293
695	20 Parts 615, 618
708	20 Parts 615, 618
719	39 Part 235
773—775	39 Part 211
799	18 Part 2
843	25 Part 150
922	27 Part 55
952	27 Part 55
1018	50 Part 259
1026	46 Part 283
	50 Part 259
1036	46 Parts 206, 207, 221, 222, 250-252, 276, 280, 283, 294, 298, 308-310, 331, 381, 385, 391
1071	15 Part 1200
1227	40 Parts 165, 240, 241, 243-247
1236	42 Part 2a
1253	21 Part 1304
1258—1259	21 Part 1304
1270	28 Part 0
1271	21 Part 1304
1289	21 Part 1304
1316	45 Parts 1385-1388
1327	49 Part 200
1338—1339	49 Part 251
1361	7 Part 760
1382	7 Part 760
1420—1421	17 Part 270
1424—1425	17 Parts 270, 274
1432—1433	17 Part 275
1509 et seq.	18 Parts 801, 803
1600	29 Part 1951
1613	29 Part 1951
1676	40 Parts 55, 81
1687	40 Part 61
1706	40 Part 54
1713	40 Parts 51, 53
1744	43 Part 1810
	44 Parts 200, 201
1848	32 Part 62
1865	24 Part 222
1880	28 Part 23
1894	7 Part 21
	40 Part 4
84 Stat.—Continued	
1909	25 Part 275
1925	25 Part 275
1975—1976	49 Part 250
2083	47 Parts 214, 215
2090	50 Part 215
85 Stat.	
38	18 Part 2
201	7 Part 796
361	32 Part 62
480	50 Parts 10, 217
492	14 Part 139
531—533	26 Part 142
619—621	12 Parts 602, 605, 613-618
688	25 Part 69
715	25 Parts 69, 123
735	15 Part 908
742	44 Parts 200, 201
743	10 Parts 205, 210, 212
751	5 Part 352
86 Stat.	
3	49 Part 1325
16	11 Parts 106, 110, 114, 115
62	32 Part 621
65	32 Part 62
88—95	45 Part 1321
216	41 Part 101-19
226	10 Part 1020
235	34 Part 222
424	33 Part 401
	46 Parts 71, 91
427	46 Parts 71, 91
461	36 Part 71
471	39 Part 232
530	43 Part 4
559—562	21 Parts 201, 207
613	36 Part 292
621	33 Part 209
623	33 Part 209
670—671	36 Part 270
734	32 Part 216
744	43 Part 4
767	49 Part 1002
770—778	29 Part 1912
770	22 Part 214
	41 Part 105-54
815	40 Part 429
816 et seq.	40 Parts 6, 125, 133, 136, 401, 405-418, 420-422, 424-428, 432, 439, 443, 446, 447, 454, 455, 457-460
816	40 Parts 21, 124, 403, 416, 419, 423, 430, 431, 434, 440, 465, 466
870	46 Part 543
871	40 Part 140
884	50 Part 220
897	40 Part 112
905	5 Part 294
	50 Part 10
909	50 Parts 251, 255, 259
919	31 Part 51

703

Exhibit 91: Table in the "Index and Finding Aids" volume of the *C.F.R.* showing statutory authority for agency regulations in *C.F.R.*

Since title numbers and section numbers of the *Code of Federal Regulations* are used in the List of C.F.R. Parts Affected of the *Federal Register* as a means of identifying subsequent changes in those sections, the *Register* is really a daily supplement to the *C.F.R.* Without the *Code* it would be virtually impossible to research federal regulations, since only it provides the current text with subject access.

In order to make a complete search for a current regulation, the researcher should follow these steps:

(a) Consult the subject index in the "Index and Finding Aids" volume of the *Code of Federal Regulations* to ascertain the relevant title and section of the *Code.*

(b) Locate the regulation itself in the latest revised volume of that title in the *Code.*

(c) Check the monthly pamphlets of the List of C.F.R. Sections Affected to determine if changes in the particular section have occurred since the last revision.

(d) Use the cumulative List of C.F.R. Parts Affected in the most recent issue of the *Federal Register.* This list updates the last pamphlet in (c), by indicating changes occurring within the current month.

(e) Locate the changes that have occurred by consulting the pages in daily issues of the *Federal Register* referred to in the Lists in steps (c) and (d).

(f) Shepardize the regulation in Shepard's *Code of Federal Regulations Citations* to obtain citations to decisions interpreting it. This procedure is described below at pp. 233–237.

Some of these steps can be avoided by using a looseleaf service (if one exists on the subject being researched) or one of the computer research services. Looseleaf services as a source of federal regulations are discussed in Section 3 below. The use of computer services for this purpose is discussed in Section 4. If either a looseleaf service or a computer is used, however, steps (d), (e) and (f) should still be employed since those services may not contain the latest text of the regulation or all of the cases carried in Shepard's.

3. Looseleaf Publication of Regulations. Administrative regulations on selected subjects, such as taxation, labor relations, securities, etc., also appear in commercially published looseleaf services which are dealt with in the next chapter. In that form, the regulations are well indexed and supplemented frequently, usually on a weekly basis. For that reason and also because of their integration with other relevant source material, regulations are widely used in this form. Unfortunately, however, looseleaf services are not available for every subject field.

4. Computer Services. Both LEXIS and WESTLAW provide direct access to the *Code of Federal Regulations,* and both include specialized data bases in a number of federal regulatory fields. These topical "libraries" (e.g., in taxation, labor law, securities, energy law, etc.) contain relevant regulations and administrative decisions, as well as statutes and judicial decisions. Searching by this means is often faster than by traditional sources, and also covers a variety of legal documents, as in the looseleaf services. The Bureau of National Affairs (B.N.A.), a major publishers of looseleaf services, now offers its own computer data bases in labor law, regulation of chemical substances, and intellectual property. These provide similar coverage of regulations and both judicial and administrative decisions.

5. **Agency Publication of Regulations.** The federal administrative agencies themselves often publish texts of their regulations—in either looseleaf or pamphlet form. However, these publications are not well supplemented and, although relatively inexpensive, are not widely used by lawyers or scholars. Information as to their availability is provided in the *Monthly Catalog of U.S. Government Publications.*

6. **Other Sources.** Major administrative regulations are also published selectively in such varied sources as West's *U.S. Code Congressional and Administrative News (U.S.C.C.A.N.),* and the General Law volume of *U.S. Law Week.*

ADMINISTRATIVE DECISIONS AND RULINGS

In addition to their promulgation of regulations, administrative agencies also issue decisions and rulings in the course of their quasi-judicial functions.

Over thirty federal agencies, including the major regulatory commissions, now publish an official edition of those decisions in a form similar to that of the official state reports of court decisions. These reports are in chronological series, usually published first in an advance sheet or slip decision form and then cumulated, though not promptly, into bound volumes. They are cited like court decisions, but with only the name of the private party involved in the proceeding, e.g. General Electric Co., 18 F.T.C. 501 (1958). Depending on the agency, the volumes of decisions may include indexes, digests and tables. However, most of these aids are non-cumulative, applying only to the decisions in the volume in which they appear, and so are of limited utility. The cumulative digest covering decisions of the National Labor Relations Board is an exception. Subject access to the decisions of most agencies is effectively provided only by the privately published looseleaf services, or by computer searching in LEXIS, WESTLAW, or the new B.N.A. regulatory data bases.

There are unofficial publications of some administrative decisions in the following forms:

1. Many looseleaf services publish decisions of administrative agencies in their subject fields (e.g., CCH *Trade Regulation Reporter* which publishes decisions of the Federal Trade Commission). These services usually contain better indexing than the official editions, appear more promptly, and contain other useful research material, such as relevant statutes, *court* decisions, regulations and news developments. However, in many of the services, the decisions appear only in a digested form. Looseleaf services will be described more fully in Chapter VII below.

2. Some unofficial topical reporters in particular subject fields include both court decisions and administrative decisions. Examples of such reporters include the CCH *Federal Occupational Safety and Health*

Decisions, Public Utilities Reports, United States Aviation Reports, and *West's Education Law Reporter.*

3. Pike and Fischer's *Administrative Law Service* is devoted to *procedural* aspects of administrative law and contains decisions of the major regulatory agencies which have been rendered on questions of procedure. These decisions, arranged according to the sections of the Federal Administrative Procedure Act, appear first in looseleaf sheets, then in bound volumes. The service also includes a digest, an index, court decisions, and rules of practice of some agencies.

4. Computer services, such as LEXIS and WESTLAW, include in their specialized regulatory data bases, described above, decisions of administrative agencies. B.N.A.'s new computer data bases, LABORLAW, CHEMLAW and PATLAW, also contain administrative decisions from the federal agencies regulating those fields.

CITATORS FOR FEDERAL ADMINISTRATIVE MATERIALS

Shepard's *Code of Federal Regulations Citations,* beginning in 1979, provides citations to federal and state court decisions and to articles in selected law journals, which have cited or discussed sections of the *Code of Federal Regulations,* Presidential proclamations, executive orders, or reorganization plans. Since *C.F.R.* provisions are frequently revised, the date of the *C.F.R.* editions being cited or of the citing authorities is indicated in this citator, so that the current relevancy of the decision can be determined. This service does not, however, indicate changes in the regulations themselves. Shepard's utilizes abbreviation symbols to indicate significant impact of the decision on the cited regulation (e.g., "u" for unconstitutional). Exhibit 92 shows a typical page in this citator, specifically listing decisions under the occupational safety and health regulations illustrated above.

Shepard's also publishes a number of topical citators which include among their cited materials the regulations of the federal agency in that subject area. These specialized citators include Shepard's *Federal Tax Citations, Federal Labor Law Citations, Bankruptcy Citations, Federal Energy Law Citations, Immigration and Naturalization Citations, Occupational Safety and Health Citations*, and *U.S. Patents and Trademarks Citations.*

In addition to these Shepard's citators, the following other research tools perform a partial citator function with respect to administrative regulations:

(a) Lists of C.F.R. Parts Affected, appearing in the Federal Register and in *C.F.R.* pamphlets.

(b) Looseleaf services in some fields.

(c) "Tables of Statutes Construed" in the National Reporter System, and "Tables of Laws and Regulations cited in *ALR Federal*" appearing in the Lawyers Co-op *Fed Tables* volume with *ALR Federal.*

TITLE 29 CODE OF FEDERAL REGULATIONS

370A2d146 Δ1977
67Geo744 •1977
27ARF950n Δ1976
35ARF54n Δ1977
38ARF511n Δ1978
39ARF144n Δ1978
FRCI§9.05
FRCI§9.11

§1910.1
et seq.
429FS908 Δ1977

§§1910.1 to 1910.1500
630F2d1099 •1979

§1910.1
526F2d58 Δ1975
609F2d1122 Δ1980

§1910.1(b)
505F2d871 Δ1974

§1910.2(c)
616F2d732 Δ1980

§1910.2(f)
526F2d57 Δ1975

§1910.2(h)
526F2d57 Δ1975

§1910.5
583F2d1369 Δ1978
616F2d732 Δ1980

§1910.5(b)
616F2d732 Δ1980
433FS919 Δ1977

§1910.5(c)
601F2d722 Δ1979

§1910.5(c)(1)
537F2d784 Δ1976
554F2d908 Δ1977
556F2d435 Δ1977
585F2d1334 •1972
601F2d722 Δ1979
608F2d581 Δ1979
613F2d121 Δ1980
613F2d1234 Δ1980

§1910.5(c)(2)
601F2d722 Δ1979
613F2d1234 Δ1980
38ARF527n Δ1978

§1910.5(d)
504F2d1260 Δ1974

§1910.5(e)
613F2d121 Δ1980

§1910.5(f)
489F2d1261 •1972
512F2d1150 Δ1975

§§1910.11 to 1910.16
609F2d1122 Δ1980

§1910.11(a)
526F2d57 Δ1975

§1910.11(b)
526F2d56 Δ1975
548F2d249 Δ1977
613F2d1231 Δ1980

§1910.12
516F2d1084 •1974
526F2d58 Δ1975
583F2d1369 Δ1978
613F2d124 Δ1980
Ore
621P2d667 Δ1980

§1910.12(a)
526F2d56 Δ1975
548F2d249 Δ1977

§1910.12(b)
495F2d1299 Δ1974
568F2d905 •1976
429FS908 Δ1977

§1910.12(c)
516F2d1087 •1974
526F2d56 Δ1975
548F2d249 Δ1977
423FS807 Δ1976

§1910.14(a)
613F2d1230 Δ1980

§1910.15
609F2d1122 Δ1980

§1910.16(b)(1)
529F2d1084 •1974
467FS982 Δ1979

§1910.17
526F2d58 Δ1975

§1910.20
496FS1189 Δ1980

§1910.20(c)(3)
496FS1191 Δ1980

§1910.20(c)(4)
496FS1191 Δ1980

§1910.20(c)(5)
496FS1191 Δ1980

§1910.20(c)(6)
496FS1191 Δ1980

§1910.20(c)(10)
496FS1191 Δ1980

§1910.20(e)(2)(i)
496FS1191 Δ1980

§1910.20(e)(2)(iii)
496FS1191 Δ1980

§1910.20(e)(3)
496FS1191 Δ1980

§1910.21
et seq.
FRCI§9.11

§1910.21(a)(4)
583F2d63 Δ1978

§1910.21(a)(6)
583F2d63 Δ1978

§1910.21(f)(21)
493F2d1029 Δ1974

§1910.21(f)(27)
540F2d70 Δ1976
47ARF810n Δ1980
47ARF816n Δ1980

§1910.21(f)(31)
492F2d1029 Δ1974

§1910.22
556F2d434 Δ1977
47ARF350n Δ1980

§1910.22(a)(1)
576F2d621 Δ1978
638F2d833 Δ1981
398FS1228 Δ1975

§1910.22(a)(2)
579F2d382 Δ1978
Ky
605SW31 Δ1980

§1910.22(b)(1)
398FS1228 Δ1975

§1910.22(c)
511F2d866 •1972
Va575F2d760 Δ1978
576F2d559 Δ1978

§1910.23(a)(5)
575F2d761 Δ1978
576F2d560 Δ1978

§1910.23(c)
47ARF351n Δ1980

§1910.23(c)(1)
487F2d440 Δ1973
540F2d70 Δ1976
576F2d559 Δ1978
583F2d63 Δ1978
630F2d629 Δ1980
31ARF572n Δ1977
47ARF349n Δ1980

§1910.25
FRCI§4.02

§1910.25(b)(3)
569F2d1309 Δ1978

§1910.25(b)(3)(ii)
40LCP(4)104 Δ1976

§1910.26
FRCI§4.02

§1910.26(c)(3)(viii)
35MdA262 Δ1977
Md
370A2d146 Δ1977

§1910.27(b)(ii)
577F2d275 Δ1978

§1910.28
540F2d70 Δ1976
47ARF810n Δ1980

§1910.28(a)
47ARF811n Δ1980

§1910.28(a)(1)
C542F2d29 Δ1976
47ARF812n Δ1980
48ARF470n Δ1980

§1910.28(a)(3)
V577F2d1116 Δ1977
V616F2d1113 Δ1980
47ARF812n Δ1980

§1910.28(a)(12)
577F2d1118 Δ1977
47ARF813n Δ1980

§1910.28(a)(17)
513F2d1037 Δ1975
47ARF813n Δ1980

§1910.28(d)(5)
45ARF808n Δ1979

§1910.28(e)(1)
47ARF812n Δ1980

§1910.28(e)(2)
47ARF812n Δ1980

§1910.28(g)(5)
492F2d1029 Δ1974
47ARF812n Δ1980

§1910.28(g)(9)
492F2d1029 Δ1974

§1910.28(h)(5)
47ARF816n Δ1980

§1910.28(j)(4)
47ARF812n Δ1980

§1910.28(s)(3)
495F2d1299 Δ1974

§1910.29
540F2d70 Δ1976

§1910.29(d)(1)(x)
487F2d440 Δ1973

§1910.36(b)(1)
624F2d39 Δ1980

§1910.66
et seq.
FRCI§9.11

§1910.66(c)(22)(i)
56TxL1387 •1977

§1910.93
545F2d1385 Δ1976
613F2d122 Δ1980
630F2d1096 Δ1980

408 • followed by a year refers to the CFR edition, if cited. If not cited, Δ followed by a year indicates the date of the citing reference

Exhibit 92: A sample page of Shepard's *Code of Federal Regulations Citations,* showing citations to 29 *C.F.R.* § 1910.

For the *decisions* of federal administrative agencies, Shepard's provides another citator, Shepard's *United States Administrative Citations,* which was introduced in 1967. Prior to that time, the decisions of some administrative agencies were covered in Shepard's *United States Citations* and *Federal Citations.* This administrative agency citator now lists citations to the decisions of over thirty federal agencies or offices. In addition, administrative decisions are covered in specialized subject fields by the various topical Shepard's citators listed above on page 234.

Some looseleaf services, particularly in the field of federal taxation, also perform a useful citator function with respect to the agency decisions included in those services.

On the state level, some of the Shepard's state case citators also cover decisions of major administrative agencies in those states.

Exhibit 93 shows a page from Shepard's *Federal Occupational Safety and Health Citations,* listing both court and agency decisions which cite O.S.H.A. cases.

Vol. 9 OSHC (BNA)

81/94/A2
10OSHC1081

– 1402 –
(81/15/F10)
(OSHD ¶25205)

– 1405 –
(81/10/E14)
(OSHD ¶25191)

– 1406 –
(81/11/C7)
(OSHD ¶25213)

– 1407 –
(81/17/E1)
(OSHD ¶25226)
81/50/A2
82/5/A2
82/30/A2
9OSHC1764
10OSHC1305
10OSHC1651

– 1409 –
(81/16/E4)
(OSHD ¶25220)

– 1412 –
(81/19/B8)
(OSHD ¶25221)

– 1415 –
(81/19/A2)
(OSHD ¶25225)

– 1417 –
(638F2d812)
(OSHD ¶25223)
(59ALRF377)
649F2d1167
d658F2d551
678F2d130
683F2d363
683F2d364
683F2d1109
81/63/F4
81/86/A2
82/46/C3
82/49/B8
9OSHC2037
9OSHC2043
9OSHC2177
10OSHC1593
10OSHC1825
10OSHC1890
10OSHC1903
10OSHC2003

– 1425 –
(645F2d103)
(OSHD ¶25278)
f666F2d1270
676F2d1336
10OSHC1561

– 1426 –
(81/19/C14)
(OSHD ¶25232)

– 1428 –
(81/13/F6)
(OSHD ¶25210)

– 1429 –
(81/21/A2)
(OSHD ¶25249)

– 1431 –
(80/13/C1)
(81/20/A2)
(OSHD ¶24242)

– 1432 –
(81/20/E9)
(OSHD ¶25245)

– 1433 –
(81/20/A11)
(OSHD ¶25248)

– 1434 –
(81/20/D3)
(OSHD ¶25243)

– 1435 –
Case 1
(81/21/C4)
(OSHD ¶25240)
Case 2
(81/20/C7)
(OSHD ¶25244)

– 1436 –
(81/21/D3)
(OSHD ¶25247)

– 1437 –
Case 1
(81/16/D3)
(OSHD ¶25217)
Case 2
(81/16/C13)
(OSHD ¶25214)

– 1438 –
(81/13/E4)
(OSHD ¶25209)

– 1439 –
(81/22/B9)
(OSHD ¶25273)

– 1440 –
(81/21/E2)
(81/21/E7)
(OSHD ¶25140)
(OSHD ¶25246)

– 1444 –
(81/23/F1)
(OSHD ¶25261)

– 1446 –
(OSHD ¶25292)

– 1448 –
(641F2d338)
(OSHD ¶25489)
81/92/D10
10OSHC1108

– 1449 –
(81/23/C6)
(OSHD ¶25264)

– 1450 –
(81/23/D14)
(OSHD ¶25272)

– 1451 –
(81/29/A2)
(OSHD ¶25281)
81/35/A2
81/58/A2
81/96/A2
82/57/D3
9OSHC1590
9OSHC1906
10OSHC1115
10OSHC2104

– 1460 –
(81/27/A2)
(OSHD ¶25300)
e81/47/A2
81/67/A12
81/105/E7
81/108/B8
j82/24/D4
82/46/C11
82/62/A2
e9OSHC1784
9OSHC2039
10OSHC1228
10OSHC1275
j10OSHC1596
10OSHC1979
10OSHC2123

– 1489 –
(81/26/B13)
(OSHD ¶25284)
s81/83/F2
81/40/B11
82/25/A2
9OSHC1803
10OSHC1613

– 1501 –
(81/24/A2)
(OSHD ¶25256)

– 1502 –
(81/22/D12)
(OSHD ¶25274)

– 1505 –
Case 1
(81/22/F11)
(OSHD ¶25275)
Case 2
(81/23/A2)
(OSHD ¶25276)

– 1507 –
(81/23/D5)
(OSHD ¶25269)

– 1508 –
(647F2d1)
673F2d1137
535FS658

– 1510 –
(647F2d96)
689F2d957
689F2d958
f693F2d1068
516FS678
535FS178
543FS57
d543FS59
9OSHC1972
10OSHC1217
d10OSHC [1217
10OSHC1450
10OSHC2057
386Mas442
Mass
436NE931
AgL§9.09

– 1515 –
(81/30/A2)
(OSHD ¶25297)
81/80/A5
81/91/A2
9OSHC2113
10OSHC1103

– 1523 –
(641F2d801)
(OSHD ¶25306)
s81/69/F1
s9OSHC2049
647F2d952
f692F2d649
694F2d589
82/69/A2
f10OSHC [2169

– 1525 –
(642F2d778)
(OSHD ¶25355)
f671F2d653
f10OSHC [1345

– 1527 –
(81/31/A2)
(OSHD ¶25283)

– 1530 –
(81/25/F2)
(OSHD ¶25286)

– 1533 –
(81/26/A2)
(OSHD ¶25293)
81/94/A2
81/98/D3
82/24/B7
10OSHC1081
10OSHC1153
10OSHC1607

– 1539 –
(81/28/A2)
(OSHD ¶25296)
81/71/E14
82/2/A2
82/8/A2
9OSHC2008
10OSHC1293
10OSHC1389

– 1542 –
(81/29/B13)
(OSHD ¶25295)

– 1549 –
(81/28/D8)
(OSHD ¶25285)

– 1553 –
(81/25/A2)
(OSHD ¶25314)

– 1554 –
(649F2d96)
673F2d1137
674F2d1185
674F2d1187
d683F2d1115
683F2d1116
688F2d89
692F2d645
564FS650
81/63/B13
81/70/D8
81/79/F4
81/101/A2
81/102/A2
82/43/A2
9OSHC1940
9OSHC2012
9OSHC2147
10OSHC1203
10OSHC1242
10OSHC1481
10OSHC1825
d10OSHC [1825
10OSHC1941
10OSHC1949
10OSHC2169

– 1562 –
(646F2d799)
683F2d1109
688F2d89
81/97/B2
10OSHC1128
10OSHC1825
10OSHC1941

– 1568 –
(642F2d768)
(OSHD ¶25325)
US cert den
in102SC389
in454US893
665F2d1235
f673F2d114
684F2d508
f693F2d1064
700F2d914
f710F2d675
527FS1326
548FS1057
558FS1150
10OSHC1801
Fla
415So2d1343

– 1575 –
(81/30/E13)
(OSHD ¶25280)
82/2/A2
82/30/C7
82/68/D4
10OSHC1293
10OSHC1678

– 1580 –
(81/32/A2)
(OSHD ¶25291)

– 1582 –
(81/24/F2)
(OSHD ¶25309)

– 1584 –
(647F2d383)
671F2d650
81/97/A9
82/45/A2
j82/45/A2
82/50/B7
10OSHC1345
10OSHC1978

– 1587 –
(643F2d230)
650F2d935
9OSHC1894
296Md56
Md
459A2d211

– 1590 –
(81/35/A2)
(OSHD ¶25323)
82/70/A2

– 1596 –
(81/49/A2)
(OSHD ¶25338)
82/45/A2

– 1608 –
(81/48/A2)
(OSHD ¶25360)
e695F2d1021
j695F2d1026
700F2d914
81/64/A2
82/23/G2
82/29/A2
e82/60/B5
f82/60/B5
9OSHC2041
10OSHC1672
10OSHC1709
e10OSHC [2097
f10OSHC [2097

– 1623 –
(81/37/A14)
(OSHD ¶25339)
f81/72/A2
81/107/F1
f9OSHC2000
10OSHC1285

– 1633 –
(81/36/B4)
(OSHD ¶25326)
81/96/A2
10OSHC1115

– 1641 –
(81/28/C2)
(OSHD ¶25282)
81/84/E1
9OSHC2160

– 1644 –
(81/24/C6)
(OSHD ¶25311)

– 1646 –
(647F2d840)
(647F2d1063)
652F2d979
653F2d1218
659F2d1279
699F2d432
81/63/B13
81/87/D5
81/89/B13
81/92/D10
81/96/A2
f81/97/B2
9OSHC1940
10OSHC1052
10OSHC1108
10OSHC1115
f10OSHC [1128
59ALRF404n

– 1652 –
(OSHD ¶25260)

– 1653 –
(81/39/A2)
(OSHD ¶25359)
81/54/A2
81/71/E14
81/86/A2
81/92/C9
81/94/A2
81/96/A2
82/30/C7
82/32/C14
f82/59/C12
9OSHC1891
9OSHC2008
9OSHC2177
10OSHC1081
10OSHC1115
10OSHC1136
10OSHC1678
10OSHC1734
f10OSHC [2086

– 1681 –
(81/45/A2)
(OSHD ¶25363)
81/63/B13
f81/79/F4
f81/101/A2
81/101/C12
81/102/A2
f81/102/A2
81/107/A2
82/11/A2
82/23/A2
82/46/F14
82/59/B3
9OSHC1940
f9OSHC2147
10OSHC1179
f10OSHC [1203
10OSHC1242
f10OSHC [1242
10OSHC1250
10OSHC1398
10OSHC1549
10OSHC1966
10OSHC2167

– 1703 –
(81/35/E11)
(OSHD ¶25324)
659F2d712

– 1707 –
(81/25/C3)
(OSHD ¶25312)

– 1709 –
(648F2d1278)
cc593F2d368
cc7OSHC [1105
652F2d979
676F2d1335

Continued

430

Exhibit 93: Sample entries in Shepard's *Federal Occupational Safety and Health Citations*, one of Shepard's Topical Citations.

EXECUTIVE DOCUMENTS

In addition to the independent agencies and executive departments, the President of the United States also functions as a law-maker in his own right. In that capacity, he issues a variety of legally significant documents, most of which (since 1965) appear promptly in an official publication, the *Weekly Compilation of Presidential Documents.* (Exhibit 94 shows remarks of the President upon the signing of the Occupational Safety and Health Act.) In addition, such documents appear as follows:

1. **Executive Orders and Presidential Proclamations:** The line dividing executive orders from proclamations is blurred, but it may be said that orders usually involve an exercise of presidential authority related to government business, while proclamations are announcements of policy or of matters requiring public notice. Orders and proclamations are found in the *Federal Register,* are cumulated in Title 3A of the *Code of Federal Regulations,* and selected ones appear in *U.S. C.C.A.N.* and in the supplements to *U.S.C.S.* Proclamations also appear in the *Statutes at Large.* See Exhibit 95 for an executive order issued in connection with the Occupational Safety and Health Act of 1970.

   Since 1981, the Office of the Federal Register has published the *Codification of Presidential Proclamations and Executive Orders.* Arranged by titles similar to those in the *C.F.R.,* this publication brings together, by subject, all proclamations and executive orders from 1961 to 1981, with updating projected for the future.

Weekly Compilation of

PRESIDENTIAL DOCUMENTS

Week Ending Saturday, January 2, 1971

Representative L. Mendel Rivers of South Carolina

Statement by the President on the Death of the Congressman. December 28, 1970

For 30 years, Mendel Rivers served the State of South Carolina and the Nation with dignity, with distinction, and with high integrity in the Congress of the United States. Throughout his career, Congressman Rivers held unswervingly to the belief that the freedom that exists in the modern world is inextricably tied to the military strength of the United States. He fought for that belief in committee, in the Congress, in the country. No shifting national opinion, no amount of hostile criticism, deterred him from the course he deemed right for America. In his death, I have lost a friend upon whom I could rely in times of grave difficulty; South Carolina has lost one of the most distinguished men in her history; and America has lost a patriot.

United States Ambassador to Western Samoa

Announcement of Intention To Nominate Ambassador Kenneth Franzheim II To Serve Concurrently as Ambassador to Western Samoa. December 28, 1970

The President today announced his intention to nominate Kenneth Franzheim II, Ambassador to New Zealand, to serve concurrently and without additional compensation as Ambassador to Western Samoa. Ambassador Franzheim will be the first United States Ambassador to Western Samoa, which achieved its independence in January 1962.

Born in New York City, September 12, 1925, Franzheim received his B.A. (1948) from Yale University. Upon graduation from college, he worked in various positions with oil field operations and joined Shell Oil Company in their gas contract department in 1952.

In 1953, Franzheim moved into independent oil operation and investment. He joined the board of directors of Southern National Bank in Houston in 1969. On August 4, 1969, Franzheim was appointed by President Nixon to serve as Ambassador to New Zealand.

Ambassador Franzheim is married and has four children. His legal residence is Houston, Tex.

Occupational Safety and Health Act of 1970

Remarks of the President and Secretary of Labor James D. Hodgson at the Signing Ceremony at the Department of Labor. December 29, 1970

SECRETARY HODGSON. *Mr. President, distinguished Members of the Senate and the House, leaders of organized labor, industry, administration officials, professionals in the field of safety and health, and ladies and gentlemen:*

Welcome to the Labor Department and to our signing ceremony.

Through the years, Federal legislation has been marked by some truly milestone measures in the field of worker protection. When you think back, there is the Social Security Act with its provisions to provide a cushion for various kinds of economic adversity; the National Labor Relations Act with provisions protecting organizing rights and concerted activity; then the Fair Labor Standards Act with provisions to prevent abuses in hours and wages and conditions of work.

Through all of this period there had been, it seems to us, a gap in the worker protection, namely, with regard to safety and health.

It is rather curious that more attention hadn't been paid to this subject earlier. Through the years a number of workers were killed, were injured, or fell ill due to working conditions on the job, but it has only been in

4

Exhibit 94: Remarks of the President at the signing of the OSHA as published in the *Weekly Compilation of Presidential Documents.*

THE PRESIDENT

EXECUTIVE ORDER 11612

Occupational Safety and Health Programs for Federal Employees

The Occupational Safety and Health Act of 1970, 84 Stat. 1590, authorizes the development and enforcement of standards to assure safe and healthful working conditions for employees in the private sector. Section 19 of that Act makes each Federal agency head responsible for establishing and maintaining an effective and comprehensive occupational safety and health program which is consistent with the standards promulgated by the Secretary of Labor for businesses affecting interstate commerce.

Section 7902 of Title 5, United States Code, authorizes the President to establish by Executive Order a safety council composed of representatives of Federal agencies and of labor organizations representing employees to serve as an advisory body to the Secretary of Labor in carrying out a Federal safety program.

As the Nation's largest employer, the Federal Government has a special obligation to set an example for safe and healthful employment. It is appropriate that the Federal Government strengthen its efforts to assure safe and healthful working conditions for its own employees.

NOW, THEREFORE, by virtue of the authority vested in me by section 7902 of Title 5 of the United States Code, and as President of the United States, it is hereby ordered as follows:

ESTABLISHMENT OF OCCUPATIONAL SAFETY AND HEALTH PROGRAMS IN FEDERAL DEPARTMENTS AND AGENCIES

SECTION 1. The head of each Federal department and agency shall establish an occupational safety and health program (hereinafter referred to as a safety program) in compliance with the requirements of section 7902 of Title 5 of the United States Code and section 19(a) of the Occupational Safety and Health Act of 1970 (which Act shall hereinafter be referred to as the Safety Act). The programs shall be consistent with the standards prescribed by section 6 of the Safety Act. In providing safety programs for Federal employees, the head of each Federal department and agency shall—

(1) Designate or appoint a qualified official who shall be responsible for the management of the safety program within his agency.

(2) Establish (A) a safety policy; (B) an organization and a set of procedures, providing for appropriate consultation with employees, that will permit that policy to be implemented effectively; (C) a safety management information system; (D) goals and objectives for reducing and eliminating employee injuries and occupational illnesses; (E) periodic inspections of workplaces to ensure compliance with standards; (F) plans and procedures for evaluating the program's effectiveness; and (G) priorities with respect to the factors which cause occupational injury and illness so that appropriate countermeasures can be developed.

(3) Correct conditions that do not meet safety and health standards.

(4) Submit to the Secretary of Labor by April 1 of each year a report containing (A) the status of his agency's safety program in reducing

FEDERAL REGISTER, VOL. 36, NO. 145—WEDNESDAY, JULY 28, 1971

Exhibit 95: Executive Order 11612 on occupational safety and health, as set out in the *Federal Register*.

2. **Presidential Messages:** These communications from the President to Congress explain proposed legislation or vetoes, report on the state of the nation, and serve other functions. Messages are found in the *Congressional Record, House* and *Senate Journals, House* and *Senate Documents,* and selectively in the advance sheets of the U.S.C.C.A.N.

3. **Reorganization Plans:** These plans contain presidential proposals for the reorganization of agencies and departments within the executive branch. When submitted to Congress, the plans are published in the *Congressional Record.* If the plans subsequently become effective, they will also appear in the *Statutes at Large,* Title 5 of the *U.S. Code,* the *Federal Register,* and Title 3 of the *Code of Federal Regulations,* as well as in *U.S.C.C.A.N.*

4. **Executive Agreements:** Executive agreements reflect diplomatic arrangements made by the President with other nations, under his power to conduct foreign affairs. Unlike treaties, these agreements do not require the advice and consent of the Senate.

   Since 1950, agreements have appeared in the official bound series, *U.S. Treaties and Other International Agreements (U.S.T.).* Prior to that date, they were published in the *Statutes at Large.* Cumulative indexes to *U.S.T.* covering 1776–1949 (4 v., Oceana, 1975, by I. Kavass & M.A. Michael), and 1950–1970 (4 v., Oceana, 1973, by I. Kavass & A. Sprudzs), with Supplement for

1971–1975 (1977), enable a researcher to locate an agreement in these sources by number, country, subject, or date. See page 283 below.

Since 1958 an official series called *Public Papers of the Presidents* has also been published by the Federal Register Division. It contains collections of presidential documents, arranged by year, for all presidents after Franklin D. Roosevelt, and for Herbert Hoover. These volumes, which are individually indexed, contain most of the documents listed above, and cumulate the contents of the *Weekly Compilation of Presidential Documents.* So far, the papers of Presidents Hoover, Truman, Eisenhower, Kennedy, Johnson, Nixon, Ford, Carter and Reagan have been published and the project will continue to issue the state papers of future presidents. Papers of most of the earlier presidents are generally available in other editions. Currently, the Library of Congress is planning to reproduce its collections of earlier presidential papers on microfilm to facilitate public access to those documents.

Since 1977, cumulative indexes for each presidential administration have been published commercially under the title, *The Cumulative Indexes to the Public Papers of the Presidents of the United States* (KTO Press, 1977-date).

ADMINISTRATIVE LAW AT THE STATE AND LOCAL LEVEL

Like the federal government, state governments have experienced in recent years an increase in the number and activity of their administrative agencies.

However, as a general rule, publication of state agency rules and decisions is far less systematic than that of the federal government.

Nearly every state publishes a state manual, variously called a redbook, a register, or a legislative manual, which parallels the *United States Government Manual,* providing quick access to information about the state's government, agencies, and officials. In addition, the Council of State Governments issues *The Book of the States,* which combines in one volume basic information on government operations in each of the fifty states.

Access to state rules and regulations themselves, although difficult in the past, has improved in recent years. Approximately thirty-eight states now issue compilations of their administrative regulations, with more or less regular supplementation. For states without such compilations, a researcher must apply to the Secretary of State or to the particular agency for a copy of a specific regulation.

Decisions of some state agencies, especially those dealing with banking, worker's compensation, public utilities, taxation, and insurance, may be published in official form in chronological series. Some looseleaf services, particularly in the tax field, also include decisions of state tribunals, but this practice is limited to a few subject areas.

Though no publication as comprehensive as the *Monthly Catalog of U.S. Government Publications* exists in any of the states, the *Monthly Checklist of State Publications,* issued by the Library of Congress, lists all state documents received by that library. The documents listed are arranged by state and agency, with a comprehensive annual index.

M.L. Fisher's *Guide to State Legislative Materials* (rev.ed., Fred B. Rothman, 1983) is also useful in this regard. It provides a state-by-state listing of selected administrative materials and attorney general opinions, and includes names and addresses of issuing agencies or publishers.

On the municipal and local level, administrative decisions are almost never published, and regulations, if published, are rarely kept up to date. One would have to request a specific regulation from a town clerk or particular agency, if it were definitely known to exist. It would be very difficult, however, to determine the existence of a particular regulation since they are not available to the public in a compiled or current text, and are rarely indexed in official files.

OPINIONS OF THE ATTORNEYS GENERAL

The opinions of the U.S. Attorney General and the attorneys general of the various states have considerable significance in legal research. These officials render formal and informal opinions of law in response to questions from their respective governments or officials. Their decisions are advisory in nature and do not have binding authority, but they are given considerable weight by the courts in interpreting statutes and regulations. Consequently they may be useful to the attorney with a similar problem or to the scholar investigating that area of law.

For the federal government, the published series of opinions is entitled *Opinions of the Attorneys General of the United States.* Opinions appear first in slip form and are then cumulated into bound volumes at a slow pace. Each volume contains its own index, and, in addition, some cumulative indexing is available. U.S. Attorney General opinions are included as cited material in *Shepard's United States Citations, U.S. Administrative Citations,* and *Federal Citations,* and in some annotated state and federal statutory codes.

Most states also issue Attorney General opinions in bound volumes, published chronologically. In some states, the opinions are published every year, but in many there is a long time lag between issuance and publication. The volumes are rarely preceded by slip opinions.

Each volume of state attorney general opinions usually contains an index but these rarely cumulate. Subject access to these rulings in all of the states was formerly provided by the *Digest of Opinions of the Attorneys General,* published by the Council of State Governments. Unfortunately, it ceased publication in 1969, and no other service has replaced it.

Many of Shepard's state citators use the opinions of the state's attorney general as cited material (with references thereunder to judicial decisions, etc.), and all of the state citators use those opinions as citing material for both cases and statutes.

The *Checklist of Basic American Legal Publications* (Fred B. Rothman, 1962, with looseleaf supplements), issued by the American Association of Law

Libraries, includes in Section III a listing of all published volumes of attorney general opinions. As noted above, current source information for state attorneys general opinions is provided in M.L. Fisher's *Guide to State Legislative Materials.*

CONCLUSION

From one of the most bibliographically inaccessible areas of law, federal administrative law has become one of the most sophisticated in its research apparatus. This development stemmed from four separate publishing innovations: first, the looseleaf services (described in the next chapter); second, the improvements brought by the Federal Register System; third, the introduction of specialized regulatory data bases in the LEXIS, WESTLAW and BNA computer systems; and finally, the expanded Shepard's coverage of administrative materials in a variety of specialized citators.

In addition to the major sources of administrative and regulatory law outlined above, there are other useful research aids of a more general nature. Kenneth C. Davis, *Administrative Law Treatise* (2d ed., K.C. Davis Publ. Co., 1978-date), a comprehensive multi-volume treatise, covers all aspects of this field, both substantive and procedural. A similar work in a looseleaf format is *Administrative Law,* by B.J. Menzines, J.A. Stein & J. Gruff (Matthew Bender, 1981) 6 vols. Schmeckebier & Eastin, *Government Publications and Their Use,* 2d ed. (Brookings, 1969), although somewhat dated, is still a useful guide to the documents of the executive and administrative branch of the federal government. A new research manual specifically devoted to this area is *Research Essentials in Administrative Law,* by H.B. Jacobini, A.P. Melone & C. Kalvelage (Palisades Publishers, 1983).

For following current developments in administrative law and federal regulation, there are several legal periodicals with that emphasis: *Administrative Law Review, Federal Bar Journal* and the *Yale Journal on Regulation.*

CHAPTER VII

LOOSELEAF SERVICES

One of the unique inventions of legal bibliography has been the looseleaf service, which offers researchers an easily supplemented tool in specific subject areas, containing legal source material of various kinds, special finding aids and secondary material. The first looseleaf services were issued just before World War I, and were designed to facilitate research in the then new federal income tax law. These publications provide *comprehensive, unified* and *current* access to selected fields of legal literature. They have become particularly popular in public law areas where government regulation is the central focus of legal development, e.g., taxation, labor, antitrust, securities, and regulated industries such as transportation, communication, banking, utilities, etc.

Services have been published in such areas of current interest as criminal law, education, environmental control, housing, health care, poverty law, and urban law. For many lawyers and other researchers specializing in those fields, the looseleaf services are their primary research tools. A selected list of looseleaf services being published at the end of 1983 in fields of major interest can be found in Appendix D, at the end of this volume.

The methods of organization of these tools vary according to the nature of the material, the requirements of the subject matter, and the publisher's predilection. In areas where one major statute dominates the legal order, the service may be arranged by statutory sections or divisions (e.g., the taxation services, which are structured according to the sections of the Internal Revenue Code). Where several statutes are significant, the service may be divided into areas by the relevant statutes (e.g., labor law services which offer separate sections for the Labor Management Relations Act, the Labor Management Reporting and Disclosure Act, the Wage and Hour Act, state laws, etc.). In other fields where common law or judicial rules predominate, or where there is a mixture of case and statutory law, the service may follow a logical arrangement of the subject matter (e.g., family law, trusts and estates, or corporations).

ADVANTAGES

The following are the major advantages of looseleaf services over separate research in each of the original primary sources. It should be noted, however, that not every service contains all of these features.

1. **Compilation of Primary Sources.** *All* relevant law is collected in one place by a convenient, compact and coordinated presentation of primary authority, regardless of its original form of publication. By using this integrated approach to varied legal sources, the researcher on a particular topic can work largely within the confines of a single tool. A lawyer can have available economically a wide range of material, which would otherwise require vast shelf space, greater costs and considerable searching time and coordination.

A typical looseleaf service may include the following primary sources:

(a) Statutes, both state and federal.

(b) Decisions, not only of state and federal courts, but also of administrative agencies which operate in that area.

(c) Rules and regulations of those administrative agencies, promulgated pursuant to their authorizing statute.

(d) Rulings of agencies on adjudicated matters or submitted questions.

Of course, most of these authorities would be available in their primary forms of publication (e.g. in statutory compilations like the *U.S. Code* and similar state codes; in official and unofficial state and federal court reporters; in the *Federal Register*, the *Code of Federal Regulations* and state administrative compilations; and in the reporters of administrative agency decisions)—but, as noted above, at far greater cost in time, space and money. However, there may be differences of treatment and coverage between the official forms of publication and the looseleaf services. For example, decisions appear in some looseleaf services only in an abbreviated form; on the other hand, some decisions, not otherwise published in official or unofficial reporters, can be found in these services. Sometimes entire classes of material are available only in a looseleaf service.

2. Secondary Material. Looseleaf services offer the following additional features, usually coordinated with, or cross-referenced to, the primary sources:

(a) Summaries of *proposed* legislation and regulations, along with their analysis, status and purpose.

(b) News coverage of the legal and general developments in the particular area covered.

(c) Editorial notes and comments, interpretations of the primary sources, projections of current trends, and related background material.

3. **Speed.** By regular supplementation, all of these materials appear promptly, frequently weekly, while there are often delays in the official publication of the primary sources. The looseleaf service cuts through these delays by offering prompt transmittals and an easy, economical means of updating by simply filing the new sheets into the service as they are received.

4. **Integrated Coverage.** The services cut across jurisdictional lines and cover their respective fields as units without regard to the source of the particular publications.

5. **Indexing.** Quick and detailed indexing coordinates the whole collection and affords convenient access at many points. A typical service may include all of the following indexes under these or similar names:

(a) **Rapid Finder Index**—using a broad, analytical approach, it divides the whole service into major areas and provides an initial orientation to its contents.

(b) **Basic or Topical Index**—using the catch word or topical approach, it provides more direct and specific reference to the service.

(c) **Finding Lists**—include different types of documentary material by their official citations, enabling the researcher to locate a specific regulation, rule, order, decision or ruling directly.

(d) **Current and Supplementary Indexes**—update the basic index and include references to the latest additions to the service.

(e) **Tables of Cases**—not only provide direct access to cases, but sometimes also provide a limited citator function.

COMMON FEATURES

A detailed and specific description of looseleaf services is impossible because of the variety and individuality of their form and content. Each publisher approaches the problem of arrangement in a slightly different way and the variations of subject material often require markedly different treatment as well. However, the following common features of most looseleaf services can be noted:

1. Looseleaf supplementation by expandable binders into which sheets are filed periodically (weekly in most services).

2. Detailed instructions for use of the service, which are set out at the beginning of the first volume.

3. Paragraph number arrangement and citation instead of page references.

4. Indexes and tables as described above.

5. Current material and news developments.

6. Commentary and editorial analysis on the primary sources.

There are two different types of looseleaf services: *cumulating* services and *interfiling* services. In the *cumulating* service, new material received to update the service is filed as a unit, usually at the end of the set, or as *several* units to be filed at the end of each of several parts of the service. These units *supplement* the existing compilation of material and do not replace pages already filed. The *interfiling* service utilizes the replacement of superseded pages or sections by new, revised pages or sections to update its contents. Some interfiling services provide for the retention of replaced material of permanent value by offering transfer binders which subscribers can use to store such material for later consultation. Both types of services reissue the decisions of courts or agencies in topical reporters, which then become a separate addition to the library, for permanent use either with the looseleaf service, or independently.

RESEARCH STEPS IN USING SERVICES

Although again it is difficult to generalize about the best procedure to be followed in working with a looseleaf service, the following steps are typical for most cases:

1. Analysis of one's problem into general areas of concern, noting the type of source material likely to be needed.

2. Perusal of the instructions at the front of the applicable service, which, in three minutes, can usually provide an adequate working orientation. This is the most neglected step and one which can save the researcher much time and trouble.

3. Use of the service's various indexes to locate the specific material for solution of the problem—generally proceeding from the Rapid Finder Index to the Basic or Topical Index and then to the Current Material Index. If the researcher has specific reference to a

relevant document (order, regulation, ruling or bulletin), the Finding Lists can be used to locate it directly.

4. Study of the actual texts of the relevant primary material, supplemented by the editorial explanation and secondary materials. It should be noted that, although many services contain only digests of court or administrative decisions, some publishers will provide the *full* text of such decisions to subscribers upon request.

5. Updating the relevant sources by use of the citators and current material sections.

AN ILLUSTRATIVE SEARCH PROBLEM

The actual research aids and procedures of a typical looseleaf service are illustrated in the following exhibits. To provide a focus for examining the service, consider the problem of determining the rights of an employee who has been discharged because of his or her observance of a Saturday Sabbath. The service used here is CCH's *Employment Practices Guide.* Note that citations within the service refer to paragraph numbers, rather than page numbers.

The search begins with several subject or topical indexes which give access to most of the material in the service, including short essays summarizing various topics in the field, federal statutes and regulations, and federal judicial and administrative agency decisions. Also included in this service, but not shown in these exhibits, are state statutes and decisions. The finding lists and tables of cases give the looseleaf paragraph number of materials cited, so that they can easily be located.

242 **Topical Index**

References are to paragraph (¶) numbers.
See also Current Topical Index at page 2651.

Exhibit 96: The search begins in the basic Topical Index of the service, where introductory or background material on a particular topic can be located by paragraph number. Here we find, under the entry "Religious observances and holidays," references to paragraph 1170 and various annotations thereunder.

Holidays—Vacations—Time Off

¶ 1170

Most of the problems surrounding the granting of time off from work for holidays and vacations involve the observance of religious holidays. The 1972 amendments to Title VII of the Civil Rights Act of 1964 contain a new definition of "religion" to include all aspects of religious observance and practice, as well as belief (.01). Under this definition, an employer is expected to recognize the reasonable religious needs of his employees, unless he can show that he is unable to reasonably accommodate an employee's or prospective employee's religious observance without undue hardship on the conduct of his business.

Religious Holidays and Beliefs—Sabbath Observance

While it is unlawful to refuse to hire or to discharge employees because of their religion, the principal problem involving religious discrimination arises in connection with the granting of religious holidays or permitting the observance of the Sabbath. According to EEOC guidelines, employers have an obligation to accommodate the reasonable religious needs of their employees and prospective employees when such accommodations can be made without undue hardship on the conduct of the employer's business (.03). According to the Commission, undue hardship may exist when an employee's job cannot be performed by another worker of substantially similar qualifications during the time when the employee is absent for religious reasons. Because of the sensitive nature of discharging or refusing to hire an employee or applicant on account of his religious beliefs, an employer has the burden of proving that an undue hardship renders the required accommodations to the religious needs of the employee unreasonable. The Commission has stated that it will review each case on an individual basis in an effort to seek an equitable application of its religious discrimination guidelines.

Similarly, government agencies are required by regulation to make reasonable accommodations to the religious needs of applicants and federal government employees, including the observance of the Sabbath on days other than Sunday, when those accommodations can be made without undue interference with the business of the agency or with the rights of other applicants and employees (.031). Government contractors and subcontractors are also prohibited from discrimination on the basis of religion (.02).

An employer established that its accommodation to the religious belief of a process engineer by allowing him time off during the winter months would have involved an undue hardship on the conduct of its business since the responsibilities of the process engineer required that he be available on a 24-hour, seven-day-a-week basis (.10). Similarly, an employer would suffer undue hardship where it was not practical for him to find a replacement for the employee, a Seventh-Day Adventist, who did not work on Saturdays during the harvest season (.11). In the absence of evidence presented by the employer, however, that its accommodation to an employee's religious beliefs, generally requiring time off for observance of Sabbaths or other religious holidays, would involve an undue hardship on the conduct of its business, discharge of the employee for observance of such holidays constituted religious discrimination (.13-.15). Another factor considered in determining whether or not an employer discriminated on a religious basis was whether its accommodation to the

Exhibit 97: Paragraph 1170 contains a background summary which provides an overview of the topic and citations to other relevant material in the service.

religious beliefs of an employee created discontent among the other employees (.16).

Refusal to allow a nurse in a hospital to wear a religious head covering, in lieu of the usual nurse's cap, forced the nurse to choose between her job and her religious conviction and this, in effect, constituted constructive discharge of the nurse when she resigned rather than make an exception to her belief (.20). Recognition of a Sunday Sabbath for certain employees who worked overtime and refusal to allow overtime work to an employee whose Sabbath was Saturday constituted unlawful discrimination by the employer (.30). Sometimes union contract provisions entered into the situation and relieved the employer (including the government as employer) of the need to accommodate to the employees' religious beliefs (.40). This was true even as to a union provision for the employee to seek his own replacement. Hence, where the employee did not find his own replacement for the time when he would be off due to religious beliefs, the employer was held to have made reasonable accommodations to such beliefs (.50).

Equal Pay for Equal Work

There can be no wage differential by employers as to vacation or holiday pay to employees of either sex if the work of both sexes is subject to the equal pay standard and the differential is not shown to come within any exception to such standard (.032). Thus, covered male and female employees performing equal work must receive equal pay for holidays not worked (.62). The same is true as to vacation pay, so that an employer violated the equal pay provisions by giving vacation pay to covered employees of only one sex (.60). Such equality, however, was not required between women employees who took six-month pregnancy leaves of absence and other employees who worked a full year (.61).

Age Discrimination in Employment

It is unlawful for an employer to discriminate against any individual because of such individual's age with respect to vacations and holidays (.033). Vacation rights based upon length of service, however, with age being no factor for consideration therein, are not violative of the age discrimination ban (.65).

Racial and National Origin Discrimination

Vacation rights of a Spanish-surnamed American employee, based upon seniority and in accordance with collective bargaining agreement provisions, did not violate the ban against national origin discrimination (.75). Time off with pay to Negro workers to observe the funeral of a slain Negro leader did not constitute racial discrimination by an employer who was willing to grant all employees (Negro and white) the same time off (.80).

.01 **Laws.**—*Civil Rights Act of 1964, Title VII*, 42 U.S.C. 2000e(j), ¶ 3048A.

.02 **Executive Orders.**—*Executive Order 11246 on Government Contractors and Subcontractors*, 3 CFR 339, Sec. 202, ¶ 3680.

.03 **Regulations.**—*EEOC, Religious Discrimination Guidelines*, 29 CFR 1605.1, ¶ 3970.

.031 *Civil Service Commission, Equal Federal Employment Opportunity*, 5 CFR 713.204(f), ¶ 3855.204(f).

.032 *Wage-Hour Division, Interpretative Bulletin on Equal Pay for Equal Work Under FLSA*, 29 CFR 800.116(c), ¶ 4750.116(c).

.033 *Wage-Hour Division, Interpretative Bulletin on Age Discrimination in Employment*, 29 CFR 860.50(c), ¶ 4770.50(c).

.10 **Undue hardship to employer.**—Reasonable cause did not exist to support belief that employer had engaged in job bias on basis of religion by refusing to hire for position of process engineer applicant whose religious beliefs required him to be absent from work

Exhibit 97: Cont'd.

2621-18 **Current Items** 109 6-76

References are to paragraph (¶) numbers.
See also Topical Indexes at pages 151, 2623 and 2651.

REL

Exhibit 98: Index to "Current Items" covers the most recent material of the four subiect indexes in this service (Exhibit 96, Topical Index, was the first or basic index of this kind). "Current Items" provides access to the latest court and agency decisions.

Conclusion

The charge against Respondent State Commissioner of Education is dismissed for lack of jurisdiction.

There is no reasonable cause to believe that Respondent Board of Education discriminated against Charging Party on the basis of sex.

[¶ 6500] FAILURE TO ACCOMMODATE EMPLOYEE'S RELIGIOUS NEEDS WAS BIAS

→ Decision of the Equal Employment Opportunity Commission, Decision No. 76-104, April 2, 1976.

Title VII—Civil Rights Act of 1964

Religious Discrimination—Lumber and Building Supply Company—Discharged Employee—Failure to Accommodate Religious Need.—By an employer failing to sustain the burden of proving that an undue hardship existed which prevented it from accommodating the religious needs of its employee not to work on the Saturday Sabbath, there was reasonable cause to believe the employer engaged in an unlawful employment practice in violation of the Act, as amended, by discriminating against claimant because of his religion.

→ Back reference.—¶ 1164.

Full Text of EEOC Decision

Summary of Charge

Charging Party alleges that Respondent has engaged in an unlawful employment practice in violation of Title VII of the Civil Rights Act of 1964, as amended, by discharging him because of his religion.

Jurisdiction

Respondent is a lumber and building supply facility engaging in interstate commerce, and is an employer within the meaning of 701(b) of the Civil Rights Act of 1964, as amended. The charge was timely filed and deferred within the time limitations as prescribed by Title VII, and all other jurisdictional requirements have been met.

Summary of Investigation

The record discloses that the facts are that Charging Party was employed by Respondent as a salesman in 1964. It is unclear when Charging Party adopted his religious philosophy, but he became a Christian and began the study of the scriptures. Although Charging Party belonged to no established religion which worshiped on Saturday he attended the Free Will Baptist Church of God which held services on Saturdays and Sundays.

It appears Charging Party's convictions about Sabbath work became more and more rigid as he became convinced that Saturday was to be observed as a day of rest. At this junction he informed his supervisor that he no longer wanted Thursdays off, but instead wanted Saturdays off to observe the Sabbath. Respondent's manager never questioned the sincerity of Charging Party's religious conviction, instead he informed him that he had the alternative to either work on Saturdays or his absence would be construed as a resignation. No attempt of any kind was made to accommodate Charging Party in order for him to have Saturdays off. Charging Party did not work on the following Saturday, and when he returned to work on the next Monday, he was considered as having resigned effective his last working day. Respondent never claimed that Charging Party's absence would cause an undue hardship on the conduct of its business.

Respondent's manager asserted in an interview with this Commission's representative that Charging Party would have been accommodated if he were either a Seventh Day Adventist or Jewish, while at the same time unequivocally emphasizing that he had previously accommodated another employee who was a member of the Seventh Day Adventist Church.

The question Respondent seems to be raising here is whether Charging Party's conviction regarding Sabbath work qualifies as an expression of a "religion" within the protection of Title VII. The Supreme Court's construction of Section 6(j) of the Universal Military Training and Service Act is instructive. In *United States v. Seeger,* 380 U. S. 163 (1965), the Court's principal statement of its test for determining whether a conscientious objector's beliefs are religious within the meaning of Section 6(j) was as follows (380 U. S. at 176):

> A sincere and meaningful belief which occupies in the life of its possessor a place parallel to that filled by the God of those admittedly qualifying for the exemption comes within the statutory definition.

Exhibit 99: This service contains decisions of the relevant administrative agency in full text. Here is a decision of the Equal Employment Opportunity Commission on the problem being researched. This paragraph reference was given in the "Current Items" index above. Note the back reference to ¶ 1164 which contains another background summary on this problem. (See Exhibit 100 below.)

The Court also held that "intensely personal" convictions which some might find "incomprehensible" or "incorrect" come within the meaning of "religious belief" in the Training and Service Act. *Welsh v. United States,* 90 S. Ct. 1792, 1796 (1970), citing 380 U. S. at 186-187. If "religion" were construed more narrowly for Title VII purposes than it is in the context of Section 6(j), then Title VII's proscription of religious discrimination would conflict with the First Amendment's Establishment Clause.

There is no contention that Charging Party's beliefs are not deeply and sincerely held religious convictions. See C. D. 71-779, CCH EEOC Decisions (1973) ¶ 6180.

These beliefs are therefore entitled to protection under the 1964 Civil Rights Act, as amended.

We also disagree with Respondent's view that Charging Party had to be of a particular faith before any attempt at accommodation is necessary. In an amendment to the Civil Rights Act of 1964, effective March 1972, Congress determined the issue of what is the meaning of "religion" in the act, by incorporating this Commission's guidelines into the federal statute. See *Commission's Guidelines on Religious Discrimination,* 29 C. F. R. 16051. The following provision was added to Section 701:

> (j) The term "religion" includes all aspects of religious observance and practice, as well as belief, unless an employer demonstrates that he is unable to reasonably accommodate to an employee's or prospective employee's religious observance or practice without undue hardship on the conduct of the employer's business.

The gravamen of the statute clearly states that Congress did not intend that employees of one religion be given preference over another. Where an employee's religious belief meets the standard set forth by the Supreme Court in *Seeger,* supra, that belief is protected by Title VII. If there is a conflict between the requirements of his protected religious belief and of his work schedule, the employer is obligated to accommodate the employee unless such accommodation would impose an undue hardship on the employer. See, *Cummins v. Parker Seal Co.,* (6th Cir. 1975) 9 EPD ¶ 10,171. Further, the employer has the burden of proving that an undue hardship renders the required accommodation to the religious need of the employee unreasonable. See *Commissions Guidelines On Religious Discrimination,* 29 C. F. R. 1605.1(c).

We do not know what kind of accommodation could have been made had the employer made a good faith effort in this direction: other employers in similar situations have arranged shift-exchanges with other employees, have gotten along with one less person on the shift, or have hired part-time help. The record shows that Respondent had hired part-time help on Saturdays in situations similar to the Charging Party's to cover a busy day.[1] It does not appear, however, that Respondent gave serious thought to any of these alternatives here.

We must conclude that where similarly placed persons of different religious beliefs are accorded dissimilar treatment, the Commission must find, in the absence of other evidence, that religion was a factor in the disparate treatment. Further, Respondent has not met the burden of proving that an undue hardship exists in rendering the required accommodation to the religious needs of Charging Party. Absent such evidence, we find Charging Party's constructive discharge constituted discrimination against him because of his religion within the meaning of Section 703(a) of Title VII.

Conclusion

There is reasonable cause to believe that Respondent engaged in an unlawful employment practice in violation of Title VII of the Civil Rights Act, as amended, by discharging Charging Party because of his religion.

---

[1] As courts have recently noted, "The regulation does not preclude some cost to the employer any more than it precludes some degree of inconvenience to effect a reasonable accommodation." *Hardison v. TWA,* — F. 2d — (10th Cir. 1975) 10 EPD ¶ 10,554; *Ward v. Allegheny Ludlum Steel Corp.,* 397 F. Supp. 375 (W. D. Pa. 1975) 10 EPD ¶ 10,327.

Exhibit 99: Cont'd. Note references in the decision to other decisions in this service and to administrative regulations or guidelines in *C.F.R.* The latter are set forth in Exhibit 103 below.

Ricans applied, their chances of consideration for employment were nil.

EEOC Decision, Case No. CC AT 7-2-112, June 30, 1969.

.88 Concerted activities.—Employer discriminatorily denied employment to two Negro carpenters because of their engagement in protected concerted activities as evidenced by employer's knowledge that they were seeking employment not only for themselves but for other Negroes. Fact that employer hired two Negro carpenters at later date did not establish that employer's earlier refusal to hire these employees was not due to racial discrimination.

Mason & Hanger-Silas Mason Co., 1969 CCH NLRB ¶ 21,323, 179 NLRB (No. 71).

.90 State agency.—Employer effectively discontinued his racially discriminatory practices of hiring directly employees needed and necessary in operation of his plant when he commenced by contract hiring of employees through state agency.

Irvin v. Mohawk Rubber Co. (DC, Ark.; 1970) 2 EPD ¶ 10,152, 308 F.Supp. 152.

Religion Discrimination

¶ 1164

Federal law makes it unlawful to refuse to hire employees because of their religion (.01). The principal problems involving religious discrimination arise in connection with observation of Sabbaths and granting of religious holidays (see ¶ 1170).

Under the 1972 amendments to Title VII of the Civil Rights Act of 1964, "religion" was defined to include all aspects of religious observance and practice as well as belief (.011). The effect of this new definition was that, unless an employer demonstrates that he is unable to reasonably accommodate to an employee's or prospective employee's religious observance without undue hardship on the conduct of his business, he will be deemed to have violated the law. Employers are expected to make reasonable accommodations for employees whose "religion" may include observances, practices and beliefs, such as Sabbath observance, which may differ from the employer's or potential employer's requirements regarding standards, schedules, or other business-related employment conditions.

The exemption from the ban on religious discrimination given to religious corporations and societies, which was formerly restricted to employees working in religious activities, was broadened by the 1972 amendments to Title VII to cover all secular activities of these institutions (.012). This means that these institutions may now employ individuals of a particular religion in all their activities, instead of only in their religious activities.

Under EEOC guidelines employers have an obligation to accommodate the reasonable religious needs of their employees and prospective employees when such accommodations can be made without undue hardship on the conduct of the employer's business (.03). Under these rules, undue hardship may exist when an employee's job cannot be performed by another worker of substantially similar qualifications during the time when the employee is absent for religious reasons. Because of the sensitive nature of refusing to hire an applicant on account of his religious beliefs, an employer has the burden of proving that an undue hardship renders the required accommodation to the religious needs of an employee as unreasonable. The Commission will review each case on an individual basis in an effort to seek an equitable application of its guidelines.

.01 Laws.—*Civil Rights Act of 1964, Title VII*, 42 U.S.C. 2000e-2(a)(1), ¶ 3051(a)(1).

.011 *Civil Rights Act of 1964, Title VII*, 42 U.S.C. 2000e(j), ¶ 3048A.

.012 *Civil Rights Act of 1964, Title VII*, 42 U. S. C. 2000e-1, ¶ 3049A.

.03 Regulations.—*EEOC, Religious Discrimination Guidelines*, 29 CFR 1605.1, ¶ 3970.

Exhibit 100: Background summary, cited in previous exhibit, refers to relevant statutes and regulations.

pursuant to this section, the head of the Federal department or agency shall file with the committees of the House and Senate having legislative jurisdiction over the program or activity involved a full written report of the circumstances and the grounds for such action. No such action shall become effective until thirty days have elapsed after the filing of such report. [July 2, 1964, P. L. 88-352, Title VI, § 602, 78 Stat. 252, 42 U. S. C. § 2000d-1.]

[¶ 3023] JUDICIAL REVIEW—ADMINISTRATIVE PROCEDURE ACT

Sec. 603. Any department or agency action taken pursuant to section 2000d-1 of this title shall be subject to such judicial review as may otherwise be provided by law for similar action taken by such department or agency on other grounds. In the case of action, not otherwise subject to judicial review, terminating or refusing to grant or to continue financial assistance upon a finding of failure to comply with a requirement imposed pursuant to section 2000d-1 of this title, any person aggrieved (including any State or political subdivision thereof and any agency of either) may obtain judicial review of such action in accordance with section 1009 of Title 5, and such action shall not be deemed committed to unreviewable agency discretion within the meaning of that section. [July 2, 1964, P. L. 88-352, Title VI, § 603, 78 Stat. 253, 42 U. S. C. § 2000d-2.]

[¶ 3024] ADMINISTRATIVE ACTION—FEDERALLY FINANCED ASSISTANCE—EMPLOYMENT AS PRIMARY OBJECTIVE

Sec. 604. Nothing contained in this subchapter [Title] shall be construed to authorize action under this subchapter [Title] by any department or agency with respect to any employment practice of any employer, employment agency, or labor organization except where a primary objective of the Federal financial assistance is to provide employment. [July 2, 1964, P. L. 880352, Title VI, § 604, 78 Stat. 253, 42 U. S. C. § 2000d-3.]

[¶ 3025] FEDERALLY FINANCED ASSISTANCE—INSURANCE AND GUARANTY PROGRAMS

Sec. 605. Nothing in this subchapter [Title] shall add to or detract from any existing authority with respect to any program or activity under which Federal financial assistance is extended by way of a contract of insurance or guaranty. [July 2, 1964, P. L. 88-352, Title VI, § 605, 78 Stat. 253, 42 U. S. C. § 2000d-4.]

→ Title VII—Equal Employment Opportunity

[¶ 3040] DEFINITIONS

Sec. 701. For the purposes of this title—

[¶ 3041] [Person]

(a) The term "person" includes one or more individuals, governments, governmental agencies, political subdivisions, labor unions, partnerships, associations, corporations, legal representatives, mutual companies, joint-stock companies, trusts, unincorporated organizations, trustees, trustees in bankruptcy, or receivers. [As amended March 24, 1972, P. L. 92-261, Title VII, 86 Stat. 103, 42 U. S. C. § 2000e(a).]

[¶ 3042] [Employer]

(b) The term "employer" means a person engaged in an industry affecting commerce who has fifteen or more employees for each working day in each of twenty or more calendar weeks in the current or preceding calendar year, and any agent of such a person, but such term does not include (1) the United States, a corporation wholly owned by the Government of the United States, an Indian tribe, or any department or agency of the District of Columbia subject by statute to procedures of the competitive service (as defined in section 2102 of Title 5 of

Exhibit 101: Here paragraphs containing relevant statutes are set forth. These documents were referred to in the earlier background summary and in the E.E.O.C. decision.

office in any State or political subdivision of any State by the qualified voters thereof, or any person chosen by such officer to be on such officer's personal staff, or an appointee on the policy making level or an immediate adviser with respect to the exercise of the constitutional or legal powers of the office. The exemption set forth in the preceding sentence shall not include employees subject to the civil service laws of a State government, governmental agency or political subdivision. [As amended March 24, 1972, P. L. 92-261, Title VII, 86 Stat. 103, 42 U. S. C. § 2000e(f).]

[¶ 3046] [Commerce]

(g) The term "commerce" means trade, traffic, commerce, transportation, transmission, or communication among the several States; or between a State and any place outside thereof; or within the District of Columbia, or a possession of the United States; or between points in the same State but through a point outside thereof. [As amended July 2, 1964, P. L. 88-352, Title VII, 78 Stat. 253, 42 U. S. C. § 2000e(g).]

[¶ 3047] [Industry Affecting Commerce]

(h) The term "industry affecting commerce" means any activity, business, or industry in commerce or in which a labor dispute would hinder or obstruct commerce or the free flow of commerce and includes any activity or industry "affecting commerce" within the meaning of the Labor-Management Reporting and Disclosure Act of 1959 and further includes any governmental industry, business, or activity. [As amended March 24, 1972, P. L. 92-261, Title VII, 86 Stat. 103, 42 U. S. C. § 2000e(h).]

[¶ 3048] [State]

(i) The term "State" includes a State of the United States, the District of Columbia, Puerto Rico, the Virgin Islands, American Samoa, Guam, Wake Island, the Canal Zone, and Outer Continental Shelf lands defined in the Outer Continental Shelf Lands Act. [As amended July 2, 1964, P. L. 88-352, Title VII, 78 Stat. 253, 42 U. S. C. § 2000e(i).]

[¶ 3048A] [Religion]

(j) The term "religion" includes all aspects of religious observance and practice, as well as belief, unless an employer demonstrates that he is unable to reasonably accommodate to an employee's or prospective employee's religious observance or practice without undue hardship on the conduct of the employer's business. [As added March 24, 1972, P. L. 92-261, Title VII, 86 Stat. 103, 42 U. S. C. § 2000e(j).]

[¶ 3049] EXEMPTION

[¶ 3049A] [Non-Resident Aliens—Religious Institutions]

Sec. 702. This title shall not apply to an employer with respect to the employment of aliens outside any State, or to a religious corporation, association, educational institution, or society with respect to the employment of individuals of a particular religion to perform work connected with the carrying on by such corporation, association, educational institution, or society of its activties. [As amended March 24, 1972, P. L. 92-261, Title VII, 86 Stat. 103, 42 U. S. C. § 2000e-1.]

[¶ 3050] DISCRIMINATION BECAUSE OF RACE, COLOR, RELIGION, SEX, OR NATIONAL ORIGIN

[¶ 3051] [Unlawful Practices of Employers]

Sec. 703. (a) It shall be an unlawful employment practice for an employer—

(1) to fail or refuse to hire or to discharge any individual, or otherwise to discriminate against any individual with respect to his compensation, terms,

Exhibit 101: Cont'd.

conditions, or privileges of employment, because of such individual's race, color, religion, sex, or national origin; [July 2, 1964, P. L. 88-352, Title VII, 78 Stat. 255, 42 U. S. C. § 2000e-2(a)(1)] or

(2) to limit, segregate, or classify his employees or applicants for employment in any way which would deprive or tend to deprive any individual of employment opportunities or otherwise adversely affect his status as an employee, because of such individual's race, color, religion, sex, or national origin. [As amended March 24, 1972, P. L. 92-261, Title VII, 86 Stat. 109, 42 U. S. C. § 2000e-2(a)(2).]

[¶ 3052] [Unlawful Practices of Employment Agencies]

(b) It shall be an unlawful employment practice for an employment agency to fail or refuse to refer for employment, or otherwise to discriminate against, any individual because of his race, color, religion, sex, or national origin, or to classify or refer for employment any individual on the basis of his race, color, religion, sex, or national origin. [July 2, 1964, P. L. 88-352, Title VII, 78 Stat. 255, 42 U. S. C. § 2000e-2(b).]

[¶ 3053] [Unlawful Practices of Labor Organizations]

(c) It shall be an unlawful employment practice for a labor organization—

(1) to exclude or to expel from its membership, or otherwise to discriminate against, any individual because of his race, color, religion, sex, or national origin [July 2, 1964, P. L. 88-352, Title VII, 78 Stat. 255, 42 U. S. C. § 2000e-2(c)(1)];

(2) to limit, segregate, or classify its membership or applicants for membership, or to classify or fail or refuse to refer for employment any individual, in any way which would deprive or tend to deprive any individual of employment opportunities, or would limit such employment opportunities or otherwise adversely affect his status as an employee or as an applicant for employment, because of such individual's race, color, religion, sex, or national origin; [As amended March 24, 1972, P. L. 92-261, Title VII, 86 Stat. 109, 42 U. S. C. § 2000e-2(c)(2)] or

(3) to cause or attempt to cause an employer to discriminate against an individual in violation of this section. [July 2, 1964, P. L. 88-352, Title VII, 78 Stat. 255, 42 U. S. C. § 2000e-2(c)(3).]

[¶ 3054] [Apprenticeship Programs]

(d) It shall be an unlawful employment practice for any employer, labor organization, or joint labor-management committee controlling apprenticeship or other training or retraining, including on-the-job training programs to discriminate against any individual because of his race, color, religion, sex, or national origin in admission to, or employment in, any program established to provide apprenticeship or other training. [July 2, 1964, P. L. 88-352, Title VII, 78 Stat. 255, 42 U. S. C. § 2000e-2(d).]

[¶ 3055] [Religion, Sex or National Origin as Occupational Qualification]

(e) Notwithstanding any other provision of this title, (1) it shall not be an unlawful employment practice for an employer to hire and employ employees, for an employment agency to classify, or refer for employment any individual, for a labor organization to classify its membership or to classify or refer for employment any individual, or for an employer, labor organization, or joint labor-management committee controlling apprenticeship or other training or retraining programs to admit or employ any individual in any such program, on the basis of his religion, sex, or national origin in those certain instances where religion, sex, or national origin is a bona fide occupational qualification reasonably necessary to the normal operation of that particular business or enterprise, and (2) it shall not be an unlawful employment practice for a school, college, university, or other educational institution or institution of learning to hire and employ employees of a particular religion if such school, college, university, or other edu-

Exhibit 101: Cont'd.

112 7-76 Finding Lists 529

Chapter XIV—Equal Employment Opportunity Commission—Continued

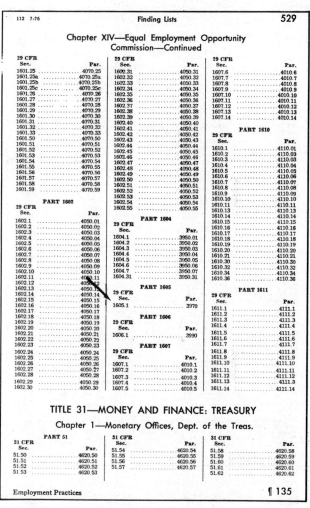

29 CFR Sec.	Par.
1601.25	4070.25
1601.25a	4070.25a
1601.25b	4070.25b
1601.25c	4070.25c
1601.26	4070.26
1601.27	4070.27
1601.28	4070.28
1601.29	4070.29
1601.30	4070.30
1601.31	4070.31
1601.32	4070.32
1601.33	4070.33
1601.50	4070.50
1601.51	4070.51
1601.52	4070.52
1601.53	4070.53
1601.54	4070.54
1601.55	4070.55
1601.56	4070.56
1601.57	4070.57
1601.58	4070.58
1601.59	4070.59

PART 1602

29 CFR Sec.	Par.
1602.1	4050.01
1602.2	4050.02
1602.3	4050.03
1602.4	4050.04
1602.5	4050.05
1602.6	4050.06
1602.7	4050.07
1602.8	4050.08
1602.9	4050.09
1602.10	4050.10
1602.11	4050.11
1602.12	4050.12
1602.13	4050.13
1602.14	4050.14
1602.15	4050.15
1602.16	4050.16
1602.17	4050.17
1602.18	4050.18
1602.19	4050.19
1602.20	4050.20
1602.21	4050.21
1602.22	4050.22
1602.23	4050.23
1602.24	4050.24
1602.25	4050.25
1602.26	4050.26
1602.27	4050.27
1602.28	4050.28
1602.29	4050.29
1602.30	4050.30
1602.31	4050.31
1602.32	4050.32
1602.33	4050.33
1602.34	4050.34
1602.35	4050.35
1602.36	4050.36
1602.37	4050.37
1602.38	4050.38
1602.39	4050.39
1602.40	4050.40
1602.41	4050.41
1602.42	4050.42
1602.43	4050.43
1602.44	4050.44
1602.45	4050.45
1602.46	4050.46
1602.47	4050.47
1602.48	4050.48
1602.49	4050.49
1602.50	4050.50
1602.51	4050.51
1602.52	4050.52
1602.53	4050.53
1602.54	4050.54
1602.55	4050.55

PART 1604

29 CFR Sec.	Par.
1604.1	3950.01
1604.2	3950.02
1604.3	3950.03
1604.4	3950.04
1604.5	3950.05
1604.6	3950.06
1604.7	3950.07
1604.31	3950.31

PART 1605

29 CFR Sec.	Par.
1605.1	3970

PART 1606

29 CFR Sec.	Par.
1606.1	3990

PART 1607

29 CFR Sec.	Par.
1607.1	4010.1
1607.2	4010.2
1607.3	4010.3
1607.4	4010.4
1607.5	4010.5
1607.6	4010.6
1607.7	4010.7
1607.8	4010.8
1607.9	4010.9
1607.10	4010.10
1607.11	4010.11
1607.12	4010.12
1607.13	4010.13
1607.14	4010.14

PART 1610

29 CFR Sec.	Par.
1610.1	4110.01
1610.2	4110.02
1610.3	4110.03
1610.4	4110.04
1610.5	4110.05
1610.6	4110.06
1610.7	4110.07
1610.8	4110.08
1610.9	4110.09
1610.10	4110.10
1610.11	4110.11
1610.13	4110.13
1610.14	4110.14
1610.15	4110.15
1610.16	4110.16
1610.17	4110.17
1610.18	4110.18
1610.19	4110.19
1610.20	4110.20
1610.21	4110.21
1610.30	4110.30
1610.32	4110.32
1610.34	4110.34
1610.36	4110.36

PART 1611

29 CFR Sec.	Par.
1611.1	4111.1
1611.2	4111.2
1611.3	4111.3
1611.4	4111.4
1611.5	4111.5
1611.6	4111.6
1611.7	4111.7
1611.8	4111.8
1611.9	4111.9
1611.10	4111.10
1611.11	4111.11
1611.12	4111.12
1611.13	4111.3
1611.14	4111.14

TITLE 31—MONEY AND FINANCE: TREASURY

Chapter 1—Monetary Offices, Dept. of the Treas.

PART 51

31 CFR Sec.	Par.
51.50	4620.50
51.51	4620.51
51.52	4620.52
51.53	4620.53
51.54	4620.54
51.55	4620.55
51.56	4620.56
51.57	4620.57
51.58	4620.58
51.59	4620.59
51.60	4620.60
51.61	4620.61
51.62	4620.62

Employment Practices ¶ 135

Exhibit 102: Finding lists enable the researcher to locate regulations and other documents within the service by references to their paragraph numbers. Here the E.E.O.C. Guidelines, referred to in the E.E.O.C. decision in Exhibit 99, can be located in ¶ 3970.

Equal Employment Opportunity Commission

Religious Discrimination Guidelines

¶ 3970

The following guidelines on religious discrimination were signed July 10, 1967, effective immediately. They replace prior guidelines,[1] issued June 15, 1966 (31 F. R. 8370), and were codified and published in the Federal Register July 13, 1967 (32 F. R. 10298) as Title 29—Labor, Chapter XIV—Equal Employment Opportunity Commission, Part 1605—Guidelines on Discrimination Because of Religion.

Section 1605.1 Observance of Sabbath and other religious holidays.—(a) Several complaints filed with the Commission have raised the question whether it is discrimination on account of religion to discharge or refuse to hire employees who regularly observe Friday evening and Saturday, or some other day of the week, as the Sabbath or who observe certain special religious holidays during the year and, as a consequence, do not work on such days.

(b) The Commission believes that the duty not to discriminate on religious grounds, required by section 703(a)(1) of the Civil Rights Act of 1964, includes an obligation on the part of the employer to make reasonable accommodations to the religious needs of employees and prospective employees where such accommodations can be made without undue hardship on the conduct of the employer's business. Such undue hardship, for example, may exist where the employee's needed work cannot be performed by another employee of substantially similar qualifications during the period of absence of the Sabbath observer.

(c) Because of the particularly sensitive nature of discharging or refusing to hire an employee or applicant on account of his religious beliefs, the employer has the burden of proving that an undue hardship renders the required accommodations to the religious needs of the employee unreasonable.

(d) The Commission will review each case on an individual basis in an effort to seek an equitable application of these guidelines to the variety of situations which arise due to the varied religious practices of the American people.

[1] Prior to amendment, Section 1605.1 read as follows:

"**Section 1605.1 Observance of Sabbath and religious holidays.**—(a)(1) Several complaints filed with the Commission have raised the question whether it is discrimination on account of religion to discharge or to refuse to hire a person whose religious observances require that he take time off during the employer's regular work week. These complaints arise in a variety of contexts, but typically involve employees who regularly observe Saturdays as the Sabbath or who observe certain special holidays during the year.

"(2) The Commission believes that the duty not to discriminate on religious grounds includes an obligation on the part of the employer to accommodate the reasonable religious needs of employees and, in some cases, prospective employees where such accommodation can be made without serious inconvenience to the conduct of the business.

"(3) However, the Commission believes that an employer is free under Title VII to establish a normal work week (including paid holidays) generally applicable to all employees, notwithstanding that this schedule may not operate with uniformity in its effect upon the religious observances of his employees. For example, an employer who is closed for business on Sunday does not discriminate merely because he requires that all his employees be available for work on Saturday.

"Likewise, an employer who closes his business on Christmas or Good Friday is not thereby obligated to give time off with pay to Jewish employees for Rosh Hashanah or Yom Kippur:

"(b) While the question of what accommodation by the employer may reasonably be required must be decided on the peculiar facts of each case, the following guidelines may prove helpful.

"(1) An employer may permit absences from work on religious holidays, with or without pay, but must treat all religions with substantial uniformity in this respect. However, the closing of a business on one religious holiday creates no obligation to permit time off from work on another.

"(2) An employer, to the extent he can do so without serious inconvenience to the conduct of his business, should make a reasonable accommodation to the needs of his employees and applicants for employment in connection with special religious holiday observances.

"(3) The employer may prescribe the normal work week and foreseeable overtime requirements, and, absent an intent on the part of the employer to discriminate on religious grounds, a job applicant or employee who accepted the job knowing or having reason to believe that such requirements would conflict with his religious obligations is not entitled to demand any alterations in such requirements to accommodate his religious needs.

"(4) Where an employee has previously been employed on a schedule which does not conflict with his religious obligations, and it becomes necessary to alter his work schedule, the employer should attempt to achieve an accommodation so as to avoid a conflict. However, an employer is not compelled to make such an accommodation at the expense of serious inconvenience to the conduct of his business or disproportionate allocation of unfavorable work assignments to other employees."

Employment Practices ¶ 3970

Exhibit 103: ¶ 3970, shown here, contains the E.E.O.C. Guidelines, referred to above.

2514 **Curre it Items to Cumulative Index** NQ 6-76

See also Cum ılative Indexes at pages 2531 and 255r.

From Compilation Paragraph No.		To New Development Paragraph No.
	Restaurant's decision to replace all waiters with waitresses was sex bias (NY SCt App Div)	10,188
1170	Ban of pay for Good Friday holiday stayed pending appeal (Cal Ct App) 5 EPD ¶ 8553.—Aff'd (Cal Ct App) 9 EPD ¶ 10,003.—Aff'd (Cal S Ct)	10,891
→	Discharge of employee was not religious bias where employer made reasonable attempt to accommodate religious needs (CA-10)	10,621
.10	Airline's failure to accommodate Sabbath justified by hardship and union rules (DC Mo) 8 EPD ¶ 9546.—Rev'd (CA-8)	10,554
.40	Union failure to accommodate Sabbath justified by seniority rules (DC Mo) 8 EPD ¶ 9546.—Aff'd on other issues (CA-8)	10,554
→ .50	Applicant had right to job if religious needs not an undue hardship (CA-6) 5 EPD ¶ 8013.—Decision on the merits (DC Tenn) 7 EPD ¶ 9206.—Rev'd on this issue (CA-6) 10 EPD ¶ 10,373.—Full court hearing on this issue denied (CA-6)	10,759
1180	Female overtime law violates sex bias bans, extension to males rejected (DC Ark)	10,675
	State female overtime laws invalid due to conflict with federal law—extension to males rejected (Ark Cir Ct)	10,675
.32	No evidence supported conclusion that Negro laborer was denied overtime opportunities because of his race (EEOC)	6472
1201	Racial bias in promotions indicated by results of subsequently instituted affirmative action plan (DC Ohio) 9 EPD ¶ 10,019.—Aff'd (CA-6)	10,741
1208	Railroad law allowing earlier female retirement constitutional and not in conflict with Title VII (DC Pa)	10,857
	Retirement plan which penalized males more heavily than females for early retirement was sex biased (EEOC)	6471
1210	Agreement allowing forced retirement at age 52 illegal (W-H Opinion Letter)	5366
	Early retirement under bona fide labor pact not age bias (DC Mich)	10,702
1230	Biased seniority practices warrant relief from layoff (DC Miss)	10,784
	Layoff and recall policy was sex biased (EEOC)	6464
	Layoff of Negro foreman under subjective standards was race bias (DC Ohio) 8 EPD ¶ 9523.—Aff'd (CA-6)	10,688
	School employees hired under affirmative action programs not entitled to preferential treatment in event of layoffs	5375
	State layoff preference for longer seniority and veterans constitutional (CA-2)	10,834
.12	Effect of past bias shown in recall from layoff (CA-7) 8 EPD ¶ 9658.—Cert den (US S Ct)	10,925
.12	Processing of layoff grievances barred by conciliation agreement (DC Miss)	10,556
.12	Proportionate layoff of women under conciliation, rather than union, agreement (DC Miss)	10,556
1240	Demotion and bias charges of nominal director dismissed as unsupported (DC Ohio)	10,926
.40	No race bias despite few Negro supervisors in paper mill (DC Ala) 6 EPD ¶ 8912.—Rev'd & rem'd (CA-5)	10,880
1250	Back pay and seniority for female flight attendants dismissed under no-marriage rule (DC Cal)	10,933
	Discharge of white female married to black victim of racial bias (Mich Cir Ct)	10,763
	Lower seniority justified wife's discharge under ban on employment of spouses (DC Mo) 9 EPD ¶ 9982.—Aff'd (CA-8)	10,498
	Policy of not hiring spouse of employee who works for company was sex discrimination (EEOC)	6492
	Requiring married females to use husband's name on personnel records was reasonable (DC Tenn)	10,548
1268	Age was occupational qualification for hiring as bus driver (DC Fla) 4 EPD ¶ 7795.—Aff'd (CA-5)	10,916
	Factual basis needed for belief that age is occupational qualification (DC Fla) 4 EPD ¶ 7795.—Aff'd (CA-5)	10,916
1290 .20	Exclusion of Negroes from jobs as welders and fabricators constitutes pattern and practice of bias (DC NC)	10,492
1295	Fire and police height rule biased and not justified by business necessity (DC Cal)	10,818
	Height requirements for police department biased against females (DC Ill)	10,597
	Rejection of blind teacher violated Rehabilitation Act (DC Pa)	10,823
1300	Apprenticeship affirmative action not unlawful reverse bias (DC Tenn)	10,846
	Black fireman promotion under affirmative action plan vacated—no showing of bias (DC Cal)	10,804
	Preferential hiring order for police and fire national origin bias (DC Cal)	10,818
	School employees hired under affirmative action programs not entitled to preferential treatment in event of layoffs	5375
1310	Denial of benefits for pregnancy barred as sex bias (DC Miss)	10,784
	Denial of pregnancy leave and termination was sex bias (DC NC)	10,651
	Denial of reemployment to teacher following pregnancy was bias (DC SC)	10,652
	Denial of sick leave for maternity purposes was sex bias (DC NC)	10,651
	Denial of sickness disability benefits for pregnancy related disability was sex bias (EEOC)	6462
	Discriminatory reinstatement policy following maternity leave was sex bias (EEOC)	6461
	Failure to rehire pregnant teacher because of impending interruption was sex bias (DC SC)	10,652
	Fixed date maternity leave for school teachers was sex bias (EEOC)	6463
	Fixed maternity leave dates and sick benefit denial for pregnancy sex bias (EEOC)	6487

Exhibit 104: By using this table, "Current Items to Cumulative Index," one gets references from an earlier background paragraph (¶ 1170, shown in Exhibit 97 above) to new material on the same subject. Note how the reference to the case in ¶ 1170.50 serves as a citator by locating later court proceedings in the same case.

— Footnotes —

[1] See *Waters v. Heublein, Inc.*, 8 EPD ¶9522 (N.D.Cal. 1974).

[2] It has been previously ruled that there is no independent cause of action against Heublein. See fn. 1, *supra*.

[3] See Exhibit A to affidavit of EEOC officer Brenda Brush filed August 14, 1973.

[4] This situation may change if it is later determined that subclasses are necessary.

[5] Since plaintiff's complaint alleges continuous violations of the law by United Vintners, she may represent a class of present and future employees. However, some past employees cannot be represented because of their failure to file charges with the EEOC.' *Wetzel v. Liberty Mutual Insurance Co.*, [9 EPD ¶9931] 508 F.2d 239, 246 (3rd Cir. 1975), *cert. denied*, [9 EPD ¶10,176] 421 U.S. 1011 (1975) (*Wetzel I*). (Another case involving the same parties, *Wetzel II*, reported at [9 EPD ¶9942] 511 F.2d 199 [3rd Cir. 1975] will be heard by the Supreme Court. 421 U.S. 987 (1975). The class action issues in *Wetzel I* are not involved in *Wetzel II*.)

However, no exact cutoff date can be established because some past employees nominally excluded from the class by the time limitations of 42 U.S.C. § 2000e-5(e) [§ 2000e-5(d) when plaintiff filed her EEOC charges] may be able to avoid operation of that limitation because of their specific individual circumstances. See *Reeb v. Economic Opportunity Atlanta, Inc.*, [10 EPD ¶10,358] 516 F.2d 924 (5th Cir. 1975).

Consequently, for present purposes, inclusion of all past employees in the class is acceptable. If plaintiff prevails on her class claims, other individuals must then prove that they are members of the class and entitled to relief. *Baxter v. Savannah Sugar Refining Corp.*, [7 EPD ¶9426] 495 F.2d 437, 443-444 (5th Cir. 1974), *cert. denied*, [8 EPD ¶9789] 419 U.S. 1033 (1974). Any statute of limitations problems can be resolved at that time. As a woman and a former employee of United Vintners, plaintiff has standing to represent the proposed class. See, e.g., *Long v. Sapp*, [8 EPD ¶9712] 502 F.2d 34, 42-43 (5th Cir. 1974).

[6] See fn. 3, *supra*.

[7] It is thus unnecessary to rely on past employees who may be barred by the statute of limitations from participating in the case, fn. 5, *supra*, to establish a class large enough to satisfy Rule 23(a)(1).

[8] Appendix to Plaintiff's Memorandum in Support of Class Certification Motion, p. A-4.

[9] Defendant asserts that only one other woman employee of United Vintners has filed such a charge. Defendant's Memorandum in Support of Motion to Strike the Class, p. 10.

[10] It is thus unnecessary to evaluate this class claim in terms of the other requirements of Rule 23. If plaintiff can correct the defect outlined above, the Court will consider the matter further.

[11] Similarly, there is no requirement that all questions of law and fact be common to the class. The existence of some common questions is sufficient. *Like v. Carter*, 448 F.2d 798, 802 (8th Cir. 1971), *cert. denied*, 405 U.S. 1045 (1972).

[¶10,621] Larry J. Williams, Plaintiff-Appellant, Cross-Appellee v. Southern Union Gas Company, Defendant-Appellee, Cross-Appellant, United States Equal Employment Opportunity Commission, *Amicus Curiae*, Newspaper Agency Corporation, *Amicus Curiae* in the CrossAppeal.

United States Court of Appeals, Tenth Circuit. Nos. 75-1104 and 75-1105. January 21, 1976.

On Appeal from United States District Court, District of New Mexico. Affirmed.

Title VII—Civil Rights Act of 1964

Court Action—Timeliness.—The statutory period of 180 days allotted the EEOC for efforts to reach a voluntary settlement of employment discrimination claims does not place a time limit on complainants for bringing court action. The complainant has 90 days in which to initiate court action after receipt of the EEOC notice of right to sue, which need not be issued on expiration of the 180-day period.

Back reference.—¶ 2420.

Court Action—Timeliness—EEOC Notice.—An EEOC notice advising a job bias claimant of the failure of conciliation efforts and of his right to request a notice of right to sue did not start running of the time period for bringing an action in court. Since the court action was brought within 90 days of receipt of the notice of right to sue, it was not to be dismissed as untimely.

Back reference.—¶ 2420.

Religious Discrimination—Saturday Sabbath—Reasonable Accommodation.—A federal trial court properly determined that an employee observing Saturdays as Sabbath days was lawfully discharged for not working on a Saturday. The employer's business required service to the public 24 hours a day, seven days per week, and the requirement of work on Saturday was occasioned by an emergency to which the employee may have contributed by taking off the preceding Wednesday for a religious holiday. Considering that the employer had a duty to serve the consuming public and to adhere to employment practices

Exhibit 105: One of the new developments cited in the last Exhibit is the U.S. Court of Appeals decision shown here in full text.

that were fair to other employees, he was properly held to have acted reasonably. 42 U.S.C. Sec. 2000e-5(f)(1).

Back reference.—¶ 1170.

Robert J. Laughlin (Ralph K. Helge, on brief), for Plaintiff-Appellant and Cross-Appellee.

Owen M. Lopez (Jeffrey R. Brannen, Montgomery, Federici, Andrews, Hannahs & Buell, on brief), for Defendant-Appellee and Cross-Appellant.

Charles L. Reischel, Assistant General Counsel (Julia P. Cooper, Acting General Counsel, Joseph T. Eddins, Associate General Counsel, Beatrice Rosenberg, Assistant General Counsel, on brief), for Equal Employment Opportunity Commission, *Amicus Curiae*.

James S. Lowrie and Edward J. McDonough (Jones, Waldo, Holbrook & McDonough), on brief, for Newspaper Agency Corporation, *Amicus Curiae*.

Before HOLLOWAY, MCWILLIAMS and BARRETT, Circuit Judges.

[*Statement of Case*]

MCWILLIAMS, C.J.: This is a Civil Rights case based on a claim of unlawful job discharge. From July 1962 until October 3, 1970, Larry Williams was employed by the Southern Union Gas Company, initially as a dehydrator repairman's helper and later as a production repairman. On October 3, 1970, a Saturday, Williams was fired by Southern Union when he refused to report for work. Williams was at that time a member of the Worldwide Church of God. One of the tenets of this church is that its members should not work on the Sabbath, and Sabbath for this church is from sundown Friday to sundown Saturday. The reason given by Williams for not reporting for work on Saturday, October 3, 1970, was that his religion forbade working on the Sabbath.

On March 26, 1971, Williams filed a complaint with the Equal Employment Opportunity Commission alleging that Southern Union in firing him had discriminated against him because of his religion and in so doing had engaged in unlawful employment practices in violation of Title VII of the Civil Rights Act of 1964. On May 30, 1973, the Commission sent a letter to Williams advising him that compliance efforts had been unsuccessful and that he could bring a private action if he so desired. More specifically, this letter of May 30, 1973, advised Williams that if he decided to sue he should request a "Right-to-Sue" letter from the Commission and that he would have 90 days from the time the "Right-to-Sue" letter was received within which to bring an action against Southern Union. Williams did request such a letter, and on December 6, 1973, the "Right-to-Sue" letter was issued. Williams instituted the present action under 42 U.S.C. § 2000(e), as amended, on March 6, 1974. On trial the trial court found for Southern Union and entered judgment dismissing the action "on the merits." Williams now appeals.

By separate appeal Southern Union seeks review of the trial court's ruling that it had subject matter jurisdiction. In this regard it is Southern Union's position that the suit was not timely brought. The background facts must be developed in some detail.

[*Background Facts*]

When Williams went to work for Southern Union in 1962 he was informed that it was a company policy that all employees should be available for work seven days a week, 24 hours per day. Southern Union felt this was necessary inasmuch as it was a public utility and as such was obligated to provide continuous and uninterrupted natural gas service to the general public. It was also Southern Union's policy, however, to schedule its employees for only five days of work each week, eight hours per day. Williams in 1962 did not belong to any church and hence was under no prohibition, religious or otherwise, from working any day in the week.

During the fall of 1969 Williams became a member of the Worldwide Church of God. He informed his supervisor of his conversion and advised him that he would no longer be able to work between Friday at sundown and Saturday at sundown. The supervisor, one Al Dean, explained that it would be difficult to promise that Williams would never be called on to work on a Saturday, but that he would do what he could. Coincidentally, or otherwise, at the time of his conversion Williams'

Exhibit 105: Cont'd.

TOPICAL REPORTERS

Most of the looseleaf services which publish the full text of judicial and administrative decisions also issue them in bound volume series for permanent retention. These volumes have a continuing reference value and are retained despite changes in the rest of the service, particularly since they frequently contain decisions not included in the standard court reporters. In many cases, these unofficial reporters duplicate official editions (e.g., the CCH *N.L.R.B. Decisions* and the BNA *Labor Relations Reference Manual* both include material which can be found in the official *Decisions of the National Labor Relations Board*). However, these reporters include better indexing and finding devices than the official editions, are issued more quickly, and are tied into the other research features of their looseleaf services.

CONCLUSION

While looseleaf services continue to provide excellent coverage and access to varied legal sources in many subject fields, the computerized research systems are rapidly duplicating their functions. These specialized mini-libraries, whether in looseleaf format or in computer data bases, offer quick and convenient access to selected areas of law. There are several different ways of determining whether a service is available on a particular topic of interest. A selective list of major services, arranged by subject, is set forth in Appendix D at the end of this volume. More extensive lists appear in the 8th edition of *How to*

Find the Law (1983) and in its paperback abridgment, *Finding the Law* (1984). The following additional sources are also recommended:

Legal Looseleafs in Print, by A.L. Stern (Infosources Publishing)—an *annual* bibliography.

Catalogs issued by the major looseleaf publishers, listing their respective services. These include Bureau of National Affairs, Commerce Clearing House and Prentice-Hall.

The card catalog and reference staff of your local law library.

CHAPTER VIII

U.S. TREATIES

Treaties are formal agreements between countries, and have legal significance for both domestic and international purposes. When they are made between two governments, treaties are called *bilateral;* when entered into by more than two governments, they are called *multilateral.* Since Article VI of the Constitution provides that treaties shall be the supreme law of the land and shall bind all judges, they have the same legal effect and status as federal statutes. Thus, treaties can supersede prior statutes and statutes can supersede treaties, when the issue is the controlling law within the United States. The Seneca Indians of New York discovered this sadly a few years ago when their lands, secured to them for over 200 years by treaty, were taken from them pursuant to a later statute. Internationally, a treaty no longer valid as the law of the land may still be binding between the United States and another country, until formally abrogated.

The treaties of the United States are published in a variety of forms—official and unofficial, national and international, current and retrospective. There are a number of useful finding tools and aids available for research in treaties, but the bibliography of this literature is somewhat complex. Most of the various publications described herein include both treaties, which require approval by two-thirds of the Senate, and executive agreements, which generally do not require

Senate consent. Executive agreements may, however, be submitted to the Senate for approval if the President so decides.

An understanding of treaty publications generally may be facilitated by a review of the following critical dates in the progress of a treaty from signing to adoption:

1. **Date of Signing.** The date on which the treaty is signed by the representatives of the U.S. and the other country is ordinarily used in citations. It is so cited by the Department of State and lawyers generally, and is also the form of listing in *Shepard's Citations.* It is not, however, the treaty's effective date, nor the date on which it becomes the "law of the land", since Senate approval and presidential ratification are required first.

2. **Date of Approval by Senate.** The date on which the Senate "consents" to the treaty by a two-thirds vote of those present.

3. **Date of Ratification by the President.**

4. **Effective Date of Treaty.** Unless the treaty provides otherwise, this is usually the date on which the President ratifies the treaty, or on which ratifications are exchanged with the other signatory.

5. **Date of Proclamation.** The date on which the President proclaims the treaty, following which it is usually published.

An executive agreement is cited by the date of its signing. Because no Senate approval is needed, it becomes effective on the date stated in the agreement itself.

CURRENT PUBLICATION OF U.S. TREATIES AND EXECUTIVE AGREEMENTS

The following are the most common forms of treaty publication:

1. **Department of State Press Releases.** The first publication of treaties and most executive agreements, these releases are usually issued on the date of signing.

2. **Department of State Bulletin.** This monthly periodical is an authoritative source of treaty information and often contains the text of treaties shortly after their signing. It also reports authoritatively on negotiations, congressional action, ratification, and other developments in the progress of a treaty from signing to proclamation, in a regular feature called "Treaties—Current Actions".

3. **Treaty Documents** (formerly called *Senate Executive Documents*). A treaty is transmitted to the Senate for its consideration in this form, which usually includes transmittal messages from the President and the Secretary of State. Some of these documents are initially confidential and are thus not available for distribution or listed in the *Monthly Catalog of U.S. Government Publications* until the Senate lifts its injunction of secrecy. Until 1980, *Senate Executive Documents* were identified by alphabetical designations. Since 1981, their successors, the *Treaty Documents,* have appeared in numerical series, reflecting the Congress and order in which they were issued. They may be pending before the Senate for many

sessions before approval, but still retain their original citation. *Senate Executive Documents* should be distinguished from *Senate Executive Reports* which contain the report of the Senate Committee on Foreign Relations on the treaty.

4. **Slip Treaty Publication.** After ratification, the first widely disseminated official publication is in the *Treaties and Other International Acts Series (T.I. A.S.),* which began in 1945 as a successor to two separate series called *Treaty Series* (1908–1945) and *Executive Agreement Series* (1929–1945). It is a pamphlet form of publication, similar to the statutory slip law. The slip treaties are consecutively numbered and separately paginated, and contain the text of each treaty or agreement in the language of all parties signing it. There is often a considerable delay between the effective date of a treaty and the publication of its slip form.

5. **U.S. Treaties and Other International Agreements (U.S.T.).** Since 1949 when the publication of treaties in the *Statutes at Large* was discontinued, this series has been the permanent form of official treaty publication. These volumes cumulate the *T.I. A.S.* pamphlets in the same way that the *Statutes at Large* collect the slip laws. Like *T.I.A.S., U.S.T.* includes both treaties and executive agreements, and provides the English language text first, followed by the texts in any other official languages of the compact. Several volumes are issued every year and each is separately indexed by subject and country. There are now several, successive commercially published cumulative indexes providing access to this material

by *T.I.A.S.* number, date, country and subject. These are described below under "Finding Tools" on page 283 below.

6. Unofficial Publications. There are some unofficial sources for U.S. treaties, but they are selective and do not offer the complete coverage of *T.I.A.S.* and *U.S.T.* *International Legal Materials,* published bimonthly since 1962 by the American Society of International Law, contains the texts of treaties of major significance and sometimes provides drafts before final agreement. Although selective, it is considerably faster than most of the other publications described in this section and is particularly useful for that reason.

There are also several treaty collections in specialized subject areas, issued by commercial publishers. For example, *Extradition Law and Treaties,* 2 vols. looseleaf (Hein, 1979) compiled by I.I. Kavass & A. Sprudzs and updated annually, contains all operative United States extradition treaties arranged by the countries with which the treaties are made. CCH *Tax Treaties* is a looseleaf service which publishes U.S. treaties relating to income and estate taxation.

U.S.C.A. and *U.S.C.S.,* like the *U.S. Code* itself, publish a few important treaties which substantially affect related *Code* provisions (e.g., the Universal Copyright Convention in Title 17). *U.S.C.C.A.N.* also publishes selected treaties after their ratification.

7. United Nations Treaty Series (U.N.T.S.). Since 1946 this series has published all treaties registered with the United Nations by member nations (including the U.S.) and some filed by non-members. It succeeds the *League of Nations Treaty Series (L.N.T.S.)* which was published on a similar basis from 1920 to 1946. The treaties appear in their original languages *and* in English and French translations. Cumulative indexes originally appeared for each one hundred volumes published and more recently for every fifty volumes. The series is the most comprehensive treaty collection and already contains over a thousand volumes, with thirty to forty new volumes being published each year. Unfortunately, there is now a time lag of approximately seven years in its publication of treaties and over ten years in its publication of indexes. For retrospective cumulative indexing to *U.N.T.S.* and *L.N.T.S.*, see P. Rohn, *World Treaty Index*, at page 287 below.

8. **Organization of American States Treaty Series.** Some individual countries and several regional organizations publish their own treaty series. The *Organization of American States Treaty Series*, formerly the *Pan American Union Treaty Series*, contains the texts of multilateral treaties entered into by its members, including the United States. It is published in English and Spanish editions, with some treaties in Portuguese and French.

RETROSPECTIVE COLLECTIONS OF U.S. TREATIES

For research in treaties of the past, the following historical sources are generally used:

1. **Bevans' Treaties and Other International Agreements of the United States of America 1776–1949** (U.S.G.P.O., 1968–75). This is the definitive retrospective compilation of treaties and other international agreements entered into by the United States

from 1776 to 1949. The set consists of thirteen volumes, the first four of which contain multilateral treaties (arranged chronologically by date of signature) and the next eight, bilateral treaties (arranged alphabetically by countries). Indexes by country and subject are included as volume 13. *Bevans* is now the definitive retrospective compilation of United States treaties, superseding its predecessors, *Malloy's Treaties, Conventions, International Acts, Protocols, and Agreements Between the U.S.A. and Other Powers* (U.S.G.P.O., 1910–1938, 4 vols.) and *Miller's Treaties and Other International Acts of the U.S.A.* (U.S. G.P.O., 1931–1948, 8 vols.)

2. **Statutes at Large.** Volume 8 of the *Statutes at Large* published a compilation of treaties entered into from 1778 to 1845. Thereafter, until 1949, treaties appeared regularly in the individual volumes of *Statutes at Large.* Volume 18 includes a collection of treaties in force as of 1873 and was published in connection with the *Revised Statutes* of 1873. Beginning in 1931 executive agreements were also included. In 1949 their publication in the *Statutes at Large* was discontinued and the *U.S.T.* took over the publication of both treaties and agreements. The last volume of the *Statutes at Large* to include treaties (vol. 64) contains a complete listing of all treaties appearing in the *Statutes,* arranged by country.

3. **Indian Treaties.** Volume 7 of the *Statutes at Large* included a collection of Indian treaties for the years 1778–1842. Thereafter, Indian treaties continued to appear with other treaties in the regular volumes of the *Statutes at Large.* The best compila-

tion of Indian treaties and related statutes is Kappler, *Indian Affairs, Laws and Treaties* (U.S.G.P.O., 1904–1941, 5 vols.). Felix Cohen's *Handbook of Federal Indian Law* 1945 revised 1971 and 1982), is a classic restatement of the law dealing with Native Americans.

4. **Unperfected Treaties of the United States of America 1776–1976** (Oceana, 1976–), edited by Christian Wiktor. This compilation contains all *unperfected* U.S. treaties, i.e., those which, for one reason or another, did not become effective. It includes legislative history and analysis of each treaty. The work is projected to include five or six volumes, with indexes.

5. **League of Nations Treaty Series.** Although not a member of the League, U.S. treaties appeared in this series during its publication from 1920 to 1946. It is now discontinued, having been succeeded by the *United Nations Treaty Series,* as noted above, but it is still the best collection for the period covered.

6. **The Inter-American System: Treaties, Conventions and Other Documents.** This new set is being published by Oceana, under the auspices of the Organization of American States. The first two volumes, covering legal and political affairs, appeared in 1983, and contain treaties and organic documents relating to the early history of the O.A.S.

7. **Consolidated Treaty Series** (Oceana, 1969–1981), edited by Clive Parry. This useful compilation includes all treaties between national states from 1648 to 1918. It is designed to provide a complete compilation of treaties (including those of the United States)

up to the beginning of the *League of Nations Treaty Series.* The series consists of 231 volumes and three volumes of indexes.

8. **Major Peace Treaties of Modern History, 1648–1979,** edited by Fred L. Israel (Chelsea, 1967–1980). This five volume compilation of peace treaties provides English translations, where necessary. The arrangement is chronological with a subject index included.

FINDING TOOLS

Because of the chronological publication of treaties, the following finding tools are generally used for subject access:

1. **Treaties in Force.** The most important current index to United States treaties and agreements in force is this annual publication of the Department of State, which has been issued since 1950. It is revised annually to include only treaties *in force,* but gives citations to earlier forms of such treaties where appropriate. It offers citations to all of the major treaty publications, including *Statutes at Large, T.I.A.S., U.S.T., Bevans, League of Nations Treaty Series,* and *U.N. Treaty Series.* The first part of the index lists bilateral treaties alphabetically by country and then, under each country, by subject. The second section lists multilateral treaties alphabetically by subject. This index is usually the starting point for searching current treaties. Its two sections are illustrated in Exhibit 106 below. *Treaties in Force* is supplemented between its annual revisions by the "Current Actions" section of the *Department of State Bulletin,* as illustrated in Exhibit 107 below.

CITIZENSHIP (See NATIONALITY)

CLAIMS (See also ARBITRATION; INVESTMENT DISPUTES; PACIFIC SETTLEMENT OF DISPUTES)

Convention for the arbitration of pecuniary claims. Signed at Buenos Aires August 11, 1910; entered into force for the United States January 1, 1913.
38 Stat. 1799; TS 594; 1 Bevans 763.
States which are parties:
Bolivia
Brazil
Costa Rica
Dominican Rep.
Ecuador
Guatemala
Honduras
Nicaragua
Panama
Paraguay
United States
Uruguay

Agreement relating to certain *Marechal Joffre* claims, with memorandum of understanding. Signed at Washington October 19, 1948; entered into force for the United States October 19, 1948.
62 Stat. 2841; TIAS 1816; 4 Bevans 783; 84 UNTS 201.
States which are parties:
Australia
France
United States

COFFEE

International coffee agreement, 1976, with annexes. Done at London December 3, 1975; entered into force for the United States provisionally October 1, 1976; definitively August 1, 1977.
28 UST 6401; TIAS 8683.
Parties:
Angola
Australia*
Austria
Belgium[1]**
Benin
Bolivia
Brazil
Burundi
Cameroon
Canada
Central African Rep.**
Colombia
Congo*
Costa Rica**
Cyprus
Denmark**
Dominican Rep.
Ecuador
El Salvador

CUBA

AVIATION

Agreement to facilitate notification of private flights between Cuba and the United States. Exchange of notes at Habana January 19 and February 26, 1953; entered into force February 26, 1953.
4 UST 210; TIAS 2779; 205 UNTS 213.

Air transport agreement. Signed at Habana May 26, 1953; entered into force June 30, 1953.
4 UST 2837; TIAS 2892; 224 UNTS 75.

Amendment:
May 21 and July 30, 1957 (8 UST 1407; TIAS 3891; 289 UNTS 322).

BOUNDARIES

Maritime boundary agreement. Signed at Washington December 16, 1977; entered into force provisionally January 1, 1978.
TIAS

Agreement extending the provisional application of the maritime boundary agreement of December 16, 1977. Exchange of notes at Washington December 16 and 28, 1981; entered into force December 28, 1981.
TIAS 10327.

CONSULS

Consular convention. Signed at Habana April 22, 1926; entered into force December 1, 1926.
44 Stat. 2471; TS 750; 6 Bevans 1149; 60 LNTS 371.

COPYRIGHT (See APPENDIX)

CUSTOMS

Agreement relating to free-entry privileges for noncommissioned personnel. Exchange of notes at Habana March 23 and May 16, 1932; entered into force May 16, 1932.
5 UST 1638; TIAS 3040; 234 UNTS 283.

DEFENSE

Agreement for the lease to the United States of lands in Cuba for coaling and naval stations. Signed at Habana February 16, 1903, and at Washington February 23, 1903; entered into force February 23, 1903.
TS 418; 6 Bevans 1113.

Agreement providing conditions for the lease of coaling or naval stations. Signed at Habana July 2, 1903; entered into force October 6, 1903.
TS 426; 6 Bevans 1120.

Agreement relating to the control of electromagnetic radiations in the event of attack. Exchange of notes at Habana December 10 and 18, 1951; entered into force December 18, 1951.
3 UST 2860; TIAS 2459; 165 UNTS 3.

Military assistance agreement. Signed at Habana March 7, 1952; entered into force March 7, 1952.
3 UST 2901; TIAS 2467; 165 UNTS 11.

Exhibit 106: Treaties in Force (1983 ed.) Bilateral Treaties on the left (arranged by country and then subject); Multilateral Treaties on the right (listed by subject).

TREATIES

Current Actions

MULTILATERAL

Atomic Energy
Protocol to suspend application of safeguards pursuant to the IAEA-U.S.-Venezuela agreement of Mar. 27, 1968 (TIAS 6433, 10096), and to provide for application of safeguards pursuant to the IAEA-Venezuela safeguards agreement (June 23, 1978) concerning the treaties on nonproliferation and prohibition of nuclear weapons in Latin America and pursuant to the IAEA-U.S. safeguards agreement of Nov. 18, 1977 (TIAS 9889). Signed at Vienna Sept. 27, 1983. Entered into force Sept. 27, 1983.

Coffee
International coffee agreement 1983, with annexes. Done at London Sept. 16, 1982.
Entered into force: Provisionally, Oct. 1, 1983.
Ratification deposited: Denmark, Ethiopia, Rwanda, Sept. 29, 1983; Dominican Republic, Sept. 30, 1983; New Zealand, Sept. 27, 1983; Tanzania, Sept. 28, 1983.
Accession deposited: Australia, Sept. 30, 1983.
Declarations of provisional application deposited: Angola, Haiti, Togo, Sept. 28, 1983; Benin, Spain, Sept. 29, 1983; Bolivia, Colombia, Liberia, Portugal, Rwanda, Sept. 27, 1983; Ecuador, European Economic Community, F.R.G., Ghana, Greece, Italy, Paraguay, Yugoslavia, Sept. 30, 1983.

Commodities—Common Fund
Agreement establishing the Common Fund for Commodities, with schedules. Done at Geneva June 27, 1980.[1]
Signature: Bhutan, Sept. 22, 1983.
Ratifications deposited: Canada, New Zealand, Sept. 27, 1983; Malaysia, Sept. 22, 1983; Nigeria, Sudan, Sept. 30, 1983; Zimbabwe, Sept. 28, 1983.

Conservation
Amendment to the convention of Mar. 3, 1973, on international trade in endangered species of wild fauna and flora (TIAS 8249). Adopted at Bonn June 22, 1979.[1]
Acceptances deposited: Egypt, Mar. 28, 1983; Finland, Apr. 5, 1983; Madagascar, Mar. 11, 1983; Niger, Apr. 8, 1983.

Consular Relations
Vienna convention on consular relations. Entered into force Mar. 19, 1967; for the U.S. Dec. 24, 1969. TIAS 6820.
Accessions deposited: Japan, Oct. 3, 1983; Togo, Sept. 26, 1983.

Optional protocol, to the Vienna convention on consular relations, concerning the compulsory settlement of disputes. Entered into force Mar. 19, 1967; for the U.S. Dec. 24, 1969. TIAS 6820.
Accession deposited: Japan. Oct. 3, 1983.

Cultural Property
Convention on the means of prohibiting and preventing the illicit import, export, and transfer of ownership of cultural property. Adopted at Paris Nov. 14, 1970. Entered into force Apr. 24, 1972.[2]
Ratification deposited: Democratic People's Republic of Korea, May 13, 1983.

Education—UNESCO
Convention on the recognition of studies, diplomas, and degrees concerning higher education in the states belonging to the Europe region. Done at Paris, Dec. 21, 1979. Entered into force Feb. 19, 1982.[2]
Ratification deposited: Malta, Mar. 24, 1983.

Energy
Agreement amending the agreement of Sept. 18, 1979 (TIAS 10188), for a program of research, development, and demonstration on hot dry rock technology. Signed at Paris Sept. 19, 1983. Entered into force Sept. 19, 1983.

Human Rights
International covenant on economic, social, and cultural rights. Done at New York Dec. 16, 1966. Entered into force Jan. 3, 1976.[2]

International covenant on civil and political rights. Done at New York Dec. 16, 1966. Entered into force Mar. 23, 1976.[2]
Accessions deposited: Congo, Oct. 5, 1983.

Judicial Procedure
Convention on the civil aspects of international child abduction. Done at The Hague Oct. 25, 1980. Entered into force Dec. 1, 1983.[2]
Ratification deposited: Portugal, Sept. 29, 1983.

Property—Intellectual
Convention establishing the World Intellectual Property Organization. Done at Stockholm July 14, 1967. Entered into force Apr. 26, 1970; for the U.S. Aug. 25, 1970. TIAS 6932.
Accession deposited: Honduras, Aug. 15, 1983.

Refugees
Protocol relating to the status of refugees. Done at New York Jan. 31, 1967. Entered into force Oct. 4, 1967; for the U.S. Nov. 1, 1968. TIAS 6577.
Accession deposited: Guatemala, Sept. 22, 1983.

Slavery
Convention to suppress the slave trade and slavery. Done at Geneva Sept. 25, 1926. Entered into force Mar. 9, 1927; for the U.S. Mar. 21, 1929. 46 Stat. 2183; TS 778.

Exhibit 107: "Treaties - Current Actions" section of the monthly *Department of State Bulletin* showing recent developments on various multilateral treaties.

2. Guide to the United States Treaties in Force (Hein, 1982). This commercially published guide to current treaties, edited by I.I. Kavass and A. Sprudzs, is scheduled to be issued annually. Part I, first published in 1982, differs from *Treaties in Force* in that it does not separate bilateral and multilateral treaties. It features numerical lists of treaties and agreements and a combined subject index. Part II will focus on multilateral treaties, listing them chronologically and indexing them by country.

3. Cumulative Indexes to United States Treaties. The major collections and series of U.S. treaties are indexed in the following works:

(a) *United States Treaties and Other International Agreements Cumulative Index 1776–1949* (Hein, 1975), by I.I. Kavass and M.A. Michael, provides a comprehensive four-volume index of the pre-*U.S.T.* treaties in the *Bevans* compilation. Each volume is a separate index, allowing access to treaties by number, date, country and topic.

(b) *U.S.T. Cumulative Index 1950–1970* (Hein, 1973), by I.I. Kavass and A. Sprudzs, provides similar four-volume coverage for the first twenty years of the *U.S.T.* series. It is supplemented by one volume for 1971 to 1975 (Hein, 1977) and a looseleaf Indexing Service for the latest *U.S.T.* volumes.

(c) *Current Treaty Index* is a cumulative index to treaties that have been published in slip form in the *T.I.A.S.* series, but have not yet appeared in the bound *U.S.T.* volumes.

4. Multilateral Treaties Deposited with the Secretary-General (United Nations). Exhibit 108 illustrates the format of this work. This annually revised, comprehensive list of multilateral treaties is arranged by subject with current information as to their status,

CHAPTER VII. TRAFFIC IN PERSONS

1. **Protocol to amend the Convention for the Suppression of the Traffic in Women and Children, concluded at Geneva on 30 September 1921, and the Convention for the Suppression of the Traffic in Women of Full Age, concluded at Geneva on 11 October 1933**

Signed at Lake Success, New York, on 12 November 1947[1]

ENTRY INTO FORCE: 12 November 1947, in accordance with article V.[2]

REGISTRATION: 24 April 1950, No. 770.

TEXT: United Nations, *Treaty Series*, vol. 53, p. 13.

State	*Signature subject to approval*	*Definitive signature (s) acceptance*
AFGHANISTAN		12 November 1947 *s*
ALBANIA		25 July 1949
AUSTRALIA		13 November 1947 *s*
AUSTRIA		7 June 1950 *s*
BELGIUM		12 November 1947 *s*
BRAZIL	17 March 1948	6 April 1950
BURMA		13 May 1949 *s*
CANADA		24 November 1947 *s*
CHINA[3]		12 November 1947 *s*
CZECHOSLOVAKIA		12 November 1947 *s*
DENMARK	12 November 1947	21 November 1949
EGYPT		12 November 1947 *s*
FINLAND		6 January 1949
GERMAN DEMOCRATIC REPUBLIC		16 July 1974
GERMANY, FEDERAL REPUBLIC OF[4]		29 May 1973
GREECE	9 March 1951	5 April 1960
HUNGARY		2 February 1950 *s*
INDIA		12 November 1947 *s*
IRAN	16 July 1953	
IRELAND		19 July 1961
ITALY		5 January 1949
IVORY COAST		5 November 1962 *s*

[1] The Protocol was approved by the General Assembly of the United Nations in resolution 126 (II) of 20 October 1947. For the text of this resolution, see *Official Records of the General Assembly, Second Session, Resolutions* (A/519), p. 32.

[2] The amendments set forth in the annex to the Protocol entered into force in respect of both Conventions on 24 April 1950, in accordance with paragraph 2 of article V of the Protocol.

[3] See note, p. iii.

[4] The instrument of acceptance by the Federal Republic of Germany was accompanied by the following declaration:

". . . The said Protocol shall also apply to Berlin (West) with effect from the date on which it enters into force for the Federal Republic of Germany."

With reference to the above declaration, the Secretary-General received the following communications:

Union of Soviet Socialist Republics (communication received on 4 December 1973):

The 1921 Convention for the Suppression of the Traffic in Women and Children and the 1933 Convention for the Suppression of the Traffic in Women of Full Age, as amended by the 1947 Protocol, and also the 1904 International Agreement for the Suppression of the White Slave Traffic and the 1910 International Convention for the Suppression of the White Slave Traffic, as amended by the 1949 Protocol, deal with matters related to the territory of the countries Parties to the Conventions and to the exercise of authority by the Parties. As is well known, the western sector of Berlin is not an integral part of the Federal Republic of Germany and cannot be governed by it. In that connexion, the Soviet Union regards the above-mentioned statement by the Federal Republic of Germany as unlawful and as having no legal force, with all the consequences that flow therefrom, since the extension of the force of the said treaty instruments to the western sector of Berlin raises questions relating to its status, thus conflicting with the relevant provisions of the Quadripartite Agreement of 3 September 1971.

[*footnote continues on following page*

Exhibit 108: *Multilateral Treaties Deposited with the Secretary-General* (United Nations); a sample entry showing only part of the information provided on the convention.

signatories, ratifications, and reservations imposed by thesignatories. It is limited to treaties concluded under U.N. auspices for which the Secretary-General acts as depository.

State	Signature subject to approval	Definitive signature (s) acceptance
JAMAICA		16 March 1965
LEBANON		12 November 1947 s
LUXEMBOURG	12 November 1947	14 March 1955
MALTA		27 February 1975
MEXICO		12 November 1947 s
NETHERLANDS	12 November 1947	7 March 1949
NICARAGUA	12 November 1947	24 April 1950
NIGER		7 December 1964
NORWAY	12 November 1947	28 November 1947
PAKISTAN		12 November 1947 s
POLAND		21 December 1950
ROMANIA		2 November 1950 s
SIERRA LEONE		13 August 1962 s
SINGAPORE		26 October 1966
SOUTH AFRICA		12 November 1947 s
SWEDEN		9 June 1948 s
SYRIAN ARAB REPUBLIC		17 November 1947 s
TURKEY		12 November 1947 s
UNION OF SOVIET SOCIALIST REPUBLICS		18 December 1947 s
YUGOSLAVIA		12 November 1947 s

footnote continued from previous page]

Czechoslovakia (communication received on 6 December 1973):

"The Czechoslovak party is willing to take due notice of the above declaration of the Government of the Federal Republic of Germany on the extension of force of the Protocol to amend the Convention for the Suppression of the Traffic in Women and Children concluded at Geneva on 30 September 1921 and of the Convention for the Suppression of the Traffic in Women of Full Age concluded at Geneva on 11 October 1933 and of the Protocol amending the International Agreement for the Suppression of the White Slave Traffic signed at Paris on 18 May 1904, and the International Convention for the Suppression of White Slave Traffic signed at Paris on 4 May 1910 to apply also to Berlin (West) only on the understanding that this extension of force is carried out in accordance with the Quadripartite Agreement of 3 September 1971 and in accordance with the established procedures."

German Democratic Republic (communication accompanying the instrument of acceptance):

With regard to the application to Berlin (West) of the Convention for the Suppression of the Traffic in Women and Children of 30 September 1921 as amended by the Protocol of 12 November 1947 the German Democratic Republic states in accordance with the Quadripartite Agreement of 3 September 1971 between the Governments of the Union of Soviet Socialist Republics, the United Kingdom of Great Britain and Northern Ireland, the United States of America and the French Republic that Berlin (West) is no constituent part of the Federal Republic of Germany and must not be governed by it. The statement of the Federal Republic of Germany that this Convention as amended by the said Protocol was also to be extended to Berlin (West) is contrary to the Quadripartite Agreement which stipulates that agreements concerning the status of Berlin (West) must not be extended to Berlin (West) by the Federal Republic of Germany. Consequently, the statement of the Federal Republic of Germany can have no legal effects.

France, United Kingdom, United States of America (communication received on 17 July 1974):

"In a communication to the Government of the Union of Soviet Socialist Republics which is an integral part (Annex IV A) of the Quadripartite Agreement of 3 September 1971, the Governments of France, the United Kingdom of Great Britain and Northern Ireland and the United States of America reaffirmed that, provided that matters of security and status are not affected, international agreements and arrangements entered into by the Federal Republic of Germany may be extended to the Western Sectors of Berlin in accordance with established procedures. For its part, the Government of the Union of Soviet Socialist Republics, in a communication to the Governments of France, the United Kingdom and the United States which is similarly an integral part (Annex IV B) of the Quadripartite Agreement of 3 September 1971, affirmed that it would raise no objection to such extension.

"The purpose and effect of the established procedures referred to above, which were specifically endorsed in Annex IV A and B to the Quadripartite Agreement, are precisely to ensure that agreements and arrangements to be extended to the Western Sectors of Berlin are extended in such a way that questions of security and status remain unaffected and to take account of the fact that these Sectors continue not to be a constituent part of the Federal Republic of Germany and not to be governed by it. The extension to the Western Sectors of Berlin of the Conventions of 1921 and 1933, as amended by the Protocol of 1947, and of the Agreement of 1904 and the Convention of 1910, as amended by the Protocol of 1949, received the prior authorization, under these established procedures, of the authorities of France, the United Kingdom and the United States. The rights and responsibilities of the Governments of those three countries remain unaffected thereby. There is thus no question that the extension to the Western Sectors of Berlin of the Conventions of 1921 and 1933, as amended by the Protocol of 1947, and the Agreement of 1904 and the Convention of 1910, as amended by the Protocol of 1949, is in any way inconsistent with the Quadripartite Agreement.

"Accordingly, the application to the Western Sectors of Berlin of the Conventions of 1921 and 1933, as amended by the Protocol of 1947, and the Agreement of 1904 and the Convention of 1910, as amended by the Protocol of 1949, continues in full force and effect."

Federal Republic of Germany (communication received on 27 August 1974):

"The Government of the Federal Republic of Germany shares the position set out in the Note of the Three Powers. The extension of the Protocols to Berlin (West) continues in full force and effect."

France, United Kingdom of Great Britain and Northern Ireland and United States of America (8 July 1975—in relation to the declaration by the German Democratic Republic received on 27 August 1974):

"The communication mentioned in [the Note] listed above refer to the Quadripartite Agreement of 3 September 1971. This Agreement was concluded in Berlin between the Governments of the French Republic, the Union of Soviet So-

[*Footnote continues on following page*

Exhibit 108: Cont'd.

Declarations and Reservations

MALTA

"In accepting the above-mentioned Protocol, Malta considers itself bound only in so far as the Protocol applies to the Convention for the Suppression of the Traffic in Women and Children concluded at Geneva on 30 September 1921 to which Malta is a party."

PAKISTAN

". . . In accordance with paragraph 4 of the *Schedule to the Indian Independence Order, 1947*, Pakistan considers herself a party to the International Convention for the Suppression of the Traffic of Women and Children concluded at Geneva on 30 September 1921 by the fact that India became a party to the above-mentioned Convention before 15 August 1947."

[footnote continued from previous page]

cialist Republics, the United Kingdom of Great Britain and Northern Ireland and the United States of America. [The Government sending these communications is not a party to the Quadripartite Agreement and is] therefore not competent to make authoritative comments on its provisions.

"The Governments of France, the United Kingdom and the United States wish to bring the following to the attention of the States Parties to the instruments referred to in the above-mentioned communications. When authorising the extension of these instruments to the Western Sectors of Berlin, the authorities of the Three Powers, acting in the exercise of their supreme authority, ensured in accordance with established procedures that those instruments are applied in the Western Sectors of Berlin in such a way as not to affect matters of security and status.

"Accordingly, the application of these instruments to the Western Sectors of Berlin continues in full force and effect.

"The Governments of France, the United Kingdom and the United States do not consider it necessary to respond to any further communications of a similar nature by States which are not signatories to the Quadripartite Agreement. This should not be taken to imply any change in the position of those Governments in this matter."

Federal Republic of Germany (19 September 1975):

"By their Note of 8 July 1975, disseminated by Circular Note . . . C.N.196.1975.TREATIES-1 of 13 August 1975, the Governments of France, the United Kingdom and the United States answered the assertions made in the communications referred to above. The Government of the Federal Republic of Germany, on the basis of the legal situation set out in the Note of the Three Powers, wishes to confirm that the application in Berlin (West) of the above-mentioned instruments extended by it under the established procedures continues in full force and effect.

"The Government of the Federal Republic of Germany wishes to point out that the absence of a response to further communications of a similar nature should not be taken to imply any change of its position in this matter."

Exhibit 108: Cont'd.

5. **Inter-American Treaties and Conventions** (Organization of American States). This volume offers substantially the same data on O.A.S. treaties as does the United Nations service described above, and is supplemented by a biennial volume of charts called *Status of Inter-American Treaties and Conventions.*

6. **Indexes to the United Nations Treaty Series.** These indexes cover many more treaties than those of the United States. As noted above, they now cumulate every fifty volumes and are useful for research in the *United Nations Treaty Series,* despite the substantial delay in their publication. The researcher should note that these indexes are not limited to

treaties in force and may refer to treaties which have been modified or renounced.

7. **World Treaty Index,** compiled by Peter H. Rohn (ABC-Clio, 2d ed., 1983). This five volume set includes citations to some 44,000 treaties, indexing the *United Nations* and *League of Nations Treaty Series,* and many other series of treaties made since 1900. It provides access by the parties to the treaty, subject keywords, date, and the name of any international organization involved.

8. **Treaties by Popular Name.** There are several ways to translate the popular name of a treaty into its official *U.S.T.* or *Statutes at Large* citation. *Shepard's Acts and Cases by Popular Names* includes treaties, and both *Bevans'* index and the *U.S.T. Cumulative Indexes* include popular names of treaties with references to their official citations.

9. **Computer Services.** Although neither *LEXIS* nor *WESTLAW* provide direct or comprehensive access to treaties, both systems have data bases of international tax agreements and conventions. The U.S. Air Force project *FLITE* has been building a large data base of international agreements for full text searching. The United Nations has been developing a computer-assisted index of international documents, including treaties, for several years.

GUIDES TO THE LEGISLATIVE HISTORY OF TREATIES

Congressional deliberations and actions on pending treaties, like the legislative histories of statutes, are often the subject of legal research. G.B. Folsom, *Legislative History, Research for the Interpretation of Laws* (University Press of Virginia, 1972; reprinted by Fred B. Rothman, 1979) includes in Chapter VII a discussion of sources for such research into the background of treaties. The following finding tools aid in locating relevant material:

1. **CCH Congressional Index.** This looseleaf service, discussed above in Chapter V, includes among its other features a table of treaties pending before the Senate. It is one of the most valuable status tables for determining actions taken on pending treaties and their present status, regardless of when they were introduced. Treaty listings include references to Executive Reports of the Senate Foreign Relations Committee, hearings, ratifications, etc. The treaties are listed chronologically by the session of transmittal and designated by their executive letter or, since 1981, by their Treaty Document number. A subject index precedes the list of treaties. The table is shown in Exhibit 109, below.

2. **Legislative Calendar of the Senate Foreign Relations Committee.** This official status table of business before the Senate committee is perhaps the best list of pending treaties with actions taken thereon, but is less accessible than the CCH service. Its information on hearings is particularly useful. The "Cumulative Record" final edition for each Congress includes a list of committee publications for the period.

3. **Congressional Information Service.** This important legislative history service, described above at

98-5, Treaty Document No. (4-25-83)—Foreign trade—wheat

Protocols for the Wheat Trade Convention, 1971, and the Food Aid Convention, 1980, were signed by the Secretary of Agriculture on April 25, 1983.

Together the Conventions are known as the International Wheat Agreement, 1971; which was negotiated as a framework for cooperation in wheat trading matters and to perpetuate the International Wheat Council and commitments made by members of the Council to provide minimum cereal food requirements to developing countries.

The Protocols would extend both Conventions through June 30, 1986.

Injunction of secrecy removed: 7/11/83

In Foreign Relations Committee: 7/11/83

98-6, Treaty Document No. (4-27-83)—Income tax—Denmark

The Convention between the Government of the United States of America and the Government of the Kingdom of Denmark for the avoidance of double taxation and the prevention of fiscal evasion with respect to taxes on estates, inheritances, gifts and certain other transfers, was signed at Washington on April 27, 1983.

Injunction of secrecy removed: 9/8/83

In Foreign Relations Committee: 9/13/83

98-7, Treaty Document No. (6-14-83)—Income tax—Canada

The Protocol to the Convention between the United States and Canada with respect to Taxes on Income and Capital resolves certain textual problems which have delayed ratification of the original Convention (96-2, Executive T).

In addition, the Protocol amends the Convention with regard to pensions, annuities, and alimony; athletic bonuses; and United States taxing rights in accordance with the provisions of the Foreign Investment in Real Property Act.

Injunction of secrecy removed: 9/21/83

In Foreign Relations Committee: 9/21/83

98-8, Treaty Document No. (10-29-82)—Corrections and correctional facilities—Thailand—sentence execution

The Treaty Between the United States of America and the Kingdom of Thailand on Cooperation in the Execution of Penal Sentences was signed at Bangkok on October 29, 1982.

The Treaty would permit citizens of either nation who had been convicted in the courts of the other country to serve their sentences in their home country. In each case the consent of the offender as well as the approval of the authorities of the two governments would be required.

Injunction of secrecy removed: 9/21/83

In Foreign Relations Committee: 9/21/83

98-9, Treaty Document No. (8-31-81)—Foreign trade—uniform law

The United Nations Convention on Contracts for the International Sale of Goods is designed to settle contract disputes between traders from different countries when the applicable domestic laws of those countries disagree with one another.

Exhibit 109: Entries in the treaty section of the CCH *Congressional Index,* listing treaties pending before the Senate.

pages 183–188, includes coverage of treaties. These appear in the subject index, in the index of document numbers, and in the summaries of actions by committee.

4. **Congressional Quarterly.** This publication, devoted to congressional activity generally, also includes useful information on treaties. In addition to occasional special reports on major treaties, its *Weekly Report* includes the actual text of important documents, chronologies, summaries of debates and messages, and general information about current treaties. The *Weekly Report* indexes offer leads to current information and documents on pending treaties.

5. **Congressional Record Indexes.** In the fortnightly indexes to the *Congressional Record* and in the bound volume index for each session there is a listing of treaty actions and discussions appearing in the *Record.* These references appear under the heading "Treaties" in the alphabetical subject index and also occasionally under the name of a particular treaty or its subject matter. The *Congressional Record* indexes are not very convenient for current use, but they are helpful for retrospective research into a particular treaty's legislative history. However, their coverage is limited to material appearing in the *Record.*

EXTRINSIC AIDS IN TREATY RESEARCH

The study of treaties often involves their history and interpretation, for which the following external sources may offer useful information:

1. Citators. The interpretation of treaties by courts provides authoritative material for the researcher who seeks information on the meaning or effect of a treaty. Citations to such decisions can be found in:

(a) **Shepard's United States Citations—Statutes Edition.** This citator is limited to *federal* court decisions, but includes all cases mentioning the treaty in addition to those actually interpreting it. For treaties up to 1949, listing is by date of signing rather than by *Statutes at Large* citation. After 1950, a separate section lists treaties by their *U.S.T.* citation. Shepard's also includes later legislation or a subsequent treaty change affecting the cited treaty.

(b) **Shepard's Citations for various states.** There are similar listings of state court decisions citing U.S. treaties in the statutes volume of every state Shepard's citator. Many more judicial interpretations of U.S. treaties occur in the state courts than in the federal courts.

(c) **U.S. Code Service.** In its volume of *Annotations to Uncodified Laws & Treaties,* this edition of the *United States Code* includes citations to both state and federal judicial decisions interpreting U.S. treaties, including those with Native Americans. The treaties are listed by date of signing, even if they are in *U.S.T.*

2. Digests of International Law. There have been a number of encyclopedic digests of international law which include material on treaties and their judicial interpretation, analytical and historic notes, and other scholarly comments. The current and now most important of these works is Whiteman's *Digest of International Law,* published by the Department of State in fifteen volumes from 1963 to 1973.

The Whiteman *Digest* is supplemented by annual volumes of a Department of State series called *Digest of United States Practice in International Law* (U.S. Govt. Printing Office, 1973–date). These volumes are updated by "Contemporary Practice of the United States Relating to International Law," which appears in each quarterly issue of the *American Journal of International Law.* "Contemporary Practices" digests current materials and is organized under the system used in the *Digest of U.S. Practice.*

Earlier *Digests of International Law* (with some variation in title) by Francis Wharton (1886, 2d ed. 1887; 3 vols.), John Bassett Moore (1906; 8 vols.), and Green H. Hackworth (1940–44; 8 vols.) have not been completely superseded by Whiteman, and remain useful for historical research.

The American Law Institute's *Restatement (Second) of the Foreign Relations Law of the United States,* (1965) is an unofficial but highly reputed summary of American law and practice in this field. Most parts of a revised edition are available in tentative drafts. The *Restatement of Conflict of Laws* (A.L.I., 1971, 1980; 4 vols.) covers private international law.

3. Documentary Compilations. There are several useful collections of documentary materials which include sources for treaty research. Most of the documents contained in these compilations are available in other primary forms of publication, but they may be more conveniently accessible through these editions.

(a) *Reports of the Committee on Foreign Relations, 1789–1901* (U.S.G.P.O., Sen.Doc. 231, 56th Congress, 2d Session, 8 vols.). This set is a handy compilation of important source material for research in the legislative history of U.S. treaties. It is an exhaustive collection of regular committee reports, executive reports and documents. There is a cumulative index in the last volume. Unfortunately, the work has not been continued beyond 1901.

(b) *American International Law Cases, 1783–1968* (Oceana, 1971–), edited initially by Francis Deak and continued by Frank S. Ruddy. This reprint collection of American federal and state court decisions relating to international law includes annotations to relevant treaties. Part of the set has been updated to 1978, and a looseleaf index began publication in 1982.

(c) *Foreign Relations of the United States* (U.S. G.P.O., 1861 to date). This continuing series of official papers is prepared by the Historical Office of the U.S. Department of State and provides a comprehensive record of material relating to treaties, their negotiation and adoption. Unfortunately, there is a time lag of about twenty-five years between issuance of these documents and their publication in this series.

(d) *American Foreign Policy.* The Department of State also publishes documentary compilations on a more current basis. This series includes: *A*

Decade of American Foreign Policy: Basic Documents, 1941–1949 (U.S.G.P.O., 1950); *American Foreign Policy, 1950–1955: Basic Documents*, 2 vols. (U.S.G.P.O., 1957); annual volumes entitled *American Foreign Policy: Current Documents*, for the years 1956 to 1967; and *American Foreign Policy: Basic Documents, 1977–1980.* A resumption of the *Current Documents* series is projected, as are *Basic Documents* volumes for 1969 to 1976. The monthly *Department of State Bulletin*, as noted above, is a useful current source for selected documents.

(e) *American Foreign Relations, A Documentary Record* (beginning in 1976, with coverage of 1971). Continuing the series *Documents on American Foreign Relations*, this privately published annual compilation was published from 1938 to 1951 by the World Peace Foundation and since then by the Council on Foreign Relations. It includes material on treaties and is similar in coverage to *American Foreign Policy: Current Documents*, above.

(f) *International Legal Materials* (American Society of International Law, 1962–date). As noted above, this bi-monthly compilation includes drafts and final texts of many treaties, as well as other documentation relating to them. It continues a similar compilation which appeared as the *Supplement* to the *American Journal of International Law.*

Additional publications from foreign and international sources, relating to international law and, incidentally, to treaties, are described in Chapter XII below.

CHAPTER IX

SECONDARY MATERIALS

Most of the materials discussed so far have been primary sources of law, that is, documents with actual legal effect (reports, statutes, regulations, treaties, etc.) or their related bibliographic apparatus (digests, indexes, citators, etc.). Primary materials may have mandatory or persuasive authority (or no authority at all) depending on their source, official status, inherent quality, the jurisdiction and tribunal in which they are presented, and their legal and factual relevance to a particular problem. We now examine the vast literature of unofficial, non-authoritative, *secondary* materials consisting of encyclopedias, treatises, periodicals and related publications. These range from scholarly writings of lasting influence, through a varied spectrum, down to hack work of low quality and fortunately short life.

When creatively and effectively exploited, the best of the secondary materials may directly affect the development of the law. Many scholarly articles have shaped law reform or stimulated new legislation (e.g., Erwin Griswold's article, "Government in Ignorance of the Law—A Plea for Better Publication of Executive Legislation", appearing in the *Harvard Law Review* in 1934, which had considerable influence in bringing about the passage of the Federal Register Act of 1935).

Secondary materials also perform several basic functions in legal research. They provide citations to primary source material, and thus serve as search books or finding tools. They can refresh the reader's recollection of a well settled but neglected area, or provide an introduction to a new or developing field of law. Handbooks and manuals provide the forms and guidelines for the operational details of daily law practice. From other sources, lawyers or scholars can construct or buttress legal arguments and enhance the effectiveness of their advocacy. Some works may describe the non-legal context or historical background of a legally significant event or state of affairs, while others illuminate the possible effects and social consequences of proposed legal action. The creative insights of some published writings can reveal trends and patterns in unsettled areas and expose incipient strains and shifts in apparently settled law.

Although secondary materials are as old as legal research, they have been used and cited more frequently in recent years by both lawyers and judges to bring non-legal scholarship to bear on legal problems. A greater interest in the social and economic consequences of particular legal actions has led to interdisciplinary cooperation between law and the other social sciences. The development of social and experimental schools of jurisprudence has further enhanced this interest in materials which are available only in secondary sources. The extension of legal concern into many new areas of human activity and the growing willingness of the courts to re-examine and revise traditional notions have increased the importance of secondary materials. Judicial and legislative history of recent years contains a scholarly documentation far more eclectic than the strictly legal references of the older literature.

The means of access to secondary sources vary widely. Some, like the encyclopedias, *Restatements of Law,* and treatises, are in effect self-indexing. Legal journals and law reviews are accessible through periodical indexes. Separately published books and non-serial publications can be identified and retrieved through several bibliographic guides (e.g. *Law Books in Print*) and, of course, the card catalogs of many libraries.

LEGAL ENCYCLOPEDIAS

Although legal encyclopedias are avidly used by law students and many lawyers, they are considered by many to be neither very scholarly nor authoritative. They lack the prestige of general encyclopedias like the older *Britannicas* or the *International Encyclopedia of the Social Sciences.* If, however, they are not used as authority in their own right, but rather as finding tools to the primary sources of authority, they can be helpful aids to legal research. Their extensive citations to judicial decisions give the encyclopedias their major value as search books, described in Chapter III above. Because of their convenience and the apparent completeness of their predigested research, they will undoubtedly continue to be used (and sometimes misused).

The two main legal encyclopedias are *Corpus Juris Secundum (C.J.S.),* published by the West Publishing Company, and *American Jurisprudence 2d (Am.Jur. 2d),* published by Lawyers' Co-operative Publishing

Company. Both employ an alphabetical arrangement of broad legal topics similar to those of the digests and provide indexing both to the entire set and to individual topics. The articles, prepared by editorial writers of each publisher and not by independent legal scholars, often lack the careful analysis and fine distinctions of a good treatise. Both *C.J.S.* and *Am. Jur.2d* are supplemented by annual pocket parts and completely revised every generation, but they are still often slow to reflect subtle changes in the law and significant trends which might be apparent to the alert scholar. Other shortcomings include both gaps and overlapping between articles; a tendency toward overgeneralization and oversimplification; neglect of statutory law and almost complete reliance on case law. This last factor results in a grossly misleading view of American law, in which statutes play a central role.

Each encyclopedia is linked by cross references to the sister publications of its respective publisher. *Corpus Juris Secundum* purports to cite in its footnotes all of the significant decisions found in the West reporters, while *American Jurisprudence 2d* provides similar leads in its references to the numerous annotations of *A.L.R.* and to other sets in the Lawyers Co-op *Total Client-Service Library.* Illustrations of the format of *C.J.S.* are shown above in Exhibits 32 and 33 at pages 85–86, while *Am.Jur.2d* is illustrated in Exhibits 34 and 35 at pages 87–88.

American Jurisprudence 2d also includes a *New Topic* service binder, allowing the set to reflect major changes in the law without reissuing entire volumes, and a *Deskbook,* which offers a variety of reference information about the legal system. The *Deskbook* includes outlines of the federal government and its court system, standards of the legal profession, financial tables, and demographic data of legal interest. There are also several multi-volume adjunct sets to *Am.Jur.2d* focusing on trial preparation and practice (*Am.Jur. Trials* and two series of *Am.Jur. Proof of Facts*) and others providing legal forms (*Am.Jur. Legal Forms 2d* and *Am.Jur. Pleading and Practice Forms*).

The West Publishing Company has published a new popular encyclopedia, *Guide to American Law: Everyone's Legal Encyclopedia* (1983–1985), with a strong historical and cultural focus. This multi-volume, illustrated encyclopedia is designed for both a lay audience and general reference use by lawyers. A similar work of English origin, with shorter articles, but broader coverage, is the one volume *Oxford Companion to Law* (1980) by David M. Walker.

Both West and Lawyers Co-op also publish several state encyclopedias similar in format to their national publications. The West encyclopedias cover Illinois, Maryland, Michigan, and Pennsylvania. Those issued by Lawyers Co-op include California, Florida, New York, Ohio, and Texas. All of these encyclopedias are updated by annual pocket parts and quarterly pamphlet supplements. They have similar utility and disadvantages as *C.J.S.* and *Am.Jur.2d.*

Words and Phrases, also described and illustrated in Chapter III, can be mentioned here as an encyclopedic collection of case abstracts construing legally significant words and phrases. These are arranged alphabetically, with constructions, interpretations and definitions culled from the cases reported in the National Reporter System and West's federal reporters. If one's research focuses on the meaning of a particular word or phrase, this set is a useful source of judicial interpretations. It is kept up to date by annual pocket parts, as well as by tables of words and phrases appearing in the advance sheets and bound volumes of the West reporters. A sample page is illustrated in Exhibit 36 at page 90 above.

TEXTS AND TREATISES

In addition to the encyclopedias, there are thousands of texts and treatises dealing with the many topics of substantive and procedural law. These include multi-volume topical encyclopedias and detailed surveys, as well as short monographs on limited aspects of single topics.

Legal treatises appeared shortly after the earliest English reports in the twelfth century *Plea Rolls.* They summarized the developing law of the English courts and statutes and contributed their own analysis and influence to this development. By restating and synthesizing decisions and statutes, texts and treatises have continued to impose order on the chaos of individual precedents. Like encyclopedias, they lack authority and legal effect and are never *binding* on courts. Some of them, however, are written by scholars of outstanding reputation and prestige and hence engender considerable judicial respect. Other texts make no pretense at scholarly analysis, but offer convenient guides by which practitioners can familiarize themselves with particular fields of law. These practice books often contain sample forms, checklists and how-to-do-it advice. The inclusion of tables of cases and other research aids can facilitate the use of treatises as finding tools.

Among the varied types of texts, the following groups can be noted:

1. Multi-volume scholarly surveys of particular fields in depth (e.g., *Wigmore on Evidence, Federal Practice and Procedure* by Wright and Miller, *Corbin on Contracts*).

2. Hornbooks, student texts and treatise abridgements (e.g., *Prosser and Keeton on Torts* and West's nutshell series).

3. Practitioners' handbooks in particular fields, many of which are published by continuing legal education groups such as California Continuing Education of the Bar, the Joint Committee on Continuing Legal Education of the American Law Institute and the American Bar Association, and the Practising Law Institute.

4. Procedural manuals, ranging from one volume compendia like the *New York Standard Civil Practice Service Desk Book* (Lawyers Co-op) and the *New York Civil Practice Annual* (Matthew Bender) to multi-volume sets like West's *Federal Practice Manual, 2d ed.* and Lawyers Co-op's *Federal Procedure.*

5. Specialized monographs on relatively narrow topics.

6. Comprehensive commentaries, histories and works of jurisprudence (e.g., Blackstone's *Commentaries on the Laws of England,* Holdsworth's *History of English Law,* and Pound's *Jurisprudence*).

These works may be supplemented by looseleaf inserts, pocket parts or bound additions. *Some* form of up-dating is usually essential however, and works which are not supplemented lose their value as to current law coverage very quickly. The bypaths of legal bibliography are cluttered with the debris of outdated and unrevised texts. The everchanging nature of law requires a literature capable of reflecting that change promptly and accurately.

It is often difficult for the researcher to evaluate texts, but the following considerations may aid selection from among the many available: the purpose of the particular publication; the reputation of the author and publisher and the standing of their previous books; the organization and scope of the work; the clarity, comprehensiveness and usefulness of its scholarly apparatus (footnotes, tables, index, bibliography, etc.); and the adequacy of supplementation and present timeliness.

RESTATEMENTS OF THE LAW

Some of the most important commentaries on American law are to be found in the series of *Restatements* prepared under the auspices of the American Law Institute and published by West. These surveys of particular legal subjects were designed:

> "To present an orderly restatement of the general common law of the United States, including in that term not only the law developed solely by judicial decision, but also law that has grown from the application by the courts of statutes that were generally enacted and were in force for many years."

They cover only ten specific fields: agency, conflict of laws, contracts, foreign relations law, judgments, property, restitution, security, torts, and trusts. All of the *Restatements*, except those on restitution and security, have been issued in second editions, to reflect new developments or later thinking, and some second editions are already undergoing further revision. While revisions are being considered and debated, tentative drafts are distributed and are of considerable interest to scholars and researchers.

The *Restatements* are divided into sections, each of which contains a "black letter" general statement of law, followed by an explanatory comment on the general principles, and then illustrated by examples of particular cases and variations on the general proposition. A general index volume is provided for all of the *Restatements* in the first series. Each *Restatement* is also separately indexed. Each of the second series of *Restatements* includes appendices containing Reporter's Notes, notes of decisions citing the first series, and cross-references to West key numbers and *A.L.R.* annotations. A glossary of terms defines the significant words appearing in the first series of *Restatements.*

A series called *Restatement in the Courts* provides annotations to court decisions (in the usual West abstracting format) which have applied or interpreted the various sections of each *Restatement,* and citations to periodical articles which have discussed the *Restatements* or particular sections. A general set covers decisions through 1977, and a few of the *Restatements* (contracts, foreign relations, property, and torts) have been updated further. Separate volumes of annotations of court decisions citing or applying the various *Restatement* sections were previously provided for many of the states, but are no longer kept up to date.

Shepard's, since 1976, has published a separate citator for the *Restatements.* This work covers all of the *Restatements* and lists citations to all reported decisions and leading law reviews which have mentioned *Restatement* sections. Shepard's *Restatement of the Law Citations* is illustrated in Exhibit 110 below.

Although they are not official and are not binding, the *Restatements* are persuasive in the courts—perhaps more so than any other secondary material. Their reporters, advisors and discussants are well known scholars and include outstanding members of the judiciary. Although some of the reporters reflected what they thought the law ought to be rather than what the law was, by and large these volumes are considered among the authoritative works of American legal scholarship.

TORTS, SECOND **§ 21**

Torts Second Series

§ 1 et seq.
41OA156
70YLJ1044

§ 1
117PaL8
38WLR426
Comment d
17CA3d1111
Calif
95CaR459

§ 2
259La443
La
250So2d397
69CR937
22MnL757
20TxL570
31TxL773
Comment a
187CA2d425
121GaA542
362Mo98
337Pa107
Calif
10CaR4
Ga
174SE368
Mo
240SW135
422SW399
Pa
9A2d367

§ 3
357Mas426
252Wis590
Mass
258NE311
Wis
32NW342
Comment a
Tex
526SW613

§ 4
489F2d1266
250FS857
17AzA125
133ALR384

184Neb572
2WAp643
Ariz
495P2d1332
Ill
272NE693
Nebr
169NW465
Wash
469P2d214
38LCP625
22MnL709
41TxL46
Comment a
133ALR384
Ill
272NE694
41TxL54
Comment b
38LCP625
41TxL46
Comment c
110NH218
NH
265A2d8
41TxL54

§ 5
68OA473
428Pa223
223Wis248
70W2d885
72W2d852
Ohio
42NE174
Pa
237A2d226
342A2d384
Wash
425P2d653
435P2d551
Wis
270NW81

§ 6
261Ia1130
87ALR217
11ALR2d392
89OA213
273Wis391
62W2d995
70W2d884
Ill
143NE680
231NE3
Iowa
156NW882
Kan
491P2d555
Ohio
101NE328
Wash
385P2d310
425P2d653
67HLR997
70HLR891
54YLJ816

Comment a
32NJ74
273Wis391
NJ
159A2d107
Tex
312SW733
Wis
78NW904

§ 7
52DC2d25
97NH57
162OS575
NH
80A2d498
Tex
456SW733
47TxL202
38WLR427
Comment a
517F2d1168
Ohio
125NE5
Comment b
47TxL203
Comment d
17CA3d1110
Calif
95CaR459

§ 8
53VaL775

§ 8A
393US311
21LE506
89SC509
43Ap2d374
49Ap2d157
48CA3d176
11C3d922
61DC2d315
122Su61
45Wis2d358
65Wis2d86
Alk
423P2d914
Calif
114CaR631
121CaR665
Fla
258So2d817
Minn
222NW340
NJ
298A2d721
NY
351S2d434
373S2d634
Wis
173NW152
221NW917
57CaL644
21StnL49
52VaL1026

Comment b
393US311
21LE506
89SC509
379FS478
122Su61
45Wis2d358
NJ
298A2d721
Ore
539P2d1151
Wis
173NW152

§ 9
417F2d610
507F2d223
292IlA508
141Kan165
192Min364
96NH385
Ill
11NE854
Kan
40P2d357
Minn
256NW903
NH
77A2d123
Pa
342A2d384
70CR1207
72HLR1252
41TxL46

§ 10
36MnL32
46WLR163

§ 12
376FS1208
15AzA500
11McA469
28NJ11
258Or143
211PaS97
92Su558
Ariz
489P2d874
Ky
453SW587
482SW569
528SW711
Mich
161NW412
Mo
443SW158
ND
226NW657
NJ
143A2d526
224A2d330
Ore
482P2d172

Pa
235A2d445
Tex
509SW563
511SW258
47CaL450
49NYL196
89PaL323
15TxL126
Comment a
248Md485
108NH378
13OrA170
49Su211
Ky
453SW588
Md
237A2d439
ND
226NW657
NH
236A2d693
NJ
139A2d449
Ore
509P2d449
49NYL196

§ 13 et seq.
56DC348
103ALR142
Ill
242NE478
47MnL87

§§ 13 to 17
Scope Note
457F2d1396
47MnL87

§§ 13 to 20
Ky
255SW495

§ 13
464F2d793
2AzA367
144Kan610
192Kan366
297Mas329
341Mas223
344Mas681
352Mas399
200Min447
68NM281
246Or204
62Wis2d245
46W2d200
69W2d106
Ariz
409P2d83
Colo
526P2d308

Kan
62P2d547
388P2d829
Mass
8NE763
168NE85
183NE867
226NE219
Minn
274NW533
Mo
419SW946
477SW79
NM
361P2d159
Ore
424P2d679
Wash
279P2d1093
417P2d368
Wis
214NW448
41MnL403
Comment c
24Ap2d288
2AzA367
50Msc2d87
101OA446
Ariz
409P2d83
NY
266S2d410
272S2d280
Ohio
140NE326
41MnL420

§ 14
103ALR143
297Mas329
341Mas223
Ill
242NE478
Mass
8NE763
168NE85
Comment b
22MnL854

§ 15
464F2d793
2AzA367
Ariz
409P2d83

§ 16
258FS413
68NM281
108Su263
DC
307A2d757
NJ
260A2d872
NM
361P2d159
49HLR1043
21MnL33
22MnL1040
41MnL420
38WLR410
Comment b
68NM281
NM

361P2d159
21MnL33
22MnL1040
Illustration 3
68NM282
NM
361P2d160

§ 18 et seq.
41TxL48

§ 18
280FS462
238CA2d445
251Md104
132PaS512
152PaS653
79Su530
58Wis2d596
73W2d583
73W2d820
Alk
430P2d917
Calif
47CaR836
Md
246A2d238
Mo
347SW402
477SW79
NJ
192A2d189
Pa
1A2d503
33A2d533
Tex
424SW629
Wash
440P2d162
440P2d828
Wis
207NW311
41MnL384
15TxL162
62YLJ708
Comment f
41MnL420
Comment g
41MnL420

§ 19
69W2d106
Mo
334SW752
Tex
424SW629
Wash
417P2d368
64HLR922
15TxL162

§ 20
259CA2d284
73W2d820
Calif
67CaR116
Wash
440P2d828
25MnL658
41MnL420

15TxL162
41TxL50
45TxL655
Comment b
25MnL658

§§ 21 to 34
54W2d447
Wash
341P2d864
30TxL122

§ 21
280FS462
373FS955
387FS540
292Mas248
344Mas681
199Min93
246Or204
149OS310
434Pa266
105RI614
20U2d28
62Wis2d245
73W2d583
Alk
430P2d917
DC
307A2d757
Iowa
271NW118
Ky
255SW495
489SW822
Mass
198NE272
183NE867
Minn
271NW118
Mo
347SW402
Ohio
121NE166
Ore
424P2d679
Pa
252A2d567
RI
254A2d290
Tex
452SW36
Utah
432P2d342
Wash
440P2d162
Wis
214NW448
47MnL74
40WLR103
62YLJ708
Comment a
Ohio
78NE739
Comment c
20U2d29
Utah
432P2d342
Comment d
20U2d29
Utah
432P2d342

249

Exhibit 110: A sample page from Shepard's *Restatement of the Law Citations.*

Model codes have also been prepared by the American Law Institute. These include the widely adopted *Uniform Commercial Code* and the *Model Penal Code* which has influenced criminal law reform on the federal and state levels.

PERIODICALS

American legal periodicals parallel in quality and variety the other secondary materials. They have been said to reflect "the law as it was, as it is, as it is tending, and as it ought to be". In recent years, legal periodicals have aroused criticism on several different, unrelated grounds—that they have had excessive influence on judicial decisions, that they encourage elitism in legal education, and that they are proliferating beyond need or reason.

1. Types of periodicals. Examples of the varied types of legal periodicals include the following:

(a) *Academic law reviews.* The most serious and highly reputed legal periodicals are those produced at the major American law schools. Law reviews are published by virtually all accredited law schools as training grounds for their best students, who serve as editors. They contain articles by established scholars and student-written comments and case notes, reflecting change and innovation in the law and describing historical developments. Both lead articles and comments are marked by extensive footnotes, and are therefore useful research tools.

In addition to general law reviews, each year sees a greater number of specialized academic journals, focusing on topics from ecology to industrial relations. Some specialized scholarly journals, such as the *American Journal of Legal History* and the *Tax Law Review,* are based at law schools but not edited by students.

(b) *Bar association journals.* The publications of the American Bar Association are the most numerous and important of the bar journals. The *A.B.A. Journal* features articles of a shorter, more popular nature than the law reviews and news of legal developments. Most A.B.A. sections issue their own publications, including several scholarly and respected journals. Several state and local bar associations and specialized bar groups also publish journals, usually of more limited scope and quality.

(c) *Commercial periodicals.* These include journals published by Commerce Clearing House, and many topical newsletters which focus on recent developments in a specific area of practice, briefly abstracting and highlighting judicial, administrative and legislative developments.

(d) *Legal newspapers.* Many large cities have daily legal newspapers, such as the *New York Law Journal* or the *Los Angeles Daily Journal.* Two newspapers, the *National Law Journal* and *Legal Times,* are national in scope and are issued weekly.

2. **Periodical indexes.** Access to this huge periodical literature is provided by the following indexes, which are similar to those in other subject fields:

(a) *Current Law Index* and *Legal Resource Index.* These companion indexes began in 1980, published under the auspices of the American Association of

Law Libraries. The *Current Law Index,* published monthly and cumulated quarterly and annually, provides access to over six hundred legal and law-related periodicals, using detailed Library of Congress subject headings. It has separate subject and author indexes, as well as case and statute tables. Exhibit 111 shows a sample page from the subject section of *Current Law Index. Legal Resource Index* is similar, but is issued monthly on a cumulated microfilm reel, which is loaded onto a motorized reader. It is somewhat broader in scope, including citations to seven legal newspapers and to relevant articles in non-law periodicals.

(b) *Index to Legal Periodicals.* Begun in 1908 and in its present series since 1926, *I.L.P.* indexes about four hundred legal periodicals, in a format similar to the *Readers Guide to Periodical Literature.* It is issued monthly and indexes by subject and author in one alphabet. Until 1983, bibliographic information, however, appeared only under the subject entries, with the author entries providing cross-references to the subject headings. *I.L.P.* includes tables of cases and statutes and a separate book review section. Exhibit 112 shows a page from its subject and author index. For the period preceding the *I.L.P.*, one can use the Jones-Chipman *Index to Legal Periodical Literature,* which covered the years 1803 to 1937, in six volumes.

(c) *Index to Foreign Legal Periodicals.* Published since 1960, this series provides comprehensive access to over three hundred periodicals and selected collections of essays, primarily from countries outside the common law system. It is divided into four sections: subject, geographic, book review and author indexes.

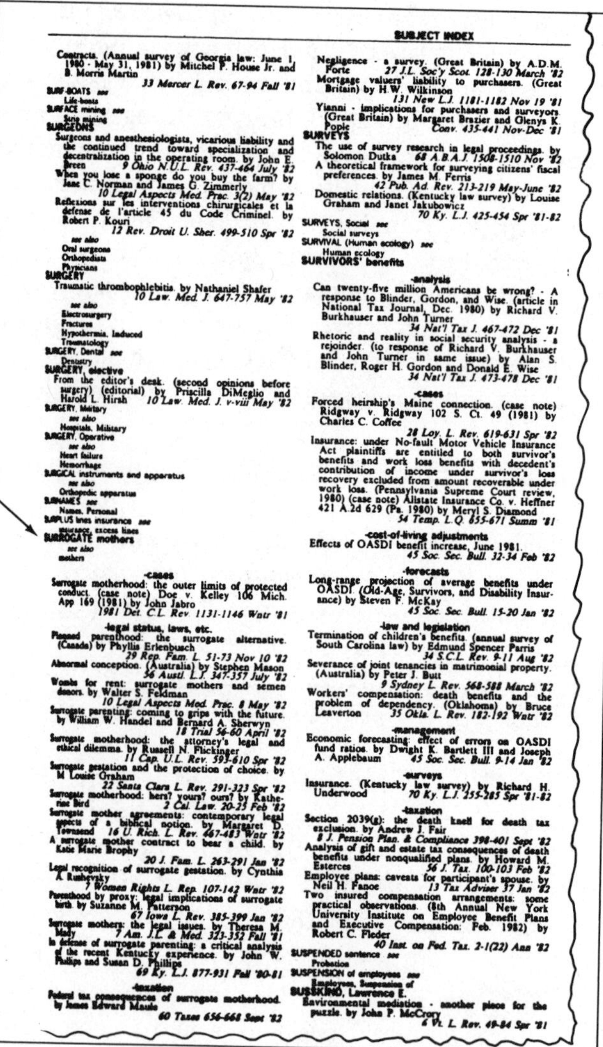

SUBJECT INDEX

Contracts. (Annual survey of Georgia law: June 1, 1980 - May 31, 1981) by Mitchel P. House Jr. and B. Morris Martin
33 Mercer L. Rev. 67-94 Fall '81

SURF-BOATS *see*
Life-boats

SURFACE mining *see*
Strip mining

SURGEONS

Surgeons and anesthesiologists, vicarious liability and the continued trend toward specialization and decentralization in the operating room. by John E. Breen *9 Ohio N.U.L. Rev. 437-464 July '82*

When you lose a sponge do you buy the farm? by Jane C. Norman and James G. Zimmerly
10 Legal Aspects Med. Prac. 3(2) May '82

Reflexions sur les interventions chirurgicales et la defense de l'article 45 du Code Criminel. by Robert P. Kouri
12 Rev. Droit U. Sher. 499-510 Spr '82

see also
Oral surgeons
Orthopedists
Physicians

SURGERY

Traumatic thrombophlebitis. by Nathaniel Shafer
10 Law. Med. J. 647-757 May '82

see also
Electrosurgery
Fractures
Hypothermia, Induced
Traumatology

SURGERY, Dental *see*
Dentistry

SURGERY, elective

From the editor's desk. (second opinions before surgery) (editorial) by Priscilla DiMeglio and Harold L. Hirsh *10 Law. Med. J. v-viii May '82*

SURGERY, Military
see also
Hospitals, Military

SURGERY, Operative
see also
Heart failure
Hemorrhage

SURGICAL instruments and apparatus
see also
Orthopedic apparatus

SURNAMES *see*
Names, Personal

SURPLUS lines insurance *see*
Insurance, excess lines

SURROGATE mothers
see also
mothers

-cases

Surrogate motherhood: the outer limits of protected conduct. (case note) Doe v. Kelley 106 Mich. App 169 (1981) by John Jabro
1981 Det. C.L. Rev. 1131-1146 Wntr '81

-legal status, laws, etc.

Planned parenthood: the surrogate alternative. (Canada) by Phyllis Erlenbusch
29 Rep. Fam. L. 51-73 Nov 10 '82

Abnormal conception. (Australia) by Stephen Mason
56 Austl. L.J. 347-357 July '82

Wombs for rent: surrogate mothers and semen donors. by Walter S. Feldman
10 Legal Aspects Med. Prac. 8 May '82

Surrogate parenting: coming to grips with the future. by William W. Handel and Bernard A. Sherwyn
18 Trial 56-60 April '82

Surrogate motherhood: the attorney's legal and ethical dilemma. by Russell N. Flickinger
11 Cap. U.L. Rev. 593-610 Spr '82

Surrogate gestation and the protection of choice. by M Louise Graham
22 Santa Clara L. Rev. 291-323 Spr '82

Surrogate motherhood: hers? yours? ours? by Katherine Bird *2 Cal. Law. 20-25 Feb '82*

Surrogate mother agreements: contemporary legal aspects of a biblical notion. by Margaret D. Townsend *16 U. Rich. L. Rev. 467-483 Wntr '82*

A surrogate mother contract to bear a child. by Katie Marie Brophy
20 J. Fam. L. 263-291 Jan '82

Legal recognition of surrogate gestation. by Cynthia A. Rushevsky
7 Women Rights L. Rep. 107-142 Wntr '82

Parenthood by proxy: legal implications of surrogate birth. by Suzanne M. Patterson
67 Iowa L. Rev. 385-399 Jan '82

Surrogate mothers: the legal issues. by Theresa M. Mady *7 Am. J.L. & Med. 323-352 Fall '81*

In defense of surrogate parenting: a critical analysis of the recent Kentucky experience. by John W. Phillips and Susan D. Phillips
69 Ky. L.J. 877-931 Fall '80-81

-taxation

Federal tax consequences of surrogate motherhood. by James Edward Maule
60 Taxes 656-668 Sept '82

Negligence - a survey. (Great Britain) by A.D.M. Forte *27 J.L. Soc'y Scot. 128-130 March '82*

Mortgage valuers' liability to purchasers. (Great Britain) by H.W. Wilkinson
131 New L.J. 1181-1182 Nov 19 '81

Yianni - implications for purchasers and surveyors. (Great Britain) by Margaret Brazier and Glenys K. Pople *Conv. 435-441 Nov-Dec '81*

SURVEYS

The use of survey research in legal proceedings. by Solomon Dutka *68 A.B.A.J. 1508-1510 Nov '82*

A theoretical framework for surveying citizens' fiscal preferences. by James M. Ferris
42 Pub. Ad. Rev. 213-219 May-June '82

Domestic relations. (Kentucky law survey) by Louise Graham and Janet Jakubowicz
70 Ky. L.J. 425-454 Spr '81-82

SURVEYS, Social *see*
Social surveys

SURVIVAL (Human ecology) *see*
Human ecology

SURVIVORS' benefits

-analysis

Can twenty-five million Americans be wrong? - A response to Blinder, Gordon, and Wise. (article in National Tax Journal, Dec. 1980) by Richard V. Burkhauser and John Turner
34 Nat'l Tax J. 467-472 Dec '81

Rhetoric and reality in social security analysis - a rejoinder. (to response of Richard V. Burkhauser and John Turner in same issue) by Alan S. Blinder, Roger H. Gordon and Donald E. Wise
34 Nat'l Tax J. 473-478 Dec '81

-cases

Forced heirship's Maine connection. (case note) Ridgway v. Ridgway 102 S. Ct. 49 (1981) by Charles C. Coffee
28 Loy. L. Rev. 619-631 Spr '82

Insurance: under No-fault Motor Vehicle Insurance Act plaintiffs are entitled to both survivor's benefits and work loss benefits with decedent's contribution of income under survivor's loss recovery excluded from amount recoverable under work loss. (Pennsylvania Supreme Court review, 1980) (case note) Allstate Insurance Co. v. Heffner 421 A.2d 629 (Pa. 1980) by Meryl S. Diamond
54 Temp. L.Q. 655-671 Summ '81

-cost-of-living adjustments

Effects of OASDI benefit increase, June 1981.
45 Soc. Sec. Bull. 32-34 Feb '82

-forecasts

Long-range projection of average benefits under OASDI. (Old-Age, Survivors, and Disability Insurance) by Steven F. McKay
45 Soc. Sec. Bull. 15-20 Jan '82

-law and legislation

Termination of children's benefits. (annual survey of South Carolina law) by Edmund Spencer Parris
34 S.C.L. Rev. 9-11 Aug '82

Severance of joint tenancies in matrimonial property. (Australia) by Peter J. Butt
9 Sydney L. Rev. 568-588 March '82

Workers' compensation: death benefits and the problem of dependency. (Oklahoma) by Bruce Leaverton *35 Okla. L. Rev. 182-192 Wntr '82*

-management

Economic forecasting: effect of errors on OASDI fund ratios. by Dwight K. Bartlett III and Joseph A. Applebaum *45 Soc. Sec. Bull. 9-14 Jan '82*

-surveys

Insurance. (Kentucky law survey) by Richard H. Underwood *70 Ky. L.J. 255-285 Spr '81-82*

-taxation

Section 2039(g): the death knell for death tax exclusion. by Andrew J. Fair
8 J. Pension Plan. & Compliance 398-401 Sept '82

Analysis of gift and estate tax consequences of death benefits under nonqualified plans. by Howard M. Esterces *56 J. Tax. 100-103 Feb '82*

Employee plans: caveats for participant's spouse. by Neil H. Fanoe *13 Tax Adviser 37 Jan '82*

Two insured compensation arrangements: some practical observations. (8th Annual New York University Institute on Employee Benefit Plans and Executive Compensation: Feb. 1982) by Robert C. Fleder
40 Inst. on Fed. Tax. 2-1(22) Ann '82

SUSPENDED sentence *see*
Probation

SUSPENSION of employees *see*
Employees, Suspension of

SUSSKIND, Lawrence E.

Environmental mediation - another piece for the puzzle. by John P. McCrory
6 Vt. L. Rev. 49-84 Spr '81

Exhibit 111: A sample page from the subject section of *Current Law Index.*

(d) *Index to Periodical Articles Related to Law.* Created in 1958 to supplement the limited coverage of *I.L.P.*, this work indexes law-related articles in journals not covered in *C.L.I.*, *I.L.P.*, or the *Index to Foreign Legal Periodicals.* It consists of a bound ten-year volume, bound five-year supplements, and quarterly issues.

(e) *Current Index to Legal Periodicals.* A weekly subject guide to the contents of law reviews and other major legal periodicals, this index fills the gap between publication of current periodical issues and their coverage by the permanent, more comprehensive indexes.

(f) There are in addition indexes to Canadian and Commonwealth legal periodicals, and indexes on specialized topics such as the *Index to Federal Tax Articles* and the *Criminal Justice Periodicals Index.*

3. **Periodical citators.** *Shepard's Law Review Citations* is a compilation of citations to articles in over 180 law reviews and legal periodicals. It shows where any article published since 1947 has been cited since 1957 in state or federal decisions or in later law review articles.

For *citing* rather than *cited* articles, Shepard's includes in each of its state citators coverage of local law reviews and of twenty national law reviews. For the federal system, it issues a separate *Federal Law Citations in Selected Law Reviews,* which indexes law review citations to federal court decisions and statutory material. Citations in the *American Bar Association Journal* are also included in the regular *U.S. Citations* and *Federal Citations* series.

426 INDEX TO LEGAL PERIODICALS 1982–1983

SURETYSHIP and guaranty—*Continued*
Recent developments under the Bankers Blanket Bond. F. L. Skillern, Jr. 17 Forum 1382-90 Summ '82
Role of bank guarantees in international trade. R. Edwards. 56 A L J 281-7 Je '82
Surety's decision on what to do. W. H. Webster. 17 Forum 1168-89 Summ '82
Surety's investigation. R. H. Britt. 17 Forum 1151-67 Summ '82
Surety's subrogation to obligee's right of setoff. E. G. Gallagher. 18 Forum 73-82 Fall '82
Trust fund provisions in indemnity agreements—their utility and enforcement. J. L. Fry. 18 Forum 512-27 Spr '83
Validity of a limitation on a claimant's right to sue contained in a construction surety bond. 32 Fed'n Ins Counsel Q 383-8 Summ '82
Violations of antifraud provisions of federal securities laws and the Stockbrokers Blanket Bond, form 14. L. J. Barbagallo. 18 Forum 417-50 Spr '83
What every real estate lawyer should know about payment and performance bonds. B. C. Hart, H. E. Kane. 17 Real Prop Prob & Tr J 674-89 Wint '82

SURRICK, R. Barclay
Damages (P)
Ind diseases (P)

SURROGATE motherhood
See also
Artificial insemination
Parent and child

Abnormal conception. S. Mason. 56 A L J 347-57 Jl '82
Federal tax consequences of surrogate motherhood. J. E. Maule. 60 Taxes 656-68 S '82
Legal recognition of surrogate gestation. C. A. Rushevsky. 7 Women's Rights L Rep 107-42 Wint '82
Surrogate gestation and the protection of choice. M. L. Graham. 22 Santa Clara L Rev 291-323 Spr '82
Surrogate mother contract in Indiana. 15 Ind L Rev 807-30 Fall '82
Surrogate motherhood: analysis of the problems and suggestions for solutions. P. Coleman. 50 Tenn L Rev 71-119 Fall '82
Surrogate motherhood and artificial insemination: contractual implications. L. J. Greenberg, H. L. Hirsh. 29 Med Trial Tech Q 149-66 Fall '82
Surrogate motherhood: the attorney's legal and ethical dilemma. 11 Cap U L Rev 593-610 Spr '82
Surrogate parenthood: a need fir legislative direction. R. D. Mawdsley. 71 Ill B J 412-17 Mr '83

SURVEYS and surveying
Damages for negligent surveys and valuations. D. C. Jess. 133 New L J 80-2 Ja 28 '83
Land surveys and the New York law of real property. B. M. Rifkin. 54 N Y St B J 443-7+ N '82

SURVIVAL OF ACTIONS; SEE REMEDIES, WRONGFUL DEATH

SUSE, Philip J.
Corp: improper payments (Q)
Middle East (Q)

SUSMAN, Stephen D.
Antitrust law: sp industries, etc (S)
Radio and tv (C)

SUSMAN, Thomas
Freedom of inf (N)
Trade secrets (N)

SUSSMAN, Daniel L.
Inc tax: employee benefits—US (I)
Investments (T)

SUSSNA, Stephen
Environ protect (N)
Land use (N)

SUTHERLAND, P.
Govt immun and liab (Int law) (R)

SUTHERLAND, P. F.
Int judicial assitance (U)

SUTTON, Kenneth C.
Contracts (U)

SUTTON, Winifred Ann
Inherit taxes (C)

SWAN, George Steven
Compar law (A)
Const law—Can (A)
Federalism (A)
Self-determination, Natl (S)
South Africa (S)
Transkei (S)

SWAN, John
Canada: S Ct (F)
Contracts (D)

SWAN, Oscar E.
Oil and gas (C)
Statutes (C)

SWANN, Jerre B.
Trademarks and trade names (A)

SWANSON, Michael J.
Hearsay (L)

SWARTZ, Mark A.
Products liab (C)

SWEDEN
Swedish press ombudsman—a model for the United States? J. W. Williams. 3 N Y L Sch J Int'l & Comp L 137-73 '82

SWEENY, John P.
Corp: improper payments (F)
Securities (S)
US: SEC (S)

SWEENEY, Mary C.
Attorneys (D)
Insurance (D)

SWEENEY, Terrance
Taxation: enforcement—Can (T)

SWEET, Allan J.
Inc tax: corp distr—US (C)

SWEET, Justin
Constr contracts (C)

SWEET, Neesa
Computers (M)

SWENNEN, Jean-Pierre
US: Claims Ct (C)

SWIDORSKI, Carl
Courts—NY (J)
Judges (J)

SWINTON, Katherine
Discrimination: sex (R)
Occup safety and health (R)

SWISHER, Peter Nash
Comity (F)
Conflict of laws: domestic relat (F)
Divorce and sep (F)
Legal educ: teaching (T)

SWITZER, Erwin O.
Due process (A)
Freedom of the press (A)
US: S Ct (A)

SWITZERLAND
Contemporary patterns of drinking in the cultures of Switzerland. R. Muller. 10 Contemp Drug Prob 155-77 Summ '81
Swiss alcohol policy: the emergence of a compromise. M. Cahannes. 10 Contemp Drug Prob 37-53 Spr '81

SWYGERT, H. Patrick
Negligence (N)
Sports (N)

SWYGERT, Luther M.
Courts—US (I)
Judicial rev (I)
Pub legal serv (S)
Right to counsel (S)

SYDOW, Michael D.
Fed juridic (A)
Maritime law (A)

Exhibit 112: A sample page from the author & subject section of the *Index to Legal Periodicals*.

OTHER MATERIALS

There are a number of other specialized types of secondary material which should also be noted:

1. **Directories** of practicing lawyers are published by state and county bar associations, and for particular fields of professional specialization. There are also a number of general bar directories which are national or international in scope. The most comprehensive of these is the *Martindale-Hubbell Law Directory* which provides a national listing of lawyers in all states, most cities, many towns, and some foreign countries. The first six volumes of *Martindale-Hubbell* provide classified listings, as well as fuller descriptions of those lawyers and law firms who purchase space beyond a simple one line entry. In addition, the last volume of the directory includes court calendars, model acts and uniform laws, brief digests of the law of every state and many foreign countries on specific substantive and procedural legal topics, and information on the organization of the jurisdiction's courts. These are usually prepared by outstanding practitioners in the area and often provide references to the primary sources on which they are based. Although they are too limited for serious research, the digests are useful for a brief statement of law on a particular point or for a reference from which further research can be undertaken.

There are also many guides to government offices and agencies at both federal and state levels. The *Federal Court Directory* (Want Publishing) and the

United States Court Directory (Legal Reporters Associates) are examples of useful annual directories.

2. **Records and Briefs.** The printed records and briefs of the parties in cases before appellate courts are distributed to a limited number of libraries around the country for research use. The records and briefs of the Supreme Court of the United States, in their official form, go to approximately twenty-five libraries around the country, while many more libraries subscribe to microform editions. A microfilm edition of the U.S. Supreme Court records and briefs from 1832 to 1925 (with hardcopy indexes) is also commercially available. Records and briefs of the various U.S. Courts of Appeals have a more limited distribution. Records and briefs of the appellate courts in most states are also distributed to local law libraries in the state.

These materials have a permanent value in that they enable attorneys and other legal researchers to study in detail the arguments and facts of significant cases decided by these courts. These documents are usually retrievable by report citation or docket number of the case in which they were submitted. The researcher typically begins with an interest in a case or decision and then seeks this additional source of material on the case. There is no direct subject approach to appellate records and briefs.

The record consists of a transcript of all proceedings below, including the trial testimony, as well as all of the previous legal papers, documents, opinions and judgments. The briefs consist of the written arguments and authorities cited by the attorneys for the respective parties on appeal.

3. **Formbooks.** Because of the repetitive occurrence of similar problems and transactions in the course of legal practice, a literature of formbooks has developed which contains sample forms of commonly used legal documents and instruments. These can be consulted by attorneys and used as the basis for the preparation of similar papers in later situations. Model forms can be found in a variety of sources, ranging from multi-volumed collections covering different types of proceedings and subjects to singly printed forms for a particular transaction or purpose which can be purchased at a legal stationary store. Annotated formbooks are also published and include citations to cases in which the particular forms have actually been litigated and upheld on appeal. Both Lawyers Co-op and West publish multi-volume collections which present forms in an encyclopedic manner with extensive indexing, notes and cross-references. Lawyers Co-op has one set, *Am.Jur.Legal Forms 2d*, for forms of instruments (contracts, leases, wills, etc.); and another, *Am.Jur.Pleading and Practice Forms*, which focuses on litigation and other practice before courts and administrative agencies. *West Legal Forms 2d* and its predecessor, *Modern Legal Forms*, include both practice forms and instruments. Both companies also issue sets devoted to forms used in federal practice, *West's Federal Forms* and *Federal Procedural Forms, Lawyers' Edition.*

There are also specialized sets or volumes for many states and for particular subject areas. In addition, manuals of practice frequently contain sample forms, and compilations of statutory forms are often issued in conjunction with state codes.

4. Bar Associations Publications. Legal materials of various kinds including the following types of publications are issued by many bar associations:

(a) Newsletters and periodicals containing reports on association activities, articles on legal topics, and notices of recent developments.

(b) Annual proceedings or yearbooks of meetings and committee reports.

(c) Texts or manuals for the continuing legal education of practitioners. The growing movement for continuing education of the bar produces a substantial literature of instructional materials. Some C.L.E. publications are substantial treatises in their own right (e.g., those of California Continuing Education of the Bar and a selected number of those published by the Practising Law Institute). Many, however, are more ephemeral pamphlets or course handbooks designed for use in seminars or teaching programs.

(d) Comments or special reports on proposed legislation or important developments in law.

5. Dictionaries. The leading American law dictionaries are *Black's Law Dictionary* (West, 5th ed., 1979) and *Ballentine's Law Dictionary* (Lawyers Co-op, 3d ed., 1969). Both cite cases; *Ballentine's* includes frequent references to *Am.Jur.2d* and *A.L.R.* *Black's* can also be searched by computer on WESTLAW. The *Modern Legal Glossary* (Michie,

1980) is considerably shorter than either *Black's* or *Ballentine's,* and is limited to the definition of legal terms, phrases and concepts. All three contain legal maxims with translations, if in Latin, and explanations. There are now also several smaller paperback dictionaries available.

W.C. Burton, *Legal Thesaurus* (Macmillan, 1980) is a useful source of alternatives for words and phrases commonly used in legal writing and argument. Organized like *Roget's Thesaurus,* it lists synonyms, related concepts, and foreign phrases under main words, and provides an index of the secondary words.

D.M. Bieber, *Dictionary of Legal Abbreviations Used in American Law Books* (Hein, 1979) provides 16,000 entries, including acronyms and abbreviations used for government agencies, organizations, court reports, and legal periodicals. Legal abbreviations and citations can also be traced in M.D. Powers, *The Legal Citation Directory* (Franas Press, 1971), D. Raistrick, *Index to Legal Citations and Abbreviations* (Professional Books, 1981), and, more selectively, in the *Uniform System of Citation,* 13th ed. (Harvard Law Review Association, 1981).

COMPUTER ACCESS TO SECONDARY MATERIALS

With the increased availability of computer data bases in legal research, new means of access to secondary materials have been developing rapidly. The incorporation of treatises, periodicals, encyclopedias, looseleaf services and dictionaries in LEXIS and WESTLAW is growing steadily and will undoubtedly expand their usefulness. Vast collections of non-legal information from other disciplines are available in Lockheed's DIALOG data bases, and can be searched from both LEXIS and WESTLAW terminals, and from many personal computers.

Among the secondary sources available on LEXIS are a number of legal treatises published by Matthew Bender; briefs in cases argued before the U.S. Supreme Court since 1979; NEXIS, a library of newspapers (including the *New York Times* and the *Washington Post*), and a number of business journals and news magazines; the *Encyclopedia Britannica;* the *Accounting Information* data base; *DISCLO*, a library of financial reports filed with the S.E.C.; and a number of major law school journals.

WESTLAW includes access to the following data bases of secondary materials: *Accountant's Index; Black's Law Dictionary; DISCLOSURE*, a collection of S.E.C. corporate filings; the Dow Jones News/Retrieval Services, which include the *Wall Street Journal* and *Barron's;* the *Forensic Services Directory;* and a number of selected full text articles from legal periodicals.

The DIALOG data bases, available from both LEXIS and WESTLAW, include the *Congressional Information Service; Legal Resource Index; Federal Index* (covering the *Congressional Record* and the *Federal Register*); *Public Affairs Information Service; Social Scisearch*, a social science indexing service; *Environline*, a comprehensive data base of primary and secondary sources dealing with environmental protection; *Criminal Justice Periodi-*

cal Index; MEDLINE, the National Library of Medicine's data base of medical literature; and on and on.

CONCLUSION

This very brief survey of secondary materials cannot reflect their full impact on the judicial process and on legal research in general. There is a growing realization that legal authority is not a simple hierarchy of sources, but rather a broad spectrum with many sources reflecting a multitude of influences on judicial decision making. Increasing attention has focused on the role of secondary sources in legal thinking and their relative authority on the courts. See, for example, two articles by J.H. Merryman: "The Authority of Authority," 6 *Stanford Law Review* 613 (1954) and "Toward a Theory of Citations . . . ," 50 *Southern California Law Review* 381 (1977). It can be expected that, particularly with their increased access by computer, all of the secondary sources described above, and the literature of other disciplines, will continue to play a large role in the research of lawyers and legal scholars.

CHAPTER X

ENGLISH LAW

INTRODUCTION TO ENGLISH LAW

Foreign law, as considered in this chapter and the next, consists of the domestic law of countries other than the United States. The forms of legal literature of most foreign legal systems parallel our own, but often with significant differences. Virtually all countries have some type of court reports, statutes, administrative decrees and decisions, finding tools, encyclopedias, treatises and periodicals, but their relative status as authority and the format of their publications may differ widely from those of the United States.

The legal systems of most foreign countries can be divided into two groups—those within the common law system and those within the civil law system. Each system has its own history, its own fundamental principles and procedures, and its own forms of publication for legal sources. The treatment of foreign law here has therefore been divided by the two systems; this chapter treats the common law system, focusing primarily on English materials, and the next chapter treats the civil law system.

There are several basic differences between the common and civil law systems, although the two systems have in recent years influenced each other and their unique characteristics have become much less absolute. The civil law system is still marked by a primary emphasis on legislation, which constitutes the basic legal norms. Judicial decisions are generally not considered primary sources of law and may be less authoritative than important commentaries on the codes by leading scholars. The codes themselves are original statutes which form a comprehensive statement of the law on their subject, as distinguished from the so-called codes of common law countries, which are usually alphabetically arranged subject compilations of previously enacted specific statutes. There are other crucial differences in terminology, in procedure and remedies, and in the status and role of judges, prosecutors, juries and even lawyers themselves.

The common law system includes the law of the United States, England and those countries which have adopted the basic structure of the English common law. This includes most of the Commonwealth of Nations and a few other jurisdictions which have directly or indirectly followed the common law structure and its basic approach. The forms of publication and research procedures under the common law most closely resemble those of the United States.

Whether one is pursuing comparative study of another country's law for academic or scholarly purposes, or preparing for a problem in law practice, it is necessary to have some knowledge of the published sources of law and of the research procedures for their use. This chapter and the next are designed as an introduction for that purpose. This chapter deals with English law as illustrative of common law countries generally, and the next chapter discusses research in the sources available for countries of the civil law system.

Among all of the foreign legal systems, the one which is closest to our own is that of England. English law and tradition still have a special relevance in this country by virtue of our common Anglo-American legal development. The American colonies inherited the English common law and a legal tradition of statutes, cases, customs, and attitudes. Although, since then, American law has developed quite separately, we still share a heritage which often gives English law a persuasive value in our courts not generally afforded to the law of other countries. In general, English legal scholarship, legislation and judicial decisions are frequently of interest here.

Although common law countries with federal systems, such as Canada and Australia, offer different research problems, this description will be limited to English sources. For an introduction to research in Canadian law, see M.A. Banks, *Using a Law Library, A Guide for Students and Lawyers in the Common Law Provinces of Canada* (Carswell, 3d ed., 1980) and D.T. MacEllven, *Legal Research Handbook* (Butterworth's, 1983). For Australia, see E. Campbell, *Legal Research: Materials and Methods* (The Law Book Company, 2d ed., 1979).

The following is a very brief outline of the main sources and forms of publication of English legal materials.

ENGLISH STATUTES

The standard historical collection of English statutes is the *Statutes of the Realm*, covering 1235 to 1713 in 9 vols. (1810–1825), with alphabetical and chronological indexes. Several other collections, all arranged chronologically, were published during the 19th century under the title, *Statutes at Large,* some of which extended coverage to 1869. The contents and coverage of these compilations and later statutory publications are more fully described in *Guide to Law Reports and Statutes* (Sweet & Maxwell, 4th ed., 1962). The *current* forms of published statutes are as follows:

1. **Slip laws,** issued by Her Majesty's Stationery Office (H.M.S.O.).
2. **Session laws:**
   (a) *Public General Acts and Measures* (H.M. S.O.), published since 1831. An annual chronological compilation of slip laws, now issued in two volumes with a non-cumulating subject index. This compilation also appears in the same form in the *Law Reports* series, described below.

   (b) *Current Law Statutes Annotated* (Sweet & Maxwell, 1948–date). A commercial annual session law compilation, chronolcgically arranged, with annotations.

   (c) *Butterworth's Annotated Legislation Service* (Butterworth, 1939–date). A *selective* annotated session law service.

3. **Compiled statutes:**

   (a) *Halsbury's Statutes of England* (Butterworth, 3rd ed., 1968–1975). An unofficial, well-indexed encyclopedic arrangement of acts in force, supplemented with annual bound volumes and two looseleaf volumes (*Current Statutes Service* and *Noter-Up*). This is the most convenient subject compilation of English statutes and includes footnote annotations to judicial decisions. It also includes an added volume, *European Continuation, 1952–1972,* which provides European community treaties and secondary legislation.

   (b) *Statutes Revised, 1235–1948* (H.M.S.O., 3rd ed., 1950). This official chronological arrangement of statutes, supplemented annually by a volume of amending acts, is out of date and has been replaced by the *Statutes in Force: Official Revised Edition.*

   (c) *Statutes in Force: Official Revised Edition* (H.M.S.O., 1972–). This official compilation replaces the 3rd ed. of the *Statutes Revised.* Each act is issued in a separate pamphlet for inclusion in looseleaf volumes by broad subject categories. A primitive form of publication as compared to *Halsbury's Statutes* or the *U.S.Code,* it will be updated by revised pamphlets as necessary. A microfiche edition is also available.

4. **Statutory Indexes.** The various session law compilations generally contain their own indexes

and, in addition, the following compiled indexes are available for English statutes:

(a) *Chronological Table of Statutes* (H.M.S.O.). Covers 1235 to date; cumulated and revised annually.

(b) *Index to the Statutes in Force* (H.M.S.O.). This companion volume to the *Chronological Table of Statutes,* above, is cumulated and revised annually and provides an excellent subject index to English statutes.

(c) *Halsbury's Statutes of England* (Butterworth). Includes a consolidated index and individual volume indexes. The general index is revised annually.

(d) *Statutes of the Realm* and *Statutes at Large.* Alphabetical and chronological indexes for historical research only.

LAW REPORTS

1. **Early Law Reports.** As described above in Chapter II (at pages 10–11, English law reporting has had a long and varied history. The recording of decisions began with the pleas rolls, then developed into the Year Books, and next into the nominative reporters. Most of the nominative reports were cumulated into the *English Reports: Full Reprint,* covering 1220 to 1865 (W. Green, 1900–1932, in 176 vols.; reprinted by Fred B. Rothman and Stevens & Sons). This invaluable set contains about 100,000 of the most important decisions, originally published in some 275 nominative reporters. The volumes are arranged by

courts, star-paged to the original reporter, and made accessible by a two volume alphabetical table of cases. A similar compilation, the *Revised Reports,* covering 1785 to 1866 (Sweet & Maxwell and Little, Brown, 1891–1917, in 149 vols.) partially duplicates the *Full Reprint,* but adds many other reporters not in the latter. A microform collection of early reports not included in either of these compilations has been issued commercially by Trans-Media Corporation.

2. Current Law Reporting. For decisions since those published in the *English Reports: Full Reprint* (i.e., since 1865), the following reporters are used:

(a) *Law Reports* (Incorporated Council of Law Reporting for England and Wales, 1865 to date). These current series have semi-official status and authority; they include four specialized reporters which cover:

Appeal Cases (from the House of Lords and the Judicial Committee of the Privy Council);

Queen's Bench Division;

Chancery Division; and

Family Division (prior to 1972, called Probate, Divorce and Admiralty Division)

(b) *Weekly Law Reports* (Incorporated Council of Law Reporting for England and Wales, 1953 to date). Most complete of all current English law reporters, it includes many decisions not appearing in the *Law Reports* series.

(c) *All England Law Reports* (Butterworth, 1936 to date). Contains more decisions than the *Law Reports,* but not always with complete text. A supplementary, retrospective set, *All England Law Reports Reprint, 1558–1935* (1957–1968) added about five thousand earlier cases.

(d) Special subject and topical reporters, similar to such specialized American reports, are currently being published in many fields.

(e) Several reporters published in conjunction with legal periodicals are now discontinued, but are still cited for early cases. These include, among others: *Law Journal Reports* (1822–1949); *Law Times Reports* (1859–1947); and *Times Law Reports* (1884–1952).

3. **Finding Tools.**

(a) *Current Law* and *Current Law Year Books* (Sweet & Maxwell, 1947–date). This comprehensive research service includes a case digest and citator, statutory digest and citator, and a limited index to British legal periodicals and texts. Issued as *Current Law Consolidation, 1947–1951,* with supplementary monthly pamphlets, annual bound volumes and periodic consolidations, it is the most effective citator for English law. Separate editions are also published for Canada and Scotland.

(b) *The Digest: Annotated British, Commonwealth and European Cases,* formerly called *English and Empire Digest* (Butterworth, 3d ed., 1971–date). This most comprehensive and popular English case digest is now being published in a new "green band" edition, replacing the 2d or "blue band" edition. In addition to digests of

English decisions, it also covers cases from the courts of Australia, Canada, Ireland, New Zealand, Scotland, and other Commonwealth countries. The arrangement is similar to American digests and it is well indexed and supplemented.

(c) *Halsbury's Laws of England* (Butterworth, 4th ed., 1973–date). Despite its title, this is a general legal encyclopedia, with references to case law, statutes, and administrative sources. It is well indexed, offers tables of cases and statutes cited, and provides cumulative annual supplements and a current looseleaf service.

(d) *Halsbury's Statutes of England* (Butterworth). See description above, at pages 324–325.

(e) *Law Reports Digest*, 1865–1949, and *Consolidated Index*, 1951–date (Incorporated Council of Law Reporting). This companion publication to the *Law Reports* began in 1892 and consists of a series of cumulations of little current use. However, its *Consolidated Index* has continued as an updated subject index and digest to the *Law Reports*, with a table of cases reported, and citators for cases, statutes, and statutory instruments. The *Index* appears currently in monthly advance sheets, annual cumulations, and five and ten year consolidations.

CITATORS

There is no equivalent of Shepard's citators for English legal bibliography, but the following tools offer citator service and can be used for that purpose.

1. Statutory Citators.

The major citator for English and Scottish statutes is *Current Law Statute Citator,* published by Sweet & Maxwell in connection with their *Current Law* service. It is issued in a cumulative volume covering 1947 to 1971, and paperback supplementation with current monthly updating thereafter. The citator consists of a list of statutes from 1235 to date, arranged by year and chapter, with references to all later statutes and cases (decided since 1947) which affect the listed statute. It also notes all statutory instruments issued under the statutes. The *Current Law Statute Citator* is illustrated in Exhibit 113 below.

In addition, the following sets also include more limited citators for statutes:

(a) *Halsbury's Statutes of England*

(b) *Law Reports Consolidated Index*

(c) *All England Law Reports*

2. Case Citators.

The major citator for English case law is the Sweet & Maxwell *Current Law Case Citator,* also published in connection with the *Current Law* service. It is issued in a cumulative volume covering 1947 to 1976, and paperback supplementation with current monthly updating thereafter. The Citator consists of an alphabetical listing of cases, with later cases which have cited the listed case indicated below. The effect of each later case on the earlier case it cites is indicated (e.g., "Overruled", "Applied", "Considered", etc.) The *Current Law Case Citator* is illustrated in Exhibit 114 below.

STATUTE CITATOR 1972–82 **1976**

CAP.

1976—cont.

71. Supplementary Benefits Act 1976—*cont.*
s. 20 amended: 1982,c.24,s.41,sch.4; repealed in pt.: 1980,c.30,sch.2.
s. 21, see *Clear* v. *Smith* [1981] 1 W.L.R. 399, D.C.
s. 21, amended: 1977, c.5,s.14; 1980, c.30,sch.2; 1981,c.33,sch.1.
s. 22, amended: 1977, c.5,s.14; 1980, c.30,sch.2; 1981, c.33,sch.1; repealed in pt.: 1980,c.30,schs.2,5.
s. 23, amended: 1977, c.5,s.14; 1981, c.33,sch.1.
s. 24, amended: 1980,c.30,sch.2; repealed in pt.: *ibid.*,schs.2,5; 1981,c.33,sch.1.
s. 25, see *Galt* v. *Turner*, 1981 S.L.T. (Notes) 99.
s. 25, amended: 1977, c.5,s.14; 1980, c.30,sch.2; 1981, c.33,sch.1; repealed in pt.: 1980, c.30,schs.2,5.
s. 27, amended: *ibid.*,sch.2.
s. 28, rules 80/1605; 82/40.
s. 29, repealed: 1977,c.5,sch.2.
s. 30, amended: 1980,c.30,sch.2; repealed in pt.: *ibid.*,schs.2,5.
s. 31, amended: *ibid.*,sch.2.
s. 32, repealed in pt.: *ibid.*,sch.5.
s. 32A, regs. 80/1774; 81/1524.
s. 32A, added: 1980,c.30,sch.2.
s. 33, regs. 81/1016, 1197; 82/1127.
s. 33, amended: 1979,c.18,sch.3; 1980,c.30,sch.2; repealed in pt.: *ibid.*,schs.2,5.
s. 34, regs. 80/982, 1774; 81/815, 1524; amended: 1980,c.30,s.6,sch.2; repealed in pt.: *ibid.*,schs.2,5.
s. 36, repealed in pt.: *ibid.*,sch.5.
sch. 1, see *R.* v. *West London Supplementary Benefits Appeal Tribunal, ex p. Wyatt* [1978] 1 W.L.R. 240, D.C.; *R.* v. *Greater Birmingham Supplementary Benefit Appeal Tribunal, ex p. Khan* [1979] 3 All E.R. 759, D.C.; *R.* v. *Bolton Supplementary Benefits Appeal Tribunal, ex p. Fordham* [1981] 1 W.L.R. 28; [1981] 1 All E.R. 50, C.A.; *McDougall* v. *Secretary of State for Social Services; McIntyre* v. *Secretary of State for Social Services*, *The Times*, May 15, 1981, H.L.; *Roberts* v. *Supplementary Benefits Commission*, Second Division, November 26, 1980; *Crake* v. *Supplementary Benefits Commission; Butterworth* v. *Supplementary Benefits Commission* [1982] 1 All E.R. 498, Woolf J.; *Pearson* v. *Secretary of State for Social Services*, Second Division, November 20, 1981.
sch. 1, regs. 77/1141, 1142; 78/913; 80/1300, 1579, 1774; 81/513, 1196, 1524, 1525, 1527; 82/1126, 1127, 1634.
sch. 1, substituted: 1980,c.30,sch.2; repealed in pt.: 1980,c.51,sch.26; amended: regs. 82/1127.

CAP.

1976—cont.

71. Supplementary Benefits Act 1976—*cont.*
schs. 2, 3, repealed: 1980,c.30,sch.5.
sch. 4, rules 80/1605; 82/40.
sch. 4, substituted: 1979,c.18,s.6,sch.2.
schs. 5, 6, amended: 1980,c.30,sch.2; repealed in pt.: *ibid.*,schs.2,5.
sch. 7, repealed in pt.: 1977,c.5,sch.2; 1978,c.22,sch.3; c.44,sch.17; order 77/2158; 1980,c.30,sch.5; c.51,sch.26; 1982,c.24,sch.5.
sch. 16, amended: *ibid.*,s.42.

72. Endangered Species (Import and Export) Act 1976.
Royal Assent, November 22, 1976.
s. 1, amended: 1979,c.2,sch.4.
ss. 1, 3, amended: 1981,c.69,sch.10.
s. 3, orders 77/153; 78/1280, 1939; 79/1054; 82/1230.
s. 4, amended and repealed in pt.: 1981,c.69,sch.10.
ss. 4, 5, amended: 1979,c.2,sch.4.
s. 10, amended: *ibid.*
s. 11, orders 77/153; 78/1939; 79/1054.
s. 13, order 77/24.
s. 13, amended: 1981,c.69,sch.10; repealed in pt.: *ibid.*,sch.17.
schs. 1–3, substituted: order 82/1230
sch. 2, amended: order 79/1054.
sch. 3, amended: orders 78/1280; 79/1054.
schs. 4, 5, added: 1981,c.69,sch.10.

73. Industry (Amendment) Act 1976.
Royal Assent, November 22, 1976.

74. Race Relations Act 1976.
Royal Assent, November 22, 1976.
s. 1, see *Singh* v. *Rowntree Mackintosh* [1979] I.C.R. 554, E.A.T.; *Panesar* v. *Nestlé Co.* [1980] I.C.R. 144, C.A.; *Owen and Briggs* v. *James* [1981] I.C.R. 377, E.A.T.; *Kingston and Richmond Area Health Authority* v. *Kaur* [1981] I.C.R. 631, E.A.T.; *Ojutiku* v. *Manpower Services Commission* [1981] I.C.R. 515, E.A.T.; *Chattopadhyay* v. *The Headmaster of Holloway School* [1981] I.R.L.R. 487, E.A.T.; *Bayoomi* v. *British Railways Board* [1981] I.R.L.R. 431, Industrial Tribunal; *Chin* v. *British Aerospace P.L.C.* [1982] I.R.L.R. 56, E.A.T.; *Ojutiku* v. *Manpower Services Commission*, *The Times*, May 28, 1982, C.A.; *Perera* v. *Civil Service Commission* [1982] I.C.R. 350, E.A.T.
ss. 1, 3, see *Commission for Racial Equality* v. *Riley*, July 5, 1982, H.H. Judge Da Cunha (sitting with assessors) Manchester C.C.; *Mandla (Sewa Singh)* v. *Dowell Lee* [1982] 3 W.L.R. 932, C.A.
ss. 1, 4, see *Zarczynska* v. *Levy* [1979] 1 W.L.R. 125, E.A.T.; *Din (Ghulam)* v. *Carrington Viyella* [1982] I.C.R. 256, E.A.T.

Exhibit 113: A sample page from the *Current Law Statute Citator*, 1982 Supplement (Sweet & Maxwell, 1983).

"CURRENT LAW"
CASE CITATOR 1977-82

Note.—The "Current Law" Case Citator, Part I, contains in a single table:
- **(a) Cases reported during 1982 and digested herein.**
- **(b) Cases judicially considered in the English courts.**
- **(c) Cases overruled, etc., by Statute.**
- **(d) Cases the subject of articles in legal periodicals.**
- **(e) Additional references for cases digested 1947-76 which are cited in the Case Citator 1947-76.**

Figures appearing in black type indicate the main substantive paragraph.

A. (A MINOR), *Re* (1978) 8 Fam. Law 201, C.A. .... *Digested*, 78/**1988**
A. (A MINOR), *Re* (1979) 10 Fam. Law 49, C.A. .... *Digested*, 80/**1798**
A. (Minors), *Re* (1978) 8 Fam. Law 247, C.A. .... *Digested*, 79/**1785**
A. (Minors), *Re* (1979) 123 S.J. 553 .... *Digested*, 79/**1812**
A.W. and E.W. (Minors) (Wardship: Jurisdiction), *Re*. *See* W. (Minors) (Wardship: Jurisdiction), *Re*.
A. *v*. A. (Children: Arrangements) [1979] 1 W.L.R. 533; [1979] 2 All E.R. 493, C.A. .... *Digested*, 79/**1799**
A. *v*. C. (1978) 8 Fam. Law 170 .... *Digested*, 78/**1967**
A. *v*. C. [1982] R.P.C. 509 Lord Hooson Q.C. [1981] 2 W.L.R. 629; [1980] 2 All E.R. 347; *sub nom*. A. and B. *v*. C., D., E., F., G. and H. [1980] 2 Lloyd's Rep. 200; affirming [1982] 1 Lloyd's Rep. 166 .... *Digested*, 82/**2571**
A. *v*. C. [1981] 2 W.L.R. 654; [1981] 2 All E.R. 126; *sub nom*. A. and B. *v*. C., D., E., F., G. and H. (No. 2) [1981] Lloyd's Rep. 559; [1981] Com.L.C. 66 .... *Digested*, 81/**2161**
A. *v*. C. (Note) [1981] Q.B. 956 .... 82/**2503**
A. *v*. C. (Note) .... *Approved in part*, 81/2159
A. *v*. C. (No. 2) Note [1981] Q.B. 961 .... 82/**2508**
A. *v*. H.M. Treasury; B. *v*. H.M. Treasury [1979] 1 W.L.R. 1056; (1979) 123 S.J. 554; [1979] 2 All E.R. 586 .... *Digested*, 79/**2274**
A. *v*. Liverpool City Council [1981] 2 W.L.R. 948; (1981) 125 S.J. 396; [1981] 2 All E.R. 385; (1981) 79 L.G.R. 621, [1982] A.C. 363, H.L. ....*Digested*, 81/**1796**, *Applied*, 81/1763, 82/2085, 2055
A. (A Juvenile) *v*. Queen, The [1978] Crim.L.R. 689, Kent Crown Ct. .... *Digested*, 78/**444**
A.C. (A Minor) *v*. Hume. *See* C. (A Minor) *v*. Hume.
A. and B. *v*. C., D., E., F., G. and H. *See* A. *v*. C.
A. & M. Records Inc. *v*. Audio Magnetics Inc. (U.K.) [1979] F.S.R. 1, D.C. ... *Digested*, 79/**356**
A.B. Motor Co. of Hull *v*. Minister of Housing and Local Government [1969] .... *Referred to*, 78/2904
A.B.C. Coupler and Engineering Co. (No. 3), *Re* [1970] .... *Applied*, 78/304
A.B.C.'s Application. *See* Associated British Combustions' Application.
A.C.T. Construction Co. *v*. Customs and Excise Commissioners [1981] 1 W.L.R. 1542; (1981) 125 S.J. 864; [1982] 1 All E.R. 84; [1982] S.T.C. 25, H.L.; affirming [1981] 1 W.L.R. 49; (1980) 124 S.J. 777; [1981] 1 All E.R. 324; [1980] T.R. 357; [1980] S.T.C. 716, C.A.; affirming [1979] 1 W.L.R. 870; (1979) 123 S.J. 217; [1979] 2 All E.R. 691; [1979] S.T.C. 358 .... *Digested*, 82/**3345**; *Applied*, 82/3319
AEI Cables *v*. McLay [1980] I.R.L.R. 84, Ct. of Session .... *Digested*, 80/**1003**
AFZAL *v*. Rochdale Metropolitan Borough (Ref./108/1979) (1980) 254 E.G. 512, Lands Tribunal .... *Digested*, 80/**312**
AMP Inc. *v*. Utilux Proprietary [1972] .... *Applied*, 78/2254; *Considered and explained*, 78/2230
A.R.W. Transformers *v*. Cupples (1977) 12 I.T.R. 355; [1977] I.R.L.R. 288, E.A.T. .... *Digested*, 78/**941**
A/S Awilco of Oslo *v*. Fulvia S.p.A. di Navigazione of Cagliari; Chikuma, The [1981] 1 W.L.R. 314; (1981) 125 S.J. 184; [1981] 1 All E.R. 652; [1981] 1 Lloyd's Rep. 371; [1981] Com.L.R. 64, H.L. 64, H.L.; [1980] 2 Lloyd's rep. 409, C.A.; reversing [1979] 1 Lloyd's Rep. 367 .... *Digested*, 81/**2486**; *Applied*, 82/96

Exhibit 114: A sample page from the *Current Law Case Citator*, 1982 Supplement (Sweet & Maxwell, 1983).

In addition, the following sets also include more limited citators for cases:

(a) *The Digest: Annotated British, Commonwealth and European Cases*

(b) *Law Reports Consolidated Index*

(c) *Halsbury's Law of England*

Both the *Statute Citator* and the *Case Citator* are updated by the *Current Law Citator,* a cumulative annual supplement. The *Current Law Citator* also notes statutory instruments since 1947 which have been amended or revoked.

ADMINISTRATIVE LAW

English administrative regulations, known since 1948 as *statutory instruments,* are issued by governmental ministries or agencies as subordinate legislation under statutory authority. Some, issued by the Queen in Council, are known as *orders in council,* and may derive their authority from the Royal Prerogative, as well as from Parliament. Prior to 1948, statutory instruments were called *statutory rules and orders.*

The last official subject compilation of these regulations, now outdated, was *Statutory Rules and Orders and Statutory Instruments, Revised to December 31, 1948,* 3rd ed. (H.M.S.O., 1949–1952), 25 vols. It included permanent rules of general application, and included a general subject index, tables, and looseleaf supplementation. The compilation is updated by annual volumes called *Statutory Instruments,* which are still issued as the official form of publication, with a delay of at least a year and a half in publication.

The government still publishes two current finding tools: the official *Table of Governmental Orders* (an annual numerical list of all general rules, orders and statutory instruments currently in force) and the *Index to Government Orders* (a biennial subject index to rules, orders and instruments in force, with a supplement in alternate years).

The most useful research source for these materials, however, is the unofficial *Halsbury's Statutory Instruments* (Butterworth, 4th ed., 1978–date) 24 vols. Similar in arrangement to *Halsbury's Statutes of England,* it is updated by replacement volumes, as needed, and a one-volume looseleaf supplement. The set also includes a second looseleaf volume updating service containing several finding aids and an *Annual Cumulative Supplement and Quarterly Survey.* A general index, with pocket part supplements, affords subject access to the set.

English administrative decisions are published in forms similar to those used in this country. Some agencies and ministries issue official texts of their decisions and rulings; some commercially published looseleaf services in public law fields include administrative tribunal decisions and rulings; and topical reporters on some specialized subjects, like those described above in Chapter II, include administrative decisions, as well as those of the courts.

BIBLIOGRAPHIC AIDS

The following bibliographies and research guides are helpful for research in English law:

(a) *A Legal Bibliography of the British Commonwealth of Nations* (Sweet & Maxwell, 2d ed., 1955–1964, 7 vols.)

(b) *Guide to Law Reports and Statutes* (Sweet & Maxwell, 4th ed., 1963).

(c) *A Bibliographic Guide to the Law of the United Kingdom*, etc., edited by A.G. Chloros (Institute of Advanced Legal Studies, 2d ed., 1973).

(d) Beale, Joseph H. *Bibliography of Early English Law Books.* (Harvard University Press, 1926; Supplement, 1943).

(e) Maxwell, Wm. Harold. *A Complete List of British & Colonial Law Reports & Legal Periodicals* (Carswell, 3rd ed., 1937).

(f) Raistrick, D. and J. Rees. *Lawyers' Law Books: A Practical Index to Legal Literature* (Professional Books, 1977).

(g) Ringrose, C.W. *Where to Look for Your Law* (Sweet & Maxwell, 14th ed., 1962).

An introductory text on English legal research, J. Dane and P.A. Thomas, *How to Use a Law Library* (Sweet & Maxwell, 1983) offers a somewhat simplified guide to legal bibliography for that jurisdiction.

COMPUTER ACCESS TO ENGLISH LAW

Computerized legal research in England and the United Kingdom has had a somewhat slower development than in the United States. Now, however, there are active and expanding systems operating there. Both LEXIS and WESTLAW offer English legal data bases from those systems, and each also offers European Community legal sources.

The LEXIS data base includes current English statutes and statutory instruments, *All England Law Reports* from 1945 to date, *Weekly Law Reports* from 1953 to date, unreported decisions from 1980 to date, and a number of specialized topical reporters beginning at various dates between 1945 and 1979.

WESTLAW offers access to the EUROLEX data base, an English service with similar United Kingdom coverage, but also including the *Current Law* service and yearbooks from 1977.

CHAPTER XI

THE CIVIL LAW SYSTEM

INTRODUCTION TO THE CIVIL LAW SYSTEM

Having focused up to now on the legal materials of the common law system as exemplified by the United States and England, we turn now to bibliography and research procedures of the civil law system.

It should be noted at the outset that the term *civil law* is used in various contexts to designate very different concepts, some quite unrelated to the *civil law system.* In Roman law, *civil law* had several different meanings, which are still of interest to historians of that system. As the canon law of the Roman Catholic Church developed, *civil law* was used to refer to the secular law of the state, in distinction to ecclesiastical law, and that dichotomy is widely used today in many legal systems. In international law, *civil law* is used to describe the domestic law of individual states, as distinguished from the law of nations, called public international law. In *common law* countries, *civil law* refers to the law governing relations between persons and private entities, in distinction to *criminal law* and *administrative law* which involve state regulation of conduct. In *civil law* countries, *civil law* is also used to describe the law applicable to private citizens in their ordinary conduct, as differentiated from *commercial law* governing trade and other business activities. In both the common and civil law systems, *civil law* describes the body of civil and criminal rules, in distinction to the rules of *military law.* Finally, in comparative law and in *this* context, *civil law* refers to the tradition, stemming historically from Roman law and in modern times from the European codes, which characterizes the legal system of the countries of continental Western Europe, Latin America, and those parts of Africa and Asia which historically were not subject to English rule.

The publications of civil law, shaped largely by the primacy of its codes, differ considerably from those of the common law. The socialist countries of Eastern Europe are usually considered to be part of the civil law system, although they have incorporated into it significant conceptual and procedural changes. Many scholars now consider the law of socialist countries, such as the Soviet Union, China, and Cuba, to constitute a new and separate legal system. There are other countries which do not fit clearly into the civil law, common law, or socialist systems, but are strongly influenced by Roman law, customary law, or traditional religious systems, particularly Hindu or Moslem law. Their legal publications tend to differ most markedly from those in this country and are the least familiar to American lawyers.

Although the law of civil law countries has in the past not been an important part of the practice of the average American lawyer, and its sources rarely appear in most small law library collections, today civil law has become a more frequent concern of the legal profession. Expanded foreign communication, travel and trade have made it increasingly significant to life in this country and frequently relevant to legal proceedings in our courts. Business transactions between Americans and the citizens, companies and governments of civil law countries have given rise to many legal problems involving the law of other countries. More and more American attorneys are required to prove the law of a foreign country in American court proceedings and many American legal scholars are now using foreign law as a basis for comparing and analyzing our own system. Foreign law sources are essential to the growing study of comparative law, by which the differences and similarities of law in different countries and systems are analyzed.

As described above in Chapter X, English Law, the differences between the common law and civil law systems have become less marked in recent years. We can note, however, the following distinctive characteristics of the law in most *civil law* countries: the predominance of generalized codes governing large fields of law (civil, criminal, commercial, civil procedure, criminal procedure, etc.); the strong influence of concepts, terms and principles from Roman law; a diminished weight for judicial decisions as legal authority; and great influence by legal scholars in interpreting, criticizing and developing the law in their writings, particularly through commentaries on the codes.

THE LANGUAGE PROBLEM

Bibliographic guides and general introductions are available in English for the law of many civil law countries, but their legal literature remains an impenetrable mystery to most American legal researchers. Part of the bibliographic problem in dealing with the civil law system stems of course from differences in language. Foreign legal dictionaries exist for many languages and they are collected in the major law libraries, but it is impossible to comprehend the law of an unfamiliar country in an unfamiliar language with only the aid of a legal dictionary.

Translations and summaries of foreign law in English may be quite helpful, but research in translated texts of legal materials is no substitute for study of the original documents. Where a lack of facility with the original language precludes the consultation of primary sources, recourse to practitioners trained in the foreign legal system will be necessary to adequately handle the interests of a client faced with a problem involving foreign law. Linguistic knowledge does not assure legal understanding and a consultant or specialist in the relevant foreign law may be desirable in any event. The use of translations can, however, provide some familiarity with the basic concepts and issues of the foreign law problem and improve the quality of discourse with the consultant or foreign law specialist.

CIVIL LAW TOOLS IN ENGLISH

Research in English language materials on civil law should begin with the many bibliographic guides which are available for references to specific publications on the country and subject involved. These generally cover both primary and secondary materials. The use of encyclopedias and treatises is also helpful for background analysis of the legal system and subjects being studied. Then research in English translations and summaries of law can be undertaken. Periodical articles can provide discussion of specific problems, comparative analysis, or leads to other sources.

1. Bibliographic Guides. Some guides consist of general legal bibliographies providing coverage of all subjects and jurisdictions. Others are specialized bibliographic surveys of the law of a particular region or country, or of a particular subject.

(a) **General bibliographic guides.**

(1) *Law Books Recommended for Libraries* (Fred B. Rothman & Co., 1967–1970, 6 vols.) and its *Supplements* (Rothman, 1974–75). Published under the auspices of the Association of American Law Schools, this looseleaf compilation of bibliographies on a wide variety of legal subjects combines the attributes of both general and specialized guides. Volume 5 is devoted entirely to the subject of foreign law while sections in other volumes of the set are devoted to the law of specific areas and systems, such as African, Chinese, Islamic, Latin American, Roman, and Russian-Soviet legal systems.

(2) Szladits, Charles. *A Bibliography on Foreign and Comparative Law. Books and Articles in English* (Oceana, 1955–1983). This excellent tool consists of ten volumes, supplemented by periodic cumulations and updated regularly in the *American Journal of Comparative Law.*

(3) Buckwalter, Robert. *Law Books in Print* (Glanville Publishers, Inc., 4th ed., 1982, 5 vols.), updated periodically by *Law Books Published* (Glanville). This bibliography of legal works in English is arranged by author/title, subject, and publishers, and includes some foreign and comparative publications.

(4) UNESCO, *Register of Legal Documentation in the World* (2d ed., 1957). This is a country-by-country survey of the important legal sources throughout the world. Although out of date, it is still useful for those countries not covered by the *International Encyclopedia of Comparative Law* (see below).

The *International Encyclopedia of Comparative Law,* described below, contains topical bibliographies for each country in its "National Reports" section, as well as general outlines of the sources of law for those countries.

(b) Specialized guides.

As noted earlier, bibliographic guides exist for specific regions, countries, and subjects. The scope of this publication does not permit a comprehensive listing of such guides. For such a list, one may consult Chapter 20, Foreign and Comparative Law, in *How to Find the Law* (West, 8th ed., 1983). A few examples for Western Europe include: *Bibliography of Translations of Codes and Other Laws of Private Law* (Council of Europe, 1975); P. Graulich, et al., *Guide to Foreign Legal Materials: Belgium, Luxembourg, Netherlands* (Oceana, 1968); and C.

Szladits, *Guide to Foreign Legal Materials: French, German, Swiss* (Oceana, 1959).

2. **Encyclopedias and Treatises.** The most extensive survey in English of the law of various nations is the *International Encyclopedia of Comparative Law* (J.C.B. Mohr, 1971–date). This comprehensive work, still in progress, is providing background material on the legal systems of many countries and detailed information and bibliographies on specific legal topics, such as contracts, torts, and civil procedure.

A more concise overview of the civil law system can be found in general treatises such as Rene David and J. Brierley, *Major Legal Systems in the World Today* (Free Press, 2d ed., 1978); John H. Merryman, *The Civil Law Tradition* (Stanford Univ. Press, 1969); and Alan Watson, *The Making of Civil Law* (Harvard Univ. Press, 1981). Some casebooks useful as introductions to foreign law are Henry DeVries, *Civil Law and the Anglo-American Lawyer* (Oceana, 1976), Rudolf Schlesinger, *Comparative Law* (Foundation Press, 4th ed., 1980) and Arthur von Mehren, *Civil Law System* (Little, Brown, 2d ed., 1977).

3. **Translations and Summaries of Foreign Law.** The growing literature on foreign law includes many translations of actual laws, as well as discussions of law on different subjects for various foreign countries. For the simplest information, English summaries of the major areas of law of many countries appear annually in the last volume *(Law Digests)* of the *Martindale-Hubbell Law Directory,* arranged first by country and then by subject.

Several commercially published series for foreign laws in translation are also available, prominent among which are *Digest of Commercial Laws of the World*, sponsored by the National Association of Credit Management (Oceana, 1966–date), eight volumes, looseleaf; *American Series of Foreign Penal Codes*, compiled by the Comparative Criminal Law Project of the New York University School of Law (Fred B. Rothman & Co., various dates); and a series of looseleaf volumes published by the Foreign Tax Law Association on the commercial and tax laws of many countries.

Similar publications have also been issued by official bodies, such as the Organization of American States (*A Statement of the Laws of . . . in Matters Affecting Business*, covering various Latin American countries) and the U.S. Bureau of Labor Statistics (*Labor Law and Practice in . . .*, covering countries throughout the world).

In addition, several American accounting firms publish series of brief guides to foreign tax and commercial law in English (e.g., Price, Waterhouse & Co., Arthur Andersen & Co., Ernst & Whinney, and Peat, Marwick, Mitchell & Co.). These are available from the issuing firm, sometimes on a complimentary basis.

A useful compilation of the constitutions of the countries of the world is A.J. Peaslee, *Constitutions of Nations* (Martinus Nijhoff, vol. 1, 4th ed., 1974; vols. 2–4, 3rd ed., 1965–1970). A later compilation is *Constitutions of the Countries of the World* edited by Albert Blaustein and G.H. Flanz (Oceana, 1971–

date, 14 vols. projected, looseleaf). A supplementary series edited by Albert Blaustein and Eric Blaustein is *Constitutions of Dependencies and Special Sovereignties* (Oceana, 1975–date, 4 vols., looseleaf); for communist countries, there is *The Constitutions of the Communist World,* edited by W.B. Simons (Oceana, 1980).

4. Periodical Guides. For periodical literature on foreign law, the following aids are helpful:

(a) Periodical indexes such as the *Index to Foreign Legal Periodicals, Index to Legal Periodicals, Current Law Index,* and *Legal Resource Index,* all of which are discussed above in Chapter IX.

(b) Szladits, Charles. *A Bibliography on Foreign and Comparative Law,* described above, also indexes periodical articles.

(c) Blaustein, Albert. *Manual on Foreign Legal Periodicals and their Index* (Oceana, 1962) contains a list of important foreign legal periodicals, providing for each the country of origin, the language in which it is written, and the subjects which it includes.

CIVIL LAW IN ORIGINAL SOURCES

1. Basic Legal Sources

(a) **Codes.** Each country in the civil law system has separately published codes, as described above. These include the basic general codes (civil, criminal, commercial, civil procedure and criminal procedure) and several minor codes which are really statutory compilations on other specific subjects (e.g., taxation, labor law, family law, etc.). The codes are usually published in a simple unadorned text, in frequent editions, and also in larger editions with scholarly commentary, annotations and other aids. There is, however, no legal distinction between a code and other legislation, and the codes are amended or repealed by ordinary statutes.

(b) **Collections of Laws.** Laws, decrees and administrative orders are typically published in comprehensive official gazettes, often appearing daily. In some countries, cumulative indexing is unfortunately infrequent. As a result, research is often carried on in periodicals which contain legislative sections, or in looseleaf services, where indexing is more effective.

(c) **Collections of Decisions.** Since there are far fewer reported judicial decisions in civil law countries, there are fewer reporters of such decisions. Both official and commercial series do exist, however, for many countries. The commercial editions are often part of larger periodical or looseleaf services, which may also include statutes, decrees, regulations, and helpful commentary.

2. Secondary Materials. As noted above, legal commentaries and treatises may have considerable weight as persuasive authority under the civil law system. The range of text material, however, as in common law countries, is quite broad, in both subject and quality. There are comprehensive scholarly treatises, highly specialized monographs on narrow topics, pragmatic manuals and guides for the practitioner, and simplified texts for students and popular use. For those with the necessary language skills, these works can offer considerable help in legal research. Information about the foreign language literature available on specific topics can be found in legal bibliographies and guides published for particular countries (e.g., Szladits' *Guide to Foreign Legal Materials: French, German, Swiss,* cited above). The introductory *National Reports* volumes of the *International Encyclopedia of Comparative Law,* as noted above, contain not only sections on "Sources of Law," but also on "Selective Bibliography," which include major treatises for many individual countries.

The literature of foreign periodicals is equally varied and frequently helpful for the treatment of specific legal problems. In addition to such English language journals as the *American Journal of Comparative Law* and the *International and Comparative Law Quarterly,* which specialize in foreign and comparative law, there are numerous journals in both English and foreign languages dealing with the law of particular civil law countries and regions. The *International Journal of Legal Information* (formerly the *International Journal of Law Libraries*) provides excellent bibliographic coverage of foreign and comparative law, as well as international law. Most of the civil law periodical literature is of course in foreign languages. In the major civil law countries, many legal periodicals focus on specific subjects, in addition to those offering general coverage. Access to foreign language periodical articles is primarily available through the *Index to Foreign Legal Periodicals* (cited above), which also covers *festschriften* and other collections of essays.

Foreign legal encyclopedias, particularly in France (*e.g.*, Dalloz *Nouveau Repertoire de droit*) are generally of much higher quality and reputation than those in this country. Although they are still basically guides to authority, their articles are written by leading experts and are usually very reliable.

3. **Research Steps.** Since the best research approach to a specific legal problem will vary from country to country, depending on the subject under consideration and the published sources available for that jurisdiction, it is impossible to offer one effective model procedure.

Background reading in an encyclopedia or looseleaf service, if available, is always helpful, both for its introductory value and as a lead to further sources. Failing that, a treatise or relevant periodical articles may serve the same purpose. The leading general French periodicals, e.g., *Recueil Dalloz Sirey* and *La Semaine Juridique*, and the French looseleaf services of the *Juris-Classeurs* system are particularly useful in offering legislative texts and judicial decisions, along with their scholarly articles.

Inevitably, however, the researcher must consult the relevant code (preferably in an edition with good commentary) or other statutes, and then refer to administrative decrees or orders which may have been promulgated on the particular problem. Judicial and administrative decisions interpreting the legislative norms must also be studied. In the absence of citators, the current authority of decisions can be determined through digests or indexes to collections of decisions, if available, or from references in recent treatises and articles.

It should be emphasized, however, that the above procedure will not apply to every civil law country. In many countries, research will begin with the code itself, but almost never, as in the United States, with a review of judicial decisions.

4. Research Aids. Citation forms for foreign legal materials can be very confusing for American lawyers. Fortunately, the *Uniform System of Citation* (the now familiar *bluebook*) includes in its latest edition citation information for ten major civil law countries and for the basic Roman law sources. Its coverage is quite limited, but still helpful.

The extensive use of abbreviations adds another difficulty to foreign law research. The following guides in English, compiled by A. Sprudsz and published by Oceana Publications, can be consulted: *Benelux Abbreviations and Symbols: Law and Related Subjects* (1971); *Foreign Law Abbreviations: French* (1967); and *Italian Abbreviations and Symbols: Law and Related Subjects* (1969). Also for France, one can use *Abbreviations, Guide to French Forms in Justice and Administration*, 2d ed., by G. Leistner (1975). For Germany, only a guide in German is available: H. Kirchner, *Abkuerzungsverzeichnis der Rechtssprache* (2d ed., 1968).

CIVIL LAW IN AMERICA

For study of a civil law jurisdiction closer to home, the state of Louisiana provides an excellent example. Its legal system was based on French law and codes, and it is still a civil law jurisdiction, although common law influences have been increasing. The early legal histories of California, Florida and Texas also had largely civil law origins—from Spain and Mexico in California and Texas, and from France and Spain in Florida. The Canadian province of Quebec remains a civil law jurisdiction, with primarily French influence.

COMPUTER ACCESS TO CIVIL LAW

WESTLAW makes available to its subscribers (at additional cost) access to the EUROLEX data base, produced by the European Law Centre in London. All documents in EUROLEX are in English. In addition to European Communities and other international materials (see Chapter XII, International Law), EUROLEX contains full-text decisions from European *national* courts in commercial cases (from 1978), and summaries of decisions in other subject areas (from 1973).

LEXIS offers its subscribers at no extra cost the full texts of French legal material, in French. Included are judicial opinions (for some courts, as far back as 1958), as well as statutes and regulations (with the *Journal Official* available from 1955).

Legal data bases are appearing with increasing frequency within Europe, providing access to such sources as decisions of the Italian Constitutional Court and abstracts of articles in Belgian legal periodicals. A listing of these files is contained on pp. 114–125 of a directory published by the Commission of the European Communities: *Data Bases in Europe 1982* (Brussels, 1982). These data bases, however, are not yet available on-line in the United States.

CHAPTER XII

INTERNATIONAL LAW

INTRODUCTION

Although this is primarily a manual of *American* legal bibliography, in addition to the discussions of *English Law* and the *Civil Law System* in Chapters X and XI, some mention must also be made of the main sources of *International Law.* As noted above in Chapter VIII, *U.S. Treaties,* the Constitution (Art. VI, Sec. 2) states that treaties are, like federal statutes, the supreme law of the land. Over the last few decades, other forms of international law have had a growing effect on day-to-day legal activities. The effective researcher today must know and be able to use the basic materials of international law. The subject deserves fuller coverage than can be given in this brief outline, but the research aids and procedures described here should be of considerable help in starting to find the law.

International law, in the traditional sense, is the law governing relations between nations. It is to be distinguished from foreign law, which refers to the domestic law of nations other than our own. Simply stated, international law deals with the external relations of nations, while foreign law refers to the internal law governing matters *within* a particular country. There is a further significant distinction in this field between *public* international law and *private* international law. The latter (in this country frequently called "conflict of laws") determines where, and by whose law, controversies involving the law of more than one jurisdiction are to be resolved, and how foreign judgments are to be enforced.

Public international law, on the other hand, traditionally only allows *states* as actors. This theoretical difference has been blurred over the last few years, in that states have entered into treaties which recognize an individual's right of action in an international forum, and in those areas where states have been full participants in traditionally private commercial enterprises. International law, for the purpose of this chapter, can be viewed as those rules, procedures and customs which regulate national states in their relations with each other.

The classic statement of the *sources* of international law is found in Article 38 the *Statute* of the International Court of Justice. The court is to apply the following sources:

"a. international *conventions,* whether general or particular, establishing rules expressly recognized by . . . states.

"b. international *custom,* as evidence of a general practice accepted as law.

"c. general *principles* of law recognized by civilized nations.

"d. . . . *judicial decisions* and *teachings* of the most highly qualified publicists of the various nations . . . " (Italics added)

It is important to remember that the judicial decisions referred to in section "d" above mean the decisions of both international tribunals and domestic courts on international law questions. "Publicists" are international law scholars and teachers.

The published forms of most of these sources can be found within the broad bibliographic categories already discussed. Treatises, periodicals, casebooks, encyclopedias, looseleaf services, treaty compilations, and digests are available for basic research in international law. The specialized literature of international organizations requires special attention, however.

RESEARCH STEPS IN INTERNATIONAL LAW

A researcher facing a problem in international law can begin in any one of a variety of sources. If the problem deals with a particular area (e.g., an international organization's activities, a treaty, foreign relations of a particular country, etc.), one can proceed directly to the relevant documentation in that field. For a general problem, without immediate references to specifically identifiable sources, recourse to the following material is suggested:

1. **Reference Works.** To obtain an overview of an area of international law, one can consult a general treatise, such as M. Akehurst's *A Modern Introduction to International Law* (Allen and Unwin, 4th ed., 1982) or I. Brownlie's *Principles of Public International Law* (Oxford Univ. Press, 3rd ed., 1979). Certain classics are still quite valuable: the elegant *The Law of Nations* by J.L. Brierly (Oxford Univ. Press, 6th ed., 1963) and *International Law*, originally by L. Oppenheim, later editions edited by H. Lauterpacht (Longmans, Green, 7th and 8th ed., 1955). Finally,

there is a new *Encyclopedia of Public International Law* (North-Holland, 1981–), edited by Rudolf Bernhardt and published under the auspices of the Max Planck Institute at Heidelberg. Although produced in West Germany, it is published in English and admirably fills a long felt need for such a comprehensive work. Six of a projected twelve volumes have been published so far. Each article is written by an expert in the field, and although the entries are rather short, they are informative, and are invariably followed by a brief bibliography for further research.

2. **The Restatement of Foreign Relations.** Since the *Digest of United States Practice in International Law* has been so slow in publishing the last few years, the American Law Institute's *Restatement of Foreign Relations, 2d* (West Publishing Company, 1965) has become the best source of U.S. international law practice. The third revision is in draft form at the moment, and is the subject of considerable debate among practitioners and scholars. As a research tool, however, the reporter's notes in all the editions are good guides to U.S. attitudes as expressed through treaties, statutes, and cases.

3. **Treaties.** When they apply to a particular problem, treaties are the preeminent expression of international law. Discussion of treaty sources and guides are found in Chapter VIII, above, and they will not be treated here.

4. **Yearbooks.** Yearbooks are of two kinds: the annual reviews of a nation's practice in international law (often combined with a selection of articles on current topics), and the annual statements of the activ-

ities of particular bodies, such as international organizations or learned associations. The first type of yearbook is especially useful when the practice of a foreign government on some international law question must be found. Some countries with publications of this type are Great Britain, France, West Germany, Japan, Canada, the U.S.S.R., and Australia. Yearbooks of the second type are the main tools for preliminary research in international organizations. These include the yearbooks described below at pages 361–362.

5. International Organizations. Because of the increasingly active role of international organizations in promulgating and administering international law, documents issued by these bodies are frequently important both as sources in their own right and as material illuminating other sources. An introduction to their literature is provided in *The World Bibliography of International Documentation* by T.D. Dimitrov, 2 volumes, (Unifo, 1981). A more complete list of bibliographic guides is set forth on pages 362–371, below.

6. International Adjudications and Arbitrations. Adjudications and arbitrations by some international bodies are recognized as authoritative in interpreting international law and resolving international disputes, although they sometimes lack effective enforcement procedures. The published opinions of such tribunals (particularly those of the International Court of Justice) may be relevant in treaty interpretation, and in defining the customary and general law of nations. Information on the publications of the I.C.J. and other international and regional organization tribunals can be found on pages 373–378, below. Sources for the decisions of international arbitrations are also summarized below.

7. **Municipal or Domestic Law.** This body of internal national law dealing with international law problems is part statutory and part judicial in nature. It can be found in the usual published sources for each country, as well as in special compilations. Often the fastest source for the more important material of this kind is *International Legal Materials* (American Society of International Law, 1962–date). Decisions and excerpts of decisions from courts all over the world are collected in the *International Law Reports,* the present title of a continuing series begun in 1919 and edited by E. Lauterpacht (Grotius Publ.). Deak, *American International Law Cases 1783–1968* (see page 293 above) collects American decisions. Similar series are available for Great Britain, West Germany, the Commonwealth, and other countries.

8. **Foreign Relations Law.** Individual countries publish documents of their foreign relations, along with digests and annuals of their international practice. These are useful in revealing both official policies of a general nature and specific handling of particular problems. *Foreign Relations of the United States,* as the series is now called (1861–date), is an example of such a collection. Many nations publish such series, and separate collections of documents relating to specific topics or periods also exist. Most can be found through the bibliographies listed below.

9. Secondary Materials. Many specialized treatises and periodical articles by scholars can provide further research leads and help in understanding the background, current state and future direction of law in this field. Bibliographies and periodical indexes for locating these sources are indicated below.

REFERENCE BIBLIOGRAPHIES

A complete survey of reference sources in international law is beyond the scope and purpose of this *Nutshell.* In addition to the other references in this chapter which contain bibliographies, the researcher is directed to the following bibliographies for references to particular problems under consideration. Unfortunately, most of these bibliographies are not updated, and hence are primarily useful for retrospective searches.

1. Retrospective Bibliographies

a. I. Delupis, *Bibliography of International Law* (Bowker, 1975).

b. S. Kleckner and B. Kudej, *Public International Law and International Organizations* (Oceana, 1984), one of a series of looseleaf bibliographies issued under the general title: *A Collection of Bibliographic and Research Resources.*

c. J.G. Merrills, *Current Bibliography of International Law* (Butterworths, 1978).

d. G. Schwarzenberger, *Manual of International Law* (Stevens, 6th ed., 1976), contains an extensive bibliography of books and periodical articles.

e. Harvard Law School Library, *Catalog of International Law and Relations,* in 20 volumes, (1965–1967). This is being supplanted by the new microfiche edition of *all* the Harvard Law School Library catalogues to be published by K.G. Saur during 1984–1985. The International Law catalogue will be the first segment distributed, and can be considered the most comprehensive historical bibliography in this field.

f. G.W. Baer, *International Organizations, 1918–1945: A Guide to Research and Research Materials* (Scholarly Resources, Inc., 1981).

g. 15 *Journal of International Law and Economics* 1–321 (1981). This entire issue is devoted to research tools in international law.

2. Current Bibliographies. A variety of bibliographies published on a current and continuing basis are available in the field of international law. These can be employed effectively to supplement the retrospective bibliographies cited above and provide subject access to current monographs and/or articles.

a. *American Journal of International Law* (quarterly). The bibliographic section of each issue is an invaluable source of information on current publications.

b. *Public International Law* (semiannually). Since starting in 1976, this index produced by the Max Planck Institute in Heidelberg has been the most comprehensive on the subject.

c. *Current Bibliographical Information* (U.N., monthly). This is the current acquisitions list of the Dag Hammarskjold Library of the United Nations, interfiled with an index of current articles. It is, as may be expected, especially strong for international organizational material. It is also useful for access to non-Western materials, especially from the U.S.S.R., the Arab states, and the Third World.

d. *International Journal of Legal Information* (quarterly). This is the journal of the International Association of Law Libraries. A recent shift in editorial policy has made this an extremely useful compilation of reviews and bibliographic lists. The material covered is primarily international and comparative law. The articles are usually bibliographic in nature.

e. R. Buckwalter, *Law Books in Print*, 5 vols. (Glanville, 4th ed., 1982–1983). Includes references to international law books in English by author, title, and subject. Updated by *Law Books Published* (quarterly).

f. Periodical indexes, such as the *Index to Legal Periodicals*, the *Index to Foreign Legal Periodicals*, and the *Current Legal Index*, all include articles in the leading international law journals.

g. *International Organization* (quarterly). Each issue of this periodical contains a useful bibliography on international organizations.

h. A new quarterly publication of the West Publishing Company called *West International Law Bulletin* includes short articles, legal news notes, brief book reviews, and bibliographies, all in the fields of foreign, comparative and international law. Its irregular publication frequency since inception make its future viability uncertain.

INTERNATIONAL ORGANIZATIONS

International organizations play an increasingly important role in the creation and enforcement of international law. The organizations may be world-wide, like the United Nations; they may be regional, like the European Communities or the Organization of American States; or they may be subject specific, like the International Maritime Organization or the Organization of Petroleum Exporting Countries. In most cases, the organizations act as forums for international politics and negotiations, and as rulemaking and enforcing bodies in international law. The ability to do research with their documents and in the general literature has become crucial for the student of international law.

There are several useful basic references on international organizations generally. These include D.W. Bowett, *The Law of International Institutions* (Stevens, 4th ed., 1982), H.G. Schermers, *International Institutional Law,* (Sijthoff, rev.ed., 1980), and Volume 5 of *The Encyclopedia of Public International Law,* (1983), described above. The organic documents of most of the important international organizations are gathered in *International Organization and Integration: Annotated Basic Documents and Descriptive Directory of International Organizations and Arrangements,* edited by P.J.G. Kapteyn et al.

(Nijhoff, 2nd rev.ed., 1981–date). Four of a projected six volumes have so far been published. A recent text which attempts to describe the work and range of a variety of international organizations through parallel analyses is *International Organizations, a Comparative Approach* by Feld, Jordan, and Hurwitz (Praeger, 1983).

In beginning work on a current problem dealing with an international organization or its activities, it is often desirable to begin with the yearbook of that organization, particularly if the primary documents of the organization are not easily accessible. These yearbooks review the activities of the organization during the preceding year and frequently provide general directory information. The existence of a relevant yearbook can be ascertained from the *Yearbook of International Organizations,* which provides data on most international organizations. If a yearbook has been located, its index will provide access to pertinent information. These volumes also have a permanent reference value, since research can be carried out retrospectively in their review sections, and citations to primary sources and documents can be found in them. Among the most useful are the following:

(a) *Yearbook of International Organizations,* (Brussels, Union of International Associations, 1951 to date, published every two years in English, now distributed by K.G. Saur). The 1983–1984 issue is in three large volumes.

(b) *Yearbook of the United Nations* (United Nations, 1946–47 to date). This is the best starting point for any retrospective research on the activities of the United Nations and its affiliated organizations. It is arranged by organization, and then by subject. After each entry there is a short bibliography of the important documents relevant to that entry. A selection of key documents is reprinted in full, including the resolutions of the appropriate bodies. Since the indexing of U.N. materials prior to 1979 is quite complicated, this is an essential tool. The index for each volume is quite complete and easy to use.

(c) *Yearbook on Human Rights* (United Nations, 1946 to date).

(d) *Yearbook of the European Convention on Human Rights* (Nijhoff, for the European Commission and European Court of Human Rights, 1959, covering 1955, to date).

(e) *Yearbook of the International Court of Justice* (1946–7 to date).

(f) *United Nations Juridical Yearbook* (United Nations, 1965 to date).

(g) *Yearbook of the International Law Commission* (United Nations, 1949 to date).

(h) *European Yearbook (Annuaire Europeen)*— published under the auspices of the Council of Europe annually at the Hague, 1955 to date, with coverage of several European organizations.

1. Bibliographic Guides to the United Nations. The publications of the United Nations are probably the most important materials in the field of international organizations. The distribution and indexing of this material is very complex, but through the years a relatively clear documentation system has developed. Basically the United Nations has two different distribution systems, a documents system and a sales system. Virtually everything offered as a sales item was issued earlier as a document, so almost every sales item also has a document number. Therefore, a single item will often have two identification numbers.

When a document is generated at the United Nations, it is immediately assigned an individual identification number. This number indicates the provenance of the document, i.e., which body, commission, subcommittee or working party produced the item, and at what point in the life of that body the item was produced. For example, a document labeled A/CN.2/AC.1/PV.26 would be interpreted as:

A	=	General Assembly
CN.2	=	Commission # 2
AC.1	=	Ad Hoc Committee # 1
PV.26	=	*Proces-verbaux* # 26

Thus the item is a transcript (*Proces-verbaux*) of the 26th meeting of the first ad hoc committee of the second commission of the General Assembly.

This numbering system is described in full in a U.N. pamphlet, *United Nations Documentation* (ST/LIB/34/Rev. 1). Another useful guide, available from the U.N., is its *List of United Nations Documents Series Symbols.*

The indexing of this material, unfortunately, has not been as simple. The United Nations, has successively used several different indexing systems, and happily the current one, UNDOC, in use since 1979, is by far the best. UNDOC is issued as a monthly publication, with annual cumulations. Its predecessors were UNDEX and the *United Nations Documents Index.* The UNDOC indexing system includes separate subject, author, and title indexes, all of high quality and simple to use. Each issue of UNDOC also contains a "Checklist of Documents and Publications", which is extremely informative, with a full descriptive entry for each document and a summary of its contents. Exhibit 115 illustrates sample document entries in UNDOC and Exhibit 116 show typical index entries.

There are two categories of U.N. publications which are not sent to the depository libraries: "L." suffix items are for limited distribution, although they often turn up reprinted in later documents; and "R." suffix items are restricted for security reasons. UNDOC also includes that distribution information.

After the closing of each session of the various organs of the United Nations, a set of *Official Records* is distributed. These are on higher quality paper than the initial distribution, and have been reviewed by the participants (this review can be quite slow: the transcripts of several debates in the Security Council and the General Assembly from October 1980 were never distributed, and have yet to be published as *Official Records*). Since the General Assembly is the paramount body of the United Nations, its *Official Records* are most important. All of the annual reports of the other organs of the U.N. are printed in this form, except the "Technical Agencies"—the affiliated organizations devoted to specific subject areas, such as the International Civil Aviation Organization or the International Monetary Fund.

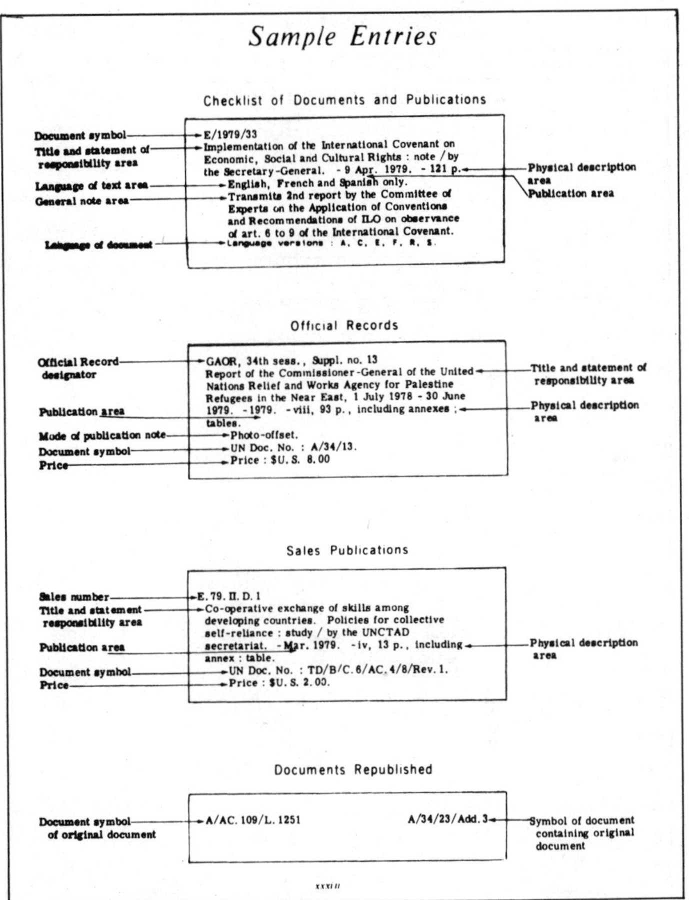

Sample Entries

Checklist of Documents and Publications

Document symbol — E/1979/33
Title and statement of responsibility area — Implementation of the International Covenant on Economic, Social and Cultural Rights : note / by the Secretary-General. - 9 Apr. 1979. - 121 p. — Physical description area; Publication area
Language of text area — English, French and Spanish only.
General note area — Transmits 2nd report by the Committee of Experts on the Application of Conventions and Recommendations of ILO on observance of art. 6 to 9 of the International Covenant.
Language of document — Language versions : A, C, E, F, R, S.

Official Records

Official Record designator — GAOR, 34th sess., Suppl. no. 13
Report of the Commissioner-General of the United Nations Relief and Works Agency for Palestine Refugees in the Near East, 1 July 1978 - 30 June 1979. - 1979. - viii, 93 p., including annexes ; tables. — Title and statement of responsibility area; Publication area; Physical description area
Mode of publication note — Photo-offset.
Document symbol — UN Doc. No. : A/34/13.
Price — Price : $U.S. 8.00

Sales Publications

Sales number — E.79.II.D.1
Title and statement responsibility area — Co-operative exchange of skills among developing countries. Policies for collective self-reliance : study / by the UNCTAD secretariat. - Mar. 1979. - iv, 13 p., including annex : table. — Publication area; Physical description area
Document symbol — UN Doc. No. : TD/B/C.6/AC.4/8/Rev.1.
Price — Price : $U.S. 2.00.

Documents Republished

Document symbol of original document — A/AC.109/L.1251
A/34/23/Add.3 — Symbol of document containing original document

xxxiii

Exhibit 115: Sample entries of documents in UNDOC.

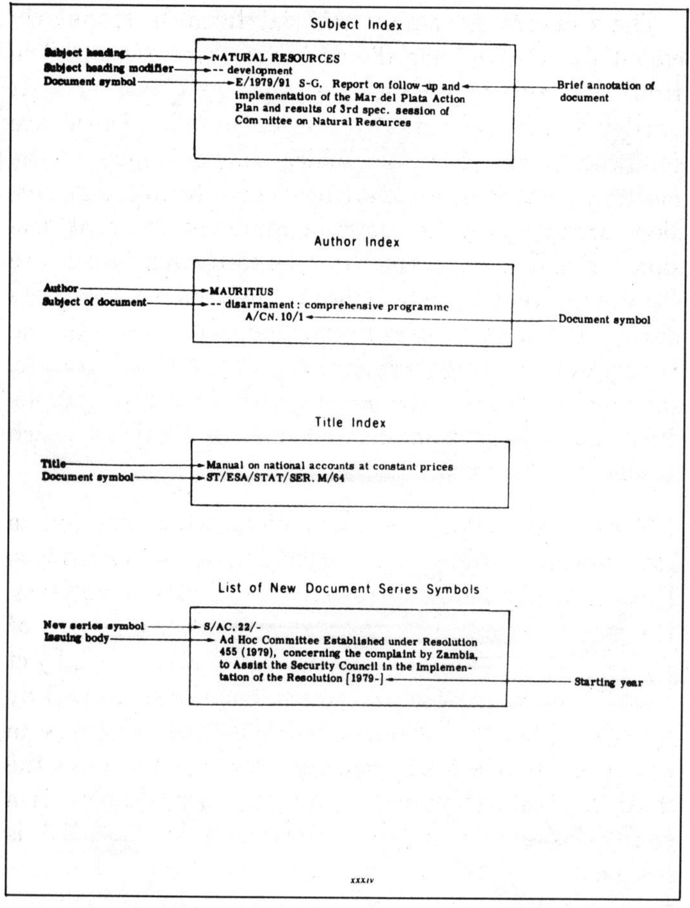

Exhibit 116: Sample entries in the various UNDOC indexes.

The General Assembly Official Records (popularly called the GAOR) are divided into three parts. The first is a record of the meetings held during that particular session, usually one each fall. These are followed by the *Annexes,* which contain copies of the more important documents produced during that session, arranged by the agenda numbers for that session. Finally, there are the *Supplements,* which are the annual reports submitted to the General Assembly during the session—from the Secretary-General, the Security Council, the International Court of Justice, the various budget committees, etc. The final supplement each year compiles all the resolutions which passed the General Assembly that session.

Those United Nations publications which are felt to have general interest are also available as sales items. These are numbered differently from the documents. The numbers are less informative as to the source of the product, but give a better indication of subject matter. Each number has four elements separated by periods. The first element indicates the language in which the item is published, the second is the year, the third is a subject indicator, and the last element is a yearly issuance number. For example, E.82.V.3 is read as:

E = English

82 = 1982

V = International Law

3 = Third item issued in 1982 under International Law

There are 17 broad subject categories represented by Roman numerals in the third element.

The fastest access to the older sales items is through *The Complete Reference Guide to U.N. Sales Publications, 1946–1978,* by M.E. Birchfield and J. Coolman, 2 vols. (Unifo, 1981). The sales section also distributes a pamphlet each year, *Catalog of U.N. Publications,* which acts as a current guide to publications.

Several other bibliographic tools are helpful for research into the earlier activities of the United Nations. These include *Checklists of United Nations Documents, 1946–49,* for the period before the development of the index: B. Brimmer, et al., *A Guide to the Use of United Nations Documents* (Oceana, 1962); and H. Winton, *Publications of the United Nations Systems* (Bowker, 1972). The Dimitrov book, *The World Bibliography of International Documentation,* mentioned earlier, is also useful for U.N. documents.

2. Special Indexes to U.N. Bodies. In many instances, indexes to the publications of specific U.N. bodies are more effective finding tools than UNDOC. Examples of such specialized indexes are the *Index to Resolutions of the General Assembly 1946–1970* (1972) and the *Index to Resolutions of the Security Council 1946–1970* (1972). Resolutions of the General Assembly and other major bodies of the U.N. are published separately as supplementary volumes to the Official Records for each session. These cumulative indexes provide convenient subject access to what are some of the most heavily used U.N. documents. A commercial reprint series of these resolutions has been issued in four subdivisions (one each for the General Assembly, the Security Council, the Economic and Social Council, and the Trusteeship Council), called *United Nations Resolutions*, edited by D.J. Djonovich (Oceana, 1973 to date), with cumulative indexes in each volume.

It must be noted that the UNDOC index does not index the subsidiary bodies of the U.N., nor does it cover the "Technical Agencies". Each of these has its own index, but none are of the quality of the United Nations tools. Some of the better systems are those of the International Labour Organization, with its *International Labour Documentation*, and UNESCO, with its *General Catalogue*. A recent publication, P.I. Hajnal's *Guide to UNESCO* (Oceana, 1983), should also prove useful for that agency.

3. Bibliographic Guides to the League of Nations. Preceding the United Nations, the League of Nations had a similar literary output and bibliographic organization. The most useful tools explaining its documentary materials are:

(a) H. Aufricht, *Guide to League of Nations Publications* (Columbia University Press, 1951; reprinted by AMS Press, 1966).

(b) A.C. Breycha-Vauthier, *Sources of Information: A Handbook on Publications of the League of Nations* (Columbia University Press, 1939).

(c) E.A. Reno, Jr., ed., *League of Nations Documents 1919–1946*, 3 vols. (Research Publications, 1973–1975).

(d) G.W. Baer, *International Organizations, 1918–1945: A Guide to Research and Research Materials* (Scholarly Resources, Inc., 1981).

4. Regional Organizations. There are a growing number of international organizations established on a regional basis. Their objectives are often based in part on those of the United Nations, and some have also patterned their organizational arrangements on selective elements of the United Nations structure. The existence of these organizations is recognized by Article 71 of the United Nations Charter. Two helpful guides to regional organizations generally are R.C. Lawson, *International Regional Organizations* (Praeger, 1962) and *Regional International Organizations and the United Nations* (U.N. Institute for Training and Research, 1978).

Most of the regional organizations and their documentation are also described in specific guides of varying scope and detail. For example, the oldest of these regional groups, the Organization of American States (established in 1890) is covered by Charles G. Fenwick, *The Organization of American States* (Washington, 1963). The documentation of the Organization of African Unity (established in 1963) and of other African groups are compiled in Louis B. Sohn, *Basic Documents of African Regional Organizations,* 4 volumes (Oceana, 1971–1972). A similar compilation for Asian organizations is M. Haas, *Basic Documents of Asian Regional Organizations,* 4 volumes (Oceana, 1974).

The separate organizational efforts of Communist states is based more on political and economic ties than on a purely regional basis. The Council for Mutual Economic Assistance (established in 1949), the counterpart to the European Communities, is the most important of these organizations. These groupings and their documents are compiled or described in English in R. Szawloski, *The System of International Organizations of the Communist Countries* (Sijthoff, 1976) and W.E. Butler, *Source Book on Socialist International Organization* (Sijthoff, 1978).

T.D. Dimitrov's *World Bibliography of International Documentation*, cited above, covers the literature of all of these regional organizations as well.

The most visible and, for United States lawyers, probably the most frequently encountered of the regional organizations are the European Communities, established in 1967 by a merger of the European Atomic Energy Community, the European Coal and Steel Community and the European Economic Community. Publications by and about the European Communities and their political counterpart, the Council of Europe (established in 1959), are numerous, and their listing is beyond the scope of this *Nutshell*. The 8th edition of *How To Find the Law* (West, 1983) contains an extensive bibliography at pp. 682–685, 691, but the literature is growing constantly.

Useful starting points for research in the law of the European Communities include:

(a) CCH *Common Market Reporter*, 4 volumes, looseleaf (Commerce Clearing House, 1962–date). For United States lawyers and researchers, this is perhaps the most useful research tool, because of its familiar format, broad scope, and frequent supplementation. In addition to its primary emphasis on the European Communities, it also provides limited coverage of many other regional organizations throughout the world, and summarizes the domestic legislation of many European countries on a variety of subjects related to doing business there.

(b) *The Law of the European Community,* by H. Smit and P. Herzog, 6 volumes, looseleaf (Bender, 1976–date). This is an article-by-article commentary on the Treaty of Rome which established the Community. The analysis contains references to current court decisions and scholarly sources, and each section is preceded by a bibliography of relevant secondary material.

(c) *Encyclopedia of European Community Law,* edited by K.R. Simmonds, et al., 11 volumes, looseleaf (Sweet & Maxwell, 1973–date). Designed primarily for British use, this work is particularly helpful for its coverage of United Kingdom legislation on European Community matters (Series A), Community treaties (Series B), and secondary legislation of the Community (Series C).

The law of the European Communities is the first substantial international law material to be available through computer data bases. As noted below, both LEXIS and WESTLAW offer European Communities files for automated research.

ADJUDICATIONS AND ARBITRATIONS

Although most international disputes are resolved by direct negotiation between the parties, some are submitted to international tribunals, arbitral bodies, or temporary commissions convened for that particular dispute.

1. International Court of Justice. Of particular interest in legal research relating to international adjudication are the publications of the International Court of Justice, which succeeded the Permanent Court of International Justice of the League of Nations. The I.C.J. meets at the Hague to settle legal controversies between countries and to resolve a limited number of other cases involving serious questions of international law. The publications of the I.C.J. include the following:

(a) *Reports of Judgments, Advisory Opinions and Orders* (issued individually in advance sheets and then in bound volumes, with both English and French texts).

(b) *Pleadings, Oral Arguments, Documents* (issued as above).

(c) *Yearbook of the I.C.J.*:

"Contains information on the composition of the Court (with biography of each Judge) . . . jurisdiction of the Court in contentious and advisory proceedings . . . it lists the states and others who are entitled to appear before the Court and matters dealt with by the Court since 1946 together with summary of judgments and advisory opinions given during the course of the year . . . digests of the decisions relating to the application of the Statute and Rules, a bibliography of works published on the Court and relevant extracts from treaties, agreements and conventions governing the jurisdiction of the Court". Published in French and English editions.

(d) *Rules of the Court* (published as Series D, although designation of Series A, B, and C is no longer used).

A similar, but somewhat more elaborate official publication scheme existed for the Permanent Court of International Justice, which was affiliated with the League of Nations and functioned as the World Court between the two World Wars. An unofficial compilation of P.C.I.J. decisions was published as *World Court Reports,* edited by Manley O. Hudson in four volumes covering 1922 to 1942 (Carnegie Endowment of International Justice, 1934–1943).

Since each year's *I.C.J. Yearbook* contains a summary of its work since 1946, it is also the easiest introductory tool. The most extensive commentary on the work of the court is S. Rosenne, *The Law and Practice of the International Court* (Sijthoff, 1965). The Court's own publication system is rather slow, so the best source for its most recent decisions tends to be *International Legal Materials* (American Society of International Law, 1962–date). The Court also regularly publishes a bibliography of secondary writings about itself, the *Bibliography of the International Court of Justice* (1946–date), prepared by the Court's library.

There are also several unofficial series of reporters for the present International Court of Justice: *Case Law of the International Court,* edited initially by Edward Hambro and continued by Arthur W. Rovine (Sijthoff, 1961–date), K. Marek, *Digest of the Deci-*

sions of the International Court (Nijhoff, Vol. 1, 1974, on the P.C.I.J.; Vol. 2, 1978, on the I.C.J.,); S. Rosenne, *Documents of the International Court of Justice* (Oceana, 2d ed., 1979); and E. Lauterpacht, *International Law Reports,* cited above (Butterworth, 1919–date) which includes P.C.I.J. and I.C.J. decisions, as well as selected decisions of national courts on international law, with several consolidated indexes.

The Law of the Sea Treaty, when ratified and in force, will be progenitor of another International Court, with jurisdiction limited to specific maritime matters.

2. Regional Organization Courts. Although a complete survey of the courts of the various regional organizations is impossible here, three such tribunals can be mentioned for illustrative purposes. The Court of Justice of the European Communities publishes its decisions in several official languages. An English edition, *Reports of Cases Before the Court,* was started in 1973, in connection with the United Kingdom's membership in the Community. Retrospective publication of earlier cases is in progress in that series. Several unofficial, commercial publishers also provide those decisions in English as part of larger services. These include the CCH *Common Market Reporter,* described above, and *Common Market Law Reports* (European Law Centre, Ltd., 1962–date). For computer access to these decisions, see pp. 379–380, below.

The European Court of Human Rights was created by most Western European countries under the European Convention of Human Rights of November 4,

1950. The Court issues two publication series covering its cases: Series A, *Judgments and Decisions,* and Series B, *Pleadings, Oral Arguments and Documents.* The Convention is unusual in having established a system for the international protection of the rights of individuals. Through the European Commission on Human Rights and, in some cases, through the European Court of Human Rights, a citizen can seek redress against the acts of his or her own government. The Commission began publication in 1975 of its own series, *Decisions and Reports.*

3. **Arbitrations.** The settlement of disputes between nations by arbitration has produced publications which constitute another important research source in international law. The awards of the Permanent Court of Arbitration and the International Commission of Inquiry, both established by the Hague International Peace Conference of 1907, were published in the *Hague Court Reports,* edited by James B. Scott (Oxford University Press, 1916, 1932). This set was continued by the United Nations in its series, *Reports of International Arbitral Awards* (1948–date). The initial coverage was retrospective in part. The awards now appear in English or French with bilingual headnotes. The set includes agreements reached by mediation or conciliation, as well as awards resulting from contested arbitrations, but is limited to disputes in which states are the parties.

A still useful historical compilation of arbitrations involving the United States is J.B. Moore's *History and Digest of the International Arbitrations . . .*, 6 vols. (Washington, U.S.G.P.O., 1898). The documents of several major arbitrations have been published separately.

Recent treatises on international arbitration include J.G. Wetter's *The International Arbitral Process, Public and Private*, 5 vols. (Oceana, 1979), and while not strictly on formal arbitration, two works reflecting modern practice are *International Claims: Their Settlement by Lump Sum Agreements*, 2 vols. (Univ. Press of Virginia, 1975) and *International Claims: Contemporary European Practice* (Univ. Press of Virginia, 1982), both by R. Lillich and B. Weston.

Although there is considerable research interest in international arbitrations between private parties, there has been little reporting of these awards. Some coverage is provided in *International Legal Materials* (American Society of International Law), cited above. *International Commercial Arbitrations*, edited by C.M. Schmitthoff in 2 vols. looseleaf (Oceana, 1974) offers a selective collection of conventions, uniform laws, enactments and arbitration rules "dealing with the settlement of international commercial disputes"—but, alas, not the awards themselves. The *Yearbook of Commercial Arbitration* (1975–date) reports extensively on current developments in this field.

4. Domestic Adjudications. Judicial decisions of the courts of individual countries on matters of international law are a valuable source of research information and are accessible through the reporters and case-finders for each country. This jurisprudence is also summarized in the yearbooks, periodicals and digests of international law published in many countries. In addition, several specialized reporters, as noted above, have been issued for such cases by Oceana Publications (*American International Law Cases, 1783–1968; British International Law Cases;* and *Commonwealth International Law Cases*). E. Lauterpacht's indispensable *International Law Reports* (cited above) includes not only decisions of international and regional organization courts and arbitration tribunals, but also selective decisions of national courts from many countries.

PRIVATE INTERNATIONAL LAW

As mentioned earlier, *private* international law is known in this country as "conflict of laws". Among the useful texts in this area are R. Leflar's *American Conflicts Law* (Bobbs-Merrill, 3d ed., 1977) and Scoles and Hay's *Hornbook on Conflict of Laws* (West, 1982). The American Law Institute's *Restatement of Conflict of Laws 2d,* 4 volumes (West, 1971–1980), is another authoritative source.

Since the American approach to conflict of laws is dominated by constitutional questions of interstate conflicts, the thorough researcher may want to augment his or her research with some foreign texts, especially a leading text for the jurisdiction involved. Useful in this regard are Dicey and Morris, *The Conflict of Laws,* 2 volumes (Stevens, 10th ed., 1980), H. Battifor and P. LaGarde, *Droit International Privé,* 2 volumes (Librarie General, 6th and 7th eds., 1976, 1981), and I. Szaszy, *International Civil Procedure, a Comparative Study* (Sijthoff, 1967).

Private international law encompasses other areas of law as well, especially those which seem to have no natural jurisdictional base. P. Vishny's *Guide to International Commercial Law* (McGraw-Hill/Shepard's, 1981) is a well annotated introductory text on the various aspects of transnational commercial activities. These may encompass problems in commercial law, taxation, trade regulation, and administrative law, which have a strong international impact. Also useful is I. Kavass's *International Business Transactions, A Guide to Research Sources* (1983).

A final example of the joining of the two aspects of international law is the recent United Nations Convention on Contracts for the International Sale of Goods (Text at A/Conf.97/19, part of the Official Records of the conference which produced the treaty, United Nations sales # E.82.V.5.). Here the full powers of the United Nations, an organization of *public* international law, were used to solve vexing questions of *private* international law. The treaty has been signed by the United States and was submitted for ratification in the fall of 1983.

COMPUTER ACCESS TO INTERNATIONAL LAW

A wide variety of European Communities material is accessible, through WESTLAW, in the European Law Centre's EUROLEX data base. (See the Chapter XI, Civil Law System, for domestic European legal material in EUROLEX.) English-language texts are available for decisions of the European Court of Justice, the Commission of the European Communities, and the European Court of Human Rights, as well as for the *Official Journal of the European Communities*

(Legislation Series) and the *Official Journal of the European Patent Office.* Full texts of conventions and agreements concluded between member states of the Council of Europe are also provided.

International tax agreements are searchable in both WESTLAW and LEXIS. LEXIS also contains European Court of Justice reports, and decisions of the European Commission on competition policy. Its French law libraries include French-language texts of bilateral fiscal agreements and the *Official Journal of the European Communities.*

In addition, both LEXIS and WESTLAW can, of course, be used to search judicial decisions, statutes, and other American materials for their treatment of international law issues or concepts.

POSTSCRIPT

It is the author's hope that this *Nutshell* will be accepted for no more than what it is—the briefest of introductions to:

"The lawless science of our law,
That codeless myriad of precedent,
That wilderness of single instances."

—Tennyson, *Aylmer's Field.*

The author concludes with this caveat from an earlier but no less cautious compiler:

> "Learned Homer sometime sleepeth, and the fastest foote sometime slyppeth, the wysest tongue may catch a tryp, and the wariest penne commit a fault, errour is as naturall, as the correction thereof commendable. Wherefore that which remaineth is, I

commit my selfe and my labour to thy good lyking, if thou lyke it, commend it, and use it, if thou dyslike it, amend it."

—William Averell, Preface to *Foure notable Histories* (1590).

*

Appendix A

LIST OF STATE RESEARCH GUIDES

Because of variations in the legal materials of the various states, a general research guide like this *Nutshell* cannot provide the necessary detail for specific state sources. Researchers and students are therefore urged to use the following guides for further information on the materials of individual states. Since new works of this kind are published from time to time, this list should be updated in local law libraries, and older guides should be used with caution.

California

Myron Fink, *Research in California Law* (Dennis, 2d ed., 1964).

Ron Granberg, *Introduction to California Law Finding* (Why Not Creations, 1977).

Dan F. Henke, *California Law Guide* (Parker & Son, 2d ed., 1976).

District of Columbia

* Carolyn Ahearn, et al., *Selected Information Sources for the District of Columbia* (American Association of Law Libraries, 1981).

Florida

Richard L. Brown, *Guide to Florida Legal Research* (Florida Bar, Continuing Legal Education, 1980).

* Prepared for the Government Documents S.I.S., American Association of Law Libraries, 75th Annual Meeting, 1982.

	Harriet French, *Research in Florida Law* (Oceana, 2d ed., 1965).
Georgia	Leah Chanin, *Reference Guide to Georgia Legal History and Legal Research* (Michie, 1980).
Illinois	Bernita J. Davies, *Research in Illinois Law* (Oceana, 1954).
	Roger F. Jacobs, et al., *Illinois Legal Research Sourcebook* (Illinois Institute for Continuing Legal Education, 1977).
Indiana	* Linda K. Fariss & Keith A. Buckley, *An Introduction to Indiana State Publications for the Law Librarian* (American Association of Law Libraries, 1982).
Louisiana	Kate Wallach, *Louisiana Legal Research Manual* (LSU Law School, Institute of Continuing Legal Education, 1972).
Maryland	* Lynda C. Davis, *An Introduction to Maryland State Publications for the Law Librarian* (American Association of Law Libraries, 1981).
Massachusetts	Margot Botsford & Ruth G. Matz, *Handbook of Legal Research in Massachusetts* (Massachusetts Continuing Legal Education, 1982), looseleaf.

Michigan Richard L. Beer, *An Annotated Guide to the Legal Literature of Michigan* (Fitzsimmons Sales, 1973).

Legal Research Guide for Michigan Libraries (Michigan Association of Law Libraries, 1983).

* Stuart D. Yoak & Margaret A. Heinen, *Michigan Legal Documents: An Annotated Bibliography* (American Association of Law Libraries, 1982).

Missouri * Patricia Aldrich, et al., *A Law Librarian's Introduction to Missouri State Publications* (American Association of Law Libraries, 1980).

New Jersey Paul Axel-Lute, *New Jersey Legal Research Handbook* (New Jersey Institute for Continuing Legal Education, 1984).

New Jersey State Law and Legislative Reference Bureau, *Legal Research Guide for the New Jersey State Library* (1957).

New Mexico Arie Poldervaart, *Manual for Effective New Mexico Legal Research* (University of New Mexico Press, 1955).

North Carolina Igor Kavass & Bruce Christensen, *Guide to North Carolina Legal Research* (Hein, 1973).

Pennsylvania	Erwin Surrency, *Research in Pennsylvania Law* (Oceana, 2d ed., 1965).
South Carolina	Robin Mills & Jon Schultz, *South Carolina Legal Research Methods* (Hein, 1973).
Tennessee	Lewis Laska, *Tennessee Legal Research Handbook* (Hein, 1977).
Texas	Marian Boner, *A Reference Guide to Texas Law and Legal History: Sources and Documentation* (University of Texas Press, 1976).
Virginia	* Margaret Aycock, et al., *A Law Librarian's Introduction to Virginia State Publications* (American Association of Law Libraries, 1981).
Washington	*Legal Research Guide* (University of Washington Law School, 1980).
Wisconsin	Richard Danner, *Legal Research in Wisconsin* (University of Wisconsin Ext., Law Dept., 1980).
	William Knudson, *Wisconsin Legal Research Guide* (University of Wisconsin—Extension Department of Law, 2d ed., 1972).

Appendix B

CONTENTS OF REPORTERS IN THE NATIONAL REPORTER SYSTEM

Atlantic Reporter (1886 to date): Includes decisions beginning with the designated volumes of the following major state reports: 53 Connecticut; 18 Connecticut Supplement; 12 Delaware (7 Houston); 6 Delaware Chancery; 77 Maine; 63 Maryland; 1 Maryland Appellate; 63 New Hampshire; 47 New Jersey Law; 40 New Jersey Equity; 108 Pennsylvania State; 102 Pennsylvania Superior; 15 Rhode Island; 58 Vermont.

North Eastern Reporter (1885 to date): 112 Illinois; 284 Illinois Appellate; 102 Indiana; 1 Indiana Appellate; 139 Massachusetts; 1 Massachusetts Appeals; 99 New York; 43 Ohio State; 20 Ohio Appellate.

North Western Reporter (1879 to date): 1 Dakota; 51 Iowa; 41 Michigan; 1 Michigan Appeals; 26 Minnesota; 8 Nebraska; 1 North Dakota; 1 South Dakota; 46 Wisconsin.

Pacific Reporter (1884 to date): 1 Arizona; 1 Arizona Appeals; 64 California; 1 California Appellate; 7 Colorado; 1 Colorado Appeals; 43 Hawaii; 1 Hawaii Appellate; 2 Idaho; 30 Kansas; 1 Kansas Appellate; 4 Montana; 17 Nevada; 3 New Mexico; 1 Oklahoma; 1 Oklahoma Criminal Appeals; 11 Oregon; 1 Oregon Appeals; 3 Utah; 1 Washington; 2 Washington Territory; 1 Washington Appellate; 3 Wyoming.

South Eastern Reporter (1887 to date): 77 Georgia; 1 Georgia Appeals; 96 North Carolina; 1 North Carolina

Appeals; 25 South Carolina; 82 Virginia; 29 West Virginia.

South Western Reporter (1887 to date): 47 Arkansas; 1 Arkansas Appellate; 1 Indian Territory; 84 Kentucky; 8 Kentucky Law Reporter; 89 Missouri; 93 Missouri Appeals; 85 Tennessee; 16 Tennessee Appeals; 66 Texas; 21 Texas Appellate; 1 Texas Civil Appeals; 31 Texas Criminal Reports.

Southern Reporter (1887 to date): 80 Alabama; 1 Alabama Appellate; 22 Florida; 104 Louisiana; 39 Louisiana Annotated; 9 Louisiana Appeals; 64 Mississippi.

California Reporter (1960 to date): 53 California 2d; 176 California Appellate 2d.

New York Supplement (1888 to date): 1 New York (1 Comstock); 1 Appellate Division; 1 Miscellaneous; and many other now discontinued lower court reporters.

Appendix C

CURRENT STATUS OF MAJOR OFFICIAL STATE REPORTS

This listing does not include *unofficial* reporters unless they have received official recognition or are generally used in place of discontinued official reporters. See the *Uniform System of Citation* (13th ed., pp. 136–176) for a fuller listing of state reports (with abbreviations), and Cohen & Berring, *How to Find the Law* (8th ed., Appendix B) for earlier reports.

Alabama: *Alabama Reports* (1840–1976) discontinued with v. 295 (1976); *Alabama Appellate Court Reports* (1910–1976) discontinued with vol. 57 (1976). Current official sources for the Supreme Court and the Court of Civil Appeals and Court of Criminal Appeals are West's *Alabama Reporter* (1976–date) and *Southern Reporter* (official since 1976).

Alaska: *Alaska Reports* (1869–1958) discontinued with vol. 17 (1958). Current official sources are West's *Alaska Reporter* (1960–date) and *Pacific Reporter* (official since 1960).

Arizona: *Arizona Reports* (1866–date) published by West since vol. 64 (1945) (includes Court of Appeals since 1976); *Arizona Appeals Reports*

(1965–1976) published by West since vol. 1.

Arkansas: *Arkansas Reports* (1837–date); *Arkansas Appellate Reports* (1979–date), bound with *Arkansas Reports.*

California: *California Reports* (1850–date); *California Appellate Reports* (1906–date).

Colorado: *Colorado Reports* (1864–1980) discontinued with v. 200 (1980); *Colorado Court of Appeals Reports* (1891–1905, 1912–1915, 1970–1980) discontinued with v. 44 (1980). Current official sources are West's *Colorado Reporter* (official since 1980) and *Pacific Reporter* (official since 1980).

Connecticut: *Connecticut Reports* (1817–date); *Connecticut Supplement* (1935–date); *Connecticut Circuit Court Reports* (1961–1977), discontinued with vol. 6 (1977).

Delaware: *Delaware Reports* (1832–1966) discontinued with vol. 59 (1966). Current official sources are West's *Delaware Reporter* (official since 1966) and *Atlantic Reporter* (official since 1966). *Delaware Chancery Reports* (1814–1968) discontinued with vol. 43 (1968). Current official sources are West's *Delaware Reporter* (official since 1968) and *Atlantic Reporter* (official since 1968).

Florida: *Florida Reports* (1846–1948) discontinued with vol. 160 (1948). Current official source is West's *Florida Cases* (official since 1948) and the *Southern Reporter* (official since 1952); *Florida Supplement* (1950–date).

Georgia: *Georgia Reports* (1846–date); *Georgia Appeals Reports* (1907–date).

Hawaii: *Hawaii Reports* (1847–date); *Hawaii Appellate Reports* (1980–date).

Idaho: *Idaho Reports* (1866–date), published by West since vol. 67 (1946).

Illinois: *Illinois Reports* (1819–date); *Illinois Appellate Court Reports* (1877–date); *Illinois Court of Claims Reports* (1889–date).

Indiana: *Indiana Reports* (1848–date); *Indiana Appellate Court Reports* (1890–date), since 1972 called *Indiana Court of Appeals Reports.*

Iowa: *Iowa Reports* (1855–1968) discontinued with vol. 261 (1968). Official source is *North Western Reporter* for both the Supreme Court and the Court of Appeals.

Kansas: *Kansas Reports* (1862–date); *Kansas Court of Appeals Reports* (1895–1901; 1977–date).

Kentucky: *Kentucky Reports* (Vol. 78, 1879–1951) discontinued with vol. 314 (1951). Current sources are West's *Kentucky Decisions* (official since 1973) and *South Western Reporter* (official since 1973).

Louisiana: *Louisiana Reports* (Vol. 104, 1901–1972) published by West since vol. 109 (1902); discontinued with vol. 263 (1972). Current sources (unofficial) are West's *Louisiana Cases* and *Southern Reporter.*

Maine: *Maine Reports* (1820–1965) discontinued with vol. 161 (1965). Current official sources are West's *Maine Reporter* (official since 1966) and *Atlantic Reporter* (official since 1966).

Maryland: *Maryland Reports* (1904–date); *Maryland Appellate Reports* (1962–date).

Massachusetts: *Massachusetts Reports* (1804–date); *Massachusetts Appeals Court Reports* (1972–date); *Massachusetts Appellate Decisions* (1941–date).

Michigan: *Michigan Reports* (1847–date); *Michigan Appeals Reports* (1965–date).

Minnesota: *Minnesota Reports* (1851–1977) discontinued with vol. 312 (1977). Current official sources are West's *Min-*

nesota Reporter and *North Western Reporter* (both official since 1978).

Mississippi: *Mississippi Reports* (1818–1966) discontinued with vol. 254 (1966). Current official sources are West's *Mississippi Cases* and *Southern Reporter* (both official since 1966).

Missouri: *Missouri Reports* (1821–1956) discontinued with vol. 365 (1956). Current official sources are West's *Missouri Cases* and *South Western Reporter* (both official since 1956). *Missouri Appeal Reports* (1876–1952) discontinued with vol. 241 (1952). Current official sources, since 1952, are West's *Missouri Decisions* and *South Western Reporter.*

Montana: *Montana Reports* (1868–date).

Nebraska: *Nebraska Reports* (1860–date).

Nevada: *Nevada Reports* (1865–date).

New Hampshire: *New Hampshire Reports* (1816–date).

New Jersey: *New Jersey Law Reports* (1790–1948, vol. 137) and *New Jersey Equity Reports* (1830–1948, vol. 142) combined and continued by *New Jersey Reports* (1948–date), published by West since vol. 53 (1968); *New Jersey Superior Court Reports*

(1948–date), published by West since vol. 103 (1968).

New Mexico: *New Mexico Reports* (1852–date), published by West since vol. 36 (1933). Includes Court of Appeals since 1967.

New York: *New York Reports* (1847–date); *Appellate Division Reports* (1896–date); *Miscellaneous Reports* (1892–date).

North Carolina: *North Carolina Reports* (1778–date); *North Carolina Court of Appeals Reports* (1968–date).

North Dakota: *North Dakota Reports* (1890–1953) discontinued with vol. 79 (1953). Current source is *North Western Reporter* (official since 1953 by designation in 1980).

Ohio: *Ohio Reports* (1821–1852) succeeded by *Ohio State Reports* (1852–date); *Ohio Official Reports, New Series* (1982–date); *Ohio Appellate Reports* (1913–date); *Ohio Miscellaneous* (1965–date).

Oklahoma: *Oklahoma Reports* (1890–1953) discontinued with vol. 208 (1953); *Oklahoma Criminal Reports* (1908–1953) discontinued with vol. 97 (1953). Current official sources are West's *Oklahoma Decisions* and *Pacific Reporter* (both official since 1969).

Oregon: *Oregon Reports* (1853–date); *Oregon Reports, Court of Appeal* (1969–date); *Oregon Tax Reporter* (1962–date).

Pennsylvania: *Pennsylvania State Reports* (1845–date) published by West since vol. 459 (1974); *Pennsylvania Superior Court Reports* (1895–date) published by West since vol. 241 (1976); *Pennsylvania Commonwealth Court Reports* (1970–date); *Pennsylvania District and County Reports* (1921–date).

Puerto Rico: *Puerto Rico Reports* (1899–1972); *Decisiones de Puerto Rico* (1899–date).

Rhode Island: *Rhode Island Reports* (1828–date).

South Carolina: *South Carolina Reports* (1868–date).

South Dakota: *South Dakota Reports* (1890–1976) discontinued with vol. 90 (1976). Current official source (since 1976) is *North Western Reporter.*

Tennessee: *Tennessee Reports* (1791–1971) discontinued with vol. 225 (1971); *Tennessee Appeals Reports* (1925–1971) discontinued with vol. 63 (1971). Current official sources, since 1972, are West's *Tennessee Decisions* and *South Western Reporter.*

Texas: *Texas Reports* (1846–1963) discontinued with vol. 163 (1961); *Texas Criminal Reports* (1876–1963) discontinued with vol. 172 (1963). Current sources (unofficial) are West's *Texas Cases* and *South Western Reporter.*

Utah: *Utah Reports* (1855–1974) published by West from vol. 1, 2d series—vol. 30, 2d series (1953–1974) and then discontinued. Current sources (official since 1974) are West's *Utah Reporter* and *Pacific Reporter.*

Vermont: *Vermont Reports* (1826–date).

Virgin Islands: *Virgin Islands Reports* (1917–date).

Virginia: *Virginia Reports* (1790–date).

Washington: *Washington Reports* (1889 to date); *Washington Appellate Reports* (1969–date).

West Virginia: *West Virginia Reports* (1864–date), not officially discontinued, but last vol. issued is 157 (1973–74); *West Virginia Court of Claims Report* 1942–date), not officially discontinued, but last vol. issued is 12 (1977–79). Current source (unofficial) is *South Eastern Reporter.*

Wisconsin: *Wisconsin Reports* (1853–date); West's *Wisconsin Reporter* (1941–date) is co-official since 1975.

Wyoming: *Wyoming Reports* (1870–1959) discontinued with vol. 80 (1959). Current official sources (official since 1959) are West's *Wyoming Reporter* and *Pacific Reporter*.

Appendix D

LOOSELEAF SERVICES

Selective List of Looseleaf Services

The following is a selective list of looseleaf services which are useful in legal research. It does not purport to include all such publications, and it should be used with caution since new services are issued frequently and others cease publication. The basic criteria for inclusion were frequent supplementation (at least monthly) and publication of primary documents (either abstracts or full texts). The many services which are published for various foreign countries and those in fields of international law are not included except for an illustrative sampling in the fields of international taxation and international trade law. For fuller lists, see the sources cited on p. 271 above.

A list of publishers and their abbreviations precedes the listing of services.

Publishers of Looseleaf Services

Abbreviation	Publisher
BNA	Bureau of National Affairs
Bender	Matthew Bender & Company
CCH	Commerce Clearing House
CIS	Congressional Information Service
CLR	Computer Law Reporter, Inc.
Callaghan	Callaghan & Company
ELI	Environmental Law Institute
IBP	Institute for Business Planning

IBFD	International Bureau of Fiscal Documentation
L–M	Legal-Medical Studies, Inc.
LC	Lawyers Co-operative Publishing Company
NCCD	National College for Criminal Defense (U. of Houston)
Oceana	Oceana Publications, Inc.
P & F	Pike & Fisher
P–H	Prentice-Hall
PLEI	Public Law Education Institute
PLR	Professional Liability Reporter (San Francisco)
RIA	Research Institute of America
UPA	University Publications of America
WSB	Washington Service Bureau (CCH)

Selected Looseleafs by Subject

ABORTION, see HUMAN REPRODUCTION

ACCOUNTING and AUDITING

Accountancy Law Reports (CCH)

Accounting Articles (CCH)

Cost Accounting Standards Guide (CCH)

Federal Audit Guides (CCH)

SEC Accounting Rules (CCH)

ADMINISTRATIVE LAW

Pike & Fischer Administrative Law (P & F)

Federal Regulatory Week (P–H)

ADMIRALTY

Shipping Regulation (P & F)

AFFIRMATIVE ACTION, see FAIR EMPLOYMENT

AMERICAN INDIANS, see NATIVE AMERICANS

ANTITRUST, see TRADE REGULATION

ARBITRATION, see LABOR AND EMPLOYMENT RELATIONS

ATTORNEYS, see also ETHICS

Manual for Managing the Law Office (P–H)

National Reporter on Legal Ethics and Professional Responsibility (UPA)

Reporter on the Legal Profession (L–M)

AVIATION

Aviation Law Reporter (CCH)

BANKING

Banking (Control of Banking; Federal Aids to Financing) (P–H)

Federal Banking Law Reports (CCH)

Washington Financial Reports (BNA)

BANKRUPTCY

Bankruptcy Law Reports (CCH)

Bankruptcy Service, Lawyer's Edition (LC)

BIOETHICS, see ETHICS

CARRIERS

Federal and State Carrier Reports (CCH)

Federal Carrier Reports

State Motor Carrier Guide

CHARITIES, see EDUCATION, FOUNDATIONS AND CHARITIES

CHEMICAL AND TOXIC SUBSTANCES, see ENVIRONMENT

COLLECTIVE BARGAINING, see LABOR AND EMPLOYMENT RELATIONS

COLLEGES AND UNIVERSITIES, see EDUCATION AND FOUNDATIONS

COMMERCIAL LAW AND CONSUMERISM, see also PRODUCTS LIABILITY

Consumer and Commercial Credit—Credit Union Guide (P–H)

Consumer and Commercial Credit—Installment Sales Service (P–H)

Consumer Credit Guide (CCH)

Secured Transactions Guide (CCH)

Uniform Commercial Code Reporting Service (Callaghan)

COMMON MARKET, see TRADE, INTERNATIONAL

COMMUNICATIONS

Communications Service (P–H)

Media Law Reporter (BNA)

Radio Regulation (P & F)

COMPENSATION, see PENSIONS AND COMPENSATION

COMPUTER LAW

Computer Law Reporter (CLR)

CONSUMERS, see COMMERCIAL LAW AND CONSUMERISM

COPYRIGHT, see PATENT AND COPYRIGHT

CORPORATIONS

Business Franchise Guide (CCH)

Capital Changes Reporter (CCH)

Corporate Practice Series (BNA)

Corporation Management Edition (P–H)

Corporation Law Guide (CCH)

Corporation Service (P–H)

Professional Corporation Guide (P–H)

Professional Corporation Handbook (CCH)

CRIMINAL LAW

Criminal Law Monthly (NCCD)

Criminal Law Reporter (BNA)

CUSTOMS AND TARIFFS, see TRADE, INTERNATIONAL

DIVORCE, see FAMILY LAW

EDUCATION, FOUNDATIONS AND CHARITIES

Charitable Giving and Solicitation (P–H)

College and University Reporter (CCH)

Exempt Organizations (CCH)

Tax-Exempt Organizations (P–H)

ELECTIONS

Federal Election Campaign Financing Guide (CCH)

ENERGY

Economic Regulation Administration Enforcement Manual . . . DOE (CCH)

Energy Controls (P–H)

Energy Management and Federal Energy Guidelines (CCH)

Energy Users Report (BNA)

Federal Energy Regulatory Commission Reports (CCH)

Federal Power Service (Bender)

Nuclear Regulation Reporter (CCH)

Oil & Gas Reporter (Bender)

ENVIRONMENT

Chemical Regulation Reporter (BNA)

Environment Reporter (BNA)

Environmental Law Reporter (ELI)

International Environment Reporter (BNA)

Noise Regulation Reporter (BNA)

Pollution Control Guide (CCH)

Water Pollution Control (BNA)

EQUAL OPPORTUNITY, see FAIR EMPLOYMENT

ESTATES—WILLS—TRUSTS, see also TAXATION, ESTATE AND GIFT

Estate Planning (IBP)

Estate Planning Review (CCH)

Financial and Estate Planning (CCH)

Successful Estate Planning Ideas and Methods (P–H)

Wills, Estates and Trusts (P–H)

ETHICS, see also MALPRACTICE

Bioethics Reporter (UPA)

Ethics in Government (WSB)

National Reporter on Legal Ethics and Professional Responsibility (UPA)

Reporter on the Legal Profession (L–M)

EXECUTIVES, see also PENSIONS AND COMPENSATION, and TAXATION

Executive Action Report (P–H)

FAIR EMPLOYMENT, see also LABOR AND EMPLOYMENT RELATIONS

Affirmative Action Compliance Manual for Federal Contractors (BNA)

EEOC Compliance Manual (BNA)

EEOC Compliance Manual (CCH)

EEOC Compliance Manual (P–H)

Employment Practices Guide (CCH)

Equal Employment Compliance Manual (Callaghan)

Fair Employment Practice Series (BNA)

FAMILY LAW, see also TAXATION

Family Law Reporter (BNA)

FEDERAL CONTRACTS, see GOVERNMENT CONTRACTS

FOOD, DRUG AND MEDICAL

Food, Drug, Cosmetic Law Reporter (CCH)

Medical Devices Reporter (CCH)

FOREIGN TAXATION, see TAXATION, INTERNATIONAL AND FOREIGN

FOUNDATIONS, see EDUCATION, FOUNDATIONS AND CHARITIES

FRANCHISES

Business Franchise Guide (CCH)

GOVERNMENT CONTRACTS

Contract Appeals Decision (CCH)

Federal Contracts Reports (BNA)

Government Contracts Reporter (CCH)

OFCCP Federal Contract Compliance Manual (CCH)

GOVERNMENT INFORMATION, see also ADMINISTRATIVE LAW

Government Disclosure (P–H)

HEALTH AND SAFETY, see OCCUPATIONAL SAFETY AND HEALTH

HOUSING, see URBAN PROBLEMS

HUMAN REPRODUCTION, see also ETHICS

Bioethics Reporter (UPA)

Family Law Reporter (BNA)

Human Reproduction Reporter (L–M)

IMMIGRATION

Federal Immigration Law Reporter (WSB)

INSURANCE, see also MEDICARE AND MEDICAID

Benefits Review Board Service (Bender)

Insurance Guide (P–H)

Insurance Law Reporter (CCH)

Automobile Law Reports

Fire & Casualty Insurance Law Reports

Life, Health & Accident Law Reports

Loss Prevention & Control (BNA)

Unemployment Insurance–Social Security Reporter (CCH)

Workmen's Compensation Law Reporter (CCH)

INTERNATIONAL TAXATION, see TAXATION, INTERNATIONAL AND FOREIGN

INTERNATIONAL TRADE, see TRADE, INTERNATIONAL

LABOR AND EMPLOYMENT RELATIONS, see also FAIR EMPLOYMENT; INSURANCE; OCCUPATIONAL SAFETY AND HEALTH; PENSIONS AND COMPENSATION

Collective Bargaining Negotiations and Contracts (BNA)

Daily Labor Report (BNA)

Employment and Training Reporter (BNA)

Employment Practices Guide (CCH)

Federal Regulation of Employment Service (LC)

Government Employee Relations Report (BNA)

Human Resources Management (CCH)

Industrial Relations Guide (P–H)

Labor Arbitration Awards (CCH)

Labor Arbitration Reports (BNA)

Labor Law Reporter—Labor Relations—Wages—Hours (CCH)

Labor Relations Guide (P–H)

Labor Relations Reporter (BNA)

Labor-Management Relations

State Laws

Fair Employment Practice

Wages and Hours

Labor Arbitration

NLRB Case Handling Manual (CCH)

Personnel Policies and Practices (P–H)

Public Employee Bargaining (CCH)

Public Personnel Administration—Labor-Management Relations (P–H)

Union Labor Report (BNA)

Wage-Hour Guide (P–H)

White Collar Report (BNA)

LEGAL PROFESSION, see ATTORNEYS and ETHICS

LEGISLATION

Advance Session Law Reporter (CCH)

Congressional Index (CCH)

Congressional Information Service/Index (CIS)

Congressional Legislative Reporting (CCH)

State Legislative Reporting Service (CCH) *

* CCH publishes a guide to each state individually.

LIQUOR CONTROL

Liquor Control Law Reporter (CCH)

MALPRACTICE

Professional Liability Reporter: Malpractice Decisions & Developments (PLR)

MEDICARE AND MEDICAID

Medicare and Medicaid Guide (CCH)

MILITARY LAW

Military Law Reporter (PLEI)

NATIVE AMERICANS

Indian Law Reporter (Amer. Indian Lawyer Training Program, Inc.)

NATURAL RESOURCES, see ENVIRONMENT

OCCUPATIONAL SAFETY AND HEALTH

Employment Safety and Health Guide (CCH)

Job Safety and Health (BNA)

Job Safety and Health Reporter (Business Publishers, Inc.)

Labor Relations Guide: Occupational Safety and Health (P–H)

Mine Safety and Health Reporter (BNA)

OSHA Compliance Guide (CCH)

Occupational Safety and Health Reporter (BNA)

PATENT AND COPYRIGHT

Copyright Law Reporter (CCH)

Patent, Trademark & Copyright Journal (BNA)

United States Patent Quarterly (BNA)

PENSIONS AND COMPENSATION

Compensation (P–H)

Compliance Guide for Plan Administrators (CCH)

ERISA Update (WSB)

Individual Retirement Plans Guide (CCH)

Pay Planning Program (IBP)

Payroll Guides (P–H)

Payroll Management Guide (CCH)

Pension and Annuity Withholding Service (RIA)

Pension and Profit Sharing (P–H)

Pension Plan Guide (CCH)

Pension Reporter (BNA)

Plan Administrator's Compliance Manual (P–H)

POLLUTION, see ENVIRONMENT

PRODUCTS LIABILITY

Consumer Product Law (P–H)

Consumer Product Safety Guide (CCH)

Product Safety and Liability Reporter (BNA)

Products Liability Reporter (CCH)

PROFIT SHARING, see PENSIONS AND COMPENSATION

PUBLIC EMPLOYMENT, see LABOR AND EMPLOYMENT RELATIONS

PUBLIC UTILITIES

Federal Power Service (Bender)

Utilities Law Reporter (CCH)

REAL PROPERTY

Real Estate Guide (P–H)

SAFETY, see OCCUPATIONAL SAFETY AND HEALTH

SECURITIES, also see ACCOUNTING

American Stock Exchange Guide (CCH)

Blue Sky Law Reporter (CCH)

Commodity Futures Law Reports (CCH) *

Corporate Capital Transactions Coordinator (RIA)

Executive Disclosure Guide—SEC Compliance (CCH)

Federal Securities Law Reporter (CCH)

MSRB Manual (CCH)

Mutual Funds Guide (CCH)

NASD Manual (CCH)

New York Exchange Guide (CCH) **

SEC Compliance—Financial Reporting and Forms (P–H)

SEC Docket (CCH)

SEC Enforcement Reporter (WSB)

SEC No-Action Letters—Index and Summaries (WSB)

SEC Today (WSB)

* CCH also publishes *Chicago Board Options Exchange Guide, New York Futures Exchange Guide,* and *Coffee, Sugar, and Cocoa Exchange, Inc., Guide.*

** CCH also publishes *Boston, Philadelphia, Midwest,* and *Pacific Stock Exchange Guides* and the *California Eligible Securities List.*

Securities Regulation and Law Report (BNA)
Securities Regulation Service and Guide (P–H)
Significant SEC Filings (WSB)
Stock Transfer Guide (CCH)

SOCIAL SECURITY, see INSURANCE

SUPREME COURT

Supreme Court Bulletin (CCH)
United States Law Week (BNA)

TAXATION

American Federal Tax Reports (P–H)
Capital Adjustments (P–H)
Code and Regulations (CCH)
Cumulative Changes (P–H)
Divorce Taxation (P–H)
Executive Tax Review (CCH)
Federal Income Tax Regulations (CCH)
Federal Tax Articles (CCH)
Federal Tax Compliance Reporter (CCH)
Federal Tax Coordinator (RIA)
Federal Tax Guide (CCH)
Federal Tax Guide (P–H)
Federal Tax Guide Reports—Control Ed. (CCH)
Federal Taxes Citator (P–H)
Federal Taxes—IRS Letter Rulings (CCH)
Federal Taxes—Private Letter Rulings (P–H)
Federal Taxes Service (P–H)

IRS Positions (CCH)

IRS Publications (CCH)

Interest Dividend—Withholding—Information Returns (CCH)

Internal Revenue Manual (CCH)

Oil and Gas—Natural Resources Taxes (P–H)

Publications of the IRS (P–H)

Standard Federal Tax Reports (CCH)

Tax Court Decisions Reports (CCH)

Tax Court Reports (CCH)

Tax Court Service (P–H)

Tax-Exempt Organizations (P–H)

Tax Guide (RIA)

Tax Ideas (P–H)

Tax Management (BNA)

U.S. Income

Primary Sources

Tax Planning (IBP)

Tax Planning Review (CCH)

TAXATION, ESTATE AND GIFT

Estate Planning (IBP)

Estate Planning Review (CCH)

Financial and Estate Planning (CCH)

Inheritance, Estate and Gift Tax Reports (CCH)

Inheritance Taxes (P–H)

Successful Estate Planning Ideas and Methods (P–H)

Tax Management—Estates, Gifts, and Trusts (BNA)

Wills, Estates and Trusts (P–H)

TAXATION, EXCISE

Excise Taxes (P–H)

Federal Excise Tax Reports (CCH)

TAXATION, INTERNATIONAL AND FOREIGN

African Tax Systems (IBFD)

Corporate Taxation in Latin America (IBFD)

European Taxation (IBFD)

Foreign Tax and Trade Briefs (Bender)

Guides to European Taxation (IBFD)

Taxation of Patent Royalties, Dividends, Interest in Europe

Taxation of Companies in Europe

Corporate Taxation in the Common Market

Taxation of Private Investment Income

Value Added Taxation in Europe

Tax Havens of the World (Bender)

Tax Management—Foreign Income (BNA)

Tax Treaties (CCH)

Tax Treaties (P–H)

U.S. Taxation of International Operations (P–H)

TAXATION, PROPERTY

Property Tax Service (P–H)

Real Estate Federal Tax Guide (P–H)

TAXATION, STATE

All-State Sales Tax Reports (CCH)

All-States Tax Guide (P–H)

Sales Taxes Service (P–H)

State and Local Taxes (P–H)

State Income Taxes (P–H)

State Tax Cases Reports (CCH)

State Tax Guide (CCH)

State Tax Reports (CCH)

TELECOMMUNICATIONS, see COMMUNICATIONS

TRADE, INTERNATIONAL

Common Market Reports (CCH)

Digest of Commercial Law of the World (Oceana)

Doing Business in Europe (CCH)

Encyclopedia of European Community Law (Sweet & Maxwell; Bender)

European Community Secondary Legislation

European Community Treaties

United Kingdom Sources

International Trade Reporter's Export Shipping Manual (BNA)

International Trade Reporter's U.S. Export Weekly (BNA)

International Trade Reporter's U.S. Import Weekly (BNA)

Investment Laws of the World: the Developing Nations (Oceana)

TRADE REGULATION

Antitrust and Trade Regulation Reporter (BNA)

Trade Regulation Reporter (CCH)

TRADEMARKS, see PATENT AND COPYRIGHT

TRUSTS, see ESTATES—WILLS—TRUSTS

UNEMPLOYMENT COMPENSATION, see INSURANCE

UNFAIR COMPETITION, see TRADE REGULATION

URBAN PROBLEMS

Equal Opportunity in Housing (P–H)

Housing and Development Reporter (BNA)

Urban Affairs Reporter (CCH)

UTILITIES, see PUBLIC UTILITIES

WILLS, see ESTATES—WILLS—TRUSTS

WOMEN AND THE LAW

Women's Rights Law Reporter (Rutgers Law School)

WORKERS' COMPENSATION, see INSURANCE

*

INDEX

INDEX

References are to Pages

INDEX

References are to Pages

INDEX

References are to Pages

INDEX

References are to Pages

INDEX

References are to Pages

INDEX
References are to Pages

INDEX

References are to Pages

INDEX

References are to Pages

INDEX

References are to Pages

INDEX

References are to Pages

INDEX

References are to Pages

INDEX

References are to Pages

INDEX

References are to Pages

INDEX

References are to Pages

INDEX
References are to Pages

INDEX

References are to Pages

†